THE
PRENTICE HALL
REGENTS
PREP BOOK
For The
TOEIC® TEST

THE
PRENTICE HALL
REGENTS
PREP BOOK
For The
TOEIC® TEST

STEVEN A. STUPAK

Prentice Hall Regents
Englewood Cliffs, New Jersey 07632

Stupak, Steven A.
    The Prentice Hall Regents prep book for the TOEIC test / Steven A.
Stupak.
    p.   cm.
    ISBN 0-13-125816-8
    1. Test of English for International Communication– –Study guides.
    2. English language– –Textbooks for foreign speakers.   3. English
language– –Examinations– –Study guides.   I. Title.
PE1128.S89   1995
428′ .0076– –dc20

94–25985
CIP

Acquisitions editor: Nancy Baxer
Director of production and manufacturing: David Riccardi
Editorial production/design manager: Dominick Mosco
Editorial/production supervision
 and interior design: Christine McLaughlin Mann
Production Coordinator: Ray Keating
Copyeditor: Sylvia Moore

Cover Design Coordinator: Merle Krumper
Cover Design: Yes Graphics
Electronic Art: Todd Ware, Rolando Corujo

© 1995 by Si-sa-yong-o-sa, Inc.
Published by Prentice Hall Regents
Prentice-Hall, Inc.
A Simon & Schuster Company
Englewood Cliffs, New Jersey 07632

TOEIC® is a registered trademark of Educational Testing Service (ETS).
No affiliation between ETS and Prentice Hall Regents is implied.

Printed in the United States of America

10   9   8   7   6   5   4   3

ISBN   0-13-125816-8

Prentice-Hall International (UK) Limited, London
Prentice-Hall of Australia Pty. Limited, Sydney
Prentice-Hall Canada Inc., Toronto
Prentice-Hall Hispanoamericana, S.A., Mexico
Prentice-Hall of India Private Limited, New Delhi
Prentice-Hall of Japan, Inc., Tokyo
Simon & Schuster Asia Pte. Ltd., Singapore
Editora Prentice-Hall do Brasil, Ltda., Rio de Janeiro

CONTENTS

FOREWORD

Any person who sits down to take a test needs to know in advance what the test is like. TOEIC examinees are no exception. They need to know what the question formats are and where their own strengths and weaknesses lie. After nearly thirty years of experience in the field of language testing, and director of the TOEIC program at Educational Testing Service during the years of the TOEIC's most rapid expansion, 1982 through 1990, Steven A. Stupak is uniquely prepared to inform readers about the TOEIC. A recognized expert in the field of language testing, Mr. Stupak conducts workshops internationally in both test development and oral proficiency testing. In this book, he shares with the reader his knowledge of the TOEIC and testing. A special section on the Language Proficiency Interview (LPI) will be of particular interest to teachers who prepare students for the LPI or for students who want to inform themselves about the LPI.

Nancy Baxer
Certified LPI Interviewer
ESL/EFL Instructor

INTRODUCTION

The purpose of this book is to familiarize the English language learner with the testing techniques employed in the Test of English for International Communication, more commonly known as the TOEIC®, and to introduce the learner to the Language Proficiency Interview (LPI) procedure for assessing oral language proficiency. The book consists of two parts: 1) TOEIC preparation materials, and 2) a discussion of the Language Proficiency Interview.

The Prentice Hall Regents Prep Book for the TOEIC® Test will be of interest to people who are learning English for use in real-life work or study situations, and who would like to have an orientation to the question formats that appear on the TOEIC® and to the techniques employed by interviewers who rate the Language Proficiency Interview (LPI). Teachers will be interested in the book because they will want to introduce their students to approaches to English-language testing that may be unfamiliar to them. Students will be interested in it because they do not want to be surprised by the question formats, the content, or the procedures they will encounter when they take either the TOEIC® or the LPI. The book, written entirely in English, is directed to an international audience.

The first part of the book consists of test questions in each of the seven question formats that appear on the TOEIC, as well as brief discussions of ways to approach the questions in each of the seven parts of the test. Included, also, are directions for each part as they appear in the actual test. Individual test questions, the correct answers and alternatives, are not discussed. The questions presented here contain original material prepared by teachers of English as a Second Language who have had many years experience teaching English to non-native speakers of the language. The concepts tested in the questions represent errors that students of English commonly make and that are likely to appear on the TOEIC at one time or another.

This book has been designed to help the student master the item formats in the TOEIC. The design of the listening section presents the student with an excellent opportunity to overcome the difficulty of failing to understand spoken English, even when what is said is not new to the student. Before attempting to answer a question, the student should challenge himself to understand the spoken language, without the benefit of reading the scripted voice material.

In this book, to begin the study of a question in the listening section of the TOEIC, the student should cover the voiced material with a card or piece of paper. After listening to the audio tape, and *without* having read the script, the student should attempt to answer the question. After attempting to answer the question, the student should uncover the script material and study it. Once the material is understood, the student should rewind the audio tape and listen once again to the voiced material for the question. If the student understands all of what he or she reads, at this point the answer to the question should become clear.

The second part of the book discusses the format and the procedure for oral proficiency testing, giving a description of each of the eleven levels of the LPI scale. Also provided is an interpretation of each level through Level 3, so that interviewees will gain an in-depth understanding of the entire oral assessment process.

Every book must have a primary purpose and the primary purpose of this book is to inform about the TOEIC® and the LPI. Books may have secondary purposes, as well. A secondary purpose of this book may be to teach English. The reader would do well to distinguish between the two, however, and recognize at the outset that the main purpose of this book is not to teach English. While a student may learn some English from studying this book, there are other books whose sole purpose is to teach the English language.

In reviewing other test preparation books that take a language teaching approach, the author has found that for the learner who is not advanced, grammatical and lexical explanations must necessarily be in the learner's native language to be of use. Since this book is not intended for students of any particular native language background, the author has chosen to leave it to the student to determine what is right with a correct answer and what is wrong with an incorrect answer. Students who make the effort to identify their weaknesses are bound to overcome them.

The student who has a question about any of the problems presented in this book should consult an English-language text or reference work that will explain in detail each of the many concepts, including exceptions, and giving examples. Were the author to undertake such explanations here, space would not allow for adequate discussion of the points considered.

This book provides the prospective test taker with over two thousand opportunities to answer questions like those found on the TOEIC®. The practice to be gained in this activity should be such that no student who studies this book diligently and then sits down to take the TOEIC® should have any question whatsoever of what to expect on the test, whether in terms of question format, presentation of material, or difficulty of language.

ACKNOWLEDGMENTS

A book is the culmination of the combined efforts of many people. During its production process there are schedules and budgets to be kept, coordination to be effected, and trade-offs and decisions to be made. The degree to which the parties work together is the degree to which they can look with satisfaction on a a job well done. This book is no exception, and the process in bringing this book to the public has been exceptionally well orchestrated.

I would like to express my appreciation to Nancy Baxer, the acquisitions editor, and her capable assistant, Terry TenBarge, who were as patient as they were helpful. I also wish to acknowledge and thank the first-rate production editors, Christine McLaughlin Mann and Jan Sivertsen, and their supervisor, Dominick Mosco.

The many people who stood behind me during the years when I honed the skills I used in preparing this book are numerous, but two cannot go without mention. When I first joined the staff Educational Testing Service I worked under Suzanne Stahl, who had fled the Holocaust and brought to America her keen intellect, a capacity for hard work, knowledge of several languages, and the patience to work with a young, inexperienced staff. I and others in the ETS Foreign Languages Test Development staff at that time owe her a great debt. The second person I need to thank is Protase E. Woodford, who hired me at ETS more than three decades ago, and under whose leadership the Foreign Language Department in ETS' Test Development Division lived its Golden Age. We were involved in many innovative undertakings, where we were challenged to devise valid and reliable measures for a great variety of language settings. Woodford delegated responsibility to all of us and gave the opportunities to expand our professional involvements.

And finally I would like to express my appreciation to my mother, for the support she has always given me, regardless of the path I chose, and without whose early touch I would never have been able to achieve what success I have. Thanks.Mom.

Steven A. Stupak

PART I: DISCUSSION

Questions in Part I of the test do not require the test taker to be able to read, write, or speak English to be able to answer them correctly. The person need only be able to understand spoken English, and see the picture printed in the test book. The format consists of a picture about which the test taker <u>hears</u> four statements, only one of which describes what is happening in the picture. The remaining three statements rely on misunderstandings of the spoken language, whether confusions of sound or of meaning, to distract the student who may not know the answer.

By TOEIC standards, the questions in Part I are quite easy. As the test taker progresses through the test, the question and question formats become more and more difficult. This notion of a test becoming progressively more difficult applies generally to each of the parts, as well. Which is to say, within a part the first items tend to be easier than those that follow.

On first listening to Part I questions, the student should cover the printed script material with a card and listen carefully to all four of the statements. One statement will describe clearly what is in the photograph. The statement will not refer to a detail in the photograph, or to some aspect that is of only minor importance. Rather, it will refer to the main topic of the photograph. In fact, the test taker should be able to look at the photograph and say what it is a picture of, and listen for that statement.

Once the student has answered all of the questions, the audiotape should be rewound and played again. This time, the student should read along as the statements are read, confirming the answers.

This part of the test consists of 20 questions.

Listening Comprehension

In this section of the test, you will have the chance to show how well you understand spoken English. There are four parts to this section, with special directions for each part.

PART I

Directions: For each question, you will see a picture in your test book and you will hear four short statements. The statements will be spoken just one time. They will not be printed in your test book so you must listen carefully in order to understand what the speaker says.

When you hear the four statements, look at the picture in your test book and choose the statement that best describes what you see in the picture. Then, on your answer sheet, find the number of the question and mark your answer. Look at the sample below.

Now listen to the four statements.

(A) They're looking out the window.
(B) They're having a meeting.
(C) They're eating in a restaurant.
(D) They're moving the furniture.

Sample Answer

Ⓐ ⬤ Ⓒ Ⓓ

Statement (B), "They're having a meeting," best describes what you see in the picture. Therefore, you should choose answer (B).

Picture 1

You hear:

Ⓐ Ⓑ Ⓒ Ⓓ

Picture 2

You hear:

2. Woman: (A) *His hand is extended*
    (B) *He is at the end.*
    (C) *The man put his hands up.*
    (D) *He is leaving the room.*

Ⓐ Ⓑ Ⓒ Ⓓ

You hear:

3. Man B: (A) *He is looking at the floor.*
    (B) *The man has fallen down.*
    (C) *The books are on the shelves.*
    (D) *The man is lifting the shelf.*

Picture 3

Ⓐ Ⓑ Ⓒ Ⓓ

Picture 4

You hear:

4. Man B: (A) *The doors are closed.*
    (B) *The boys are looking out the window.*
    (C) *The entrance is being held open.*
    (D) *They have walked past the building.*

Ⓐ Ⓑ Ⓒ Ⓓ

Picture 5

Ⓐ Ⓑ Ⓒ Ⓓ

You hear:

5. Woman:
    (A) *Dinner has been served.*
    (B) *The chef is preparing a dish.*
    (C) *The man does not want to cook.*
    (D) *The first shift is about to begin.*

You hear:

6. Woman:
    (A) *The man is very tall.*
    (B) *There is nothing more to do.*
    (C) *They are building a house.*
    (D) *The house needs paint.*

Ⓐ Ⓑ Ⓒ Ⓓ

Picture 6

Picture 7

Ⓐ Ⓑ Ⓒ Ⓓ

You hear:

7. Woman:
    (A) *The children are playing together.*
    (B) *The boy has lost his toys.*
    (C) *They are playing in the field.*
    (D) *The children are very upset.*

Picture 8

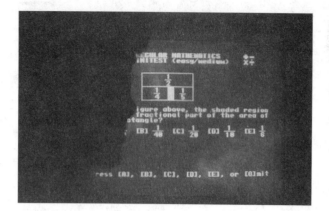

You hear:

8. Man B:
    (A) The computer is down.
    (B) The program does not work.
    (C) The monitor will have to be turned on.
    (D) There is an image on the screen.

Picture 9

You hear:

9. Woman:
    (A) The girls are enjoying their ice cream.
    (B) It is a cold and wet day.
    (C) All the stores are closed.
    (D) They are going out the back door.

Ⓐ Ⓑ Ⓒ Ⓓ

Picture 10

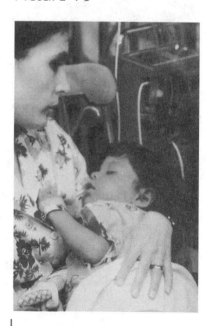

You hear:

10. Man B:
    (A) The woman is holding a sheep.
    (B) The children are sleeping together.
    (C) The field is full of sheep.
    (D) The child is asleep.

Ⓐ Ⓑ Ⓒ Ⓓ

Picture 11

You hear:

11. Woman:
    (A) *The man is retired.*
    (B) *The car door is open.*
    (C) *The taxi has already left.*
    (D) *The man is changing the tire.*

You hear:

12. Man B:
    (A) *The mountain is high*
    (B) *The water is moving fast.*
    (C) *One fountain is higher than the other.*
    (D) *This is not the right time to go.*

Picture 12

Ⓐ Ⓑ Ⓒ Ⓓ

Picture 13

You hear:

13. Woman:
    (A) *The women are arguing.*
    (B) *There are few people in the store.*
    (C) *They have chosen not to go.*
    (D) *People are walking into the shoe store.*

Ⓐ Ⓑ Ⓒ Ⓓ

Picture 14

Ⓐ Ⓑ Ⓒ Ⓓ

You hear:

14. Woman:

You hear:

15. Man B:

(A) The man is wearing a hat.
(B) The men are walking along.
(C) The man is reading the pape
(D) The men are waiting for a
ride.

Picture 15

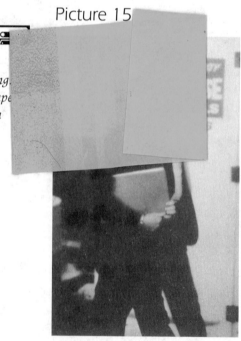

Picture 16

You hear:

16. Man B :

Ⓐ Ⓑ Ⓒ Ⓓ

Picture 17

Ⓐ Ⓑ Ⓒ Ⓓ

You hear:

17. Man B: ed.

You hear:

18. Woman: (A) Th
                (B) The
                (C) The
                (D) The b

Picture 18

Ⓐ Ⓑ Ⓒ Ⓓ

Picture 19

You hear:

19. Man B:

Picture 20

You hear:

20. Man B:
    (A) They are at the end.
    (B) The roof is finished.
    (C) The building is under construction.
    (D) The people have to go very far.

Ⓐ Ⓑ Ⓒ Ⓓ

Picture 21

You hear:

21. Man B:
    (A) The truck is being loaded.
    (B) The men have stopped working.
    (C) The wheels are turning.
    (D) The tractor is pushing the truck.

Ⓐ Ⓑ Ⓒ Ⓓ

Picture 22

You hear:

22. Man B:
    (A) The driver is turning right.
    (B) The man is wearing a headset.
    (C) The manager is looking at the machine.
    (D) The man is opening the window.

Ⓐ Ⓑ Ⓒ Ⓓ

Picture 23

You hear:

23. Woman: (A) People are in line to board the bus.
            (B) The buses are in a row.
            (C) The bus door is closed to passengers.
            (D) The bus is entering the park.

Ⓐ Ⓑ Ⓒ Ⓓ

You hear:

24. Man B: (A) The road has been cleared.
            (B) The cars are waiting to go.
            (C) The man is watching from the street.
            (D) The car is being cleaned.

Picture 24

Ⓐ Ⓑ Ⓒ Ⓓ

Picture 25

Ⓐ Ⓑ Ⓒ Ⓓ

You hear:

25. Woman: (A) They want to fly.
            (B) The wood is in a pile.
            (C) He would not be very good.
            (D) The board is meeting today.

Picture 26

You hear:

26. Woman: (A) The man is holding his ear.
                (B) The man is leaving the store.
                (C) The man is handing over the phone.
                (D) The man is making a call.

Ⓐ Ⓑ Ⓒ Ⓓ

Picture 27

You hear:

27. Woman: (A) It is already fall.
                (B) The boy is sitting in the water.
                (C) He is refusing to go.
                (D) The boy is careful not to fall.

Ⓐ Ⓑ Ⓒ Ⓓ

Picture 28

You hear:

28. Woman: (A) They are trying on the clothes.
                (B) Clothes are hanging on the line.
                (C) The people are wearing new clothes.
                (D) They have been put in a row.

Ⓐ Ⓑ Ⓒ Ⓓ

Picture 29

You hear:

29. Man B: (A) The man is working alone.
             (B) People are crowded in the street
             (C) The man is walking along the road.
             (D) Traffic from the right is very heavy.

Ⓐ Ⓑ Ⓒ Ⓓ

You hear:

30. Woman: (A) The bicycle is about to be run into.
             (B) The rider is turning over the bicycle.
             (C) The bicyclist is at the corner.
             (D) There are some twenty bicycles here.

Picture 30

Ⓐ Ⓑ Ⓒ Ⓓ

Picture 31

You hear:

31. Man B: (A) The shovels are in a bundle.
             (B) Customers are holding the shovels.
             (C) The shovel has been broken.
             (D) The shopkeeper is working with a shovel.

Ⓐ Ⓑ Ⓒ Ⓓ

Picture 32

You hear:

32. Woman: (A) The man is looking at a hat.
(B) The man is working on a brick wall.
(C) The workers are making bricks.
(D) They have grown a lot lately.

Ⓐ Ⓑ Ⓒ Ⓓ

You hear:

33. Woman: (A) The lights are very bright.
(B) The car is coming off the road.
(C) The rain has washed away the road.
(D) The car is parked in the shade.

Picture 33

Ⓐ Ⓑ Ⓒ Ⓓ

Picture 34

Ⓐ Ⓑ Ⓒ Ⓓ

You hear:

34. Man B: (A) People are walking in the street.
(B) They are running to catch the bus.
(C) Everyone is in the store.
(D) Rain has driven people into the market.

Picture 35

You hear:

35. Woman: (A) *The shop is just opening.*
            (B) *The doors are ajar.*
            (C) *The doors are locked shut.*
            (D) *The shop is closing.*

Picture 36

You hear:

36. Man B: (A) *The man works in the bank.*
            (B) *The worker is looking for a light.*
            (C) *The man is working at the bench.*
            (D) *The man's account is not current.*

Picture 37

You hear:

37. Woman: (A) *Men are watching the film.*
            (B) *The film is being shown during the day.*
            (C) *The men are fighting over the camera.*
            (D) *The crew is filming in the street.*

Picture 38

You hear:

38. Woman: (A) *It's ten past five.*
(B) *It's ten-o-five.*
(C) *It's five-ten.*
(D) *It's five till ten.*

Ⓐ Ⓑ Ⓒ Ⓓ

You hear:

39. (Man B) (A) *The truck is hauling logs.*
(B) *The road goes through timber country.*
(C) *The driver is trying to pass.*
(D) *The truck would like to turn left.*

Picture 39

Ⓐ Ⓑ Ⓒ Ⓓ

Picture 40

You hear:

40. Man B: (A) *An umbrella has been left on the floor.*
(B) *People want a place for their umbrellas.*
(C) *Umbrellas are standing in the rack.*
(D) *The room is full of umbrellas.*

Ⓐ Ⓑ Ⓒ Ⓓ

ANSWER KEY—PART I

1. D Several people are holding a meeting.
2. A His hand is extended
3. C The books are on the shelves.
4. A The doors are closed.
5. B The chef is preparing a dish.
6. C They are building a house.
7. A The children are playing together.
8. D There is an image on the screen.
9. A The girls are enjoying their ice cream.
10. D The child is asleep.
11. D The man is changing the tire.
12. C One fountain is higher than the other.
13. B There are few people in the store.
14. B The man is carrying the child.
15. B The men are walking along.
16. D There is a lock on the gate.
17. A The pool surface is undisturbed.
18. C The boys are playing ball.
19. B Travelers are waiting for their baggage.
20. C The building is under construction.

21. A The truck is being loaded.
22. B The man is wearing a headset.
23. A People are in line to board the bus.
24. D The car is being cleaned.
25. B The wood is in a pile.
26. D The man is making a call.
27. D The boy is careful not to fall.
28. B Clothes are hanging on the line.
29. A The man is working alone.
30. C The bicyclist is at the corner.
31. A The shovels are in a bundle.
32. B The man is working on a brick wall.
33. D The car is parked in the shade.
34. A People are walking in the street.
35. C The doors are locked shut.
36. C The man is working at the bench.
37. D The crew is filming in the street.
38. B It's ten-o-five.
39. A The truck is hauling logs.
40. C Umbrellas are standing in the rack.

PART II: DISCUSSION

The questions in this part of the test, as in Part I, are referred to as "pure listening" questions, meaning that the test taker need not be able to read English in order to answer them. While all other parts of the TOEIC® have four alternatives for each question, the questions in this part have only three alternatives. The reason for this is that the designers of the test did not want to test the examinees' ability to remember, but only their comprehension of spoken English.

The stimulus, or lead statement, for this part is in spoken English, followed by three possible responses, also in spoken English. One response is appropriate, while the other two alternatives clearly would not be appropriate.

As a test taker, when responding to questions in this part, you must listen carefully to the stimulus, or lead statement. You should not form a reply in your mind beforehand, but rather you should listen to the three suggested responses identified by voice on the audiotape as (A), (B), and (C). While keeping the stimulus or lead statement in mind, you must decide which of the suggested responses is appropriate. When you hear one that is appropriate, mark your answer sheet. The responses are spoken only one time, so you must make your decision immediately upon hearing each response. Do not hesitate to mark your answer, because the next question will be spoken just five seconds after alternative (C) is voiced.

Remember, this part has only *three* possible responses for each question. Do not wait for a fourth response. When you do not know an answer, guess. Be sure you make a mark for each question, leaving none unanswered.

On the TOEIC® , this part of the test consists of thirty questions.

The directions for this part of the test read as follows:

PART II

Directions: In this part of the test, you will hear a question spoken in English, followed by three responses, also spoken in English. The question and the responses will be spoken just one time. They will not be printed in your test book so you must listen carefully to understand what the speaker says. You are to choose the best response to each question.

Now listen to a sample question.

You will hear: **Man B:** *Good morning, John. How are you?*

You will also hear: **Man A:** *(A) I am fine, thank you.*

       (B) I am in the living room.

       (C) My name is John.

Sample Answer

Ⓐ Ⓑ Ⓒ

The best answer to the question "How are you?" is choice (A), "I am fine, thank you." Therefore, you should choose answer (A).

You hear:

1. **Man A:**   *Where do you go to school?*
   Man B: *(A) On the subway.*
       (B) At the National University.
       (C) Turn right at the next corner.

   1. Mark your answer on your answer sheet.
   Ⓐ Ⓑ Ⓒ

2. **Man A:**   *Do you want me to phone him?*
   Man B: *(A) No, you can't go.*
       (B) Yes, that's a good idea.
       (C) That's nice.

   2. Mark your answer on your answer sheet.
   Ⓐ Ⓑ Ⓒ

3. **Woman:**   *It's sure warm, isn't it?*
   Man A: *(A) Yes, it is. Very.*
       (B) I think it's interesting.
       (C) That's wrong.

   3. Mark your answer on your answer sheet.
   Ⓐ Ⓑ Ⓒ

4. **Man A:**   *Do you know where the train station is?*
   Man B: *(A) I don't know what that is.*
       (B) On East Gate Road.
       (C) About three-thirty.

   4. Mark your answer on your answer sheet.
   Ⓐ Ⓑ Ⓒ

5. **Woman:**   *How've you been?*
   Man B: *(A) For a few weeks.*
       (B) I can't remember.
       (C) Pretty good, thank you.

   5. Mark your answer on your answer sheet.
   Ⓐ Ⓑ Ⓒ

6. Woman: What can I do for you?
Man A:
  (A) May I help you, too?
  (B) What would you like to see?
  (C) Could you show me that camera in the window?

6. Mark your answer on your answer sheet.

  Ⓐ Ⓑ Ⓒ

7. Woman: Would you like another piece of cake?
Man B:
  (A) I'm sorry, I can't go.
  (B) Yes, I'll get you some.
  (C) No, thanks. I've had enough.

7. Mark your answer on your answer sheet.

  Ⓐ Ⓑ Ⓒ

8. Man A: How do you get to work?
Man B:
  (A) About half an hour.
  (B) It'll cost about $15.00.
  (C) I drive.

8. Mark your answer on your answer sheet.

  Ⓐ Ⓑ Ⓒ

9. Woman: Where's the orange juice?
Man A:
  (A) On Main Street.
  (B) It's in the refrigerator.
  (C) I bought some yesterday.

9. Mark your answer on your answer sheet.

  Ⓐ Ⓑ Ⓒ

10. Woman: Why don't we reduce the size of our sales staff?
Man A:
  (A) It's not possible right now.
  (B) We forgot about it.
  (C) They don't have time to go.

10. Mark your answer on your answer sheet.

  Ⓐ Ⓑ Ⓒ

11. Man B: Now, does anybody else have anything to say?
Man A:
  (A) Yes, I already told them.
  (B) Yes, everybody agrees.
  (C) No, I think that's all.

11. Mark your answer on your answer sheet.

  Ⓐ Ⓑ Ⓒ

12. Man A: Can we postpone our meeting until Friday?
Man B:
  (A) No, I'm busy on Friday.
  (B) No, I wasn't here last Friday
  (C) Yes, I phoned him myself.

12. Mark your answer on your answer sheet.

  Ⓐ Ⓑ Ⓒ

13. Man B: Do you plan to work overtime tonight?
Man A:
  (A) Yes, I worked overtime.
  (B) No, I don't have the plans.
  (C) Yes, I have a lot to do.

13. Mark your answer on your answer sheet.

  Ⓐ Ⓑ Ⓒ

14. Man A: Where did you put the files?
Woman:
  (A) They're waiting out front.
  (B) I don't think so.
  (C) I put them back in the cabinet.

14. Mark your answer on your answer sheet.

  Ⓐ Ⓑ Ⓒ

You hear:

15. **Man A:** *Would you ask him to check the figures?*
    Woman: (A) *Yes, he's received the check.*
    (B) *I will, but I know they're right.*
    (C) *Yes, he figures it's all right.*

15. Mark your answer on your answer sheet.

Ⓐ Ⓑ Ⓒ

16. **Man A:** *What do you think of my cousin?*
    Woman: (A) *I don't like him.*
    (B) *I don't think so.*
    (C) *I don't know how.*

16. Mark your answer on your answer sheet.

Ⓐ Ⓑ Ⓒ

17. **Man B:** *How long has he been here?*
    Man A: (A) *He's been here a few times.*
    (B) *He's about 180 centimeters.*
    (C) *Since two o'clock.*

17. Mark your answer on your answer sheet.

Ⓐ Ⓑ Ⓒ

18. **Woman:** *Have you been to the top of the tower?*
    Man A: (A) *Yes, I've seen her.*
    (B) *Yes, I went up it last summer.*
    (C) *No, I don't know her.*

18. Mark your answer on your answer sheet.

Ⓐ Ⓑ Ⓒ

19. **Man B:** *What do they look like?*
    Woman: (A) *They're both very tall.*
    (B) *They like to play golf.*
    (C) *They say they're interested.*

19. Mark your answer on your answer sheet.

Ⓐ Ⓑ Ⓒ

20. **Man A:** *Could you please speak a little slower?*
    Man B: (A) *Not at all.*
    (B) *Of course. I'm sorry.*
    (C) *Yes, I can do it.*

20. Mark your answer on your answer sheet.

Ⓐ Ⓑ Ⓒ

21. **Man A:** *What's today's date?*
    Woman: (A) *It's the twenty-second.*
    (B) *I think it's Friday.*
    (C) *No, I'm staying home to watch the game.*

21. Mark your answer on your answer sheet.

Ⓐ Ⓑ Ⓒ

22. **Woman:** *Good evening. I'm sorry to bother you.*
    Man A: (A) *That's O.K. What do you need?*
    (B) *You shouldn't have telephoned him.*
    (C) *Yes, I saw you there.*

22. Mark your answer on your answer sheet.

Ⓐ Ⓑ Ⓒ

23. **Man A:** *Do you work near here?*
    Woman: (A) *Yes, I've been asked to work today.*
    (B) *Yes, I like to go for walks.*
    (C) *Yes, I work in that building across the street.*

23. Mark your answer on your answer sheet.

Ⓐ Ⓑ Ⓒ

You hear:

24. **Man A:** *What does Biff do for a living?*
    Man B: (A) *He's an airplane mechanic.*
    (B) *He's reading a novel.*
    (C) *He likes to play baseball.*

24. Mark your answer on your answer sheet.

Ⓐ Ⓑ Ⓒ

25. **Man A:** *Do you live by yourself?*
    Man B: (A) *Yes, I made it yesterday.*
    (B) *No, I have a house.*
    (C) *No, I have a roommate.*

25. Mark your answer on your answer sheet.

Ⓐ Ⓑ Ⓒ

26. **Woman:** *Are you sure it's not out of your way?*
    Man A: (A) *You're welcome.*
    (B) *Not at all. Come along.*
    (C) *No, I don't mind taking orders.*

26. Mark your answer on your answer sheet.

Ⓐ Ⓑ Ⓒ

27. **Man B:** *Are you new with the company?*
    Woman: (A) *No, but I'm new in this office.*
    (B) *Yes, I live in town.*
    (C) *I'm not sure.*

27. Mark your answer on your answer sheet.

Ⓐ Ⓑ Ⓒ

28. **Man B:** *Could you do me a favor?*
    Man A: (A) *Sure. What is it?*
    (B) *Sure. To whom?*
    (C) *Sure. How much?*

28. Mark your answer on your answer sheet.

Ⓐ Ⓑ Ⓒ

29. **Woman:** *Why did he leave?*
    Man A: (A) *He left a few minutes ago.*
    (B) *I think he was very upset.*
    (C) *It was around ten o'clock.*

29. Mark your answer on your answer sheet.

Ⓐ Ⓑ Ⓒ

30. **Man B:** *Have you decided what you're going to do now?*
    Man A: (A) *I work and study.*
    (B) *I usually go to my friend's place.*
    (C) *I plan to get a job as soon as I can.*

30. Mark your answer on your answer sheet.

Ⓐ Ⓑ Ⓒ

31. **Man B:** *Is there anything I can do?*
    Woman: (A) *I don't think so, but thanks anyway.*
    (B) *There's some cake left.*
    (C) *That sounds like a good idea.*

31. Mark your answer on your answer sheet.

Ⓐ Ⓑ Ⓒ

32. **Man A:** *What are you doing over the holidays?*
    Man B: (A) *I've bought a lot of presents.*
    (B) *I don't know yet.*
    (C) *I visited my girl friend's home.*

32. Mark your answer on your answer sheet.

Ⓐ Ⓑ Ⓒ

You hear:

33. **Man A:** Could you show me how the computer works?
Woman:
(A) Yes, it does work.
(B) I'd be glad to.
(C) Thanks a lot.

33. Mark your answer on your answer sheet.

Ⓐ Ⓑ Ⓒ

34. **Man B:** When did you make the reservation?
Woman:
(A) Sometime, I believe.
(B) I haven't made it yet.
(C) Maybe I should leave now.

34. Mark your answer on your answer sheet.

Ⓐ Ⓑ Ⓒ

35. **Man A:** Who's that over there?
Man B:
(A) It's my bus.
(B) It's a bird.
(C) It's my brother.

35. Mark your answer on your answer sheet.

Ⓐ Ⓑ Ⓒ

36. **Man A:** Right now I'm looking for a hospital job.
Man B:
(A) Are you sick?
(B) I'm sorry to hear that.
(C) Well, I hope you find something.

36. Mark your answer on your answer sheet.

Ⓐ Ⓑ Ⓒ

37. **Man A:** May I please speak with Mr. Kim?
Woman:
(A) I'm sorry, he isn't in yet.
(B) Of course, he's out.
(C) He says he doesn't know how.

37. Mark your answer on your answer sheet.

Ⓐ Ⓑ Ⓒ

38. **Man B:** What are you going to do this weekend?
Man A:
(A) I don't know. I don't have any plans.
(B) I went to the zoo with my family.
(C) We would be happy to join you.

38. Mark your answer on your answer sheet.

Ⓐ Ⓑ Ⓒ

39. **Man A:** Are you going to the football match tomorrow night?
Man B:
(A) What do you mean?
(B) No, I don't smoke.
(C) I wouldn't miss it.

39. Mark your answer on your answer sheet.

Ⓐ Ⓑ Ⓒ

40. **Man B:** Will the construction be finished on time?
Man A:
(A) Yes, it's time to go.
(B) I hope you're ready for dessert.
(C) I'm sure it will be.

40. Mark your answer on your answer sheet.

Ⓐ Ⓑ Ⓒ

41. **Woman:** Won't you need these documents today?
Man A:
(A) He's the only doctor I know.
(B) I may. I'll take them in my briefcase.
(C) They're loading it now.

41. Mark your answer on your answer sheet.

Ⓐ Ⓑ Ⓒ

42. **Man A:** *I think the profit margin is too small.*
    Man B: (A) *It's already in the machine.*
    (B) *It ought to fit all right.*
    (C) *No. We'll do all right with it.*

42. Mark your answer on your answer sheet.

Ⓐ Ⓑ Ⓒ

43. **Woman:** *They've been overseas for quite a while, haven't they?*
    Man A: (A) *I sent it while you were gone.*
    (B) *Yes, for about ten years now.*
    (C) *International trade is important to everyone.*

43. Mark your answer on your answer sheet.

Ⓐ Ⓑ Ⓒ

44. **Man A:** *Is there any food in the refrigerator?*
    Man B: (A) *I'll eat it at lunchtime.*
    (B) *I'm sure I can fix it.*
    (C) *I'm sure we can find something to eat.*

44. Mark your answer on your answer sheet.

Ⓐ Ⓑ Ⓒ

45. **Man B:** *Could you let me know when the shipment comes in?*
    Man A: (A) *It's the only one I have.*
    (B) *Last year.*
    (C) *Sure, I'll phone you.*

45. Mark your answer on your answer sheet.

Ⓐ Ⓑ Ⓒ

46. **Woman:** *If they're worried, why don't they just buy out the competition?*
    Man A: (A) *Competition is the answer.*
    (B) *They don't have enough money.*
    (C) *We have to be competitive.*

46. Mark your answer on your answer sheet.

Ⓐ Ⓑ Ⓒ

47. **Man A:** *Can you help me now, or are you busy?*
    Woman: (A) *He's always helpful.*
    (B) *Yes, please help me with this.*
    (C) *No, I'm not doing anything.*

47. Mark your answer on your answer sheet.

Ⓐ Ⓑ Ⓒ

48. **Woman:** *When did you last visit Los Angeles?*
    Man A: (A) *Yes, but I found it later.*
    (B) *My entire family went.*
    (C) *It was nearly five years ago.*

48. Mark your answer on your answer sheet.

Ⓐ Ⓑ Ⓒ

49. **Man B:** *Are you ever going to finish that job?*
    Man A: (A) *I guess I'm not very good at this work.*
    (B) *I always buy the same ones.*
    (C) *Yes, we expect him before long.*

49. Mark your answer on your answer sheet.

Ⓐ Ⓑ Ⓒ

50. Woman: What do you have in mind to improve our international sales?

     Man B: (A) Oh, do you need to buy a present?

            (B) I plan to set up more overseas offices.

            (C) I don't know why he doesn't want to join sales.

50. Mark your answer on your answer sheet.

Ⓐ Ⓑ Ⓒ

51. Woman: Did you tell the editor that we haven't yet finished the layout on the Gibbs brochure?

     Man A: (A) That's too bad. I hope he gets better.

            (B) No, but I'll tell him later today.

            (C) Yes, and it's a good thing we finished it early.

51. Mark your answer on your answer sheet.

Ⓐ Ⓑ Ⓒ

52. Man A: Do you speak Chinese?

     Woman: (A) No, he's Japanese.

           (B) Just a little.

           (C) I've been to China only once.

52. Mark your answer on your answer sheet.

Ⓐ Ⓑ Ⓒ

53. Man B: Have you mailed that package yet?

     Man A: (A) No, not yet.

           (B) I should receive it tomorrow.

           (C) I think I have it.

53. Mark your answer on your answer sheet.

Ⓐ Ⓑ Ⓒ

54. Man A: What do you plan to do on Saturday?

     Woman: (A) I went to a movie.

           (B) I'd like to go to the library.

           (C) I spoke with him yesterday.

54. Mark your answer on your answer sheet.

Ⓐ Ⓑ Ⓒ

55. Man B: How do you like working for an advertising firm?

     Woman: (A) For about four years.

           (B) I find it very interesting.

           (C) A friend told me about the job.

55. Mark your answer on your answer sheet.

Ⓐ Ⓑ Ⓒ

56. Man A: Have you ever been to Canada?

     Man B: (A) No, but I've always wanted to go.

           (B) No, but may I please have some?

           (C) No, but I think we can do it.

56. Mark your answer on your answer sheet.

Ⓐ Ⓑ Ⓒ

57. Man B: Would you like me to explain how this machine works?

     Man A: (A) I know he's a good worker.

           (B) Yes, that's what I thought.

           (C) Yes, please do.

57. Mark your answer on your answer sheet.

Ⓐ Ⓑ Ⓒ

58. **Woman:** *Is there something I can do for you?*
Man A: *(A) No. What happened?*
(B) You're welcome.
(C) Yes. Could you please call my office.

58. Mark your answer on your answer sheet.

Ⓐ Ⓑ Ⓒ

59. **Woman:** *Did you hear about Han's father?*
Man B: *(A) Yes, I've met him.*
(B) That's nice.
(C) No. What happened?

59. Mark your answer on your answer sheet.

Ⓐ Ⓑ Ⓒ

60. **Man A:** *Do you know anyone there?*
Man B: *(A) He's from Jakarta.*
(B) Yes. A friend from college lives there.
(C) Oh, it's a beautiful place.

60. Mark your answer on your answer sheet.

Ⓐ Ⓑ Ⓒ

61. **Man B:** *Who's your favorite singer?*
Woman: *(A) I like jazz the best.*
(B) I guess I'd have to say it's Elton John.
(C) I don't sing if I don't have to.

61. Mark your answer on your answer sheet.

Ⓐ Ⓑ Ⓒ

62. **Woman:** *How long have you been waiting?*
Man A: *(A) Since five o'clock.*
(B) Two hours ago.
(C) Every morning at the same time.

62. Mark your answer on your answer sheet.

Ⓐ Ⓑ Ⓒ

63. **Man B:** *Did you like London better than Paris?*
Woman: *(A) Oh, I don't know. It's hard to say.*
(B) London is a large city.
(C) Madrid, too, is a good place to visit.

63. Mark your answer on your answer sheet.

Ⓐ Ⓑ Ⓒ

64. **Man A:** *How are things going at work?*
Man B: *(A) For the past year.*
(B) Pretty well, considering everything.
(C) They left yesterday.

64. Mark your answer on your answer sheet.

Ⓐ Ⓑ Ⓒ

65. **Man B:** *What have you been doing lately?*
Man A: *(A) I'm sorry. I was busy.*
(B) Nothing much, really.
(C) He's never late.

65. Mark your answer on your answer sheet.

Ⓐ Ⓑ Ⓒ

66. **Woman:** *Do you know if this store is looking for help?*
Man A: *(A) I've been told that they are.*
(B) Yes, I'd be glad to help.
(C) Why don't they go over there?

66. Mark your answer on your answer sheet.

Ⓐ Ⓑ Ⓒ

67. Woman: Are you a good swimmer?
Man B: (A) I studied math in school.
(B) Yes. I think I can see him.
(C) Not very, but I won't drown.

67. Mark your answer on your answer sheet.

Ⓐ Ⓑ Ⓒ

68. Woman: How's your sister?
Man A: (A) She's only twenty-one.
(B) She's doing fine, thanks.
(C) I'd say she's about average height.

68. Mark your answer on your answer sheet.

Ⓐ Ⓑ Ⓒ

69. Man A: Excuse me. Can you change this bill?
Man B: (A) No. I'm sorry, I can't.
(B) I'm happy to meet you.
(C) No. I don't know him.

69. Mark your answer on your answer sheet.

Ⓐ Ⓑ Ⓒ

70. Woman: More coffee, Mr. Brown?
Man A: (A) No, thank you. I have to go.
(B) Yes, but only the first page.
(C) I'll have copies made at the office.

70. Mark your answer on your answer sheet.

Ⓐ Ⓑ Ⓒ

71. Man A: How're your children?
Man B: (A) They're four and six.
(B) I have two children.
(C) They're all doing well.

71. Mark your answer on your answer sheet.

Ⓐ Ⓑ Ⓒ

72. Man A: Can you tell me where the park is?
Woman: (A) It's over in that direction somewhere.
(B) Yes. Is it near here?
(C) You can park anywhere.

72. Mark your answer on your answer sheet.

Ⓐ Ⓑ Ⓒ

73. Man A: Would you like to leave a message?
Woman: (A) I'll leave in ten minutes.
(B) No. I'll call back later.
(C) May I go with you?

73. Mark your answer on your answer sheet.

Ⓐ Ⓑ Ⓒ

74. Man B: The meeting is supposed to start soon, isn't it?
Man A: (A) That meeting was one of the worst.
(B) Yes, but we're waiting for the president.
(C) I'll be in the coffee shop.

74. Mark your answer on your answer sheet.

Ⓐ Ⓑ Ⓒ

75. Man A: By the way, are you still a loan officer at City Bank?

    Man B: (A) No, I'm working at the National Bank now.
(B) I've tried, but my credit isn't good.
(C) No, I'm sorry. I don't know where it is.

75. Mark your answer on your answer sheet.

Ⓐ Ⓑ Ⓒ

76. Man A: Do you have a pen I could borrow?

    Woman: (A) Yes. Do you have one I can use?
(B) Yes. You may use this one.
(C) Oh, there's my pen.

76. Mark your answer on your answer sheet.

Ⓐ Ⓑ Ⓒ

77. Man B: What's wrong?

    Man A: (A) I can't find my wallet.
(B) I bought a wallet.
(C) My wallet's on the table.

77. Mark your answer on your answer sheet.

Ⓐ Ⓑ Ⓒ

78. Man B: That's a very nice dress you have on.

    Woman: (A) Yes, I turned it on.
(B) Why, thank you.
(C) Yes, I put it there.

78. Mark your answer on your answer sheet.

Ⓐ Ⓑ Ⓒ

79. Woman: Where are the elevators?

    Man B: (A) They're visiting friends this week.
(B) Down the hall and to the left.
(C) They're on their way home.

79. Mark your answer on your answer sheet.

Ⓐ Ⓑ Ⓒ

80. Man A: Why don't we go to the Culture Center this evening?

    Woman: (A) That's too bad.
(B) That was last night.
(C) That's a good idea.

80. Mark your answer on your answer sheet.

Ⓐ Ⓑ Ⓒ

81. Woman: Do you know him?

    Man B: (A) Yes, very well.
(B) Sometimes I do.
(C) For about a year.

81. Mark your answer on your answer sheet.

Ⓐ Ⓑ Ⓒ

82. Man A: Where are you from?

    Man B: (A) To the bathroom.
(B) I think from outside the city.
(C) Manchester, England.

82. Mark your answer on your answer sheet.

Ⓐ Ⓑ Ⓒ

83. Man B: How was the concert?

    Man A: (A) I thought it was great.
(B) About two hours.
(C) It was a string quartet.

83. Mark your answer on your answer sheet.

Ⓐ Ⓑ Ⓒ

You hear:

84. **Man A:** When do you expect to give me the new specifications?
    Man B: (A) I totally agree.
    (B) That usually happens early.
    (C) Later today, if I get them done.

84. Mark your answer on your answer sheet.

Ⓐ Ⓑ Ⓒ

85. **Man A:** Do you mind if I bring a friend?
    Woman: (A) I don't know him.
    (B) Of course not. Please do.
    (C) Yes, thank you.

85. Mark your answer on your answer sheet.

Ⓐ Ⓑ Ⓒ

86. **Man A:** How often do you go to the beach?
    Woman: (A) Every weekend.
    (B) In the summer.
    (C) For four or five hours.

86. Mark your answer on your answer sheet.

Ⓐ Ⓑ Ⓒ

87. **Man B:** You look upset. Is anything wrong?
    Man A: (A) I've been promoted.
    (B) Anything will do.
    (C) I can't find my house keys.

87. Mark your answer on your answer sheet.

Ⓐ Ⓑ Ⓒ

88. **Man A:** What do you do?
    Man B: (A) I'm writing a letter to my mother.
    (B) I can't decide.
    (C) I work in a pharmacy.

88. Mark your answer on your answer sheet.

Ⓐ Ⓑ Ⓒ

89. **Woman:** Why did he do that?
    Man A: (A) I think so.
    (B) I don't know why.
    (C) He shouldn't have done it.

89. Mark your answer on your answer sheet.

Ⓐ Ⓑ Ⓒ

90. **Man B:** Have you found a job yet?
    Woman: (A) No, I'm still looking.
    (B) I've been working there for years.
    (C) Oh, all right.

90. Mark your answer on your answer sheet.

Ⓐ Ⓑ Ⓒ

91. **Man A:** What did you think about the proposal?
    Man B: (A) In the factory.
    (B) That's understandable.
    (C) It seems reasonable.

91. Mark your answer on your answer sheet.

Ⓐ Ⓑ Ⓒ

92. **Woman:** Hasn't the company put a ceiling on the number of employees they'll hire?
    Man A: (A) I don't know, but they keep on hiring.
    (B) They're all in the basement.
    (C) I did a job for them back in 1986.

92. Mark your answer on your answer sheet.

Ⓐ Ⓑ Ⓒ

93. Woman: *How do you like the new shopping center?*
       Man B: *(A) I really like it.*
       (B) I went there a few years ago.
       (C) I think it's somewhere in the middle.

93. Mark your answer on your answer sheet.

Ⓐ Ⓑ Ⓒ

94. Woman: *Where did you go last weekend?*
       Man A: *(A) To the amusement park.*
       (B) Yes, I took my wife there.
       (C) I don't know where to begin looking.

94. Mark your answer on your answer sheet.

Ⓐ Ⓑ Ⓒ

95. Man A: *When did they arrive?*
       Man B: *(A) In a taxi.*
       (B) Only about five minutes ago.
       (C) Since last year.

95. Mark your answer on your answer sheet.

Ⓐ Ⓑ Ⓒ

96. Man B: *Do you think this contract is fair to us?*
       Man A: *(A) The weather should be good.*
       (B) On Thursday nights.
       (C) No, but it's the best we could do.

96. Mark your answer on your answer sheet.

Ⓐ Ⓑ Ⓒ

97. Man A: *How about something cold to drink?*
       Man B: *(A) Yes, that would be good.*
       (B) This must be your refrigerator.
       (C) Yes, it is getting a bit cool.

97. Mark your answer on your answer sheet.

Ⓐ Ⓑ Ⓒ

98. Man B: *Would you like to play golf with us?*
       Man A: *(A) I've never been there.*
       (B) No, I won't be able to, thank you.
       (C) I don't know where it is.

98. Mark your answer on your answer sheet.

Ⓐ Ⓑ Ⓒ

99. Man A: *Why don't you wait until tomorrow to turn in the report?*
       Man B: *(A) The ship is already in port.*
       (B) I don't think I can get it done even then.
       (C) That's no secret to me.

99. Mark your answer on your answer sheet.

Ⓐ Ⓑ Ⓒ

100. Man B: *At night, they usually put the money in the safe, don't they?*
       Man A: *(A) No, they leave it in the cash register.*
       (B) Yes, it's a good idea to count the money.
       (C) Employee safety has to come first.

100. Mark your answer on your answer sheet.

Ⓐ Ⓑ Ⓒ

You hear:

101. **Man B:** *Where do you plan to go for your vacation?*

Woman: (A) *Nothing in particular.*
(B) *Nowhere special. I'll just stay home.*
(C) *We went to visit my parents.*

101. Mark your answer on your answer sheet.

Ⓐ Ⓑ Ⓒ

102. **Man A:** *Could I use your typewriter for a while?*
Man B: (A) *You're welcome.*
(B) *That's a very good idea.*
(C) *Sure. Keep it as long as you like.*

102. Mark your answer on your answer sheet.

Ⓐ Ⓑ Ⓒ

103. **Man A:** *May I speak with Anna?*
Woman: (A) *She's already here.*
(B) *Yes. Just a minute, please.*
(C) *Ask her when you see her next week.*

103. Mark your answer on your answer sheet.

Ⓐ Ⓑ Ⓒ

104. **Man B:** *How long does it take you to get home?*
Woman: (A) *I take the bus.*
(B) *Only twenty minutes.*
(C) *Less than three kilometers.*

104. Mark your answer on your answer sheet.

Ⓐ Ⓑ Ⓒ

105. **Woman:** *What do you usually do on your vacation?*

Man A: (A) *I go to the ocean.*
(B) *I'm a sales executive.*
(C) *I take it with me.*

105. Mark your answer on your answer sheet.

Ⓐ Ⓑ Ⓒ

106. **Woman:** *How do I get to the Midway Cinema?*
Man B: (A) *Next time you can go alone.*
(B) *Turn right at the next light and go straight ahead.*
(C) *First you must submit an application.*

106. Mark your answer on your answer sheet.

Ⓐ Ⓑ Ⓒ

107. **Man A:** *I'm going to the market. Do you want to come?*

Woman: (A) *Why don't we go to the market?*
(B) *Of course I don't mind.*
(C) *No, thanks. I don't need anything.*

107. Mark your answer on your answer sheet.

Ⓐ Ⓑ Ⓒ

108. **Man B:** *Were you able to go to the baseball game last night?*
Man A: (A) *No, I had to work late.*
(B) *No, I went with a friend.*
(C) *Yes, I'm sure he did.*

108. Mark your answer on your answer sheet.

Ⓐ Ⓑ Ⓒ

109. **Man A:** *Why did he buy on credit?*
Woman: *(A) He always does the right thing.*
(B) I hope he gets credit for his work.
(C) As I understand it, he didn't have any cash.

109. Mark your answer on your answer sheet.

Ⓐ Ⓑ Ⓒ

110. **Man B:** *Do you want to see the rest of the plant?*
Man A: *(A) Maybe some other time.*
(B) Why, is he tired?
(C) We water it every day.

110. Mark your answer on your answer sheet.

Ⓐ Ⓑ Ⓒ

111. **Man B:** *You do understand our position, don't you?*
Man A: *(A) Yes, it's true.*
(B) Please repeat, more slowly.
(C) Yes, but I don't agree with you.

111. Mark your answer on your answer sheet.

Ⓐ Ⓑ Ⓒ

112. **Man A:** *Did you hear whether they are ready to ship?*
Man B: *(A) Yes, it's a very large ship.*
(B) They said they'd be ready last week.
(C) I'm sorry, I don't hear very well.

112. Mark your answer on your answer sheet.

Ⓐ Ⓑ Ⓒ

113. **Woman:** *Would you rather send this letter by regular mail or registered?*
Man B: *(A) Yes, that's just fine.*
(B) That's the normal size for this item.
(C) Registered, please.

113. Mark your answer on your answer sheet.

Ⓐ Ⓑ Ⓒ

114. **Man A:** *The new equipment works beautifully, don't you agree?*
Man B: *(A) It sure does.*
(B) No, he doesn't work very hard.
(C) I expect him to disagree.

114. Mark your answer on your answer sheet.

Ⓐ Ⓑ Ⓒ

115. **Man B:** *What time did the conference end?*
Man A: *(A) Last week.*
(B) On Tuesday.
(C) At around five o'clock.

115. Mark your answer on your answer sheet.

Ⓐ Ⓑ Ⓒ

116. **Man A:** *What price are you looking for?*
Man B: *(A) Did I win?*
(B) Fifty percent of retail.
(C) I can't find it anywhere.

116. Mark your answer on your answer sheet.

Ⓐ Ⓑ Ⓒ

117. **Man B:** *Can you show that this approach is really cost effective?*

    Man A: (A) *Yes, it's the most expensive one on the market.*

    (B) *My brother just bought fifty shares.*

    (C) *I can prove it with figures for the last six months.*

117. Mark your answer on your answer sheet.

Ⓐ Ⓑ Ⓒ

118. **Woman:** *How did you ever come up with that information?*

    Man A: (A) *I came by car.*

    (B) *I read it in the quarterly report.*

    (C) *It was heavy, but I was able to.*

118. Mark your answer on your answer sheet.

Ⓐ Ⓑ Ⓒ

119. **Woman:** *What do you think of our new promotional literature?*

    Man A: (A) *You deserve it. You work very hard.*

    (B) *I knew he was a student, but I didn't know where.*

    (C) *We should do very well with it.*

119. Mark your answer on your answer sheet.

Ⓐ Ⓑ Ⓒ

120. **Woman:** *What makes you think it's a wholly owned subsidiary?*

    Man A: (A) *I understand they have several sheep.*

    (B) *I read that it can be used instead of sugar.*

    (C) *I met yesterday with the president of the company.*

120. Mark your answer on your answer sheet.

Ⓐ Ⓑ Ⓒ

121. **Woman:** *A computer would be a useful addition, don't you think?*

    Man A: (A) *Yes, it probably would be.*

    (B) *Yes, it was extremely useful.*

    (C) *Yes, it was done on the new calculator.*

121. Mark your answer on your answer sheet.

Ⓐ Ⓑ Ⓒ

122. **Man B:** *Would you look over the contract one more time?*

    Man A: (A) *Yes, I'll let him know.*

    (B) *No, it's not finished yet.*

    (C) *Of course, if you want me to.*

122. Mark your answer on your answer sheet.

Ⓐ Ⓑ Ⓒ

123. **Man A:** *How did you get into the seminar?*

    Man B: (A) *I had a special invitation.*

    (B) *We'll take a taxi to the airport.*

    (C) *I wasn't very careful.*

123. Mark your answer on your answer sheet.

Ⓐ Ⓑ Ⓒ

124. Woman: How many times do you think you'll have to go?

Man B: (A) At 2:00 o'clock.
(B) Three or four.
(C) Two and one half hours.

124. Mark your answer on your answer sheet.

Ⓐ Ⓑ Ⓒ

125. Man A: Will the research be completed this month?

Woman: (A) I expect they can.
(B) I've been looking all over for it.
(C) I certainly hope so.

125. Mark your answer on your answer sheet.

Ⓐ Ⓑ Ⓒ

126. Man B: You haven't been to the new office yet, have you?

Woman: (A) Yes, I visited there on Monday.
(B) Thank you very much.
(C) Yes, they've opened a new office.

126. Mark your answer on your answer sheet.

Ⓐ Ⓑ Ⓒ

127. Woman: When was the telex sent?

Man A: (A) Since yesterday.
(B) In a few days.
(C) On Wednesday, the twelfth.

127. Mark your answer on your answer sheet.

Ⓐ Ⓑ Ⓒ

128. Man A: Should we talk about this today or postpone the decision until everyone can be here?

Man B: (A) We need a decision on this right away.
(B) I don't know why the mail is so slow.
(C) I'm not very hungry right now.

128. Mark your answer on your answer sheet.

Ⓐ Ⓑ Ⓒ

129. Man B: When was the last time you checked the inventory?

Man A: (A) Every three days.
(B) Two weeks ago.
(C) Until yesterday.

129. Mark your answer on your answer sheet.

Ⓐ Ⓑ Ⓒ

130. Man A: Is the accounting department still working on the invoice?

Woman: (A) No, he isn't.
(B) Yes, I think so.
(C) No, it broke down earlier today.

130. Mark your answer on your answer sheet.

Ⓐ Ⓑ Ⓒ

131. Man B: Can you prepare the report on the merger?

Man A: (A) Since noon.
(B) I already have a draft.
(C) I didn't know it needed repair.

131. Mark your answer on your answer sheet.

Ⓐ Ⓑ Ⓒ

You hear:

132. **Man A:** Do you have the technical data or is it still unavailable?
 Man B: (A) Yes, that's correct.
 (B) No, it's technical.
 (C) No, I have it.

132. Mark your answer on your answer sheet.

Ⓐ Ⓑ Ⓒ

133. **Man B:** What time did you get out of the meeting?
 Man A: (A) Last Tuesday morning.
 (B) It was nearly three o'clock.
 (C) I was sick that day.

133. Mark your answer on your answer sheet.

Ⓐ Ⓑ Ⓒ

134. **Man A:** Would you care to see the results of the experiment?
 Man B: (A) Yes, I've seen the results.
 (B) Yes, if you have time to show them to me.
 (C) Yes, I'd like to have seen them.

134. Mark your answer on your answer sheet.

Ⓐ Ⓑ Ⓒ

135. **Man B:** Is anyone monitoring the new system?
 Man A: (A) Yes, the engineer is.
 (B) Yes, the monitor is new.
 (C) No, it's being monitored already.

135. Mark your answer on your answer sheet.

Ⓐ Ⓑ Ⓒ

136. **Man A:** How can we find out if the blueprints are finished?
 Man B: (A) I know it.
 (B) It was painted this year.
 (C) We have to call.

136. Mark your answer on your answer sheet.

Ⓐ Ⓑ Ⓒ

137. **Man A:** Can you return it before lunch?
 Woman: (A) I can't promise, but I'll try.
 (B) I'm sorry, I have plans.
 (C) He's already returned.

137. Mark your answer on your answer sheet.

Ⓐ Ⓑ Ⓒ

138. **Man B:** You calculated the profit margin, didn't you?
 Woman: (A) Yes, thank you.
 (B) Yes, I did.
 (C) Yes, it did.

138. Mark your answer on your answer sheet.

Ⓐ Ⓑ Ⓒ

139. **Man A:** Do you expect to have the data by Wednesday?
 Woman: (A) Yes, I think today's Wednesday.
 (B) I certainly hope we do.
 (C) I'm responsible for quality control.

139. Mark your answer on your answer sheet.

Ⓐ Ⓑ Ⓒ

You hear:

140. **Man B:** *How about getting together with the sales people at the same time?*
    Woman: (A) *They asked me to go.*
    (B) *We didn't do that.*
    (C) *That's a good suggestion.*

140. Mark your answer on your answer sheet.

Ⓐ Ⓑ Ⓒ

141. **Man A:** *Is there another alternative?*
    Man B: (A) *There doesn't seem to be.*
    (B) *Yes, there it goes now.*
    (C) *It's only an alternative.*

141. Mark your answer on your answer sheet.

Ⓐ Ⓑ Ⓒ

142. **Woman:** *When is the next staff meeting?*
    Man A: (A) *Ten days ago.*
    (B) *By 2:00 P.M., Monday.*
    (C) *A week from today.*

142. Mark your answer on your answer sheet.

Ⓐ Ⓑ Ⓒ

143. **Man A:** *How will the results be presented?*
    Man B: (A) *About twenty five, in all.*
    (B) *In a comprehensive written report.*
    (C) *In about two months.*

143. Mark your answer on your answer sheet.

Ⓐ Ⓑ Ⓒ

144. **Man A:** *The manager is out of the office. May I help you?*
    Woman: (A) *I'm sorry. I can't help you.*
    (B) *No, thank you. I'll call again.*
    (C) *No, thank you. I've had lunch.*

144. Mark your answer on your answer sheet.

Ⓐ Ⓑ Ⓒ

145. **Man B:** *Can we look at that data again? I don't think it's right.*
    Man A: (A) *Sure. Let's do it now.*
    (B) *Yes, I'm sure the check is all right.*
    (C) *No, it hasn't been checked.*

145. Mark your answer on your answer sheet.

Ⓐ Ⓑ Ⓒ

146. **Man A:** *When did the mail come?*
    Woman: (A) *In a few hours.*
    (B) *About an hour ago.*
    (C) *Since noon, yesterday.*

146. Mark your answer on your answer sheet.

Ⓐ Ⓑ Ⓒ

147. **Woman:** *Would you ask him to make corrections on the newsletter?*
    Man A: (A) *Yes, you can ask him.*
    (B) *I asked him yesterday.*
    (C) *You're welcome.*

147. Mark your answer on your answer sheet.

Ⓐ Ⓑ Ⓒ

148. **Man A:** *What did you think of the presentation?*
    Woman: (A) *We discussed the new program.*
    (B) *It should last all day.*
    (C) *I found it very informative.*

148. Mark your answer on your answer sheet.

Ⓐ Ⓑ Ⓒ

You hear:

149. **Man B:** *Will you be able to go out for lunch?*
     Woman: (A) *Yes, we did.*
     (B) *In the cafeteria.*
     (C) *I'm afraid not.*

149. Mark your answer on your answer sheet.

Ⓐ Ⓑ Ⓒ

150. **Man B:** *Can you ask him to call me?*
     Man A: (A) *He doesn't know.*
     (B) *Yes, I can call him.*
     (C) *Yes, I'll give him the message.*

150. Mark your answer on your answer sheet.

Ⓐ Ⓑ Ⓒ

151. **Man A:** *How about opening next month?*
     Man B: (A) *No, that's too early.*
     (B) *No, I was busy then.*
     (C) *No, it's closed today.*

151. Mark your answer on your answer sheet.

Ⓐ Ⓑ Ⓒ

152. **Man A:** *Mr. Lee would make a good branch manager, don't you think?*
     Man B: (A) *Yes, it would be good.*
     (B) *Yes, he was a good manager.*
     (C) *Yes, I think he would.*

152. Mark your answer on your answer sheet.

Ⓐ Ⓑ Ⓒ

153. **Man B:** *Does your advertising bring in any business?*
     Man A: (A) *It's the best transportation we have.*
     (B) *Yes, those new ads really work for us.*
     (C) *Yes, we ought to, before it starts to rain.*

153. Mark your answer on your answer sheet.

Ⓐ Ⓑ Ⓒ

154. **Man A:** *When did you discuss this?*
     Man B: (A) *Tomorrow night.*
     (B) *Only yesterday.*
     (C) *Until a week ago.*

154. Mark your answer on your answer sheet.

Ⓐ Ⓑ Ⓒ

155. **Man B:** *Is the accounting report ready yet?*
     Woman: (A) *No, it hasn't been counted yet.*
     (B) *No, there's still a lot to be done.*
     (C) *No, it hasn't been reported.*

155. Mark your answer on your answer sheet.

Ⓐ Ⓑ Ⓒ

156. **Man A:** *You spoke to the customer yourself, didn't you?*
     Woman: (A) *Yes, I'll speak to him myself.*
     (B) *No, but my assistant did.*
     (C) *I'm sorry, I don't.*

156. Mark your answer on your answer sheet.

Ⓐ Ⓑ Ⓒ

157. Man B: *What makes you so sure the market is saturated?*

      Man B: (A) *We've conducted extensive surveys.*

            (B) *I'll try to change the prices today.*

            (C) *I can only hope he'll keep searching.*

157. Mark your answer on your answer sheet.

Ⓐ Ⓑ Ⓒ

158. Man A: *Do you save money by scheduling production this way?*

      Man B: (A) *Yes, our losses have increased considerably.*

            (B) *Yes, quality is more important than production.*

            (C) *Yes, we've found it really pays off.*

158. Mark your answer on your answer sheet.

Ⓐ Ⓑ Ⓒ

159. Man B: *Do your retail outlets carry replacement parts?*

      Man A: (A) *He can carry anything.*

            (B) *They are supposed to, but some may not.*

            (C) *Yes, we've been able to get them out quickly.*

159. Mark your answer on your answer sheet.

Ⓐ Ⓑ Ⓒ

160. Man A: *Are the officers of your company in close touch with the government?*

      Man B: (A) *No, I haven't been in touch with him.*

            (B) *What exactly is the role of the military?*

            (C) *I think they want to keep their distance.*

160. Mark your answer on your answer sheet.

Ⓐ Ⓑ Ⓒ

161. Man B: *Who quoted those prices to you?*

      Man A: (A) *It's been moving up and down all day.*

            (B) *They came in over the telex yesterday.*

            (C) *I think he picked it up at the airport.*

161. Mark your answer on your answer sheet.

Ⓐ Ⓑ Ⓒ

162. Man B: *Why did they take them to court?*

      Man A: (A) *They're trying to get their money back.*

            (B) *They only had one pint left.*

            (C) *They didn't want to be alone.*

162. Mark your answer on your answer sheet.

Ⓐ Ⓑ Ⓒ

You hear:

163. Man A: *You've been told about the new contract, haven't you?*
Man B: *(A) Yes, we've heard all about it.*
(B) No, I didn't want to do that.
(C) Yes, I've been told to contact him.

163. Mark your answer on your answer sheet.

Ⓐ Ⓑ Ⓒ

164. Woman: *The staff reduction won't be a big one, will it?*
Man A: *(A) No, I will.*
(B) Yes, I'm afraid it will.
(C) I'll help him carry it.

164. Mark your answer on your answer sheet.

Ⓐ Ⓑ Ⓒ

165. Woman: *He's busy right now. Would you like to make an appointment?*
Man B: *(A) No, I'm not busy now.*
(B) No, I don't have an appointment.
(C) Yes. When would he be free?

165. Mark your answer on your answer sheet.

Ⓐ Ⓑ Ⓒ

166. Man A: *Is there any time left?*
Man B: *(A) I'm sorry, there isn't.*
(B) You can leave at seven o'clock.
(C) Any time is fine with me.

166. Mark your answer on your answer sheet.

Ⓐ Ⓑ Ⓒ

167. Man B: *Do you think the trade fair gave us much exposure?*
Man A: *(A) It's been open for two years.*
(B) I expect to receive orders from it any day.
(C) Produce displays are on the left as you enter.

167. Mark your answer on your answer sheet.

Ⓐ Ⓑ Ⓒ

168. Man A: *What do you think about the first of June for a target date to launch the product?*
Man B: *(A) That doesn't give us enough lead time for advertising.*
(B) I don't think she should go along.
(C) He would be my second choice, I'm afraid.

168. Mark your answer on your answer sheet.

Ⓐ Ⓑ Ⓒ

169. Man A: *Aren't we asking for trouble by doing this?*
Man B: *(A) No, I think we'll be better off in the long run.*
(B) No, I didn't ask him yet.
(C) No, I didn't ask to talk to John.

169. Mark your answer on your answer sheet.

Ⓐ Ⓑ Ⓒ

You hear:

170. **Man B:** *May I ask you for some advice?*
    Man A: *(A) I don't know where to get it.*
           (B) You may have whichever one you'd like.
           (C) Yes, go right ahead.

170. Mark your answer on your answer sheet.

Ⓐ Ⓑ Ⓒ

171. **Man A:** *Where will you spend your vacation next month?*
    Woman: *(A) I'm planning to go to Indonesia.*
           (B) I went to the mountains.
           (C) The hotel was too expensive.

171. Mark your answer on your answer sheet.

Ⓐ Ⓑ Ⓒ

172. **Man A:** *Who was that you were just talking to?*
    Man B: *(A) I told him I was busy.*
           (B) That's Bill, from the Shipping Department.
           (C) He said he'd be right back.

172. Mark your answer on your answer sheet.

Ⓐ Ⓑ Ⓒ

173. **Man B:** *Did you see the jumping competition?*
    Woman: *(A) No, I saw it.*
           (B) Yes, I was there.
           (C) No, I don't know.

173. Mark your answer on your answer sheet.

Ⓐ Ⓑ Ⓒ

174. **Man A:** *Do you know if the agenda has been set?*
    Man B: *(A) Yes, that's right.*
           (B) Sometime tomorrow.
           (C) Yes, it has.

174. Mark your answer on your answer sheet.

Ⓐ Ⓑ Ⓒ

175. **Woman:** *You've heard about the new policy changes, haven't you?*
    Man A: *(A) No, not yet.*
           (B) No, it hasn't changed.
           (C) No, I'm going dressed as I am.

175. Mark your answer on your answer sheet.

Ⓐ Ⓑ Ⓒ

176. **Man B:** *At what time were the negotiations concluded?*
    Man A: *(A) In February.*
           (B) Last week.
           (C) Sometime in the afternoon.

176. Mark your answer on your answer sheet.

Ⓐ Ⓑ Ⓒ

177. **Woman:** *Will you be able to participate in the workshop?*
    Man B: *(A) Yes, they can participate.*
           (B) Yes. I'm looking forward to it.
           (C) I'll use it to do metal sculptures.

177. Mark your answer on your answer sheet.

Ⓐ Ⓑ Ⓒ

You hear:

178. **Woman:** *Do you want me to make a reservation on the train or are you going to drive?*
   Man A: (A) *He's a fast learner, so it won't take long.*
   (B) *I have to drive, because I'll need my car.*
   (C) *Yes, if you want to call him.*

   178. Mark your answer on your answer sheet.
   Ⓐ Ⓑ Ⓒ

179. **Man A:** *When was the last time the board met?*
   Man B: (A) *In February.*
   (B) *Once a week.*
   (C) *Since 1986.*

   179. Mark your answer on your answer sheet.
   Ⓐ Ⓑ Ⓒ

180. **Man A:** *Is this seat taken?*
   Man B: (A) *You have to take a taxi to get there.*
   (B) *It will take at least three months to grow.*
   (C) *No, please sit down.*

   180. Mark your answer on your answer sheet.
   Ⓐ Ⓑ Ⓒ

181. **Man B:** *Has there been a maintenance check recently?*
   Man A: (A) *Yes, it's been maintained.*
   (B) *No, it's already been done.*
   (C) *Yes, in fact, just last week.*

   181. Mark your answer on your answer sheet.
   Ⓐ Ⓑ Ⓒ

182. **Man A:** *I don't see any way they can go through with the merger, do you?*
   Man B: (A) *I'm afraid it doesn't look good.*
   (B) *I think it merged.*
   (C) *I've seen it before, thank you.*

   182. Mark your answer on your answer sheet.
   Ⓐ Ⓑ Ⓒ

183. **Man A:** *Did you do this work yourself, or did somebody help you?*
   Man B: (A) *Yes, I helped a little.*
   (B) *I worked on it alone.*
   (C) *I'm finishing it now.*

   183. Mark your answer on your answer sheet.
   Ⓐ Ⓑ Ⓒ

184. **Man A:** *Do you know where the new office will be located?*
   Woman: (A) *It should be sometime this year.*
   (B) *I have no idea.*
   (C) *I think it will be Mr. Smith.*

   184. Mark your answer on your answer sheet.
   Ⓐ Ⓑ Ⓒ

185. **Man B:** *When do they plan to begin building?*
   Man A: (A) *A few weeks ago.*
   (B) *They've already begun.*
   (C) *At the new site.*

   185. Mark your answer on your answer sheet.
   Ⓐ Ⓑ Ⓒ

You hear:

186. **Man B:** *Are you sure there won't be any delay in getting to the airport?*

    Man A: *(A) Yes, I heard the traffic report on the radio just now.*
(B) Yes, I'd like to accompany you.
(C) Somebody said it's a 747, but I'm not sure.

186. Mark your answer on your answer sheet.

Ⓐ Ⓑ Ⓒ

187. **Man A:** *Do you know of a good restaurant nearby?*

    Man B: *(A) I think it's quite expensive.*
(B) I prefer Japanese food, thank you.
(C) There's one just across from the hotel.

187. Mark your answer on your answer sheet.

Ⓐ Ⓑ Ⓒ

188. **Man A:** *What do you think of his suggestion for the ad campaign?*

    Man B: *(A) I think it's a great idea.*
(B) I'm sorry, you'll have to wait.
(C) He doesn't know how to respond.

188. Mark your answer on your answer sheet.

Ⓐ Ⓑ Ⓒ

189. **Man A:** *Do you understand the risks involved, if you go through with this?*

    Man B: *(A) Yes, I've lost a lot of money.*
(B) Yes, I'd like to with you.
(C) Yes, but I don't think I have a choice.

189. Mark your answer on your answer sheet.

Ⓐ Ⓑ Ⓒ

190. **Man B:** *How long has it been since we last spoke?*

    Woman: *(A) Several months, at least.*
(B) Two meters, maybe three, at most.
(C) Yes, I think we should have it fixed.

190. Mark your answer on your answer sheet.

Ⓐ Ⓑ Ⓒ

191. **Man A:** *What time does the next train arrive?*

    Man B: *(A) It takes about twenty minutes to reach the station.*
(B) It will be here in twelve minutes.
(C) The train arrives on Track 14.

191. Mark your answer on your answer sheet.

Ⓐ Ⓑ Ⓒ

192. **Man A:** *When does Art think he will be promoted?*

    Man B: *(A) He has promised to return before Saturday.*
(B) Not until he brings in more clients.
(C) Our new promotion will begin right after the holidays.

192. Mark your answer on your answer sheet.

Ⓐ Ⓑ Ⓒ

You hear:

193. **Man B:** *You've been a member of the Association for many years, haven't you?*

    Man A: *(A) Yes, he is forty years old.*
(B) Yes, I'm a lifetime member.
(C) Yes, now I remember who he is.

193. Mark your answer on your answer sheet.

Ⓐ Ⓑ Ⓒ

194. **Man A:** *Is it possible that we've met before?*

    Woman: *(A) No, I can't meet you until later.*
(B) I can meet you at seven o'clock.
(C) Yes, I think we were introduced at a dinner once.

194. Mark your answer on your answer sheet.

Ⓐ Ⓑ Ⓒ

195. **Man B:** *When do you plan to visit our main office?*

    Man A: *(A) I visited there three years ago.*
(B) He visits us quite frequently.
(C) I was planning to go there next week.

195. Mark your answer on your answer sheet.

Ⓐ Ⓑ Ⓒ

196. **Man A:** *Can I help you find something?*

    Woman: *(A) Yes, I'm looking for a gift for a friend.*
(B) It can't be helped, I'm afraid.
(C) Sure, I'd be glad to help you, if I can.

196. Mark your answer on your answer sheet.

Ⓐ Ⓑ Ⓒ

197. **Man B:** *Do you know whether he plans to expand his business in the next five years?*

    Woman: *(A) Yes, he's said something to that effect.*
(B) He went out of business last year.
(C) Bad weather affects every business.

197. Mark your answer on your answer sheet.

Ⓐ Ⓑ Ⓒ

198. **Man A:** *Do you have any suggestions for improving sales?*

    Man B: *(A) I think we should increase our retail outlets.*
(B) Sales were quite bad last month.
(C) I bought it on sale at a department store.

198. Mark your answer on your answer sheet.

Ⓐ Ⓑ Ⓒ

199. **Woman:** *Can you tell me where I can find a post office?*

    Man A: *(A) The mail arrives in the morning.*
(B) My office is downtown.
(C) There's one at the next corner, down the street.

199. Mark your answer on your answer sheet.

Ⓐ Ⓑ Ⓒ

200. **Man A:** *May I borrow some money for lunch?*
Man B: *(A) Sure. How much do you need?*
(B) Yes, please lend me some.
(C) That lunch was quite inexpensive.

200. Mark your answer on your answer sheet.

Ⓐ Ⓑ Ⓒ

201. **Man B:** *That was a good movie, don't you think?*
Woman: *(A) I'm not moving until next week.*
(B) Yes, I enjoyed it.
(C) I'm not sure. Maybe tomorrow.

201. Mark your answer on your answer sheet.

Ⓐ Ⓑ Ⓒ

202. **Woman:** *How long has he been attending that church?*
Man A: *(A) Ever since it opened.*
(B) Every Sunday morning.
(C) Services are over by noon.

202. Mark your answer on your answer sheet.

Ⓐ Ⓑ Ⓒ

203. **Man B:** *I see it as a great opportunity, don't you?*
Man A: *(A) I couldn't agree more.*
(B) Whenever you're ready, we'll go.
(C) My sight seems to be getting worse.

203. Mark your answer on your answer sheet.

Ⓐ Ⓑ Ⓒ

204. **Woman:** *Could you please turn down the radio?*
Man A: *(A) Yes, it is too expensive.*
(B) Thank you, I would like to try one.
(C) I'm sorry. I'll turn it off.

204. Mark your answer on your answer sheet.

Ⓐ Ⓑ Ⓒ

205. **Woman:** *You know, you really should see a doctor about that pain in your chest.*
Man A: *(A) Yes, my best friend from high school is in the hospital.*
(B) Yes, I'll call for an appointment.
(C) I've known him for many years.

205. Mark your answer on your answer sheet.

Ⓐ Ⓑ Ⓒ

206. **Woman:** *Are you Tom Smith?*
Man A: *(A) Yes. Do I know you?*
(B) Nice to meet you.
(C) Right over there, I believe.

206. Mark your answer on your answer sheet.

Ⓐ Ⓑ Ⓒ

207. **Woman:** *Do you have breakfast every morning?*
Man B: *(A) I'm very sorry about it.*
(B) It's in the kitchen.
(C) Usually, but not always.

207. Mark your answer on your answer sheet.

Ⓐ Ⓑ Ⓒ

208. **Man A:** *Where do you live?*
Man B: *(A) From the airport.*
(B) A few blocks from here.
(C) On the street.

208. Mark your answer on your answer sheet.

Ⓐ Ⓑ Ⓒ

209. **Man B:** *Do you play any sports?*
     Man A: (A) *No, I'm not at all athletic.*
             (B) *Any time at all.*
             (C) *Yes. I like to watch football on television.*

209. Mark your answer on your answer sheet.

Ⓐ Ⓑ Ⓒ

210. **Woman:** *I have a terrible cold.*
     Man A: (A) *That's great!*
             (B) *I'm a little cold myself.*
             (C) *You should probably be in bed.*

210. Mark your answer on your answer sheet.

Ⓐ Ⓑ Ⓒ

211. **Man A:** *Could I please speak with Mr. Jones?*
     Woman: (A) *I'll dial again.*
             (B) *There's no one here by that name.*
             (C) *Hello, Mr. Jones.*

211. Mark your answer on your answer sheet.

Ⓐ Ⓑ Ⓒ

212. **Man B:** *What are you looking for?*
     Woman: (A) *My purse. I've misplaced it.*
             (B) *No, I think I'll need five.*
             (C) *Look in the drawer.*

212. Mark your answer on your answer sheet.

Ⓐ Ⓑ Ⓒ

213. **Woman:** *How late are you open today?*
     Man B: (A) *We open at ten.*
             (B) *We're close to the station.*
             (C) *Until eight o'clock.*

213. Mark your answer on your answer sheet.

Ⓐ Ⓑ Ⓒ

214. **Woman:** *Whose umbrella is this?*
     Man A: (A) *It's hers.*
             (B) *They're mine.*
             (C) *He's my younger brother.*

214. Mark your answer on your answer sheet.

Ⓐ Ⓑ Ⓒ

215. **Man B:** *Do you need any help with those bags?*
     Woman: (A) *No, that's O.K. I can manage.*
             (B) *I think I can get up, but it hurts.*
             (C) *Yes, I think they live near here.*

215. Mark your answer on your answer sheet.

Ⓐ Ⓑ Ⓒ

216. **Woman:** *What do you want to do tonight?*
     Man A: (A) *I knew he would call.*
             (B) *Oh, nothing. I'm really tired.*
             (C) *No, tomorrow night.*

216. Mark your answer on your answer sheet.

Ⓐ Ⓑ Ⓒ

217. **Man B:** *What's it like out?*
     Man A: (A) *It's windy and cold.*
             (B) *It's large, but not heavy.*
             (C) *It didn't cost very much.*

217. Mark your answer on your answer sheet.

Ⓐ Ⓑ Ⓒ

218. **Man A:** *Where are you from?*
    Woman: (A) *I'm going to work.*
          (B) *I was born in Germany, but I grew up here.*
          (C) *They're in the closet.*

218. Mark your answer on your answer sheet.

Ⓐ Ⓑ Ⓒ

219. **Man B:** *How many eggs do we need?*
    Woman: (A) *He was going very fast.*
          (B) *Ten or twelve.*
          (C) *They're not hungry yet.*

219. Mark your answer on your answer sheet.

Ⓐ Ⓑ Ⓒ

220. **Man B:** *What did you think of the movie?*
    Man A: (A) *That's a good idea.*
          (B) *I don't know. It didn't occur to me.*
          (C) *I didn't like it at all.*

220. Mark your answer on your answer sheet.

Ⓐ Ⓑ Ⓒ

221. **Man A:** *When did the accident happen?*
    Woman: (A) *The day before yesterday.*
          (B) *That's too bad.*
          (C) *Right in front of my house.*

221. Mark your answer on your answer sheet.

Ⓐ Ⓑ Ⓒ

222. **Man B:** *I called you last night, but you weren't home.*
    Man A: (A) *I'm going to speak with him about it.*
          (B) *No. We went to visit my wife's parents.*
          (C) *I'll send somebody to pick it up.*

222. Mark your answer on your answer sheet.

Ⓐ Ⓑ Ⓒ

223. **Man B:** *Where did you learn Spanish?*
    Man A: (A) *I lived in Mexico for a while.*
          (B) *I studied business in college.*
          (C) *Sometimes it's very painful.*

223. Mark your answer on your answer sheet.

Ⓐ Ⓑ Ⓒ

224. **Man A:** *How far is the bus stop from here?*
    Man B: (A) *It's quite high up.*
          (B) *Two blocks, in that direction.*
          (C) *I think it's a new record!*

224. Mark your answer on your answer sheet.

Ⓐ Ⓑ Ⓒ

225. **Woman:** *Did anyone call?*
    Man A: (A) *Yes, but no one got hurt.*
          (B) *No, we all lost.*
          (C) *Somebody named Tom asked for you.*

225. Mark your answer on your answer sheet.

Ⓐ Ⓑ Ⓒ

226. **Man B:** *How often do you exercise?*
    Man A: (A) *I run at least two laps.*
          (B) *Every day, for about an hour.*
          (C) *It's not very difficult.*

226. Mark your answer on your answer sheet.

Ⓐ Ⓑ Ⓒ

227. **Man A:** *Can you drive a car with a manual transmission?*

   Woman: *(A) Yes, in fact, I've never had an automatic.*

   (B) He's been on the police force a long time.

   (C) Six, maybe seven, but no more.

227. Mark your answer on your answer sheet.

   Ⓐ Ⓑ Ⓒ

228. **Man B:** *What's wrong with your phone?*

   Man A: *(A) I'll phone Mr. Charles.*

   (B) I don't know how to sing very well.

   (C) Nothing, that I know of.

228. Mark your answer on your answer sheet.

   Ⓐ Ⓑ Ⓒ

229. **Man A:** *May I help you with your bags?*

   Woman: *(A) Yes, please. My car is parked just over there.*

   (B) Yes, I love the flowers in spring.

   (C) Sure, take some of each kind.

229. Mark your answer on your answer sheet.

   Ⓐ Ⓑ Ⓒ

230. **Man A:** *Do you know how to operate a word processor?*

   Man B: *(A) Not very well, but I'm learning.*

   (B) Yes, your orders been processed.

   (C) Yes, people say I'm quite a good cook.

230. Mark your answer on your answer sheet.

   Ⓐ Ⓑ Ⓒ

231. **Man A:** *How much does that radio cost?*

   Woman: *(A) Thirty-five dollars.*

   (B) Nearly one kilo per day

   (C) Everything I had in my purse.

231. Mark your answer on your answer sheet.

   Ⓐ Ⓑ Ⓒ

232. **Man B:** *Does the coat fit?*

   Woman: *(A) I think it's windy right now.*

   (B) Yes, very nicely.

   (C) Not very hard.

232. Mark your answer on your answer sheet.

   Ⓐ Ⓑ Ⓒ

233. **Woman:** *Are you going to go out later?*

   Man B: *(A) Yes, but I'm only going to the store.*

   (B) No, it's already gone.

   (C) I don't think I should mail it.

233. Mark your answer on your answer sheet.

   Ⓐ Ⓑ Ⓒ

234. **Man A:** *How does the coffee maker work?*

   Woman: *(A) She works many hours each day.*

   (B) He takes the bus.

   (C) Just put in coffee and water, and turn it on.

234. Mark your answer on your answer sheet.

   Ⓐ Ⓑ Ⓒ

235. **Man B:** *Are you ready to order?*

   Man A: *(A) Yes, do as I told you.*

   (B) No, not yet. I need a little more time.

   (C) No, it's still far away.

235. Mark your answer on your answer sheet.

   Ⓐ Ⓑ Ⓒ

ANSWER KEY—PART II

1. (B) At the National University.
2. (B) Yes, that's a good idea.
3. (A) Yes, it is. Very.
4. (B) On East Gate Road.
5. (C) Pretty good, thank you.
6. (C) Could you show me that camera in the window?
7. (C) No, thanks. I've had enough.
8. (C) I drive.
9. (B) It's in the refrigerator.
10. (A) It's not possible right now.
11. (C) No, I think that's all.
12. (A) No, I'm busy on Friday.
13. (C) Yes, I have a lot to do.
14. (C) I put them back in the cabinet.
15. (B) I will, but I know they're right.
16. (A) I don't like him.
17. (C) Since two o'clock.
18. (B) Yes, I went up it last summer.
19. (A) They're both very tall.
20. (B) Of course. I'm sorry.
21. (A) It's the twenty-second.
22. (A) That's O.K. What do you need?
23. (C) Yes, I work in that building across the street.
24. (A) He's an airplane mechanic
25. (C) No, I have a roommate.
26. (B) Not at all. Come along.
27. (A) No, but I'm new in *this* office.
28. (A) Sure. What is it?
29. (B) I think he was very upset.
30. (C) I plan to get a job as soon as I can.
31. (A) I don't think so, but thanks anyway.
32. (B) I don't know yet.
33. (B) I'd be glad to.
34. (B) I haven't made it yet.
35. (C) It's my brother.
36. (C) Well, I hope you find something.
37. (A) I'm sorry, he isn't in yet.
38. (A) I don't know. I don't have any plans.
39. (C) I wouldn't miss it.
40. (C) I'm sure it will be.
41. (B) I may. I'll take them in my briefcase.
42. (C) No. We'll do all right with it.
43. (B) Yes, for about ten years now.
44. (C) I'm sure we can find something to eat.
45. (C) Sure, I'll phone you.
46. (B) They don't have enough money.
47. (C) No, I'm not doing anything.
48. (C) It was nearly five years ago.
49. (A) I guess I'm not very good at this work.
50. (B) I plan to set up more overseas offices.
51. (B) No, but I'll tell him later today.
52. (B) Just a little.
53. (A) No, not yet.
54. (B) I'd like to go to the library.
55. (B) I find it very interesting.
56. (A) No, but I've always wanted to go.
57. (C) Yes, please do.
58. (C) Yes. Could you please call my office.

59. (C) No. What happened?
60. (B) Yes. A friend from college lives there.
61. (B) I guess I'd have to say it's Elton John.
62. (A) Since five o'clock.
63. (A) Oh, I don't know. It's hard to say.
64. (B) Pretty well, considering everything.
65. (B) Nothing much, really.
66. (A) I've been told that they are.
67. (C) Not very, but I won't drown.
68. (B) She's doing fine, thanks.
69. (A) No. I'm sorry, I can't.
70. (A) No, thank you. I have to go.
71. (A) They're all doing well.
72. (A) It's over in that direction somewhere.
73. (B) No. I'll call back later.
74. (B) Yes, but we're waiting for the president.
75. (A) No, I'm working at the National Bank now.
76. (B) Yes. You may use this one.
77. (A) I can't find my wallet.
78. (B) Why, thank you.
79. (B) Down the hall and to the left.
80. (C) That's a good idea.
81. (A) Yes, very well.
82. (C) Manchester, England.
83. (A) I thought it was great.
84. (C) Later today, if I get them done.
85. (B) Of course not. Please do.
86. (A) Every weekend.
87. (C) I can't find my house keys.
88. (C) I work in a pharmacy.
89. (B) I don't know why.
90. (A) No, I'm still looking.
91. (C) It seems reasonable.
92. (A) I don't know, but they keep on hiring.
93. (A) I really like it.
94. (A) To the amusement park.
95. (B) Only about five minutes ago.
96. (C) No, but it's the best we could do.
97. (A) Yes, that would be good.
98. (B) No, I won't be able to, thank you.
99. (B) I don't think I can get it done even then.
100. (A) No, they leave it in the cash register.
101. (B) Nowhere special. I'll just stay home.
102. (C) Sure. Keep it as long as you like.
103. (B) Yes. Just a minute, please.
104. (B) Only twenty minutes.
105. (A) I go to the ocean.
106. (B) Turn right at the next light and go straight ahead.
107. (C) No, thanks. I don't need anything.
108. (A) No, I had to work late.
109. (C) As I understand it, he didn't have any cash.
110. (A) Maybe some other time.
111. (C) Yes, but I don't agree with you.
112. (B) They said they'd be ready last week.
113. (C) Registered, please.
114. (A) It sure does.
115. (C) At around five o'clock.
116. (B) Fifty percent of retail.

117. (C) I can prove it with figures for the last six months.
118. (B) I read it in the quarterly report.
119. (C) We should do very well with it.
120. (C) I met yesterday with the president of the company.
121. (A) Yes, it probably would be.
122. (C) Of course, if you want me to.
123. (A) I had a special invitation.
124. (B) Three or four.
125. (C) I certainly hope so.
126. (A) Yes, I visited there on Monday.
127. (C) On Wednesday, the twelfth.
128. (A) We need a decision on this right away.
129. (B) Two weeks ago.
130. (B) Yes, I think so.
131. (B) I already have a draft.
132. (C) No, I have it.
133. (B) It was nearly three o'clock.
134. (B) Yes, if you have time to show them to me.
135. (A) Yes, the engineer is.
136. (C) We have to call.
137. (A) I can't promise, but I'll try.
138. (B) Yes, I did.
139. (B) I certainly hope we do.
140. (C) That's a good suggestion.
141. (A) There doesn't seem to be.
142. (C) A week from today.
143. (B) In a comprehensive written report.
144. (B) No, thank you. I'll call again.
145. (A) Sure. Let's do it now.
146. (B) About an hour ago.
147. (B) I asked him yesterday.
148. (C) I found it very informative.
149. (C) I'm afraid not.
150. (C) Yes, I'll give him the message.
151. (A) No, that's too early.
152. (C) Yes, I think he would.
153. (B) Yes, those new ads really work for us.
154. (B) Only yesterday.
155. (B) No, there's still a lot to be done.
156. (B) No, but my assistant did.
157. (A) We've conducted extensive surveys.
158. (C) Yes, we've found it really pays off.
159. (B) They are supposed to, but some may not.
160. (C) I think they want to keep their distance.
161. (B) They came in over the telex yesterday.
162. (A) They're trying to get their money back.
163. (A) Yes, we've heard all about it.
164. (B) Yes, I'm afraid it will.
165. (C) Yes. When would he be free?
166. (A) I'm sorry, there isn't.
167. (B) I expect to receive orders from it any day.
168. (A) That doesn't give us enough lead time for advertising.
169. (A) No, I think we'll be better off in the long run.
170. (C) Yes, go right ahead.
171. (A) I'm planning to go to Indonesia.
172. (B) That's Bill, from the Shipping Department.
173. (B) Yes, I was there.
174. (C) Yes, it has.
175. (A) No, not yet.
176. (C) Sometime in the afternoon.
177. (B) Yes. I'm looking forward to it.
178. (B) I have to drive, because I'll need my car.
179. (A) In February.
180. (C) No, please sit down.
181. (C) Yes, in fact, just last week.
182. (A) I'm afraid it doesn't look good.
183. (B) I worked on it alone.
184. (B) I have no idea.
185. (B) They've already begun.
186. (A) Yes, I heard the traffic report on the radio just now.
187. (C) There's one just across from the hotel.
188. (A) I think it's a great idea.
189. (C) Yes, but I don't think I have a choice.
190. (A) Several months, at least.
191. (B) It will be here in twelve minutes.
192. (B) Not until he brings in more clients.
193. (B) Yes, I'm a lifetime member.
194. (C) Yes, I think we were introduced at a dinner once.
195. (C) I was planning to go there next week.
196. (A) Yes, I'm looking for a gift for a friend.
197. (A) Yes, he's said something to that effect.
198. (A) I think we should increase our retail outlets.
199. (C) There's one at the next corner, down the street.
200. (A) Sure. How much do you need?
201. (B) Yes, I enjoyed it.
202. (A) Ever since it opened.
203. (A) I couldn't agree more.
204. (C) I'm sorry. I'll turn it off.
205. (B) Yes, I'll call for an appointment.
206. (A) Yes. Do I know you?
207. (C) Usually, but not always.
208. (B) A few blocks from here.
209. (A) No, I'm not at all athletic.
210. (C) You should probably be in bed.
211. (B) There's no one here by that name.
212. (A) My purse. I've misplaced it.
213. (C) Until eight o'clock.
214. (A) It's hers.
215. (A) No, that's O.K. I can manage.
216. (B) Oh, nothing. I'm really tired.
217. (A) It's windy and cold.
218. (B) I was born in Germany, but I grew up here.
219. (B) Ten or twelve.
220. (C) I didn't like it at all.
221. (A) The day before yesterday.
222. (B) No. We went to visit my wife's parents.
223. (A) I lived in Mexico for a while.
224. (B) Two blocks, in that direction.
225. (C) Somebody named Tom asked for you.
226. (B) Every day, for about an hour.
227. (A) Yes, in fact, I've never had an automatic.
228. (C) Nothing, that I know of.
229. (A) Yes, please. My car is parked just over there.
230. (A) Not very well, but I'm learning.
231. (A) Thirty-five dollars.
232. (B) Yes, very nicely.
233. (A) Yes, but I'm only going to the store.
234. (C) Just put in coffee and water, and turn it on.
235. (B) No, not yet. I need a little more time.

PART III: DISCUSSION

The questions in this section of the test are a combination of listening and reading. Test takers will hear a conversation between two people and are asked a question about the conversation. The questions do not deal with trivial or unimportant points of the conversation, but rather are designed to determine whether you, the listener, can understand the main point or points, as if you were "eavesdropping" on a talk between the speakers.

You will be asked to read a question regarding the conversation. For those who understand the conversation, but who are unable to read the question, this part of the listening test becomes a test of reading. Upon studying this part of the test, however, you will learn that the reading is not very difficult. It should not present problems to most people who have studied English formally and who are able to understand spoken English at the level of the language in this part of the test.

To answer these questions, you should listen to the speakers as if you were standing with them in a room, on a street corner, or wherever they might be, and participate in the conversation with them. As part of the group, you will understand what is happening and will be able to understand the question that follows.

On the TOEIC®, this part of the test consists of twenty questions.

The directions for Part III of the TOEIC read as follows:

PART III

Directions: In this part of the test, you will hear 200 short conversations between two people. The conversations will not be printed in your test book. You will hear the conversations only once so you must listen carefully to understand what the speakers say.

You will read a question about each conversation. The question will be followed by four answers. You are to choose the best answer to each question and mark it on your answer sheet.

You hear:

1. **Man A:** *I'd like to make reservations for 7:00 P.M., Saturday, the twentieth.*

   Woman: *How many people will be dining, sir?*

   Man A: *There'll be only two of us. It's our anniversary.*

1. What is the man planning to do?
   - (A) Go to the theater.
   - (B) Take a plane trip.
   - (C) Go to a restaurant.
   - (D) Hold a conference.

You hear:

3. **Man A:** *Before you go home today, I'd like you to check these figures. We need them for the meeting tomorrow.*

   Man B: *I'll be glad to, but I'm working on that other report for you. I'm not going to have time before the meeting.*

   Man A: *O.K. then don't worry about it. I'll get Lee to look at them.*

3. Who will check the figures?
   - (A) The supervisor.
   - (B) The employee.
   - (C) Lee.
   - (D) Nobody.

You hear:

2. **Man A:** *Sorry to have kept you waiting.*

   Man B: *Where have you been?*

   Man A: *In my office. I was working on my report and just forgot what time it was.*

2. Why was the man late?
   - (A) He was in a meeting.
   - (B) He was on the telephone.
   - (C) He was looking for a report he needed.
   - (D) He was not paying attention to time.

You hear:

4. **Man A:** *I'd like to see the new release that just opened at the Capitol. My favorite actor is in it.*

   Woman: *I saw it last night. It's not very good.*

   Man A: *Oh, really? Well, maybe I'll go see it anyway.*

4. What does the man want to do?
   - (A) Buy a book.
   - (B) See a film.
   - (C) Go to a play.
   - (D) Watch a television show.

You hear:

5. ...d. Can

...hind in

...a to have

som...

...le somewhere.

5. What d... ...when the ...st?

(A) A rid... ...

(B) To know ... seminar is.

(C) For the woma... to attend a seminar.

(D) Help with his work.

You hear:

6. **Man A:** *The corporation budget's been cut again this year.*

Man B: *So we'll have even less money than before, is that right?*

Man A: *No, not really. I've been told that it won't affect our department one way or the other.*

6. What will be the result on the department because of a change in the budget?

(A) Their budget will be smaller.

(B) Their budget will be larger.

(C) Their budget will remain unchanged.

(D) Nobody knows what the impact will be.

You hear:

7. **Man A:** *We would like a double room.*

Man B: *I'm sorry, but we don't have any more doubles. How about a room with two singles?*

Man A: *Well, if that's all there is, it'll have to do.*

7. Where are the speakers?

(A) In a hotel.

(B) In a concert.

(C) At an airport.

(D) At a movie theater.

You hear:

8. **Woman:** *My flight was overbooked again, and it made us late getting off the ground.*

Man A: *That's strange. I've never had a problem with reservations on that airline.*

Woman: *If it happens once more, I'll never fly with them again.*

8. Why is the woman upset?

(A) Her reservation was lost.

(B) Her flight was canceled.

(C) Too many tickets were issued for her flight.

(D) The crew was late arriving at the airport.

You hear:

9. **Woman:** *Why didn't you make it in to work yesterday?*

Man B: *I had some bad food at a restaurant the night before. I was very sick.*

Woman: *I'm glad you're feeling better today. We have to work on those figures later on.*

9. Where was the man the day before?

(A) At his desk.

(B) At a meeting.

(C) Sick at home.

(D) At a restaurant.

You hear:

10. **Man A:** *You called the building office about a problem. What seems to be the matter?*

Woman: *My television doesn't work.*

Man A: *I'm sorry, ma'am. There's nothing I can do about that. I only take care of repairs to the apartment itself.*

10. What is the man's job?

(A) He is a television repairman.

(B) He is responsible for apartment repairs.

(C) He does not have a job.

(D) He designs offices.

You hear:

11. **Man A:** *Shall we ship this stock over to you, or can you pick it up? It looks like a big order.*

    Woman: *It is. We'll send some of my men over for it.*

    Man A: *Be sure to let us know when they're coming. It'll take us a while to get it ready.*

11. How will the woman receive her shipment?
    - (A) It will be sent to her.
    - (B) She will call later to arrange for delivery.
    - (C) She will have some men pick it up.
    - (D) The man will drop it off.

You hear:

12. **Woman:** *Who typed this report?*

    Man B: *The new temporary employee. Why do you ask?*

    Woman: *I've found three mistakes in the first paragraph alone.*

12. What is the woman complaining about?
    - (A) She has been left alone.
    - (B) She has made a mistake.
    - (C) A report is poorly typed.
    - (D) She lost a report.

You hear:

13. **Man A:** *Prepare a memorandum of the details, when you know them, and send them to me in Paris.*

    Woman: *Do you want me to call you?*

    Man A: *No. It's expensive and not necessary. Writing is fast enough.*

13. How will the man learn of the matter?
    - (A) By mail.
    - (B) By phone.
    - (C) By telex.
    - (D) By messenger.

You hear:

14. **Woman:** *Do you get over to the branch office very often?*

    Man B: *Oh, usually only once or twice a year. Not as much as I should.*

    Woman: *Well, I was just there, and they're doing fine.*

14. How often does the man visit the branch office?
    - (A) Never.
    - (B) Occasionally.
    - (C) Quite often.
    - (D) All the time.

You hear:

15. **Man A:** *Have you heard about Andy?*

    Man B: *No, is there some problem?*

    Man A: *He's announcing his retirement at the board meeting tomorrow. He says he wants more time to himself.*

15. What does Andy plan to do?
    - (A) Change jobs.
    - (B) Stop working.
    - (C) Become a board member.
    - (D) Not go to the board meeting.

You hear:

16. **Man A:** *I can't believe it! We lost the K.L. contract because our bid arrived late!*

    Man B: *That's twice in one month that our bids haven't been considered. Why do we keep doing this?*

    Man A: *I don't know. There's no good reason for it.*

16. Why did the speakers lose the K.L. contract?
    - (A) Their bid was late.
    - (B) There was no reason for it.
    - (C) Their bid was lost somewhere.
    - (D) They had forgotten about it.

You hear:

17. Man A: *I can't understand this drop in quality.*

Woman: *Well, we have a lot of new employees.*

Man A: *That's true. They don't take the care that our older workers do and make a lot of mistakes.*

17. What are the speakers discussing?

(A) The need to hire more workers.

(B) The reason quality has gone down.

(C) Training new employees.

(D) Parking lot expansion for new staff.

You hear:

18. Woman: *When do you think we can take Charles home from the hospital?*

Man B: *He may be well enough in three or four weeks, but certainly not before.*

Woman: *That seems like an awfully long time.*

18. When can Charles leave the hospital?

(A) In a few hours.

(B) In a few days.

(C) In a few weeks.

(D) In a few months.

You hear:

19. Woman: *It's after six. Where've you been? I've been so worried!*

Man A: *I was at the doctor's office, remember?*

Woman: *Oh, of course. I made the appointment!*

19. Where has the man been?

(A) At the races.

(B) At his office.

(C) At the doctor's.

(D) At a golf course.

You hear:

20. Man B: *I've misplaced my umbrella and it's raining out.*

Woman: *What color is it?*

Man B: *It's black, just like everybody else's.*

20. What happened to the man?

(A) He bought a new car.

(B) He lost his umbrella.

(C) He solved the problem.

(D) He was late for work.

You hear:

21. Man A: *I'm not used to this weather!*

Woman: *Take it easy. Like everything, it's not so bad after you're here for a while.*

Man A: *That's what they tell me every time I transfer, but I never feel at home anywhere but my home town.*

21. What can be said about the man?

(A) He does not like to move.

(B) He enjoys cold weather.

(C) He does not like foreign food.

(D) He always feels at home.

You hear:

22. Woman: *Oh, no! I have only one glove in my purse!*

Man B: *Is this your glove, here on the chair?*

Woman: *Oh, yes. Thank you so much.*

22. What had the woman done?

(A) She lost her way.

(B) She dropped a glove.

(C) She bought a new purse.

(D) She left home without money.

You hear:

23. **Man A:** *I'm getting hungry. Shall we have dinner?*

    Woman: *Sure. What would you like to have?*

    Man A: *The seafood around here is supposed to be very good. Let's try it.*

23. What is the couple about to do?
    (A) Get on a boat.
    (B) Eat dinner.
    (C) Leave for vacation.
    (D) Visit friends.

You hear:

24. **Man A:** *It's freezing in here. Can't we turn up the heat?*

    Man B: *I don't think it'll go up any higher. These old windows let in a lot of cold air.*

    Man A: *I knew there had to be something wrong, or the rent here wouldn't have been so inexpensive.*

24. What can be said about the apartment?
    (A) It is new.
    (B) It is not clean.
    (C) It is on the top floor.
    (D) It is not comfortable.

You hear:

25. **Man A:** *Do you have any onions?*

    Woman: *No, but we have some good peppers and tomatoes.*

    Man A: *Yes, but I don't like peppers and tomatoes without onions. I'll come back tomorrow.*

25. What can be said about the man?
    (A) He does not sell many vegetables.
    (B) He likes onions.
    (C) He is just passing by.
    (D) He does not know what he wants.

You hear:

26. **Woman:** *May I help you?*

    Man A: *I need some sunglasses. I've been invited skiing and I understand the snow can be very bright.*

    Woman: *We have some very good ones that are designed for winter sports.*

26. Where does the man intend to go?
    (A) Sailing.
    (B) Skiing.
    (C) Golfing.
    (D) Traveling.

You hear:

27. **Man A:** *What's the matter?*

    Man B: *I can't find my ticket or my passport!*

    Man A: *It says our flight is delayed and won't leave for two hours. Let's call the hotel, and see if you left them on the counter.*

27. Where are the two men?
    (A) In a hotel.
    (B) In a restaurant.
    (C) At an airport.
    (D) At a police station.

You hear:

28. **Woman:** *Jim and I went to dinner last night at that new restaurant just outside town.*

    Man B: *How was it?*

    Woman: *The waiters are inexperienced and nothing worked right, but they're trying. If it survives, in six months it should do well.*

28. What does the woman say about the restaurant?
    (A) It was excellent.
    (B) It was very crowded.
    (C) The service was good, but the food was not.
    (D) It will improve with time.

29. Woman: *Why have you come to Hawaii?*

Man B: *We're here on our honeymoon.*

Woman: *Many young couples come here from all over the world. I wish you both much happiness.*

29. What is the man doing?
   (A) He is studying.
   (B) He is on business.
   (C) He is visiting friends.
   (D) He is on vacation with his wife.

30. Man A: *How do you get to work?*

Man B: *I drive. It takes me an hour and a half each way.*

Man A: *An hour and a half! I come by train in forty minutes, door to door.*

30. What are the men discussing?
   (A) Work they do at home.
   (B) Time spent in meetings.
   (C) Time spent going to and from work.
   (D) Work they do while commuting.

31. Man A: *I'm getting too fat. I'm going to join a club and get some exercise.*

Woman: *You should expect to put on weight as you get older. I like you the way you are.*

Man A: *Maybe, but I don't think it's healthy to be overweight.*

31. What are the couple discussing?
   (A) His work.
   (B) His weight.
   (C) Her cooking.
   (D) His age.

32. Woman: *Cities are so noisy . . . and it's so quiet in the suburbs, which is why I live here.*

Man B: *It's quiet all right, and there's nothing to do.*

Woman: *When I want excitement, I go into town. It's not so far.*

32. Why does the woman prefer the suburbs?
   (A) Housing is less expensive.
   (B) Schools are better than in the city.
   (C) It allows for a peaceful life.
   (D) She has no interest in excitement.

33. Man A: *We're all going out for Chinese food. Would you like to join us?*

Woman: *I'd like to, but I can't. My mother's expecting me to go shopping with her right after work.*

Man A: *Well, maybe some other time.*

33. Why will the woman not join her friends?
   (A) She has to work late.
   (B) She has an exercise class.
   (C) Her mother will be waiting for her.
   (D) She does not care for Chinese food.

34. Man A: *How do you like working here?*

Man B: *They pay better than other places, but everything else is worse. I don't like it.*

Man A: *They have to pay well, because people keep quitting. This is my last day.*

34. What can be said about the men's employment?
   (A) The working conditions are quite good.
   (B) Nobody enjoys working there.
   (C) The work is better than in other places.
   (D) It is dull, but management tries to make it interesting.

You hear:

35. **Woman:** *That's a nice suit. You look good in blue.*

   Man A: *Thank you. It's one of my favorites.*

   Woman: *It goes well with your hair color.*

35. What did the woman do?

   (A) She paid the man a compliment.

   (B) She sold the man a suit.

   (C) She cut the man's hair.

   (D) She admired the man's child.

You hear:

36. **Woman:** *Did you read my report? What did you think of it?*

   Man B: *Well, you filled 300 pages with words, but I have yet to figure out what you're saying. I don't know how you do it.*

   Woman: *I guess I should rewrite it, eh?*

36. What does the man think of the report?

   (A) He likes it.

   (B) He has not yet read it.

   (C) He suggests some changes.

   (D) He does not understand it.

You hear:

37. **Man A:** *You're always willing to help a person out.*

   Man B: *I'm happy to help people out whenever I can.*

   Man A: *Well I appreciate it and would like to do something for you. Come to dinner next Saturday night and bring a friend.*

37. Why is the man being invited to dinner?

   (A) To celebrate his birthday.

   (B) Because he is new in the neighborhood.

   (C) Because he has done someone a favor.

   (D) To be introduced to somebody.

You hear:

38. **Man B:** *I was going to ask you to lend me some money.*

   Woman: *And why didn't you?*

   Man B: *I decided it wasn't enough to bother you about.*

38. Why did the man NOT borrow money from the woman?

   (A) His friend had none to lend him.

   (B) He no longer needed the money.

   (C) He thought it would be a bother to her.

   (D) Someone else lent him the money he needed.

You hear:

39. **Man A:** *If you help me, this work won't be nearly as unpleasant.*

   Woman: *I think you're fooling yourself. There's an awful lot there to do.*

   Man A: *Maybe, but I don't like to work alone.*

39. Why does the man say he is asking for help?

   (A) With help the work will go fast.

   (B) He likes company when he works.

   (C) He does not know what he's doing.

   (D) He is late for a meeting.

You hear:

40. **Woman:** *When are you going to Manila next?*

   Man B: *I don't know. My travel hasn't been approved.*

   Woman: *I hope you go soon. They need you. The project is experiencing a lot of difficulties.*

40. Why should the man travel to Manila?

   (A) To approve project changes.

   (B) To solve some problems.

   (C) To get back to work.

   (D) To deliver something.

You hear:

41. Man A: *Interesting series of presentations, isn't it?*

Woman: *Yes, very. I thought the last speaker was especially good.*

Man A: *Oh, by the way. Let me introduce myself. My name's Carl Brown.*

41. Where are the people?
(A) At a party.
(B) At a sporting event.
(C) At a picnic.
(D) At a conference.

You hear:

42. Woman: *And what's your occupation?*

Man B: *I build highways and bridges, mostly, but right now I'm working on a tunnel.*

Woman: *That must be very interesting.*

42. What does the man do?
(A) He is an architect.
(B) He is a truck driver.
(C) He is an engineer.
(D) He is a soldier.

You hear:

43. Man A: *Good morning. May I help you?*

Woman: *Yes, please. I'd like to rent an apartment, but it must have two bedrooms.*

Man A: *Fine. Please sit down. I'll need to ask you a few questions.*

43. Where are the speakers?
(A) In a real estate office.
(B) In a police station.
(C) In a department store.
(D) In a doctor's office.

You hear:

44. Woman: *Welcome to Hong Kong, sir. May I have your disembarkation card?*

Man B: *I'm sorry. What would you like to see?*

Woman: *Your disembarkation card. A little white card. They should have given you one on the plane.*

44. What is the man attempting to do?
(A) Explain who he is.
(B) Enter a foreign land.
(C) Ask directions.
(D) Buy an airline ticket.

You hear:

45. Man B: *I understand there's a new movie playing at the Cinema One theater.*

Woman: *There is, but I don't recommend it. I saw it yesterday and it was terrible.*

Man B: *Maybe I'd be better off reading a book.*

45. What is the man looking for?
(A) A friend.
(B) Something he lost.
(C) Some money he has lost.
(D) A way to entertain himself.

You hear:

46. Man A: *Why don't we go out dancing, for a change. We haven't done that for a long time.*

Woman: *That would be fine, but I have a lot of work I have to get done before tomorrow.*

Man A: *Well, we'll just stay home, then. Maybe some other time.*

46. Where are the speakers?
(A) At the office.
(B) In a store.
(C) At home.
(D) At a disco.

You hear: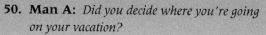

47. Man A: *Do you really think you can do that experiment?*

Man B: *I did it once, but I haven't been able to do it again. I think I've been applying too much heat. I get an unexpected reaction.*

Man A: *Let's do it together to see what the problem is.*

47. Where are the speakers?

(A) At a construction site.

(B) In a laboratory.

(C) At a stadium.

(D) In a kitchen.

You hear:

48. Man A: *Would you care to order now, sir?*

Man B: *Yes, please. I'll have the broiled fish.*

Man A: *Very good. And what vegetables would you like with it?*

48. Where are the speakers?

(A) At a restaurant.

(B) On a street corner.

(C) At home.

(D) In a store.

You hear:

49. Man A: *How many times did you get to the European office this year?*

Man B: *Not even once. Nobody in Product Development has done any overseas travel lately. They claim it's not necessary.*

Man A: *That's too bad. I know in the field they always find your visits helpful.*

49. Why has the man not traveled recently?

(A) He has no time.

(B) It costs too much.

(C) He has not been feeling well.

(D) His supervisors think it serves no purpose.

You hear:

50. Man A: *Did you decide where you're going on your vacation?*

Man B: *I want to go to the beach, but my wife and the children want to go to the mountains. They have more votes than I do, so they win.*

Man A: *I'm sure you don't mind. It will be a lot of fun.*

50. What are the speakers discussing?

(A) Education.

(B) Work.

(C) Vacations.

(D) Entertainment.

You hear:

51. Woman: *I have to go out for some office supplies. Do you need anything?*

Man B: *We could use some large envelopes for mailing brochures, maybe fifty of them.*

Woman: *That's on my list already. I won't be long.*

51. Where is the woman about to go?

(A) To the post office.

(B) To an office supply store.

(C) To pick up brochures.

(D) Home from work.

You hear:

52. Woman: *Did you mean it when you said you were quitting?*

Man B: *Yes, I find it impossible to work here. It is so unpleasant, it's ruining my health.*

Woman: *Then maybe you should leave. Nothing is so important that it should make you sick.*

52. What is the man about to do?

(A) Go to the hospital.

(B) Quit his job.

(C) Visit a friend.

(D) Leave on vacation.

You hear:

53. Man B: *Did you find my report at all useful?*

Woman: *You put a lot of work into it, I know, but I didn't think it was well organized.*

Man B: *Somebody else made the same comment. Maybe you're right.*

53. How does the man feel about his work?
   - (A) He could have done better.
   - (B) He is pleased with what he did.
   - (C) He does not know what is wrong.
   - (D) He is happy for his friend.

You hear:

54. Man A: *If you give me a chance, I know I can increase your sales by 20%.*

Man B: *I would, if you had more experience, but I need people who have proven themselves.*

Man A: *Doesn't a college degree count for anything? I tell you, I can do it.*

54. Why is the applicant being rejected?
   - (A) He is not needed.
   - (B) He wants too much money.
   - (C) He does not have experience.
   - (D) He does not have enough education.

You hear:

55. Man A: *Make sure you're on time tomorrow. We have a lot of work to do in the morning.*

Woman: *Why do you say that? Have I ever been late?*

Man A: *No, but we can't risk not finishing this job on time.*

55. How often does the woman arrive late for work?
   - (A) Never.
   - (B) Sometimes.
   - (C) Often.
   - (D) Always.

You hear:

56. Man B: *I'll need to see the Saudi file, to work on the new contract.*

Woman: *I'm sorry. It's locked up and the boss has the key. He says nobody is to see it.*

Man B: *I'll talk to him about that. How am I supposed to do my work?*

56. What is the man's problem?
   - (A) He and his boss are arguing.
   - (B) He is not allowed to see a file he needs.
   - (C) The secretary has misplaced a key.
   - (D) Nobody will talk to him.

You hear:

57. Man A: *I'd like to join you for lunch, but I really can't take the time.*

Man B: *Look, it'll do you good to get out for an hour.*

Man A: *I know, but I'm supposed to give this speech tonight, and it has to be good.*

57. Why will the man not join his friend for lunch?
   - (A) He is preparing a presentation.
   - (B) He has another lunch appointment.
   - (C) He is not hungry.
   - (D) He will leave work early and must miss his lunch.

You hear:

58. Man B: *Don't you want to tell me about your promotion?*

Woman: *No. It hasn't been approved yet, and I'm afraid it might not be.*

Man B: *Take my word for it. Don't worry. I know something you don't.*

58. What information does the man have?
   - (A) That the woman will be hired.
   - (B) That he is being given a new assignment.
   - (C) That the woman is to be promoted.
   - (D) That the company is being sold.

You hear:

59. **Man A:** *I have something I'd like to talk about with you.*

    Woman: *Sure. What is it?*

    Man A: *I'd prefer not to discuss it here, where all these people can hear. Let's go in the other room, where there're fewer people.*

59. What does the man say he wants to do?
    (A) Make an announcement to everyone.
    (B) Leave the party early.
    (C) Talk about something in private.
    (D) Introduce the woman to a friend.

You hear:

60. **Man A:** *How much food do we need for the picnic?*

    Man B: *I'm not sure. We can figure it out when we know how many people are going.*

    Man A: *I thought I'd go to the market this afternoon. There's not much time.*

60. What must be decided upon?
    (A) How many people to invite.
    (B) How much food to buy.
    (C) Where to hold the picnic.
    (D) When to go shopping.

You hear:

61. **Man B:** *Look, let me sell you some of this stock today and in ten years you'll be rich.*

    Woman: *That's easy for you to say. I have no money.*

    Man B: *You don't need a lot. Any little bit can give you great returns.*

61. What does the man want the woman to do?
    (A) Pay some of the expenses.
    (B) Invest in stock.
    (C) Lend him money.
    (D) Give up a good job to work for him.

You hear:

62. **Man A:** *I'm sorry I missed you yesterday.*

    Woman: *What happened? I waited twenty minutes outside the building.*

    Man A: *No, really? I was waiting inside and thought you didn't come.*

62. What happened to the speakers?
    (A) They had an argument.
    (B) They could not agree on where to have dinner.
    (C) They went to the wrong building.
    (D) They failed to meet one another.

You hear:

63. **Man A:** *Your garden is so beautiful; do you read Green Garden magazine?*

    Woman: *That's a terrible magazine. They tell you all the wrong things to do.*

    Man A: *That's probably why I've never been able to grow a garden.*

63. Why does the man say he is not a good gardener?
    (A) He gets the wrong advice.
    (B) He has no interest in gardening.
    (C) He does not have much spare time.
    (D) He does not use the right fertilizers.

You hear:

64. **Man B:** *I should write to the newspaper about that incident.*

    Man A: *Why don't you? It would make people more aware of a dangerous situation.*

    Man B: *The editors would never publish my letter. They only write about good things, because they don't want to upset people.*

64. Why does the man decide not to write to the newspaper?
    (A) It would upset people.
    (B) He thinks nobody wants to read his comments.
    (C) He does not want his name in print.
    (D) He says the editors would not print his letter.

You hear:

65. **Man A:** *You know, you really shouldn't walk in that area at night.*

   Woman: *But I have to. It's the only way to get home.*

   Man A: *It's only that I've read about some very unpleasant things that have happened there lately and I worry.*

65. Why is the man concerned?

   (A) He was attacked recently.

   (B) He has read about bad things happening.

   (C) His friend was hurt in a robbery.

   (D) He wants the woman to move elsewhere.

You hear:

66. **Man A:** *How much do you think Mrs. Roberts has insured all those beautiful diamonds for?*

   Woman: *She has <u>no</u> insurance on them. They're not real.*

   Man A: *That's a good reason.*

66. Why did Mrs. Roberts not insure the jewelry?

   (A) It is not hers.

   (B) It is not valuable.

   (C) She does not believe in insurance.

   (D) She has so much money, she does not care.

You hear:

67. **Man B:** *How long should my presentation be?*

   Man A: *Only long enough to say what you have to say. If you talk longer, people will become bored and forget the important part.*

   Man B: *That's good advice. Twenty minutes should be plenty of time.*

67. What are the speakers discussing?

   (A) Speaking in public.

   (B) Meeting people.

   (C) Giving advice.

   (D) Buying presents.

You hear:

68. **Woman:** *You look exhausted. You should get some rest.*

   Man B: *No, really, I'm just hungry. I haven't eaten since this morning.*

   Woman: *We can take care of that. Just sit down for a few minutes.*

68. What is the woman going to do?

   (A) Telephone a doctor.

   (B) Prepare some food.

   (C) Take a nap.

   (D) Give the man some water.

You hear:

69. **Man A:** *Do you know a good investment counselor? I have some ideas I'd like to pursue.*

   Man B: *That depends. Are you interested in long term investments or quick in-and-out speculation?*

   Man A: *I want my money to work for me. I don't really care how, just so it does as well as it can.*

69. What does the man say he wants to do with his money?

   (A) Invest it in real estate.

   (B) Save for his children's education.

   (C) Protect it against inflation.

   (D) Earn as much with it as possible.

You hear:

70. **Man A:** *Do you smoke?*

   Man B: *I used to, but I gave it up because I could tell it was ruining my health.*

   Man A: *I think it's ruining mine, too, but I'm unable to stop. Tell me what you did to stop.*

70. Why does the man say he wants to give up smoking?

   (A) Because his wife does not like it.

   (B) Because his doctor advised him to.

   (C) Because he feels it is bad for his health.

   (D) Because he is no longer allowed to smoke at work.

You hear:

71. Woman: *When are you leaving for London?*

Man B: *I'm not sure. I've misplaced my itinerary and don't remember.*

Woman: *I hope it's not before the 14th. There's a program we're supposed to attend that evening.*

71. Why does the woman want to know the man's schedule?
- (A) There is something they must do, and he should not be out of town.
- (B) She needs to make reservations.
- (C) She wants to know if he will be away on his birthday.
- (D) She would like to go to London with him.

You hear:

72. Man A: *How do you think you did on the exam?*

Man B: *I either did very well or very poorly. I have no idea, but the last time I felt this way about an exam I got the best grade in the class.*

Man A: *Then I'm sure you have nothing to worry about.*

72. What are the two men talking about?
- (A) Money.
- (B) Health.
- (C) Test grades.
- (D) Job opportunities.

You hear:

73. Woman: *Whew! I'm really tired. I work all day and now I have to go home and cook .*

Man B: *Do you make dinner every night?*

Woman: *Usually, and my roommate washes the dishes, but that's only because she can't cook. If she could cook, my life would be a lot easier.*

73. How can the woman solve her problem?
- (A) Invite the man to join her.
- (B) Teach her roommate to cook.
- (C) Cancel her reservation.
- (D) Move to a new apartment.

You hear:

74. Man B: *Do you play any sports?*

Woman: *Yes, I play tennis twice a week.*

Man B: *That must keep you healthy. I used to play, but I hurt my back and lately haven't been able to do a thing.*

74. Why does the man not play tennis?
- (A) He is not healthy.
- (B) He does not like to play tennis.
- (C) He is too busy.
- (D) He never learned.

You hear:

75. Man A: *My wife has been trying to get a job working at the newspaper.*

Woman: *That would be an interesting job. Any luck?*

Man A: *Not so far. There's a lot of competition, and we don't know anybody who works there. It always helps, you know.*

75. What would the man like to do?
- (A) Convince his wife she should not work.
- (B) Help his wife get a job.
- (C) Send his children to a good school.
- (D) Enter the competition.

You hear:

76. Man A: *Ah, you have a high temperature and it looks like the flu. There's a lot going around right now.*

Man B: *What should I do?*

Man A: *It's nothing serious. Fill this prescription, go home, go to bed, and get plenty of sleep. Your body will do the rest.*

76. Where does this conversation take place?
- (A) At a repair shop.
- (B) At a doctor's office.
- (C) At a gas station.
- (D) At a furniture store.

You hear:

77. **Woman:** *This is a picture of my sister Kate.*

    Man A: *Are you twins? You look an awful lot alike.*

    Woman *Do you really think so? Everybody says that, but I'm three years older than she.*

77. What is the woman doing?
    (A) Applying for a position.
    (B) Showing family photographs.
    (C) Talking to her father.
    (D) Explaining a problem.

You hear:

78. **Man A:** *How often does the express train leave?*

    Man B: *Every hour on the hour. The next one is at three o'clock. That's in ten minutes.*

    Man A: *Good. Two seats in First Class to Buffalo.*

78. When will the traveler leave?
    (A) In three hours.
    (B) At one o'clock.
    (C) In twenty minutes.
    (D) In ten minutes.

You hear:

79. **Woman:** *Excuse me, are you looking for something?*

    Man B: *Yes, a telephone. I have to make a call.*

    Woman: *Come in and use ours, as long as it's a local call.*

79. What does the man need to do?
    (A) Find out directions.
    (B) Make a telephone call.
    (C) Get in his house.
    (D) Find his friend.

You hear:

80. **Man A:** *Do you think I should get rid of my old car and get a new one?*

    Woman: *It may not look good, but it's paid for and it runs well. I think it would be a waste of money to buy a new one.*

    Man A: *Maybe you're right. There's nothing wrong with it. I just thought I could use a change.*

80. What does the man want to do?
    (A) Get a new car.
    (B) Take a vacation.
    (C) Get a new television.
    (D) Buy a new suit.

You hear:

81. **Man B:** *I really feel awful.*

    Woman: *I'm sorry to hear that. What's wrong?*

    Man B: *My body aches, my head is stuffed up, I have no energy, and I don't want to do a thing.*

81. What should the man do?
    (A) Change jobs.
    (B) Call for a dinner reservation.
    (C) See a doctor.
    (D) Find somebody to talk to.

You hear:

82. **Man A:** *Hello, may I please speak to Mary?*

    Woman: *I'm sorry. There's nobody here by that name. You must have the wrong number.*

    Man A: *Oh, I'm sorry. I'll check the number.*

82. Why can the man not speak with Mary?
    (A) Mary is busy.
    (B) Mary is not at home right now.
    (C) Mary no longer lives in the house.
    (D) The man called the wrong number.

You hear:

83. **Man B:** *What's this briefcase made of?*

Man A: *It's a new kind of very hard plastic. It doesn't scratch easily, which is the most common complaint with other briefcase coverings.*

Man B: *If it's that good, I'm sure everybody'll want one.*

83. What is an advantage of this briefcase over other briefcases?

(A) It is less expensive.

(B) It is lighter weight.

(C) It has more compartments.

(D) It will not damage as easily.

You hear:

84. **Woman:** *Did the sweater that your mother sent fit you?*

Man A: *No, it was a little tight. She must have made a mistake and picked up the wrong size.*

Woman: *She gave me the receipt so we can take it back to the store to exchange, if necessary.*

84. What will the man do?

(A) Ask his mother for a sweater.

(B) Buy his wife the sweater she wants.

(C) Return the sweater to the store.

(D) Wear his new sweater when he goes out.

You hear:

85. **Man B:** *What's the weather like there today?*

Woman: *It's dreadful. Hot, and very humid.*

Man B: *Sounds like a good day to be in an air-conditioned office.*

85. What would the man do?

(A) Go to the beach.

(B) Stay inside.

(C) Repair the air conditioner.

(D) Buy an umbrella.

You hear:

86. **Man A:** *Are you on your way home now?*

Man B: *In a couple of minutes. I still have one more thing to do. I won't be long.*

Man A: *I'd like to go with you, if it's O.K. I'll be waiting outside.*

86. What will the men do?

(A) Leave for home.

(B) Have a meeting.

(C) Go shopping.

(D) Visit a friend.

You hear:

87. **Man B:** *Is this a new kind of video player?*

Man A: *Yes, it is. It has few moving parts and should never need to be repaired. We sell a lot of them.*

Man B: *Of course, for the same price I could buy two of the old ones, couldn't I?*

87. What comment does the customer make about the video player?

(A) It is small.

(B) It is expensive.

(C) It is attractive.

(D) It is hard to operate.

You hear:

88. **Man A:** *Welcome back, Jana. How was your vacation?*

Woman: *It was great! I had a chance to really relax.*

Man A: *Good, because we have a lot of work to do. Do you see those files over there? They're all yours.*

88. What will Jana have to do?

(A) Find a way to get home.

(B) Leave late on her vacation.

(C) Work hard to catch up.

(D) Look for a new job.

You hear:

89. **Woman:** *What kind of work do you do?*

    Man A: *I'm an airline pilot. I fly trans-Pacific routes mostly, but sometimes I fly to Europe.*

    Woman: *That's a job with a lot of responsibility.*

89. What does the woman say about the man's work?

    (A) She would not want it.

    (B) It involves great responsibility.

    (C) The work lets the man travel.

    (D) He is paid very well.

You hear:

90. **Man A:** *I'm sorry, but I can't leave until after my eleven o'clock meeting with the boss.*

    Man B: *We should be going. How long will that take?*

    Man A: *No more than an hour, and maybe only ten minutes, if he agrees to what I want to do.*

90. What are the men trying to do?

    (A) Go somewhere together.

    (B) Convince their boss about something.

    (C) Arrange to have a meeting.

    (D) Catch an eleven o'clock train.

You hear:

91. **Woman:** *I don't like to say it, but this computer work is just too much for only three people. We need to get some help in to catch up.*

    Man B: *Isn't there anyone available?*

    Woman: *There are people, but nobody who is willing to work only a couple of weeks.*

91. What is the woman's problem?

    (A) The man refuses to help her.

    (B) Nobody wants to work short term.

    (C) The computers are too complicated.

    (D) Her best computer person has just quit.

You hear:

92. **Man A:** *Did you get to the Motor Show this year?*

    Man B: *Yes, but I spent most of my time in the motorcycle exhibition. I wanted to see what my design competition is.*

    Man A: *If the motorcycles are anything like the automobiles, you will have to work very hard to compete.*

92. Why did the man attend the Motor Show?

    (A) To see what kind of a car he should buy.

    (B) To learn what is new in motorcycles.

    (C) To watch the motorcycle race.

    (D) To learn how to stage an exhibition.

You hear:

93. **Woman:** *I haven't seen you for a long time. What have you been doing?*

    Man B: *Last year I went to Africa on a project and got sick. For a while they didn't think I would survive. I was in the hospital for two months.*

    Woman: *Well, I'm glad to see you're back and you're O.K.*

93. What had the man been doing?

    (A) He lost his job.

    (B) He was on vacation.

    (C) He had been ill.

    (D) He was assigned to a new office.

You hear:

94. **Woman:** *Are we still getting together for lunch on Friday to discuss the AJAX matter?*

    Man B: *We can, but I would prefer Thursday. On Friday I may have to take my wife to the doctor.*

    Woman: *Sorry, I can't make it on Thursday at all. I'm busy all day.*

94. What is the woman trying to do?

    (A) Meet the man for lunch.

    (B) Introduce the man to a friend.

    (C) Take the man to the doctor.

    (D) Spend the day with the man.

You hear:

95. **Man A:** *When do we expect that shipment of engine parts? We can't keep our generators going without them.*

    Man B: *I called the air freight company. They said we can expect it any time.*

    Man A: *I hope they come soon. If one more unit goes out, we shut down the plant.*

95. What is the man's concern?

    (A) His customers want delivery.

    (B) His workers are dissatisfied.

    (C) He is waiting for some visitors.

    (D) He expects a shipment that has not arrived.

You hear:

96. **Woman:** *Have you noticed that sales are up 6% this quarter?*

    Man A: *That's fine, but expenses are up 4%.*

    Woman: *Look, work on sales, and it won't matter how much expenses go up.*

96. What does the woman advise the man to do?

    (A) Sell more product.

    (B) Reduce costs.

    (C) Improve quality.

    (D) Reduce waste.

You hear:

97. **Man A:** *Did you hear that James argued with the Director about how to deal with delinquent accounts?*

    Man B: *Yes, but they're always arguing about something.*

    Man A: *Well, they won't argue any more. James has resigned.*

97. What will happen next?

    (A) James will look for a new job.

    (B) The company will pay its debts.

    (C) Delinquent accounts will be collected.

    (D) The Director will speak with employees.

You hear:

98. **Man A:** *I think we should sign that contract before they change their minds.*

    Man B: *Maybe, but I don't think everybody would agree. It's going to be risky and may not be as good as it looks.*

    Man A: *Anybody can do the easy jobs. It's the hard ones that take talent, and that's where the money is.*

98. What are the men discussing?

    (A) A meeting of the directors.

    (B) Whether to accept a contract.

    (C) A new piece of equipment.

    (D) Whether to hire some new employees.

You hear:

99. **Man A:** *Have we opened any new accounts lately?*

    Woman: *We haven't had a new account in two months, and we're losing some of our old ones.*

    Man A: *Well, let's not worry about it. I'm sure there's some explanation.*

99. What is the man's position on accounts?

    (A) He asks what the competition is doing.

    (B) He requires two new accounts per week out of his sales force.

    (C) He does not seem to worry or care about new accounts.

    (D) He is concerned that customers do not receive good service.

You hear:

100. **Man B:** *Hi, what are you reading?*

    Woman: *Oh, it's just an old mystery, Death on the Nile. Have you read it?*

    Man B: *No, I've never read it, but I saw the movie.*

100. What is the woman doing?

    (A) Going to a movie.

    (B) Telling about a trip.

    (C) Writing a letter.

    (D) Reading a book.

You hear:

101. Man B: *You know, I don't think people in this office work hard enough.*

Man A: *I agree, but what are you going to do about it?*

Man B: *I'm going to move my desk out into the work area and tell people I want to see them working.*

101. What are the men concerned about?

(A) The office is too small.

(B) Employees who do not work hard.

(C) The office needs more lighting.

(D) One of the employees is a troublemaker.

You hear:

102. Woman: *Did we put that ad to buy a used delivery van in the paper this week?*

Man A: *Yes, but it's been three days, and we've had no calls yet.*

Woman: *Well, if nobody calls, we have to go out and buy one off a lot. We need to get this stock out to customers.*

102. What do the speakers need?

(A) More time to improve sales.

(B) A way to deliver goods.

(C) To place an ad in the newspaper.

(D) More operators to take calls.

You hear:

103. Man B: *I want to thank you for your help on my report. I couldn't have done it without you.*

Woman: *That's O.K.. I enjoyed having a chance to do some writing for a change. All I ever do is add columns of figures.*

Man B: *Well if you'd like more, I'm sure we could arrange it.*

103. What will happen to the woman?

(A) She will join the shipping department.

(B) She will be asked to do more writing.

(C) She will receive the report.

(D) She will be promoted to manager.

You hear:

104. Man A: *Why has Mr. Connors been so quiet lately?*

Woman: *I think he's worried about something personal.*

Man A: *That's too bad. It might be better if he were to take a few days off to deal with whatever it is, don't you think?*

104. What do the speakers want Mr. Connors to do?

(A) Arrive at work on time.

(B) Overcome his problem.

(C) Return to work.

(D) Take a business trip.

You hear:

105. Woman: *What is the weather going to be like tomorrow?*

Man A: *They say it's going to rain in the morning, and clear up by noon.*

Woman: *Do you think we ought to call off the picnic or will we be O.K.?*

105. What is the woman worried about?

(A) The weather.

(B) A phone call.

(C) A schedule.

(D) The time.

You hear:

106. Man B: *What do you think of those customer complaints we've been getting, Bob?*

Man A: *It's never good when a customer complains. We have to look into them and make sure we're doing all we can to avoid them.*

Man B: *Let's put somebody on it to find out what the real problem is.*

106. What is the concern of the speakers?

(A) Corporate debt.

(B) Quality control.

(C) Customer satisfaction.

(D) Delivery schedules.

You hear:

107. Man B: *Did you make it to the concert last night?*

Woman: *I went, but when I got there I discovered I'd lost my ticket. I wasn't able to get in.*

Man B: *That's too bad. You missed a fine performance.*

107. What happened at the concert?
   (A) The performance was canceled.
   (B) The woman did not see it.
   (C) The electricity went out.
   (D) The critics did not like it.

You hear:

108. Man A: *When is that shipment coming?*

Man B: *I don't know. Today's the twenty-eighth. We placed our order on the sixth.*

Man A: *Well, it must be lost. Ask for it to be reshipped, but have it sent the fastest and surest way.*

108. How are the speakers solving their problem?
   (A) They asked for a short-term bank loan.
   (B) They will visit the manufacturing plant.
   (C) They are moving their operations.
   (D) They ordered a second shipment.

You hear:

109. Man A: *We should submit a bid on that project. I think we can get it.*

Woman: *We've never done that kind of work before. I can't imagine why they'd give it to us.*

Man A: *We'd get it because we've never failed in anything we've tried. All of our projects come out just the way we say.*

109. Why does the man think he could win the contract?
   (A) Because he has had similar projects.
   (B) Because he is always successful.
   (C) Because he has been told he would win.
   (D) Because he is part owner of the company.

You hear:

110. Woman: *Congratulations on your promotion.*

Man A: *It's only a title. The pay is no better than before. Everything is the same as always.*

Woman: *That's O.K. It's better than nothing.*

110. What is good about the man's promotion?
   (A) The pay.
   (B) The office.
   (C) The title.
   (D) The hours.

You hear:

111. Man A: *You'll never guess who phoned me this week.*

Man B: *I bet it was John. He's been calling everybody asking about a job. He was fired from his job at Slimco.*

Man A: *You're right. Should we hire him?*

111. What is happening?
   (A) A new company is being organized.
   (B) A man is looking for work.
   (C) A factory is being closed.
   (D) A new phone system is being installed.

You hear:

112. Man B: *What happened to the record of this order? It's not here.*

Man A: *What is it, the L-MAX account?*

Man B: *Yes. They're on the phone and want to know what's become of it.*

112. What is the inquiry about?
   (A) A competitor.
   (B) A new account.
   (C) A new product.
   (D) A misplaced order.

You hear:

113. **Woman:** *I'll go for a while, but I can't stay long.*

    Man A: *The Wangs will be disappointed. It was you they really wanted to see.*

    Woman: *I know, but I have so much to do this weekend, that if I don't get started, it'll never finish.*

113. Why does the woman not want to visit for long?

    (A) She does not enjoy visiting the Wangs.

    (B) She has another appointment.

    (C) She has a lot to do.

    (D) She is leaving on a trip.

You hear:

114. **Man A:** *It's past time to go, are you ready?*

    Man B: *In just a minute. I need these copies for the meeting, and this machine is very slow.*

    Man A: *Isn't there a copier in the meeting room? We can do that later.*

114. What do the speakers want to do?

    (A) Buy a new copying machine.

    (B) Call a meeting.

    (C) Order lunch.

    (D) Go to a meeting.

You hear:

115. **Woman:** *Did you try to reason with him, to tell him why you want to go over to the other department?*

    Man B: *Sure, but you know how he is. He wouldn't listen and became very angry. And he's the boss.*

    Woman: *He's the same with me. I can't talk to the man without him starting an argument.*

115. What can be said about the supervisor?

    (A) He refuses to listen to others.

    (B) He does not like to make decisions.

    (C) He is easy to work with.

    (D) He is never available.

You hear:

116. **Man A:** *Excuse me, does anybody know what time it is?*

    Man B: *Yes, I believe it's—almost—5:30.*

    Man A: *I'm sorry. I'm supposed to be somewhere at six o'clock. Tom, can you take over the meeting and come to some agreement on what we want this book to look like?*

116. What is the speaker's problem?

    (A) He does not agree with the others.

    (B) He does not feel well.

    (C) He has to leave a meeting.

    (D) He needs to borrow a car.

You hear:

117. **Man B:** *You know, I really feel awful. I have that article to write, and it's not getting done.*

    Man A: *That's easy enough. Just sit down and do it.*

    Man B: *It's not that easy. I have no idea what I'm going to say.*

117. Why does the man say he does not feel well?

    (A) He has a cold.

    (B) He has avoided doing something.

    (C) His friend is in the hospital.

    (D) He did not return a phone call.

You hear:

118. **Man A:** *Lady, you're in a bad place. What's the matter with your car?*

    Woman: *I don't know. The engine made a strange noise and stopped. Now it won't start.*

    Man A: *Well, you can't stay here in the middle of the street. Get in and I'll push you off to the side.*

118. What is the man worried about?

    (A) What makes the noise.

    (B) The woman's health.

    (C) He is late.

    (D) The woman is in a dangerous place.

119. Woman: *I think I sprained my ankle when I slipped out there on the front steps of your building.*

Man B: *Oh, I'm sorry. What can we do for you?*

Woman: *Find a place for me to lie down, and call a doctor. I don't think I can walk.*

119. Why is the woman complaining?

(A) She is hurt.

(B) She wants better service.

(C) She is tired of walking.

(D) She says the man is not telling the truth.

120. Man A: *Have you had lunch yet?*

Woman: *No, I'm too busy to stop for lunch. I'm O.K.*

Man A: *I'm going now. Would you like me to bring you back something?*

120. What is the man doing?

(A) Inviting the woman out to lunch.

(B) Offering to bring the woman lunch.

(C) Helping the woman with her work.

(D) Giving the woman a ride home after work.

121. Woman: *What are you reading? Is that a good book?*

Man A: *No, it's not, but I have nothing else, and I can't just sit here doing nothing.*

Woman: *I know what you mean. I love to read. It takes my mind off everything else.*

121. What are the speakers discussing?

(A) How they keep healthy.

(B) How to enjoy travel.

(C) How they spend free time.

(D) How to avoid high prices.

122. Man A: *There was a call while you were out. Rankin wants you to call him back.*

Man B: *Oh, I don't want to talk to him. He always takes twenty minutes to say what he could say in ten seconds.*

Man A: *Look, he's a good customer. He orders regularly and he pays on time. For that, you can talk to him. Call him.*

122. What are the speakers talking about?

(A) Contacting a client.

(B) Collecting money owed to them.

(C) An advertisement for a conference.

(D) How to get somewhere.

123. Man B: *I'm sorry. Mr. Sked is out on vacation this week. Can I help you?*

Man A: *No, I'm afraid not. It's a personal matter, involving his son.*

Man B: *Then perhaps I can help you. You see, I am his son.*

123. What can be said about the speakers?

(A) They are old friends.

(B) They seem to have a problem.

(C) They have arranged to meet.

(D) They are planning to go somewhere.

124. Man A: *Do you know Mr. Vin, who works at the music store?*

Man B: *Yes. In fact, I sold him my old car when I bought my new one.*

Man A: *You sold that car! It was so old, I couldn't imagine it running another two weeks.*

124. What has surprised the speaker?

(A) That his friend had sold his car.

(B) That Mr. Vin is such a good musician.

(C) That his friend has won another race.

(D) That time has gone by so quickly.

You hear:

125. Man A: *What happened to Bill? He looks as if he's been in an accident.*

Man B: *Yes, he was riding his bicycle at night and a car ran into him.*

Man A: *Nobody should ride a bicycle at night. They're too hard to see. What did he expect?*

125. What did Bill do wrong?

(A) He ate too much.

(B) He slept too late.

(C) He did something that was not safe.

(D) He forgot where he left his money.

You hear:

126. Woman: *When are they going to do something about these traffic jams? Don't they know how much time people waste just sitting here?*

Man B: *They must. The people who make the decisions drive to work. I doubt that they know how to solve the problem.*

Woman: *Then they should be replaced by someone who does.*

126. What are the speakers discussing?

(A) The high cost of living.

(B) The unemployment rate.

(C) Traffic congestion in the city.

(D) A sharp increase in crime.

You hear:

127. Woman: *Do you accept credit cards?*

Man A: *No, I'm sorry, we don't. If we were to, we would have to raise our prices to cover the cost.*

Woman: *Then I think you're smart not to.*

127. What is the shopkeeper attempting to do?

(A) Offer the latest fashions.

(B) Keep prices down.

(C) Stay open late.

(D) Train staff to be more polite.

You hear:

128. Man A: *I'm really looking forward to the opening of our new office. It's closer to my house, and we'll have a lot more room.*

Woman: *It may be better for you, but most of us will spend at least another hour a day to get to work and back.*

Man A: *I guess that's the price you have to pay for living in the city these days.*

128. Why is the woman disappointed?

(A) Her car needs repairs.

(B) Her new house is too small.

(C) She does not make enough money.

(D) She will live farther from her office.

You hear:

129. Man B: *Say, would you like to play a round of golf tomorrow morning?*

Man A: *I would, but I have to go out of town for a couple of days. How about next week?*

Man B: *O.K. Give me a call when you get back. We'll set it up.*

129. What are the speakers doing?

(A) Arranging to get together.

(B) Discussing a business deal.

(C) Making travel arrangements.

(D) Talking about a new machine.

You hear:

130. Man A: *I'd like to talk to somebody about taking out advertising in your newspaper. I need a half-page ad, to appear for three consecutive Sundays.*

Woman: *I assume this is for a commercial ad. Is that right?.*

Man A: *Yes, it's our once-a-year sale and is a major event for us.*

130. What is the man going to advertise?

(A) A house.

(B) An international airline.

(C) A department store sale.

(D) A reward for return of a valuable object.

You hear:

131. Woman: *Ms. Jones is going to have to improve her work.*

Man B: *Why? What did she do now?*

Woman: *She sent that mailing out yesterday to the wrong list. It'll cost us a lot in printing and postage, not to mention the time lost and the embarrassment.*

131. What is Ms. Jones' problem?
  (A) She is always late for work.
  (B) She made a very costly mistake.
  (C) She said the wrong thing to the boss.
  (D) She spoke disrespectfully to a major client.

You hear:

132. Man A: *I've lived in this city for eight years and I still get lost.*

Man B: *You're not alone. I was born here, and I'm no better. They keep changing streets to one way, then reversing them, then closing them. I can't keep up.*

Man A: *Well, maybe I shouldn't worry about it then.*

132. What are the speakers talking about?
  (A) Getting older.
  (B) Changes in the city.
  (C) High taxes.
  (D) Their families.

You hear:

133. Man A: *What did you think of the director's presentation on the budget?*

Woman: *I guess it was all right, but I didn't follow the numbers. He made it too complicated.*

Man A: *I thought so too, and it wasn't necessary. I don't think he wanted us to understand.*

133. What did the speakers think of the presentation?
  (A) It was difficult to follow.
  (B) It was too long.
  (C) It was too serious.
  (D) It was on the wrong subject.

You hear:

134. Man B: *Have you finished packing yet?*

Woman: *Finished? I haven't started. What time do we have to leave to make our plane?*

Man B: *If we leave in one hour, we should be all right.*

134. What are the speakers about to do?
  (A) Go to work.
  (B) Go home.
  (C) Take a trip.
  (D) Have dinner.

You hear:

135. Man A: *Does it look as if we'll be able to finish this job on time? We promised to have everything ready in eight days.*

Man B: *We'll finish on time and under budget. All we have to worry about is delivery. I think the truck drivers are on strike.*

Man A: *We'll deliver, if I have to drive the truck myself.*

135. What is the problem the speakers face?
  (A) They are late.
  (B) They have spent too much money.
  (C) They cannot find workers.
  (D) They may have difficulty making a delivery.

You hear:

136. Woman: *I see you have tulips, carnations, and mums. Do you have any other fresh flowers?*

Man B: *Yes, but we keep them in the back because we don't have enough room out here.*

Woman: *Could you make me up a bouquet, with something small, and put some green around it. And maybe a little pink ribbon. I want to take it to a young friend who isn't well.*

136. What does the woman want to do?
  (A) Rent an apartment.
  (B) Take flowers to a friend.
  (C) Plant a garden.
  (D) Visit her parents on their anniversary.

You hear:

137. Woman: *I think I've read nearly everything she's written. I really like her style.*

Man A: *Her first novel was* The Moon of Moons. *Most people have never heard of it. Have you read it?*

Woman: *Yes. In fact, I think it's one of her best.*

137. What does the woman enjoy doing?

(A) Reading about other lands.

(B) Reading novels by a particular author.

(C) Writing books about space.

(D) Helping young writers publish their books.

You hear:

138. Man B: *I wish I didn't have to take a test to replace my lost driver's license. Why can't they just give me a new one?*

Man A: *They don't keep good records and they don't know that you've ever had a license.*

Man B: *When I do something wrong they have a complete record on me. I don't see this as any different.*

138. What is bothering the man?

(A) He is afraid he could fail the driver's test.

(B) He does not want to pay a fee for his new license.

(C) He thinks it is wrong to take a test to replace a lost license.

(D) He is worried because he has broken the law.

You hear:

139. Man A: *Chad has been servicing this account for two years and his sales to them have fallen since day one. Yet the company's doing just fine.*

Man B: *Yes, I understand they're not happy with the service they get from him.*

Man A: *Then take him off it. We can't afford to have our customers go to the competition.*

139. Why are sales to the customer going down?

(A) The customer is experiencing problems.

(B) The customer no longer needs the product.

(C) The customer is not pleased with the salesman.

(D) The customer has no credit, because he did not pay his bill.

You hear:

140. Man A: *We've been having difficulty making weather forecasts because we're not getting good information.*

Man B: *There's nothing wrong with the information. We just don't know how to interpret it.*

Man A: *You may be right. Let's have another look at it.*

140. What are the speakers trying to do?

(A) Project sales.

(B) Predict the weather.

(C) Find new jobs.

(D) Find something they lost.

You hear:

141. **Woman:** *These photocopies are not very clear. Can't you adjust the setting on the machine so they're darker?*

   Man B: *We could, but if we do, we use too much toner. We don't have any more and haven't ordered it.*

   Woman: *You mean we're running out, and there's none to be had? How can that be?*

141. What has happened?
   (A) The photocopy machine is broken.
   (B) Supplies have not been ordered.
   (C) The colors were not the right ones.
   (D) It is late and there is much work to do.

You hear:

142. **Man A:** *I thought you were satisfied with your work, Jim. Why did you leave the company?*

   Man B: *I did a great job. Everybody else was promoted, but I wasn't. So I quit.*

   Man A: *If you felt that strongly about it, you probably did the right thing.*

142. Why did Jim leave the company?
   (A) He was offered a job elsewhere.
   (B) He was asked to leave.
   (C) He did not like the work.
   (D) He wanted a promotion.

You hear:

143. **Man B:** *Which film would you prefer to see?*

   Woman: *I'm sure they're both good. I think this one is probably more violent than I enjoy.*

   Man B: *Well, then let's just go see the other one. It's all the same to me.*

143. What are the speakers trying to decide?
   (A) Which restaurant to go to.
   (B) Which movie to see.
   (C) Who to invite to dinner.
   (D) Where to go on vacation.

You hear:

144. **Man A:** *The doctor says he can't operate for a couple of days.*

   Woman: *Why doesn't he do it now? She's in a lot of pain.*

   Man A: *They have to wait for the swelling to go down. They're giving her pain killers and doing everything they can.*

144. When will the doctor operate?
   (A) Immediately.
   (B) As soon as possible.
   (C) After he consults a specialist.
   (D) He may not have to operate at all.

You hear:

145. **Man B:** *How important is it that this shipment go out on Tuesday? It won't be easy to do.*

   Man A: *This one has to go out. Work all weekend, if you have to, but have it on the truck by ten o'clock Tuesday morning.*

   Man B: *O.K. We'll do it. Tell them to expect it.*

145. What will the employee do?
   (A) He will do everything he needs to do.
   (B) He will quit rather than work harder.
   (C) He will pretend to be sick.
   (D) He will send out the shipment late.

You hear:

146. **Woman:** *You know, young people are really rude these days. We never behaved that way.*

   Man B: *No. Neither did we. But young people are always the same. You notice the rude ones, but they are the few. Most are really quite nice.*

   Woman: *I suppose, but they make me so mad.*

146. What about young people has made the woman upset?
   (A) The way they dress.
   (B) The way they treat others.
   (C) They refuse to work.
   (D) Their language.

You hear:

147. **Man A:** *Have you completed your customs declaration?*

    Woman: *No, I have nothing to declare.*

    Man A: *You must complete a form anyway, saying that you are bringing nothing into the country. Here is a form.*

147. What was the woman's problem?

    (A) She did not declare her valuables.

    (B) She did not understand what was said to her.

    (C) She had not completed a customs declaration.

    (D) She made a mistake on her customs declaration form.

You hear:

148. **Man A:** *Let's get out of here as fast as we can.*

    Woman: *Why, what's going on? Is there a problem?*

    Man A: *Yes. There's a man over there with a knife. He's angry at some people, and they're not going to leave him alone. I'm afraid he'll attack them.*

148. Why does the man want to leave?

    (A) There has been an accident.

    (B) There is going to be a fight.

    (C) Somebody is going to ask him for money.

    (D) He sees somebody that he does not want to talk to.

You hear:

149. **Man A:** *Look at this place! Everything's on sale. These are real bargains.*

    Woman: *We're on vacation and have to save our money. Come on. Let's go!*

    Man A: *I can't believe you want to leave here! Don't you even want to look around?*

149. What have the speakers come upon?

    (A) A luxury hotel.

    (B) A place to shop.

    (C) A beautiful beach.

    (D) A museum in a palace.

You hear:

150. **Man B:** *Why does Mr. Batts talk so much when we meet with him? Nobody else has a chance to say anything.*

    Man A: *I don't think he respects anybody else's opinion.*

    Man B: *I don't think I'll ever agree to meet with him again. It's not worth the effort and I don't like to listen to him.*

150. What do the speakers say about Mr. Batts?

    (A) He is a brilliant speaker.

    (B) He enjoys exchanging ideas.

    (C) He talks too much.

    (D) He talks only about his family.

You hear:

151. **Man A:** *I would like to buy some stock, but I know nothing about it. Can you help me?*

    Woman: *Perhaps I can. Are you interested in speculative stocks, blue chip, or what?*

    Man A: *What do you suggest? I don't even know what questions to ask.*

151. What has been the man's experience with stocks?

    (A) He has done well in the stock market.

    (B) He says he wants to "buy low and sell high."

    (C) He expects to hold onto his stock to collect dividends.

    (D) He knows nothing about buying stocks.

You hear:

152. **Man A:** *Excuse me, are these seats taken?*

    Man B: *There are season ticket holders who sometimes sit there, but they're hardly ever here.*

    Man A: *Well, we'll sit and watch the play. If they come, we'll move.*

152. What are the speakers discussing?

    (A) Seats on a plane.

    (B) Seats on a subway.

    (C) Theater seats.

    (D) Circus seats.

You hear:

153. **Woman:** *How much does this melon cost? And do you have any others?*

     Man A: *I'm sorry, I can't sell you that one. It's not good quality, and I haven't any others.*

     Woman: *Well, thank you for being so honest. I'll be sure to come <u>here</u> to buy my fruit.*

153. Why will the woman return to the fruit stand?
     (A) The man will sell only quality fruit.
     (B) The prices are lower than elsewhere.
     (C) The stand is across from her apartment.
     (D) The stand opens early and closes late.

You hear:

154. **Woman:** *Where can I buy a bus ticket to go into the city?*

     Man B: *They sell tickets in that store over there, but they're closed right now, so you can get your ticket from the driver.*

     Woman: *Thank you. That's very convenient.*

154. What can be said about the woman?
     (A) She takes this bus often.
     (B) She has been visiting her daughter.
     (C) She has never been on this bus.
     (D) She and the man are traveling together.

You hear:

155. **Man A:** *I have to go to the bank. Do you need anything while I'm out?*

     Woman: *Yes, I could use some tissues to clean my glasses, if you go past a drugstore.*

     Man A: *There's one just beyond the bank. I'll be back in a half hour or so.*

155. What will the man do for the woman?
     (A) Bring her something to drink.
     (B) Pick up her clothes at the dry cleaners.
     (C) Go with her to the bank.
     (D) Buy something she asks for.

You hear:

156. **Man B:** *Who's next please? You, madam?*

     Woman: *Yes, I would like to send this package surface mail and buy ten international airmail stamps, please.*

     Man B: *This package is too large to mail, but there are delivery services that'll take it. Here are your stamps.*

156. Where does this conversation take place?
     (A) At an airport.
     (B) In a train station.
     (C) At a post office.
     (D) In a travel office.

You hear:

157. **Woman:** *John, could you please help me with this table? It's too heavy for me, and I want to put it upstairs before we open.*

     Man B: *I'd like to, but I hurt my back yesterday, and I don't dare strain it.*

     Woman: *Oh, that must really hurt. I'll wait for Hal to arrive. He shouldn't be long.*

157. What is the woman trying to do?
     (A) Make an appointment with a doctor.
     (B) Move some furniture.
     (C) Prepare lunch for a group.
     (D) Close the shop to run some errands.

You hear:

158. **Man A:** *Did you hear about David? He didn't get invited back to any of the companies that interviewed him.*

Man B: *I think he's looking at the wrong kind of company. He's too independent a thinker for most places. Of course, that's not how others see him.*

Man A: *No. I think they just see him as peculiar.*

158. What are the speakers discussing?

   (A) Employment for a friend.

   (B) University courses.

   (C) An invitation to a party.

   (D) A new management consultant.

You hear:

159. **Man B:** *I heard this morning that Professor Mun died yesterday. He'd been sick for about a week and went into the hospital only two days ago.*

Woman: *I think it was expected. He's been in and out of hospitals for several years.*

Man B: *I suppose so, but that doesn't make it any easier on the people close to him.*

159. What are the speakers discussing?

   (A) A health insurance plan.

   (B) The death of a friend.

   (C) A program at the university.

   (D) Plans for the future.

You hear:

160. **Man A:** *What do you have that's fresh?*

Woman: *Everything. The whiting is very good right now. This salmon just came in.*

Man A: *Your salmon's expensive, but give me three nice cuts of it. I have a good friend coming over. I guess I'll worry about the price later.*

160. What does the man want to do?

   (A) Invite a lot of people to dinner.

   (B) Buy the fish at a lower price.

   (C) Prepare dinner for a guest.

   (D) Celebrate a special event.

You hear:

161. **Man B:** *I'm going on a ten-day tour to Paris and London next month. I've never been outside the country and I'm really looking forward to it.*

Woman: *I'm sure you are. The food's great, and there are so many beautiful things to see.*

Man B: *If you have any places to recommend, I'd like to know about them.*

161. What is the man going to do?

   (A) Host visitors on behalf of his company.

   (B) Attend an orchestra performance.

   (C) Take a trip to a place he has never been.

   (D) Meet some friends at the airport.

You hear:

162. **Man A:** *Excuse me, aren't you John Everett?*

Man B: *Yes. Do I know you? I don't remember seeing you before.*

Man A: *I'm Tom Martin; you were two years ahead of me in college. We were in the same dormitory.*

162. Who are the speakers?

   (A) They attended the same college.

   (B) They met one time at a wedding.

   (C) They were in the army together.

   (D) They once worked for the same company.

You hear:

163. **Man A:** *Excuse me, are you from the Health Club?*

Woman: *Yes, I'm the director. What can I do for you?*

Man A: *I think I'd like to join. I need a place inside where I can get exercise during the winter months. Can you give me some information?*

163. What does the man want to do?

   (A) Travel to a warmer climate.

   (B) Join a health club.

   (C) Get directions.

   (D) Find a part-time job.

You hear:

164. **Man B:** *I'd like to make an appointment to see the doctor.*

    Woman: *Well, let's see. He has no time free from Monday to Thursday. How about Friday? Could you come at nine o'clock?*

    Man B: *I guess I can fit that in, as long as I get out by ten. I have a meeting at ten-thirty and the rest of the day is taken up.*

164. What can be said about the man?
    - (A) He is very busy.
    - (B) He must see the doctor quickly.
    - (C) He will join the doctor for golf.
    - (D) He will not be able to see the doctor.

You hear:

165. **Woman:** *Do you have that guide book to Mexico handy?*

    Man A: *Yes, what would you like to know? Ruins? Food? Flights? Language?*

    Woman: *No. All I care about is the beaches, how warm the water is, and how far away it is from this cold weather!*

165. What does the woman want to do?
    - (A) Study a language.
    - (B) Visit someplace warm.
    - (C) Meet interesting people.
    - (D) Write a book.

You hear:

166. **Man B:** *Paul, can you help me with this job? I have about three more hours' work on it, and the boss wants it for a meeting in an hour.*

    Man A: *I'd like to, but I have something I'm working on for the same meeting.*

    Man B: *Maybe I can find somebody else.*

166. What is the man's problem?
    - (A) He cannot go to the meeting.
    - (B) He has just had a long meeting with the boss.
    - (C) He has a lot of work to do in little time.
    - (D) He has to leave work to help a friend.

You hear:

167. **Woman:** *Could we have the check, please?*

    Man B: *Yes, of course. Would you care for some more coffee?*

    Woman: *No, we're about to leave, thank you.*

167. Where are the speakers?
    - (A) In an office.
    - (B) In a restaurant.
    - (C) On an airplane.
    - (D) In a bank.

You hear:

168. **Man A:** *I really do have to get a new stereo. This one doesn't work very well.*

    Man B: *It sounds fine to me. Why don't you get a CD player, if you're going to spend the money?*

    Man A: *If I were to do that, what would I do with all these albums? I'll just buy another one like the one I have.*

168. What are the speakers discussing?
    - (A) Equipment to play music.
    - (B) Books they would like to read.
    - (C) A clothing sale.
    - (D) Store clerks who are unattentive.

You hear:

169. **Woman:** *Is this computer working all right?*

    Man B: *Yes, but it isn't printing out. You'll have to wait.*

    Woman: *I'll use the one in the other building. I'm in a hurry to run this job.*

169. What does the woman want to do?
    - (A) Use the computer.
    - (B) Take part in an athletic event.
    - (C) Leave work early.
    - (D) Meet some friends.

You hear:

170. **Man A:** *Can you give me a price list for those materials we want to order?*

    Man B: *I don't have it yet, but I've asked for one to be sent over by fax this morning.*

    Man A: *Good. Show it to me as soon as it comes. I want to compare it to the other one before we send in our order.*

170. What do the speakers want to know?
    - (A) When their materials will arrive.
    - (B) How much their order will cost.
    - (C) Who their competition is.
    - (D) How much their competitors charge.

You hear:

171. **Woman:** *Does this bus go as far as the open market?*

    Man A: *No, we go only as far as City Hall. Then we turn and go back to the railroad station.*

    Woman: *I'll go as far as City Hall.*

171. What does the woman want to do?
    - (A) Go to the railroad station.
    - (B) Wait for the next bus.
    - (C) Go to the bus station.
    - (D) Ride as far as City Hall.

You hear:

172. **Man A:** *Do you mind if I take a picture of you and your bicycle?*

    Woman: *Why do you want it? I'm not from here.*

    Man A: *I collect photos of all forms of transportation and the people who use them.*

172. What does the man do for a hobby?
    - (A) He rides a bicycle.
    - (B) He collects postcards.
    - (C) He photographs ways to travel.
    - (D) He asks travelers about far away places.

You hear:

173. **Man B:** *You know, I've always thought your red shoes are really attractive.*

    Woman: *Well, thank you. I particularly like them, too.*

    Man B: *They always add so much color and brighten the office.*

173. What is the man doing?
    - (A) Selling the woman a pair of shoes.
    - (B) Asking the woman for her opinion.
    - (C) Admiring the woman's shoes.
    - (D) Hiring the woman for the office.

You hear:

174. **Man A:** *We'll have to remove some of these limbs before they fall and hurt someone.*

    Man B: *Do you think we can save the tree?*

    Man A: *Oh, sure, but we can't wait another year to do it. We should do it before winter comes.*

174. What are the speakers discussing?
    - (A) A hospital patient.
    - (B) A tree that needs work.
    - (C) The seasons of the year.
    - (D) Dental care for one of them.

You hear:

175. **Woman:** *I'm sorry, but this pasta is cold. Could you bring me a hot one?*

    Man A: *But that's impossible! It just came from the kitchen.*

    Woman: *That may be, but it is still cold and I would like another.*

175. What does the woman want?
    - (A) To go to a different restaurant.
    - (B) To sit at a different table.
    - (C) To order dessert.
    - (D) To exchange her dinner for a hot one.

You hear:

176. Man B: *How did Vinny get hurt?*

Woman: *He was riding his motorcycle and wasn't wearing a helmet. He was hit by a truck.*

Man B: *That's strange. Vinny's a very careful rider, and I've never seen him ride without his helmet.*

176. Which of the following statements applies to Vinny?
    (A) He has had many accidents.
    (B) Nobody would have expected him to have an accident.
    (C) He had never ridden a motorcycle before.
    (D) He was aware of the need to wear a helmet.

You hear:

177. Man A: *I always enjoy coming to this park. They have good refreshments, and it's always so quiet.*

Woman: *No question about it. It's quiet—too quiet. I like places that are a little more lively.*

Man A: *I do too, usually, but sometimes it's good to get away.*

177. What does the woman say she prefers?
    (A) People and noise.
    (B) Travel abroad.
    (C) Parks and refreshments.
    (D) Quiet evenings at home.

You hear:

178. Woman: *Do you have change for a 10,000 Yen note?*

Man A: *No, it's too early in the day. I rarely have any sales before noon.*

Woman: *Of course, I should have thought of that.*

178. Which of the following statements is true?
    (A) The store is not yet open.
    (B) The customer needs smaller bills.
    (C) The shopkeeper is very busy.
    (D) It is almost closing time.

You hear:

179. Man A: *I've read where they're going to raise the price of rice, sugar, and tea.*

Man B: *People always say that, but it will never happen.*

Man A: *I agree, it would be political suicide for anybody who voted for it. But I don't know how they can continue to pay these farm subsidies.*

179. What are the speakers discussing?
    (A) Food prices.
    (B) A death.
    (C) An election.
    (D) An argument they had.

You hear:

180. Man A: *Here, try sitting in this chair and tell me what you think.*

Woman: *O.K. Well, this one is more comfortable than the others, but I don't care for the shape.*

Man A: *Let's keep looking. We're in no hurry to buy.*

180. What are the speakers doing?
    (A) Arranging their furniture.
    (B) Looking for a chair to buy.
    (C) Getting on a bus.
    (D) Visiting a friend's house.

You hear:

181. **Man A:** *I can't get this drawer to slide in.*

Woman: *I'm not surprised. It's so full, something must be blocking it.*

Man A: *I guess you're right. But where am I supposed to put all these important papers?*

181. What is the man's problem?

  (A) He is lost.

  (B) He has eaten too much.

  (C) He has broken the drawer.

  (D) He has no place to keep his papers.

You hear:

182. **Man A:** *I want to go to the bookstore to get that new book by Mishu. The critics say it's great.*

Woman: *I have a copy I can lend you. Better yet, you can keep it. It's terrible.*

Man A: *If it's that bad, maybe you should keep it. There are other books I can read.*

182. What does the woman say about the new book?

  (A) She has not yet read it.

  (B) She agrees with the critics.

  (C) She did not like it.

  (D) It is not as good as the author's last book.

You hear:

183. **Man A:** *We plan to go out in our motorboat this weekend. Would you like to come along?*

Man B: *Would you believe it? I'm afraid of water and can't swim.*

Man A: *That's too bad. We have a lot of fun with the boat, but I suppose it would be no fun for you.*

183. What will happen on the weekend?

  (A) The men will work on the boat.

  (B) The men will go out on the boat.

  (C) One man may buy a new boat.

  (D) One man will not go on the boat.

You hear:

184. **Man A:** *Your coat looks awfully warm.*

Woman: *As a matter of fact, it's too warm for this weather.*

Man A: *That may be, but I wish I were wearing more than this light sweater.*

184. What is the weather like?

  (A) It is cool.

  (B) It is rainy.

  (C) It is very cold.

  (D) It is a hot day.

You hear:

185. **Woman:** *Do you have any idea how many nations there are in the world?*

Man B: *No, but why would anybody want to know such a fact? What does it matter?*

Woman: *The fact, itself, is not important, but if you don't interest yourself in the world around you, you become a very dull person.*

185. What does the woman want the man to do?

  (A) Answer her question.

  (B) Use his mind.

  (C) Help her find some information.

  (D) Look at something she has to show him.

You hear:

186. **Man A:** *Have you noticed? It's snowing out.*

Man B: *That's all I need! The last time it snowed I crashed my car, and I fell down on the ice. What I wouldn't give for warm weather right now.*

Man A: *C'mon. I don't like it either, but there's nothing we can do about winter. You should stop complaining and enjoy it.*

186. What can be said about the speakers?

  (A) They disagree.

  (B) They are planning a trip.

  (C) They wish it were summer.

  (D) They have a lot of work to do.

You hear: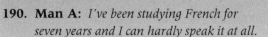

187. Man B: *When is your birthday?*

Woman: *Why do you want to know?*

Man B: *Because The General Store is announcing that people born on the same date as the store's anniversary, September 6, can get a gift by going in this week.*

187. What are the speakers discussing?

    (A) A party for the woman.

    (B) How birthdays are special.

    (C) The man's last birthday.

    (D) An opportunity for people born on September 6.

You hear:

188. Woman: *Is there anything I can do to make you more comfortable?*

Man B: *I don't think so. I hurt from head to foot, the food is terrible here, and I have a lot of work to do at the office.*

Woman: *After your accident, you're lucky to be alive. Don't worry about your work. Rest, and you'll be out of here in no time.*

188. Where does this conversation take place?

    (A) In a car.

    (B) In an office.

    (C) In a hospital.

    (D) In a restaurant.

You hear:

189. Woman: *Do you think it needs more color, or should I leave it as it is?*

Man A: *No, the problem is you drew the figure too small on the page. You should fill the page with the image and the color!*

Woman: *That's what you said about my last drawing. I don't seem to be improving.*

189. Where does this situation take place?

    (A) In a bank.

    (B) In an art class.

    (C) In a museum.

    (D) In a newspaper office.

You hear:

190. Man A: *I've been studying French for seven years and I can hardly speak it at all.*

Man B: *I know just how you feel. I've been studying Chinese for five years. It's very hard to learn another language as an adult.*

Man A: *We should have started when we were much younger. We had more free time then, and I know I didn't use it very wisely.*

190. What are the speakers discussing?

    (A) Travel experiences.

    (B) An international incident.

    (C) The international political situation.

    (D) The difficulty of learning a language.

You hear:

191. Man A: *I read today that the government spends 25% of its revenue on employee salaries.*

Man B: *That sounds like a lot to me, but I suppose it's not impossible.*

Man A: *I don't know if public employees are overpaid, but it's <u>not</u> a job I would enjoy. I'm happy right where I am.*

191. What are the speakers discussing?

    (A) Their work.

    (B) High taxes.

    (C) Public employment.

    (D) The defense budget.

You hear:

192. Man A: *We had lunch at that new Japanese restaurant down the street from the office.*

Woman: *How was it? I've been meaning to ask whether you've been there.*

Man A: *It's really very good, and much better than the place we used to go to. Let's go there soon.*

192. What does the man say about the new restaurant?

    (A) Few people eat there.

    (B) He recommends it.

    (C) It was too expensive.

    (D) He prefers their old restaurant.

You hear:

193. Man A: *We bought a set of new chairs for our kitchen. My wife wants you to come over to see them.*

Woman: *I'd love to. I've been looking for some myself, but new ones are so expensive. Would you want to sell me your old ones?*

Man A: *That's an idea. We were wondering what we should do with them.*

193. What is the woman considering doing?
    (A) Buying the man's old chairs.
    (B) Returning the chairs to the store.
    (C) Selling the man some chairs.
    (D) Buying her chairs at the man's store.

You hear:

194. Woman: *I'm sorry. This card number is not recognized by the credit card company, and we can't accept it.*

Man B: *It was just issued to me! I knew I shouldn't trust it—from now on I pay only with cash.*

Woman: *That's not necessary. This sometimes happens with new cards, but it gets straightened out in time.*

194. What are the speakers discussing?
    (A) The man's credit card is not valid.
    (B) The store does not accept credit cards.
    (C) The man was overcharged on his credit card.
    (D) The man is surprised at how convenient the credit card is.

You hear:

195. Man B: *I would like to make a reservation for round trip, Tokyo to Sydney, to depart on the fourteenth and return on the twenty-seventh.*

Woman: *What class would you like, and what time would you like to depart?*

Man B: *Business class. I would like to take the earliest flight available.*

195. What is the man trying to do?
    (A) Cancel a flight reservation.
    (B) Reserve a flight.
    (C) Learn the price of a business class ticket.
    (D) Change a flight reservation.

You hear:

196. Man A: *Where can I get a hat like that one? It's really nice.*

Man B: *I got this one in Russia. I don't think you'll find one like it here. At least, I haven't seen any.*

Man A: *If you ever go back, get me one. I've always liked that style, and I'll never get there.*

196. What does the man want?
    (A) To travel abroad.
    (B) To have a hat like his friend's.
    (C) To hear about his friend's trip.
    (D) To import hats from Russia.

You hear:

197. Man B: *This pen has leaked and ruined my shirt!*

Woman: *Don't you think the ink will come out? Wash it right away in cold water.*

Man B: *This is the second time this has happened. Why do I buy these cheap pens, anyway?*

197. What is the man's problem?

(A) His pen has stopped writing.

(B) He needs to get to a store before it closes.

(C) Ink from his pen has made a spot on his shirt.

(D) He was caught in the rain without an umbrella.

You hear:

198. Man A: *The glazing on these cups is not good. Look at these cracks. Our managers would complain.*

Man B: *Those are not first quality, sir. Look at these over here. They're much better. We can ship in any amount.*

Man A: *These are much better, but still not good enough for our stores. Is this the best you have?*

198. What is happening?

(A) The buyer will order a shipment of cups.

(B) The buyer wants to test the glaze before ordering.

(C) The manufacturer does not produce cups good enough for the buyer.

(D) The buyer wants to return some defective cups to the factory.

You hear:

199. Man B: *How are these windows better than other windows?*

Woman: *They are double paned, with a vacuum between the panes to serve as insulation. They are 80% more efficient than standard storm windows.*

Man B: *That would make it easier and cheaper to keep the house warm in winter, but I'm afraid I can't afford them. They're just too expensive.*

199. What would the man like to do?

(A) Buy a new house.

(B) Sell his house before winter.

(C) Hire someone to repair his house.

(D) Replace the windows in his house.

You hear:

200. Man B: *How far out do we have to go to find fish?*

Man A: *About ten kilometers out there's a bank, where the water is shallow and fish come to feed. We should do well there.*

Man B: *We can go pretty fast, if the waves don't get any bigger.*

200. How are the speakers traveling?

(A) By car.

(B) By boat.

(C) By plane.

(D) By train.

ANSWER SHEET—PART III

1. Ⓐ Ⓑ Ⓒ Ⓓ
2. Ⓐ Ⓑ Ⓒ Ⓓ
3. Ⓐ Ⓑ Ⓒ Ⓓ
4. Ⓐ Ⓑ Ⓒ Ⓓ
5. Ⓐ Ⓑ Ⓒ Ⓓ
6. Ⓐ Ⓑ Ⓒ Ⓓ
7. Ⓐ Ⓑ Ⓒ Ⓓ
8. Ⓐ Ⓑ Ⓒ Ⓓ
9. Ⓐ Ⓑ Ⓒ Ⓓ
10. Ⓐ Ⓑ Ⓒ Ⓓ
11. Ⓐ Ⓑ Ⓒ Ⓓ
12. Ⓐ Ⓑ Ⓒ Ⓓ
13. Ⓐ Ⓑ Ⓒ Ⓓ
14. Ⓐ Ⓑ Ⓒ Ⓓ
15. Ⓐ Ⓑ Ⓒ Ⓓ
16. Ⓐ Ⓑ Ⓒ Ⓓ
17. Ⓐ Ⓑ Ⓒ Ⓓ
18. Ⓐ Ⓑ Ⓒ Ⓓ
19. Ⓐ Ⓑ Ⓒ Ⓓ
20. Ⓐ Ⓑ Ⓒ Ⓓ
21. Ⓐ Ⓑ Ⓒ Ⓓ
22. Ⓐ Ⓑ Ⓒ Ⓓ
23. Ⓐ Ⓑ Ⓒ Ⓓ
24. Ⓐ Ⓑ Ⓒ Ⓓ
25. Ⓐ Ⓑ Ⓒ Ⓓ
26. Ⓐ Ⓑ Ⓒ Ⓓ
27. Ⓐ Ⓑ Ⓒ Ⓓ
28. Ⓐ Ⓑ Ⓒ Ⓓ
29. Ⓐ Ⓑ Ⓒ Ⓓ
30. Ⓐ Ⓑ Ⓒ Ⓓ
31. Ⓐ Ⓑ Ⓒ Ⓓ
32. Ⓐ Ⓑ Ⓒ Ⓓ
33. Ⓐ Ⓑ Ⓒ Ⓓ
34. Ⓐ Ⓑ Ⓒ Ⓓ
35. Ⓐ Ⓑ Ⓒ Ⓓ
36. Ⓐ Ⓑ Ⓒ Ⓓ
37. Ⓐ Ⓑ Ⓒ Ⓓ
38. Ⓐ Ⓑ Ⓒ Ⓓ
39. Ⓐ Ⓑ Ⓒ Ⓓ
40. Ⓐ Ⓑ Ⓒ Ⓓ
41. Ⓐ Ⓑ Ⓒ Ⓓ

42. Ⓐ Ⓑ Ⓒ Ⓓ
43. Ⓐ Ⓑ Ⓒ Ⓓ
44. Ⓐ Ⓑ Ⓒ Ⓓ
45. Ⓐ Ⓑ Ⓒ Ⓓ
46. Ⓐ Ⓑ Ⓒ Ⓓ
47. Ⓐ Ⓑ Ⓒ Ⓓ
48. Ⓐ Ⓑ Ⓒ Ⓓ
49. Ⓐ Ⓑ Ⓒ Ⓓ
50. Ⓐ Ⓑ Ⓒ Ⓓ
51. Ⓐ Ⓑ Ⓒ Ⓓ
52. Ⓐ Ⓑ Ⓒ Ⓓ
53. Ⓐ Ⓑ Ⓒ Ⓓ
54. Ⓐ Ⓑ Ⓒ Ⓓ
55. Ⓐ Ⓑ Ⓒ Ⓓ
56. Ⓐ Ⓑ Ⓒ Ⓓ
57. Ⓐ Ⓑ Ⓒ Ⓓ
58. Ⓐ Ⓑ Ⓒ Ⓓ
59. Ⓐ Ⓑ Ⓒ Ⓓ
60. Ⓐ Ⓑ Ⓒ Ⓓ
61. Ⓐ Ⓑ Ⓒ Ⓓ
62. Ⓐ Ⓑ Ⓒ Ⓓ
63. Ⓐ Ⓑ Ⓒ Ⓓ
64. Ⓐ Ⓑ Ⓒ Ⓓ
65. Ⓐ Ⓑ Ⓒ Ⓓ
66. Ⓐ Ⓑ Ⓒ Ⓓ
67. Ⓐ Ⓑ Ⓒ Ⓓ
68. Ⓐ Ⓑ Ⓒ Ⓓ
69. Ⓐ Ⓑ Ⓒ Ⓓ
70. Ⓐ Ⓑ Ⓒ Ⓓ
71. Ⓐ Ⓑ Ⓒ Ⓓ
72. Ⓐ Ⓑ Ⓒ Ⓓ
73. Ⓐ Ⓑ Ⓒ Ⓓ
74. Ⓐ Ⓑ Ⓒ Ⓓ
75. Ⓐ Ⓑ Ⓒ Ⓓ
76. Ⓐ Ⓑ Ⓒ Ⓓ
77. Ⓐ Ⓑ Ⓒ Ⓓ
78. Ⓐ Ⓑ Ⓒ Ⓓ
79. Ⓐ Ⓑ Ⓒ Ⓓ
80. Ⓐ Ⓑ Ⓒ Ⓓ
81. Ⓐ Ⓑ Ⓒ Ⓓ
82. Ⓐ Ⓑ Ⓒ Ⓓ

83. Ⓐ Ⓑ Ⓒ Ⓓ
84. Ⓐ Ⓑ Ⓒ Ⓓ
85. Ⓐ Ⓑ Ⓒ Ⓓ
86. Ⓐ Ⓑ Ⓒ Ⓓ
87. Ⓐ Ⓑ Ⓒ Ⓓ
88. Ⓐ Ⓑ Ⓒ Ⓓ
89. Ⓐ Ⓑ Ⓒ Ⓓ
90. Ⓐ Ⓑ Ⓒ Ⓓ
91. Ⓐ Ⓑ Ⓒ Ⓓ
92. Ⓐ Ⓑ Ⓒ Ⓓ
93. Ⓐ Ⓑ Ⓒ Ⓓ
94. Ⓐ Ⓑ Ⓒ Ⓓ
95. Ⓐ Ⓑ Ⓒ Ⓓ
96. Ⓐ Ⓑ Ⓒ Ⓓ
97. Ⓐ Ⓑ Ⓒ Ⓓ
98. Ⓐ Ⓑ Ⓒ Ⓓ
99. Ⓐ Ⓑ Ⓒ Ⓓ
100. Ⓐ Ⓑ Ⓒ Ⓓ
101. Ⓐ Ⓑ Ⓒ Ⓓ
102. Ⓐ Ⓑ Ⓒ Ⓓ
103. Ⓐ Ⓑ Ⓒ Ⓓ
104. Ⓐ Ⓑ Ⓒ Ⓓ
105. Ⓐ Ⓑ Ⓒ Ⓓ
106. Ⓐ Ⓑ Ⓒ Ⓓ
107. Ⓐ Ⓑ Ⓒ Ⓓ
108. Ⓐ Ⓑ Ⓒ Ⓓ
109. Ⓐ Ⓑ Ⓒ Ⓓ
110. Ⓐ Ⓑ Ⓒ Ⓓ
111. Ⓐ Ⓑ Ⓒ Ⓓ
112. Ⓐ Ⓑ Ⓒ Ⓓ
113. Ⓐ Ⓑ Ⓒ Ⓓ
114. Ⓐ Ⓑ Ⓒ Ⓓ
115. Ⓐ Ⓑ Ⓒ Ⓓ
116. Ⓐ Ⓑ Ⓒ Ⓓ
117. Ⓐ Ⓑ Ⓒ Ⓓ
118. Ⓐ Ⓑ Ⓒ Ⓓ
119. Ⓐ Ⓑ Ⓒ Ⓓ
120. Ⓐ Ⓑ Ⓒ Ⓓ
121. Ⓐ Ⓑ Ⓒ Ⓓ
122. Ⓐ Ⓑ Ⓒ Ⓓ
123. Ⓐ Ⓑ Ⓒ Ⓓ

124. Ⓐ Ⓑ Ⓒ Ⓓ
125. Ⓐ Ⓑ Ⓒ Ⓓ
126. Ⓐ Ⓑ Ⓒ Ⓓ
127. Ⓐ Ⓑ Ⓒ Ⓓ
128. Ⓐ Ⓑ Ⓒ Ⓓ
129. Ⓐ Ⓑ Ⓒ Ⓓ
130. Ⓐ Ⓑ Ⓒ Ⓓ
131. Ⓐ Ⓑ Ⓒ Ⓓ
132. Ⓐ Ⓑ Ⓒ Ⓓ
133. Ⓐ Ⓑ Ⓒ Ⓓ
134. Ⓐ Ⓑ Ⓒ Ⓓ
135. Ⓐ Ⓑ Ⓒ Ⓓ
136. Ⓐ Ⓑ Ⓒ Ⓓ
137. Ⓐ Ⓑ Ⓒ Ⓓ
138. Ⓐ Ⓑ Ⓒ Ⓓ
139. Ⓐ Ⓑ Ⓒ Ⓓ
140. Ⓐ Ⓑ Ⓒ Ⓓ
141. Ⓐ Ⓑ Ⓒ Ⓓ
142. Ⓐ Ⓑ Ⓒ Ⓓ
143. Ⓐ Ⓑ Ⓒ Ⓓ
144. Ⓐ Ⓑ Ⓒ Ⓓ
145. Ⓐ Ⓑ Ⓒ Ⓓ
146. Ⓐ Ⓑ Ⓒ Ⓓ
147. Ⓐ Ⓑ Ⓒ Ⓓ
148. Ⓐ Ⓑ Ⓒ Ⓓ
149. Ⓐ Ⓑ Ⓒ Ⓓ
150. Ⓐ Ⓑ Ⓒ Ⓓ
151. Ⓐ Ⓑ Ⓒ Ⓓ
152. Ⓐ Ⓑ Ⓒ Ⓓ
153. Ⓐ Ⓑ Ⓒ Ⓓ
154. Ⓐ Ⓑ Ⓒ Ⓓ
155. Ⓐ Ⓑ Ⓒ Ⓓ
156. Ⓐ Ⓑ Ⓒ Ⓓ
157. Ⓐ Ⓑ Ⓒ Ⓓ
158. Ⓐ Ⓑ Ⓒ Ⓓ
159. Ⓐ Ⓑ Ⓒ Ⓓ
160. Ⓐ Ⓑ Ⓒ Ⓓ
161. Ⓐ Ⓑ Ⓒ Ⓓ
162. Ⓐ Ⓑ Ⓒ Ⓓ
163. Ⓐ Ⓑ Ⓒ Ⓓ
164. Ⓐ Ⓑ Ⓒ Ⓓ

165. Ⓐ Ⓑ Ⓒ Ⓓ   174. Ⓐ Ⓑ Ⓒ Ⓓ   183. Ⓐ Ⓑ Ⓒ Ⓓ   192. Ⓐ Ⓑ Ⓒ Ⓓ
166. Ⓐ Ⓑ Ⓒ Ⓓ   175. Ⓐ Ⓑ Ⓒ Ⓓ   184. Ⓐ Ⓑ Ⓒ Ⓓ   193. Ⓐ Ⓑ Ⓒ Ⓓ
167. Ⓐ Ⓑ Ⓒ Ⓓ   176. Ⓐ Ⓑ Ⓒ Ⓓ   185. Ⓐ Ⓑ Ⓒ Ⓓ   194. Ⓐ Ⓑ Ⓒ Ⓓ
168. Ⓐ Ⓑ Ⓒ Ⓓ   177. Ⓐ Ⓑ Ⓒ Ⓓ   186. Ⓐ Ⓑ Ⓒ Ⓓ   195. Ⓐ Ⓑ Ⓒ Ⓓ
169. Ⓐ Ⓑ Ⓒ Ⓓ   178. Ⓐ Ⓑ Ⓒ Ⓓ   187. Ⓐ Ⓑ Ⓒ Ⓓ   196. Ⓐ Ⓑ Ⓒ Ⓓ
170. Ⓐ Ⓑ Ⓒ Ⓓ   179. Ⓐ Ⓑ Ⓒ Ⓓ   188. Ⓐ Ⓑ Ⓒ Ⓓ   197. Ⓐ Ⓑ Ⓒ Ⓓ
171. Ⓐ Ⓑ Ⓒ Ⓓ   180. Ⓐ Ⓑ Ⓒ Ⓓ   189. Ⓐ Ⓑ Ⓒ Ⓓ   198. Ⓐ Ⓑ Ⓒ Ⓓ
172. Ⓐ Ⓑ Ⓒ Ⓓ   181. Ⓐ Ⓑ Ⓒ Ⓓ   190. Ⓐ Ⓑ Ⓒ Ⓓ   199. Ⓐ Ⓑ Ⓒ Ⓓ
173. Ⓐ Ⓑ Ⓒ Ⓓ   182. Ⓐ Ⓑ Ⓒ Ⓓ   191. Ⓐ Ⓑ Ⓒ Ⓓ   200. Ⓐ Ⓑ Ⓒ Ⓓ

Answer Key—Part III

1. (C) Go to a restaurant.
2. (D) He was not paying attention to time.
3. (C) Lee.
4. (B) See a film.
5. (C) For the woman to attend a seminar.
6. (C) Their budget will remain unchanged.
7. (A) In a hotel.
8. (C) Too many tickets were issued for her flight.
9. (C) Sick at home.
10. (B) He is responsible for apartment repairs.
11. (C) She will have some men pick it up.
12. (C) A report is poorly typed.
13. (A) By mail.
14. (B) Occasionally.
15. (B) Stop working.
16. (A) Their bid was late.
17. (B) The reason quality has gone down.
18. (C) In a few weeks.
19. (C) At the doctor's.
20. (B) He lost his umbrella.
21. (A) He does not like to move.
22. (B) She dropped a glove.
23. (B) Eat dinner.
24. (D) It is not comfortable.
25. (B) He likes onions.
26. (B) Skiing.
27. (C) At an airport.
28. (D) It will improve with time.
29. (D) He is on vacation with his wife.
30. (C) Time spent going to and from work.
31. (B) His weight.
32. (C) It allows for a peaceful life.
33. (C) Her mother will be waiting for her.
34. (B) Nobody enjoys working there.
35. (A) She paid the man a compliment.
36. (D) He does not understand it.
37. (C) Because he has done someone a favor.
38. (C) He thought it would be a bother to her.
39. (B) He likes company when he works.
40. (B) To solve some problems.
41. (D) At a conference.
42. (C) He is an engineer.
43. (A) In a real estate office.
44. (B) Enter a foreign land.
45. (D) A way to entertain himself.
46. (C) At home.
47. (B) In a laboratory.
48. (A) At a restaurant.
49. (D) His supervisors think it serves no purpose.
50. (C) Vacations.
51. (B) To an office supply store.
52. (B) Quit his job.
53. (A) He could have done better.
54. (C) He does not have experience.
55. (A) Never.
56. (B) He is not allowed to see a file he needs.
57. (A) He is preparing a presentation.
58. (C) That the woman is to be promoted.
59. (C) Talk about something in private.
60. (B) How much food to buy.
61. (B) Invest in stock.
62. (D) They failed to meet one another.
63. (A) He gets the wrong advice.
64. (D) He says the editors would not print his letter.
65. (B) He has read about bad things happening.
66. (B) It is not valuable.
67. (A) Speaking in public.
68. (B) Prepare some food.
69. (D) Earn as much with it as possible.
70. (C) Because he feels it is bad for his health.
71. (A) There is something they must do, and he should not be out of town.
72. (C) Test grades.
73. (B) Teach her roommate to cook.
74. (A) He is not healthy.
75. (B) Help his wife get a job.
76. (B) At a doctor's office.
77. (B) Showing family photographs.
78. (D) In ten minutes.
79. (B) Make a telephone call.
80. (A) Get a new car.
81. (C) See a doctor.
82. (D) The man called the wrong number.
83. (D) It will not damage as easily.
84. (C) Return the sweater to the store.
85. (B) Stay inside.
86. (A) Leave for home.
87. (B) It is expensive.
88. (C) Work hard to catch up.
89. (B) It involves great responsibility.
90. (A) Go somewhere together.
91. (B) Nobody wants to work short term.
92. (B) To learn what is new in motorcycles.
93. (C) He had been ill.
94. (A) Meet the man for lunch.
95. (D) He expects a shipment that has not arrived.
96. (A) Sell more product.
97. (A) James will look for a new job.
98. (B) Whether to accept a contract.
99. (C) He does not seem to worry or care about new accounts.
100. (D) Reading a book.
101. (B) Employees who do not work hard.
102. (B) A way to deliver goods.
103. (B) She will be asked to do more writing.
104. (B) Overcome his problem.
105. (A) The weather.
106. (C) Customer satisfaction.
107. (B) The woman did not see it.
108. (D) They ordered a second shipment.
109. (B) Because he is always successful.
110. (C) The title.
111. (B) A man is looking for work.
112. (D) A misplaced order.
113. (C) She has a lot to do.
114. (D) Go to a meeting.
115. (A) He refuses to listen to others.
116. (C) He has to leave a meeting.

117. (B) He has avoided doing something.
118. (D) The woman is in a dangerous place.
119. (A) She is hurt.
120. (B) Offering to bring the woman lunch.
121. (C) How they spend free time.
122. (A) Contacting a client.
123. (B) They seem to have a problem.
124. (A) That his friend had sold his car.
125. (C) He did something that was not safe.
126. (C) Traffic congestion in the city.
127. (B) Keep prices down.
128. (D) She will live farther from her office.
129. (A) Arranging to get together.
130. (C) A department store sale.
131. (B) She made a very costly mistake.
132. (B) Changes in the city.
133. (A) It was difficult to follow.
134. (C) Take a trip.
135. (D) They may have difficulty making a delivery.
136. (B) Take flowers to a friend.
137. (B) Reading novels by a particular author.
138. (C) He thinks it is wrong to take a test to replace a lost license.
139. (C) The customer is not pleased with the salesman.
140. (B) Predict the weather.
141. (B) Supplies have not been ordered.
142. (D) He wanted a promotion.
143. (B) Which movie to see.
144. (B) As soon as possible.
145. (A) He will do everything he needs to do.
146. (B) The way they treat others.
147. (C) She had not completed a customs declaration.
148. (B) There is going to be a fight.
149. (B) A place to shop.
150. (C) He talks too much.
151. (D) He knows nothing about buying stocks.
152. (C) Theater seats.
153. (A) The man will sell only quality fruit.
154. (C) She has never been on this bus.
155. (D) Buy something she asks for.
156. (C) At a post office.
157. (B) Move some furniture.
158. (A) Employment for a friend.
159. (B) The death of a friend.

160. (C) Prepare dinner for a guest.
161. (C) Take a trip to a place he has never been.
162. (A) They attended the same college.
163. (B) Join a health club.
164. (A) He is very busy.
165. (B) Visit someplace warm.
166. (C) He has a lot of work to do in little time.
167. (B) In a restaurant.
168. (A) Equipment to play music
169. (A) Use the computer.
170. (B) How much their order will cost.
171. (D) Ride as far as City Hall.
172. (C) He photographs ways to travel.
173. (C) Admiring the woman's shoes.
174. (B) A tree that needs work.
175. (D) To exchange her dinner for a hot one.
176. (B) Nobody would have expected him to have an accident.
177. (A) People and noise.
178. (B) The customer needs smaller bills.
179. (A) Food prices.
180. (B) Looking for a chair to buy.
181. (D) He has no place to keep his papers.
182. (C) She did not like it.
183. (D) One man will not go on the boat.
184. (A) It is cool.
185. (B) Use his mind.
186. (C) They wish it were summer.
187. (D) An opportunity for people born on September 6.
188. (C) In a hospital.
189. (B) In an art class.
190. (D) The difficulty of learning a language.
191. (C) Public employment.
192. (B) He recommends it.
193. (A) Buying the man's old chairs.
194. (A) The man's credit card is not valid.
195. (B) Reserve a flight.
196. (B) To have a hat like his friend's.
197. (C) Ink from his pen has made a spot on his shirt.
198. (C) The manufacturer does not produce cups good enough for the buyer.
199. (D) Replace the windows in his house.
200. (B) By boat.

PART IV: DISCUSSION

This part of the test is designed to test your global understanding of spoken English. In it you will hear a short statement, followed by up to four questions. Again, the questions do not ask about unimportant information that you may hear. Rather, they test your understanding of major points in the statements. The questions relate to the kind of information that you would need to make a decision, or to take some action, were you to hear it in a real life situation.

To answer these questions correctly you must listen carefully to the English spoken, following the speaker's *intention*. Ask yourself, "What does the speaker want me to learn from the statement?"

Many of the questions in this part of the test are quite difficult, so you should not be discouraged if you find you cannot answer all of them correctly. In this part of the test, as in all parts, if you do not know the correct answer, *you must always guess an answer*.

Remember that for the listening section of the test it will do you no good to leave a question blank, to go back and read the question later, *before* answering it. Therefore, for each question, it is important that you always guess the answer you do not know before moving on to the next question.

Each statement is prefaced with an introductory statement, telling you which questions, and how many, refer to that particular statement. It will tell you whether the statement will be an announcement, a notice, a report, or a presentation, or it may refer to it as merely a statement or a talk.

On the TOEIC®, this part of the test consists of twenty questions.

The directions for this part of the test read as follows:

PART IV

Directions: In this part of the test, you will hear several short talks. Each will be spoken just one time. They will not be printed in your test book, so you must listen carefully to understand and remember what is said.

In your test book, you will read two or more questions about each short talk. The questions will be followed by four answers. You are to choose the best answer to each question and mark it on your answer sheet.

Questions 1–2 refer to the following explanation.

You hear:

(Woman) *This is a picture of Jack, my husband, with Linda. Linda's sixteen now, and she's very bright—makes top marks at school. She wants to be a doctor someday, and I think she'll make it. . . . Here she is at summer camp three years ago. That's her friend Mary, on the left, and I don't know any of the other girls. . . Do you remember when girls wanted to be nurses and boys wanted to be doctors? Things really have changed since I was a girl.*

1. What is happening in the conversation?
   (A) A graduation is taking place.
   (B) The people are looking at family photographs
   (C) Somebody is being met at a station.
   (D) The woman is telling about her new job.

2. What does Linda do?
   (A) She is a doctor.
   (B) She works at a camp.
   (C) She is a student.
   (D) She is a nurse.

Questions 3–4 refer to the following report.

You hear:

(Man A) *The Jones Mansion was built in 1718 and was used as a hotel for over 150 years. George Washington stayed here in 1782. The building was owned by the Jones family until the 1930's, 1932 to be exact, when it was sold to the Hood family. Five years ago it was made into an apartment building for the elderly, and today it houses forty of our senior citizens, thirty-two of whom are over eighty years old.*

3. When did the Jones family sell the Jones Mansion?
   (A) In the 1830's.
   (B) In the 1930's.
   (C) In the 1950's.
   (D) In the 1980's.

4. For what is the building currently used?
   (A) Apartments for old people.
   (B) Condominiums for wealthy people.
   (C) A luxury hotel.
   (D) An office building.

Questions 5–7 refer to the following report.

You hear:

(Man B) *Here is a follow-up report on the four-alarm blaze earlier today at the new City Hospital. Several fire companies were called to the scene. When Fire Chief Andrew Barnes was asked how the fire started, he answered that most likely it was caused by the cigarette of a patient smoking in bed in a back room on the fourth floor. Fire companies responded quickly to the emergency, and there were no injuries. Chief Barnes promised a complete investigation, but at the scene he stated that the circumstances did not lead him to believe that arson was involved.*

5. What was the response to the alarm?
   (A) Only one fire company was needed.
   (B) Several fire companies responded quickly.
   (C) Seven pieces of fire-fighting equipment were called to the scene.
   (D) Firemen from neighboring towns came to fight the fire.

6. What was the probable cause of the fire?
   (A) Children playing with matches.
   (B) A stove exploded.
   (C) Somebody set the fire on purpose.
   (D) Smoking in bed.

7. What kind of building caught fire?
   (A) A library.
   (B) A hospital.
   (C) A school.
   (D) A restaurant.

Questions 8–9 refer to the following announcement.

You hear:

(Woman) *Flight 217 with nonstop service to Miami and connecting with flights for South America, the Caribbean, and Europe, is boarding at Gate 34. The flight, scheduled to depart at three-thirty, is ten minutes behind schedule and will depart at three-forty. All passengers please report to the gate for boarding.*

8. Where is flight 217 going?
   (A) The Caribbean.
   (B) Miami.
   (C) Europe.
   (D) South America.

9. What time was the flight originally scheduled to depart?
   (A) Three o'clock.
   (B) Three-ten.
   (C) Three-thirty.
   (D) Three-forty.

Questions 10–12 refer to the following talk.

You hear:

(Woman) *Tonight's first-aid topic is about handling a choking incident. In terms of the environment in which it occurs, choking is one of the strangest and most unusual of medical emergencies. First, it generally occurs in happy, lighthearted circumstances, when everything appears to be going right. For example, choking incidents often take place at parties, where there are lots of people laughing and having a good time. Second, choking can happen to anyone, young or old, sick or well, alone or with others, at any time. Everybody should know what action to take in the event of a choking incident. It could happen to someone you know, or even to you, at any time.*

10. According to the statement, what kind of medical emergency is choking?
    (A) Serious.
    (B) Unusual.
    (C) Common.
    (D) Undefinable.

11. Where does the speaker say choking incidents often take place?
    (A) In violent circumstances.
    (B) In stressful circumstances.
    (C) In pleasant situations.
    (D) In quiet situations.

12. Who is most likely to become a choking victim?
    (A) A child.
    (B) An elderly person.
    (C) A sick person.
    (D) Anyone.

Questions 13–15 refer to the following talk.

You hear:

(Man A) *Welcome to "Do you know your city?" the spontaneous and unrehearsed show that asks you about the city in which you live. We broadcast from a different city every week, and this week we come to you from Binghamton. And now to our studio audience: This is the only show where you can qualify to win fabulous prizes for answering one-two-three simple questions about your city. Our contestants each week are taken from the studio audience, and this week we have four eager contestants.*

13. What kind of a show is described?
    (A) A comedy show.
    (B) A news show.
    (C) An adventure show.
    (D) A game show.

14. What is the main focus of the show?
    (A) Animals.
    (B) Foreign lands.
    (C) People.
    (D) Cities.

15. What is the show format?
    (A) A film presentation.
    (B) It is unrehearsed.
    (C) A discussion among experts.
    (D) Well-known people speak.

Questions 16–17 refer to the following presentation.

You hear:

(Man B) *O.K., stand still a minute. Now. . . . Stand up straight with your arms over your head . . . . That's right . . . stand with arms over your head, like this . . . . Now you're going to bend forward and touch your toes, then return to the up position. Remember! Knees straight. Touch your toes with your fingers like this . . . if it doesn't hurt, it's not doing you any good. O.K., now you do it. One . . . Two . . . One . . .*

16. What is this a lesson in?
    (A) Acting.
    (B) Boxing.
    (C) Dancing.
    (D) Exercising.

17. According to the speaker, to start, where are the arms to be placed?
    (A) Out in front.
    (B) By the sides.
    (C) Over the head.
    (D) On the head.

Questions 18–19 refer to the following introduction.

You hear:

(Woman) *The next speaker on this afternoon's program is Professor Helen Peterson, from City University. Professor Peterson is one of the nation's leading authorities on local tax policy. She has recently published a book on the history of local taxation. Today Professor Peterson will report on recent changes in the tax laws and the way those changes may affect you and your money.*

18. What is Helen Peterson's occupation?
    (A) Publishing executive.
    (B) University professor.
    (C) Government official.
    (D) Newspaper reporter.

19. What is the subject of Helen Peterson's talk?
    (A) Tax policy.
    (B) Book publishing.
    (C) Local history.
    (D) Changes in laws.

Questions 20–21 refer to the following announcement.

You hear:

(Man A) *Remember, this is a limited opportunity to purchase our remaining stocks of last year's models at a 50 percent, that's a 50 percent discount. That is unheard of, ladies and gentlemen. Everything must go to make room for new models. Choose from the widest selection. All sales are cash only, and all sales are final. This offer expires September 1, so you must act now.*

20. What goods are being sold?
    (A) Goods damaged in shipment.
    (B) Models from the previous year.
    (C) Overproduction on the latest models.
    (D) Everything, because the store needs cash.

21. What may a customer do with a purchase, if the customer is not satisfied with it?
    (A) It can be returned for the money paid.
    (B) It can be returned for credit at the store.
    (C) It can be exchanged for other goods.
    (D) It cannot be returned under any circumstances.

Questions 22–24 refer to the following announcement.

You hear:

(Man A) *All passengers on Sunbird Airlines flight 22 are requested to go to the Sunbird Airlines ticket counter. Due to a delay caused by the weather conditions, you will receive a voucher for a complimentary dinner in the airport restaurant. Boarding time has been rescheduled for 8:30 P.M. You will be advised if there are any further schedule changes. We sincerely regret any inconvenience caused by this delay.*

22. What are passengers to do?
    (A) Go to the ticket counter.
    (B) Board the airplane.
    (C) Go home and return the next day.
    (D) Report to another airline.

23. What will passengers be given?
    (A) A ticket.
    (B) A boarding pass.
    (C) A dinner.
    (D) A report.

24. What caused the problem?
    (A) Airplane equipment failure.
    (B) Too many tickets were sold.
    (C) A computer error.
    (D) Weather conditions.

Questions 25–27 refer to the following notice.

You hear:

(Man B) *Give us six hours of your time, and we'll show you how to get eleven hours of work out of an eight-hour day. Let our consultants show your managers how to use their time more effectively. An independent survey has shown that 90 percent of the participants in our six-hour time management seminar say they learn valuable techniques that enhance their effectiveness on the job. We design programs for organizations of all sizes, scheduled for a single day or in one-, two-, or three-hour sessions. Let us visit you in your office to show you what we can do for your company.*

25. Who are these seminars intended for?
    (A) Managers.
    (B) Clerical staff.
    (C) Consultants.
    (D) Technicians.

26. How long does the seminar last?
    (A) Three hours.
    (B) Six hours.
    (C) Eight hours.
    (D) Eleven hours.

27. What do participants learn?
    (A) How to work with others.
    (B) How to use new equipment.
    (C) How to manage time.
    (D) How to negotiate.

Questions 28–30 refer to the following talk.

You hear:

(Man A) *Of your customers surveyed by our consulting group, 1,750, or 18 percent, said they* always *buy your brand. Sixty-three percent said they buy it occasionally, and the remainder said they bought it only one time. Our consulting group analyzed the data carefully, looking at both the local and the national market. The group's opinion is that you could increase your sales by nearly 40 percent, in a two-year period, by concentrating advertising on those customers who purchase your brand only occasionally.*

28. Who was surveyed?
    (A) Store managers.
    (B) Television viewers.
    (C) Sales people.
    (D) Customers.

29. Who conducted the survey?
    (A) A consumer group.
    (B) The manufacturer.
    (C) A consulting group.
    (D) A business school class.

30. What is recommended as the result of the survey?
    (A) A more in-depth survey.
    (B) That the company concentrate on attracting new customers.
    (C) That the company focus advertising on current customers.
    (D) That the company redesign the package and carry out national advertising.

Questions 31–33 refer to the following announcement.

You hear:

(Woman) *This is the schedule we have planned for you. When you get in on Tuesday night you'll be met at the airport by our representative and driven to your hotel, where you'll have the evening free. The first meeting is scheduled for the next day, Wednesday morning at ten o'clock. Your presentation is planned*

for two o'clock, but it may be rescheduled if lunch runs late. In any case, we hope to get through with everything by Friday noon, to leave you some time to see the city. Your departure is scheduled for Saturday morning. Does this sound all right with you?

31. When is the presentation scheduled?
    (A) Tuesday night.
    (B) Wednesday morning.
    (C) Wednesday afternoon.
    (D) Friday afternoon.

32. Under what conditions would the presentation be rescheduled?
    (A) If other presentations are too long.
    (B) If a meal is too long.
    (C) If people do not show up.
    (D) If participants need to leave early.

33. When will the program end?
    (A) Sunday night.
    (B) Before the weekend.
    (C) Tuesday.
    (D) Wednesday.

Questions 34–36 refer to the following talk.

You hear:

(Man B) *According to our studies, 55 percent or the great majority of service calls on computer equipment were the result of user unfamiliarity, while only 10 percent were the result of electronic failure. The remaining 35 percent were due to a wide range of mechanical problems having nothing to do with the electronic circuitry. We plan to deal with the electronics problem by imposing more rigid quality control standards on our suppliers. The mechanical problems we will deal with immediately. All employees will undergo comprehensive workshop training for their jobs, and supervisors will receive training on how to ensure closer on-the-job supervision.*

34. What led to the most service calls of computer equipment?
    (A) Mechanical problems.
    (B) User unfamiliarity.
    (C) Damage caused in shipping.
    (D) Electronic circuitry failure.

35. How will the company deal with problems in circuitry?
    (A) Establish in-house workshops.
    (B) Change suppliers.
    (C) Set higher quality control standards.
    (D) Revise equipment specifications.

36. What will happen to supervisors?
    (A) They will be fired and replaced.
    (B) They will work on the assembly line to learn what employees do.
    (C) They will receive special training.
    (D) They will go on service calls with technicians.

Questions 37–38 refer to the following message.

You hear:

(**Woman**) *The number you have reached, 437-5206, is not in service. Please check the number and try your call again. Thank you.*

37. Why was this message necessary?
    (A) A number has been changed.
    (B) A party is unable to answer the phone.
    (C) A telephone number is not in service.
    (D) A customer has not paid his bill.

38. What is a caller supposed to do?
    (A) Call back later when someone is available.
    (B) Inform the company that the phone is out of order.
    (C) Confirm that the number dialed is correct.
    (D) Ask the operator for assistance.

Questions 39–40 refer to the following announcement.

You hear:

(**Man A**) *It is my pleasure to introduce to you this evening our guest speaker, Dr. Raj Suwantra. Dr. Suwantra is a longtime activist in the worldwide cause for human rights and has received several international awards in recognition of his distinguished record of public service. He has been a*

close friend of many of us here this evening, as well as our inspiration to work on behalf of our fellow man. Please welcome . . . Dr. Raj Suwantra.

39. In what field does Dr. Suwantra work?
    (A) Tropical medicine.
    (B) Contagious diseases of all kinds.
    (C) Human rights.
    (D) Nuclear physics.

40. For what reason does the speaker say Dr. Suwantra has received international awards?
    (A) For his discoveries in science.
    (B) For his public service.
    (C) For his many sacrifices.
    (D) For his inspiration of young scientists.

Questions 41–43 refer to the following report.

You hear:

(**Man B**) *City traffic control has announced that due to roadway construction on Highway 4, the incoming lanes of Highway 4 will be closed to traffic beginning tomorrow morning at six o'clock, that's beginning at 6:00 A.M., for the next twelve days. As an alternate route, people coming into the city by Highway 4 are advised to travel on Highway 3 as far as the Green River Bridge, then take the Parkway to the old highway.*

41. Who does this report mostly affect?
    (A) People who need to go to the airport.
    (B) People entering the city by Highway 4.
    (C) People who must cross the Green River Bridge.
    (D) People who work outside the city.

42. What does traffic control recommend that people do?
    (A) Restrict travel to certain hours.
    (B) Use special public transportation.
    (C) Follow directions provided.
    (D) Find an alternate route.

43. Why is this disruption necessary?
    (A) There has been a bad accident.
    (B) A bridge has fallen down.
    (C) There is roadway construction.
    (D) The old highway is in poor condition.

Questions 44–46 refer to the following announcement.

You hear:

(Man A) *The entire business community is invited to join Dr. Kim and a panel of seven of Harristown's leading publishing experts for a discussion about how to produce a successful print advertising campaign. At the discussion, local business people may arrange for a free appointment to discuss specific advertising needs. The panel discussion will take place in Able Hall and begin at two P.M., giving everybody plenty of time for lunch. Following will be a question and answer period. Refreshments will be served. To enter, you must leave your calling card at the door.*

44. Who is invited to attend the meeting?
    (A) The medical profession.
    (B) Reporters.
    (C) Business people.
    (D) Bankers.

45. What must people do to be admitted?
    (A) Pay a small fee.
    (B) Identify themselves.
    (C) Call in advance to reserve space.
    (D) Present an advertisement from the newspaper.

46. What time does the meeting begin?
    (A) 9:00 A.M.
    (B) 11:00 P.M.
    (C) 2:00 P.M.
    (D) 7:00 P.M.

Questions 47–49 refer to the following advertisement.

You hear:

(Woman) *Find the art supplies you need with only a glance at the O-Mart Graphic Arts catalog. The catalog contains 240 pages full of art supplies for the amateur and the professional, for the fine and the commercial artist. Plus! Don't miss out on receiving free coupons for valuable discounts on art supplies, available only to catalog-order customers. Pick up*

your catalog at either of our two convenient O-Mart locations, our new store in the Metropolitan Mall or our original store in suburban Millerville.

47. What is being offered?
    (A) Discount prices.
    (B) A catalog.
    (C) Lessons by professionals.
    (D) Valuable prizes.

48. How many O-Mart locations are there?
    (A) One.
    (B) Two.
    (C) Three.
    (D) Four.

49. Who will receive discounts?
    (A) Radio listeners.
    (B) Catalog order customers.
    (C) Everybody.
    (D) Art students.

Questions 50–51 refer to the following notice.

You hear:

(Man A) *Your attention please. The visit of the government inspection team to Mak Chemicals, scheduled for three o'clock today, has been postponed until tomorrow morning at ten o'clock. Please be sure that your work area is clean and in order and report to your supervisor anything about our plant that might create a negative impression. Our Chairman has asked that we maintain our record of maximum points with regard to these inspections. Thank you.*

50. What is expected?
    (A) A visit from the Chairman.
    (B) An inspection by government observers.
    (C) A visit from the Board of Directors.
    (D) A special team of safety experts.

51. What has prompted this notice?
    (A) A postponement.
    (B) A chemical accident.
    (C) A recent report on the environment.
    (D) A warning from an alert employee.

Questions 52–54 refer to the following announcement.

You hear:

(**Woman**) *Now in its sixteenth year, this year's Women's Club ten-K run will take place on Saturday, April 14. As in the past, proceeds will go to inform the public, and particularly women, about the dangers of cancer and the importance of early detection. To enter, runners must be female, at least eleven years of age, and in good health. The run will begin at the Monument at ten A.M. and follow a course along the river to the Aquarium. From there it will turn north to the park and finish at the Monument. Besides the usual t-shirts, participants who finish will be eligible for cash prizes.*

52. For whom is this notice of particular interest?
    (A) The general public.
    (B) Club members.
    (C) Women runners.
    (D) All women.

53. What will the money be used for that is earned by this event?
    (A) Cancer research.
    (B) Public information.
    (C) Medical expenses.
    (D) Detection equipment.

54. What is the minimum age for participants?
    (A) Ten.
    (B) Eleven.
    (C) Fourteen.
    (D) Sixteen.

Questions 55–57 refer to the following talk.

You hear:

(**Woman**) *One of the most enchanting locations to visit in the area is the island of Chara, located far off the mainland. The inhabitants of Chara have always believed that their remote jungle island and their very lives are dominated by a spirit world and have built over 250 temples for the spirits to reside in. Unique in the world, however, is the notion on Chara that there are only* good *spirits—there* are *no evil spirits. On Chara there are no wars, little sickness, no volcanoes or typhoons, and there has always been abundant food. In such a place, who could believe that evil exists?*

55. Why have the people of Chara built temples?
    (A) For their priests to live in.
    (B) As residences for spirits.
    (C) As a place to gather for daily rituals.
    (D) As a place for weddings, funerals, and special events.

56. What does the speaker say is unique about Chara?
    (A) The number of temples for the size of the population.
    (B) The absence of wars and natural disasters.
    (C) The belief that there are no evil spirits.
    (D) The Chara population has no chief or other ruler.

57. What is Chara?
    (A) A region high in the mountains.
    (B) A city deep in the jungle.
    (C) A city that exists only in the imagination.
    (D) A distant island.

Questions 58–60 refer to the following talk.

You hear:

(Man B) *Ladies, take your husband off on that weekend vacation you've always dreamed about. Sunray Tour weekend travel packages will make it both fun and affordable. Choose from seventeen distinctive adults-only resorts in five idyllic locations, far from the children, traffic, and telephones. We even make available a car, free, for you to use during your stay with us, should you want to visit the surrounding countryside. Don't wait any longer. Phone your travel agent now and ask about the Sunray Tour weekend travel package. And when your husband gets home from work tonight, surprise him with the tickets as he comes in the door. For two days at Sunray, he'll thank you for years.*

58. What does the announcer tell women to do?
    (A) Take their husbands to talk to the travel agent.
    (B) Travel to Sunray resorts without their husbands.
    (C) Buy Sunray resort tickets without discussing it with their husbands.
    (D) Earn a free trip by forming a group to visit a Sunray resort.

59. What does the announcer say is provided free with a Sunray visit?
    (A) All food.
    (B) All entertainment.
    (C) An automobile.
    (D) Accommodations for children.

60. What Sunray tours are being promoted?
    (A) Two-day.
    (B) Five-day.
    (C) Seven-day.
    (D) Fourteen-day.

Questions 61-63 refer to the following announcement.

You hear:

(Man A) *The Galaxy Cinema is now showing two first-run feature films. In Galaxy One we present "The Moonling," a story about a child moon creature.*

Showtimes are at five, seven, and nine P.M. In Galaxy Two we present "Five Figure Fingers," a fictional life-story about an accomplished pianist. Show times are at six, eight, and ten P.M. Saturday is special at the Galaxy. We show both films in a popular late showing, at midnight. Admission for all seats, all showings, every day, is three dollars. Free parking is always available across from the Galaxy.

61. How many films are being shown at the Galaxy Cinema?
    (A) One.
    (B) Two.
    (C) Three.
    (D) Four.

62. What is special about Saturday at the Galaxy?
    (A) The price is reduced.
    (B) Films are shown at midnight.
    (C) Parking is free.
    (D) There is a stage show.

63. What is "The Moonling" about?
    (A) A man who walks about at night.
    (B) Images in the skies at night.
    (C) A fictional animal that comes to life.
    (D) A child from the moon.

Questions 64–65 refer to the following announcement.

You hear:

(Man B) *Ladies and gentlemen. May I have your attention, please? I have just been given the results of the Mr. and Miss Everything contest, the male and female who are the most beautiful, most intelligent, most accomplished, and most personable among the nominees sent to us from our child-care centers all over the country. Of course, ladies and gentlemen, to qualify for their prizes our contestants must meet some very strict requirements, not the least of which is that they cannot be more than 12 months old as of today.*

64. What is the purpose of this announcement?

(A) To outline contest rules.

(B) To correct an earlier statement.

(C) To open the judging.

(D) To name the winners.

65. What sort of contest does this notice concern?

(A) A body-building contest.

(B) A beauty contest.

(C) An athletic contest.

(D) A baby contest.

Questions 66–67 refer to the following announcement.

You hear:

(Man A) *We interrupt this broadcast to bring you a special announcement of the event of the century. The spaceship Stellar Probe has just landed safely on the planet Mars. In a moment, on this station, the President will speak directly to the nation concerning this historic event. Meanwhile, on Mars, the Astronauts will prepare to leave shortly from their home of the past three months and venture onto* terra firma.

66. What does this announcement concern?

(A) An address by the President.

(B) A successful space mission.

(C) The loss of a space ship.

(D) Plans for space travel.

67. Where are the Astronauts?

(A) Getting into a rocket on Earth.

(B) On the planet Mars.

(C) Somewhere in space.

(D) Leaving the moon.

Questions 68–69 refer to the following announcement.

You hear:

(Man A) *My name's Bill Davis. I'm offering the best deals in town on late model used cars at BD's Budget Auto Lot. "BD," that's me. No one can sell cars at prices lower than mine. Come out today and test drive one of these beautiful domestic or imported cars. I have all sizes, colors, and shapes, they speak every language a car can speak, and they're all just like*

new. Don't delay. Meet me today, this beautiful sunny Sunday, at BD's Budget Auto Lot.

68. What is being advertised?

(A) Auto repair service.

(B) New cars.

(C) Auto rentals.

(D) Used cars.

69. What does BD stand for?

(A) Beautiful Day.

(B) Bill Davis.

(C) Buy Domestic.

(D) Budget.

Questions 70–72 refer to the following report.

You hear:

(Woman) *And now for the art investment report. Color Field paintings have been gaining in popularity among art collectors and museums for the past decade. Over this ten-year period the value of these works has appreciated greatly. Indeed, anyone who purchased a Color Field painting more than five years ago today would have realized an increase in value of up to five times the original price. It is not clear what the future of this market will be, but one expert believes that it will continue to improve.*

70. For how long has Color Field painting been gaining popularity?

(A) Five years.

(B) Ten years.

(C) Twenty-five years.

(D) Fifty years.

71. According to the announcer, what has been the increase in value of Color Field paintings in recent years?

(A) Up to two times.

(B) Up to three times.

(C) Up to four times.

(D) Up to five times.

72. What is the prediction for the future of the Color Field painting market?

(A) It can only increase.

(B) It will remain steady.

(C) It will rise and fall in cycles.

(D) It is uncertain.

Questions 73–74 refer to the following notice.

You hear:

(Man B) *Are your valuables safe? If you have them at home, they are not. Why not stop by your local National Trust bank and rent a safety deposit box? You will sleep more soundly, knowing that your jewelry, gold, cash, documents, and other valuables are protected by us. Visit any of our more than twenty conveniently located branches throughout the city. Speak with one of our friendly and capable staff at any location to learn how we can serve you.*

73. What does this advertisement offer?
    (A) Security.
    (B) Low prices.
    (C) Valuable prizes.
    (D) Fast personal service.

74. What should listeners do to learn more?
    (A) Visit the main office.
    (B) Inquire at one of twenty branch offices.
    (C) Telephone a special number.
    (D) Apply at any of several department stores.

Questions 75–77 refer to the following notice.

You hear:

(Man A) *Good morning. My name is Will Roberts. I work in the planning division. As you know, our section has been working with the problem of how to increase production without sacrificing product quality or plant safety. We're organizing a committee to come up with an approach to recommend to management, and we ask all work units to send one person from each shift to the twice-weekly meetings. Section quotas plantwide will be reduced for the planning period.*

75. What is the problem to be discussed?
    (A) How to improve quality.
    (B) How to increase production.
    (C) How to reduce waste.
    (D) How to improve safety.

76. Who comprises the group?
    (A) Management.
    (B) Worker committees.
    (C) Outside consultants.
    (D) A combination of union and management.

77. What will happen during the planning period?
    (A) There will be no pay increases.
    (B) There will be no overtime.
    (C) Quotas will be reduced.
    (D) Supervisors will submit reports.

Questions 78–79 refer to the following notice.

You hear:

(Man A) *End-of-the-year holidays are coming, and before they get here, I would like to inform employees that we did not meet our production goals for the year. We have an 8 percent shortfall. This is not our fault, I know. Strikes at our suppliers and a fire in one of our warehouses made our goals impossible, and until those events occurred at mid-year we were ahead by 5.5 percent, which is substantial, when you consider our total effort. Nevertheless, your bonuses will be smaller than usual, and for this the management apologizes.*

78. What is the occasion of this presentation?
    (A) Introduction of a new president.
    (B) Awarding of a large contract.
    (C) End-of-the-year holidays.
    (D) Resolution of a strike.

79. What has been the factory's recent performance?
    (A) Production has been lower than planned.
    (B) Quality has not improved.
    (C) Lack of orders for goods required layoffs.
    (D) Employees have been uncooperative.

Questions 80–83 refer to the following information.

You hear:

(Woman) *Mike Billings, of Madison, Wisconsin, does "comfort-first" designing. Recently he designed a detachable computer keyboard. A special transmitter built into the keyboard transmits the typed characters to the computer. With other computers, the keyboard is attached, and operators have to sit at a desk, bent over, and often suffer from backaches and eyestrain. But this is not Mike's first such design. All of Billings' designs begin with the premise that people come first, machines second. Hence, the name, Comfort-First Designs.*

80. What name does Billings give to his design styles?
    (A) Unit designs.
    (B) People designs.
    (C) Comfort-first designs.
    (D) Component designs.

81. What is the premise that Billings uses in his design concept?
    (A) Machines make people productive.
    (B) People are more important than machines.
    (C) Function and form are one.
    (D) Machines have feelings too.

82. Which of Billings designs is reported?
    (A) A small portable computer.
    (B) A detachable computer keyboard.
    (C) A computer for use in bed.
    (D) A computer for the blind.

83. What is an advantage of Billings' designs?
    (A) People make fewer mistakes.
    (B) Lower operating costs.
    (C) Greater productivity.
    (D) More physical comfort for users.

Questions 84–85 refer to the following talk.

You hear:

(Woman) *There are few things that make us feel so warm inside as a sincere compliment from someone whose opinion we respect. Unfortunately, many*

people are concerned only with their own welfare. That drives them to appear very cold and uncaring. It's clear that people who love life, as well as other people, get more out of life than those who are concerned only with themselves. And these loving people always have more friends. My advice—think about others. They will take far better care of you than you can.

84. According to the speaker, what do people like to hear?
    (A) Their name.
    (B) Good news.
    (C) Soft music.
    (D) Compliments.

85. What is the speaker's message to the listener?
    (A) Never betray a trust.
    (B) Take care of your family.
    (C) People who care are rewarded.
    (D) Never lend money.

Questions 86–88 refer to the following advertisement.

You hear:

(Man B) *Welcome, ladies and gentlemen, to this, our first night, the opening of our new theater. Tonight the management has a surprise for you. Before you enjoy the film you came to see, we have invited Chano the Magician to perform for you his acts of prestidigitation and sleight of hand. Chano the Magician has performed in private shows at parties in many of your homes, but this is his first public appearance. We look for great things from this young man. So please, ladies and gentlemen, join me in our opening night for . . . Chano . . . the Magician.*

86. What event is being held?
    (A) A national holiday.
    (B) A theater opening.
    (C) A birthday.
    (D) A surprise party.

87. What does Chano do?
    (A) He sings and dances.
    (B) He performs a magic act.
    (C) He tells fortunes.
    (D) He is a film star.

Questions 88–90 refer to the following announcement.

You hear:

(**Man A**) *All personnel are invited to an open-house demonstration of the new PDQ 1500 series computer system. This is a state-of-the-art system, unique in that before designing it, PDQ Systems surveyed the needs of offices—and then designed their computer to meet those needs. Of special interest to all will be the PDQ 1500 software that will enable the user to identify software problems. It is expected that maintenance costs for the PDQ system will be less than one tenth of those of other office systems over the life of the equipment. The open-house demonstration will be held today, beginning at 3 P.M. in the main cafeteria.*

88. What is this an announcement for?
    (A) An offer for a free computer.
    (B) An advertisement for a computer sale.
    (C) A press release on a new computer system.
    (D) A computer demonstration.

89. How was the computer in the announcement designed?
    (A) By copying the best from other computers.
    (B) By surveying office needs.
    (C) By taking advantage of new computer chip technology.
    (D) By reducing a large computer to office size.

90. What is a unique advantage of the PDQ 1500 series computer?
    (A) Low purchase price.
    (B) Simplicity of operation.
    (C) Low maintenance costs.
    (D) Compatibility with other systems.

Question 91 refers to the following announcement.

You hear:

Man B: *This is an emergency! There is no immediate danger. Do not panic. Please look for the nearest exit, stand up, and move in an orderly fashion toward it and the street. Do not push. Parents, please carry small children. If you need help, ask someone near you to help. There is no immediate danger. Please move slowly, but deliberately. Thank you.*

91. What are people being asked to do?
    (A) Go to an air-raid shelter.
    (B) Leave a building.
    (C) Get off the street.
    (D) Abandon a demonstration.

Questions 92–94 refer to the following talk.

You hear:

(**Woman**) *A study recently concluded that the public in industrialized nations are becoming more interested than before in helping the less fortunate people of developing nations. This newfound altruism has not resulted in personal giving of money, but rather in individual efforts to give aid through service—which is far more important than money. Most volunteers have been professionals. Doctors and nurses have volunteered for medical duty, engineers for building roads and bridges, and teachers and others have made themselves available for a variety of international assignments.*

It is not clear why this phenomenon is taking place. There has been speculation that international developments in recent years have played down nationalism and have underlined the importance of all humanity working together for a better world.

92. What is the subject of this talk?
    (A) A couple's experience as volunteers
    (B) The need for volunteers in the Third World.
    (C) A new public emphasis on volunteering.
    (D) The rewards of volunteering.

93. What kind of volunteering is discussed?

    (A) Worker.

    (B) Manager.

    (C) Professional.

    (D) Personal.

94. What reason for volunteering is given?

    (A) Unemployment

    (B) Adventure

    (C) Dissatisfaction

    (D) Feeling for humanity

Questions 95–97 refer to the following advertisement.

You hear:

(Man B) Are you looking for great lasagna? Or any Italian dish, for that matter? Try The Sorrento at 722 Third Street. The minute you walk in the door, you feel like you're in a South Italian villa, looking over the Bay of Naples. The Sorrento is open every day except Wednesday until midnight. During the week, reservations are not necessary, but on weekends, to dine before ten P.M. you should phone ahead to assure yourself a table. The Sorrento can accommodate groups of up to twenty-eight in its new Neapolitan Reception Room.

95. What kind of a place is the speaker talking about?

    (A) A hotel.

    (B) An villa.

    (C) A market.

    (D) A restaurant.

96. What day is The Sorrento closed?

    (A) Sunday.

    (B) Tuesday.

    (C) Wednesday.

    (D) Friday

97. For which of the following times are reservations suggested?

    (A) Mondays.

    (B) Saturdays.

    (C) All the time.

    (D) Never.

Questions 98–100 refer to the following talk.

You hear:

(Man A) Sometimes the simplest of tools is the most useful. Consider, for example, the ruler. A ruler is mainly used to measure and to draw straight lines on flat surfaces. It does not have a great many uses, especially since parents and teachers have given up trying to instruct children through spankings. Some rulers are transparent, some made of metal (and therefore can be used to cut straight lines), and some provide both metric and American measurements. People carry them in their shirt pockets, briefcases, or purses, to have them available for use any time.

Of course, the ruler is not the only simple but very useful device. Consider, for instance, the pencil, the doorknob and hinges, and glass. Jet planes and computers are fine, but not necessary for survival. Who, on the other hand, could survive without the simple tools mentioned here?

98. What is the subject of this talk?

    (A) Simple tools are necessary for mankind.

    (B) In a modern world, we need modern technology.

    (C) Even simple tools can be made complicated.

    (D) Modern society has forgotten how to use simple tools.

99. Which of the following statements is made about rulers?

    (A) They have many uses.

    (B) People often carry rulers with them.

    (C) Every schoolchild has a ruler.

    (D) Rulers are rarely used today.

100. How does the speaker refer to jet planes?

    (A) As necessary for modern man.

    (B) As a simple machine, once it is understood.

    (C) As unnecessary for survival.

    (D) As dangerous instruments that should not be permitted.

ANSWER SHEET—PART IV

1. Ⓐ Ⓑ Ⓒ Ⓓ
2. Ⓐ Ⓑ Ⓒ Ⓓ
3. Ⓐ Ⓑ Ⓒ Ⓓ
4. Ⓐ Ⓑ Ⓒ Ⓓ
5. Ⓐ Ⓑ Ⓒ Ⓓ
6. Ⓐ Ⓑ Ⓒ Ⓓ
7. Ⓐ Ⓑ Ⓒ Ⓓ
8. Ⓐ Ⓑ Ⓒ Ⓓ
9. Ⓐ Ⓑ Ⓒ Ⓓ
10. Ⓐ Ⓑ Ⓒ Ⓓ
11. Ⓐ Ⓑ Ⓒ Ⓓ
12. Ⓐ Ⓑ Ⓒ Ⓓ
13. Ⓐ Ⓑ Ⓒ Ⓓ
14. Ⓐ Ⓑ Ⓒ Ⓓ
15. Ⓐ Ⓑ Ⓒ Ⓓ
16. Ⓐ Ⓑ Ⓒ Ⓓ
17. Ⓐ Ⓑ Ⓒ Ⓓ
18. Ⓐ Ⓑ Ⓒ Ⓓ
19. Ⓐ Ⓑ Ⓒ Ⓓ
20. Ⓐ Ⓑ Ⓒ Ⓓ
21. Ⓐ Ⓑ Ⓒ Ⓓ
22. Ⓐ Ⓑ Ⓒ Ⓓ
23. Ⓐ Ⓑ Ⓒ Ⓓ
24. Ⓐ Ⓑ Ⓒ Ⓓ
25. Ⓐ Ⓑ Ⓒ Ⓓ

26. Ⓐ Ⓑ Ⓒ Ⓓ
27. Ⓐ Ⓑ Ⓒ Ⓓ
28. Ⓐ Ⓑ Ⓒ Ⓓ
29. Ⓐ Ⓑ Ⓒ Ⓓ
30. Ⓐ Ⓑ Ⓒ Ⓓ
31. Ⓐ Ⓑ Ⓒ Ⓓ
32. Ⓐ Ⓑ Ⓒ Ⓓ
33. Ⓐ Ⓑ Ⓒ Ⓓ
34. Ⓐ Ⓑ Ⓒ Ⓓ
35. Ⓐ Ⓑ Ⓒ Ⓓ
36. Ⓐ Ⓑ Ⓒ Ⓓ
37. Ⓐ Ⓑ Ⓒ Ⓓ
38. Ⓐ Ⓑ Ⓒ Ⓓ
39. Ⓐ Ⓑ Ⓒ Ⓓ
40. Ⓐ Ⓑ Ⓒ Ⓓ
41. Ⓐ Ⓑ Ⓒ Ⓓ
42. Ⓐ Ⓑ Ⓒ Ⓓ
43. Ⓐ Ⓑ Ⓒ Ⓓ
44. Ⓐ Ⓑ Ⓒ Ⓓ
45. Ⓐ Ⓑ Ⓒ Ⓓ
46. Ⓐ Ⓑ Ⓒ Ⓓ
47. Ⓐ Ⓑ Ⓒ Ⓓ
48. Ⓐ Ⓑ Ⓒ Ⓓ
49. Ⓐ Ⓑ Ⓒ Ⓓ
50. Ⓐ Ⓑ Ⓒ Ⓓ

51. Ⓐ Ⓑ Ⓒ Ⓓ
52. Ⓐ Ⓑ Ⓒ Ⓓ
53. Ⓐ Ⓑ Ⓒ Ⓓ
54. Ⓐ Ⓑ Ⓒ Ⓓ
55. Ⓐ Ⓑ Ⓒ Ⓓ
56. Ⓐ Ⓑ Ⓒ Ⓓ
57. Ⓐ Ⓑ Ⓒ Ⓓ
58. Ⓐ Ⓑ Ⓒ Ⓓ
59. Ⓐ Ⓑ Ⓒ Ⓓ
60. Ⓐ Ⓑ Ⓒ Ⓓ
61. Ⓐ Ⓑ Ⓒ Ⓓ
62. Ⓐ Ⓑ Ⓒ Ⓓ
63. Ⓐ Ⓑ Ⓒ Ⓓ
64. Ⓐ Ⓑ Ⓒ Ⓓ
65. Ⓐ Ⓑ Ⓒ Ⓓ
66. Ⓐ Ⓑ Ⓒ Ⓓ
67. Ⓐ Ⓑ Ⓒ Ⓓ
68. Ⓐ Ⓑ Ⓒ Ⓓ
69. Ⓐ Ⓑ Ⓒ Ⓓ
70. Ⓐ Ⓑ Ⓒ Ⓓ
71. Ⓐ Ⓑ Ⓒ Ⓓ
72. Ⓐ Ⓑ Ⓒ Ⓓ
73. Ⓐ Ⓑ Ⓒ Ⓓ
74. Ⓐ Ⓑ Ⓒ Ⓓ
75. Ⓐ Ⓑ Ⓒ Ⓓ

76. Ⓐ Ⓑ Ⓒ Ⓓ
77. Ⓐ Ⓑ Ⓒ Ⓓ
78. Ⓐ Ⓑ Ⓒ Ⓓ
79. Ⓐ Ⓑ Ⓒ Ⓓ
80. Ⓐ Ⓑ Ⓒ Ⓓ
81. Ⓐ Ⓑ Ⓒ Ⓓ
82. Ⓐ Ⓑ Ⓒ Ⓓ
83. Ⓐ Ⓑ Ⓒ Ⓓ
84. Ⓐ Ⓑ Ⓒ Ⓓ
85. Ⓐ Ⓑ Ⓒ Ⓓ
86. Ⓐ Ⓑ Ⓒ Ⓓ
87. Ⓐ Ⓑ Ⓒ Ⓓ
88. Ⓐ Ⓑ Ⓒ Ⓓ
89. Ⓐ Ⓑ Ⓒ Ⓓ
90. Ⓐ Ⓑ Ⓒ Ⓓ
91. Ⓐ Ⓑ Ⓒ Ⓓ
92. Ⓐ Ⓑ Ⓒ Ⓓ
93. Ⓐ Ⓑ Ⓒ Ⓓ
94. Ⓐ Ⓑ Ⓒ Ⓓ
95. Ⓐ Ⓑ Ⓒ Ⓓ
96. Ⓐ Ⓑ Ⓒ Ⓓ
97. Ⓐ Ⓑ Ⓒ Ⓓ
98. Ⓐ Ⓑ Ⓒ Ⓓ
99. Ⓐ Ⓑ Ⓒ Ⓓ
100. Ⓐ Ⓑ Ⓒ Ⓓ

ANSWER KEY—PART IV

1. (B) The people are looking at family photographs.
2. (C) She is a student.
3. (B) In the 1930's.
4. (A) Apartments for old people.
5. (B) Several fire companies responded quickly.
6. (D) Smoking in bed.
7. (B) A hospital.
8. (B) Miami.
9. (C) Three-thirty.
10. (B) Unusual.
11. (C) In pleasant situations.
12. (D) Anyone.
13. (D) A game show.
14. (D) Cities.
15. (B) It is unrehearsed.
16. (D) Exercising.
17. (C) Over the head.
18. (B) University professor.
19. (D) Changes in laws.
20. (B) Models from the previous year.
21. (D) It cannot be returned under any circumstances.
22. (A) Go to the ticket counter.
23. (C) A dinner.
24. (D) Weather conditions.
25. (A) Managers.
26. (B) Six hours.
27. (C) How to manage time.
28. (D) Customers.
29. (C) A consulting group.
30. (C) That the company focus advertising on current customers.
31. (C) Wednesday afternoon.
32. (B) If a meal is too long.
33. (B) Before the weekend.
34. (B) User unfamiliarity.
35. (C) Set higher quality control standards.
36. (C) They will receive special training.
37. (C) A telephone number is not in service.
38. (C) Confirm that the number dialed is correct.
39. (C) Human rights.
40. (B) For his public service.
41. (B) People entering the city by Highway 4.
42. (C) Follow directions provided.
43. (C) There is roadway construction.
44. (C) Business people.
45. (B) Identify themselves.
46. (C) 2:00 P.M.
47. (B) A catalog.
48. (B) Two.
49. (B) Catalog order customers.
50. (B) An inspection by government observers.

51. (A) A postponement.
52. (C) Women runners.
53. (B) Public information.
54. (B) Eleven.
55. (B) As residences for spirits.
56. (C) The belief that there are no evil spirits.
57. (D) A distant island.
58. (C) Buy Sunray resort tickets without discussing it.
59. (C) An automobile.
60. (A) Two-day.
61. (B) Two.
62. (B) Both films are shown at midnight.
63. (D) A child from the moon.
64. (D) To name the winners.
65. (D) A baby contest.
66. (B) A successful space mission.
67. (B) On the Planet Mars.
68. (D) Used cars.
69. (B) Bill Davis.
70. (B) Ten years.
71. (D) Up to five times.
72. (D) It is uncertain.
73. (A) Security.
74. (B) Inquire at one of twenty branch offices.
75. (B) How to increase production.
76. (B) Worker committees.
77. (C) Quotas will be reduced.
78. (C) End of the year holidays.
79. (A) Production has been lower than planned.
80. (C) Comfort-first designs.
81. (B) People are more important than machines.
82. (B) A detachable computer keyboard.
83. (D) More physical comfort for users.
84. (D) Compliments.
85. (C) People who care are rewarded.
86. (B) A theater opening.
87. (B) He performs a magic act.
88. (D) A computer demonstration.
89. (B) By surveying office needs.
90. (C) Low maintenance costs.
91. (B) Leave a building.
92. (C) A new public emphasis on volunteering.
93. (C) Professional.
94. (D) Feeling for humanity.
95. (D) A restaurant.
96. (C) Wednesday.
97. (B) Saturdays.
98. (A) Simple tools are necessary for mankind.
99. (B) People often carry rulers with them.
100. (C) As unnecessary for survival.

NOTE TO THE READER:

At this point, when taking the test, you will turn the page and continue to work on the next part. Begin by reading carefully the directions for Part V. Those directions are reproduced in this book *exactly* as they appear in the test. Make sure you understand what you are to do before continuing.

The following section of this book should provide you with sufficient information to allow you to continue working on the test uninterrupted.

Reading

PART V: DISCUSSION

This is the first part of the Reading Section of the test. Between the Listening Section and the Reading Section there is no pause or rest period. Upon completion of the Listening Section, you must continue on to the next page and begin work on the Reading Section. You will have seventy-five minutes to answer one hundred questions. That should be enough time, but use your time wisely. The questions that appear in Part VII will require more time than questions that appear in Part V and Part VI.

There is a sample question for each of the parts in the Reading Section of the test. Read them carefully and make sure you understand what you are to do for each part. The questions in Part V require you to read printed statements, each of which has a blank or a space where nothing is written. After each question you are given four possible answers, or alternatives, marked (A), (B), (C), and (D). You are to choose the word or phrase that completes the sentence correctly, and mark the answer on your answer sheet. There is only one correct answer. The other three answers, or alternatives, are wrong.

For each question in Part V, you must read and understand the entire sentence to be able to answer it correctly. Rarely is the answer obvious, and the wrong answers would often be correct except for something that is said in the sentence that makes them incorrect. The problem may be with a preposition or a verb that is used earlier in the statement, or it may be an adverb of time that appears to have little to do with the sentence.

On the TOEIC®, this part of the test consists of thirty questions.

In this section of the test you will have the chance to show how well you understand written English. There are three parts to this section, with special directions for each part.

Following are the directions as they appear before Part V of the TOEIC®:

YOU WILL HAVE ONE HOUR AND FIFTEEN MINUTES TO COMPLETE PARTS V, VI, AND VII OF THE TEST.

PART V

Directions: Questions 101–140 are incomplete sentences. Four words or phrases, marked (A), (B), (C), (D), are given beneath each sentence. You are to choose the <u>one</u> word or phrase that best completes the sentence. Then, on your answer sheet, find the number of the question and mark your answer.

Example

Because the equipment is very delicate, it must be handled with _____.

    (A) caring

    (B) careful   **Sample Answer**

    (C) care   Ⓐ Ⓑ ● Ⓓ

    (D) carefully

The sentence should read, "Because the equipment is very delicate, it must be handled with care." Therefore you should choose answer (C).

Now begin work on the questions.

1. The leader of the project was an intelligent man _____ only weakness was that he hated to fail.

    (A) whose
    (B) who
    (C) whom
    (D) who's

2. The child looked _____ of the small window in the roof.

    (A) in
    (B) out
    (C) back
    (D) into

3. The field of biotechnology _____ to research that could reduce the incidence of heart attacks.

    (A) leading
    (B) has led
    (C) had led
    (D) have been leading

4. They stopped along the road to watch the _____ birds feeding in the swamp.

    (A) color
    (B) colored
    (C) colorful
    (D) coloring

5. Some people are _____ reliable and trustworthy as the sunrise.

    (A) so
    (B) as
    (C) too
    (D) like

6. The accountant did everything he _____ to avoid making a mistake with the figures.

    (A) can
    (B) could
    (C) would
    (D) should

7. The boy was _____ ashamed of what he had done.

   (A) awful
   (B) terrible
   (C) terribly
   (D) terrifically

8. _____ mounted as time and again their designs were rejected by the sales force.

   (A) Disappoint
   (B) Disappointing
   (C) Disappointedly
   (D) Disappointment

9. As onlookers watched, the thief _____ the fence and fled his pursuers.

   (A) leap
   (B) leaps
   (C) leaped
   (D) is leaping

10. _____ new developments make these appliances more attractive to home makers.

    (A) Few
    (B) Many
    (C) Much
    (D) A little

11. The product's _____ formula has been patented in many countries.

    (A) special
    (B) especial
    (C) specially
    (D) especially

12. _____ power failure, test and change batteries regularly.

    (A) Avoid
    (B) To avoid
    (C) Avoiding
    (D) Having avoided

13. Consumers have expressed confidence and satisfaction _____ this item.

    (A) to
    (B) of
    (C) from
    (D) with

14. Now is the time to modernize your office system for greater _____.

    (A) efficient
    (B) efficiency
    (C) efficacious
    (D) efficiently

15. After leaving home, the children _____ wrote to their parents.

    (A) hardly
    (B) hard ever
    (C) hardly ever
    (D) hardly never

16. We provide a limited warranty _____ damage from shipping.

    (A) to
    (B) with
    (C) from
    (D) against

17. These cabinets offer an inexpensive, effective way _____ the quality of your home.

    (A) improving
    (B) to improve
    (C) improvement
    (D) for improvement

18. Yesterday he _____ a stern warning from his doctor.

    (A) receives
    (B) received
    (C) was receiving
    (D) had to receive

19. His pride, instinct, _____ sense of obligation helped him to be successful.

    (A) or
    (B) and
    (C) but
    (D) also

20. The weather report said it would _____ rain in the afternoon.

    (A) may
    (B) can
    (C) could
    (D) probably

21. In court, the man said he could not remember the _____.

   (A) incident
   (B) happened
   (C) incidental
   (D) opportune

22. A crowd gathered to _____ the government's action.

   (A) detest
   (B) protest
   (C) register
   (D) demonstrate

23. The employees greatly _____ management's understanding.

   (A) thank
   (B) grateful
   (C) thankful
   (D) appreciate

24. It will be difficult _____ a new telephone operator.

   (A) get
   (B) to get
   (C) for getting
   (D) having to get

25. He worked in the shipping department _____ seven years.

   (A) for
   (B) ago
   (C) since
   (D) during

26. People do not like to say how they _____ about the campaign.

   (A) say
   (B) feel
   (C) worked
   (D) opinion

27. This device will help many people who thought they could _____ lead useful lives.

   (A) no
   (B) ever
   (C) never
   (D) always

28. The small chair was a lot _____ than the large one.

   (A) comfortable
   (B) more comfortable
   (C) more comfort
   (D) the most comfortable

29. They arrived sometime _____ 7:00 and 8:00 P.M.

   (A) at
   (B) from
   (C) after
   (D) between

30. They could not see _____ in the yard.

   (A) who
   (B) nobody
   (C) anybody
   (D) somebody

31. A side _____ of the modern age is noise pollution.

   (A) affect
   (B) result
   (C) factor
   (D) effect

32. The driver said he would return _____ noon.

   (A) by
   (B) on
   (C) for
   (D) until

33. Turn _____ the lights upon leaving the room.

   (A) in
   (B) off
   (C) over
   (D) under

34. The salesman left a good _____ on his customers.

   (A) idea
   (B) feeling
   (C) impression
   (D) expression

35. The assembly instructions will provide you all the information you _____.

   (A) need
   (B) needs
   (C) needful
   (D) necessary

36. The radio is _____ to fit in a shirt pocket.

   (A) very small
   (B) not enough
   (C) small enough
   (D) smallest

37. Patients are told to follow their doctor's _____.

   (A) words
   (B) advice
   (C) advise
   (D) advising

38. The student decided to study _____ than before.

   (A) hard
   (B) harder
   (C) hardly
   (D) hardest

39. People who suffer from stress should give _____ a good rest.

   (A) theirs
   (B) himself
   (C) oneself
   (D) themselves

40. He said _____ he would send them no more invoices.

   (A) how
   (B) that
   (C) what
   (D) when

41. There is a chance they _____ be telling the truth.

   (A) may
   (B) can
   (C) are
   (D) should

42. Please _____ your name, number and the time of your visit, and somebody will contact you.

   (A) will leave
   (B) are leaving
   (C) leave
   (D) left

43. The office began to prepare for the move _____.

   (A) in two months
   (B) for two months
   (C) two months ago
   (D) since two months

44. He is going to _____ to Australia next year.

   (A) traveling
   (B) take a trip
   (C) take a travel
   (D) taking a trip

45. Although he once worked for us, Mr. Tish is _____ working at the bank.

   (A) yet
   (B) still
   (C) no longer
   (D) this time

46. The manager can speak five languages _____.

   (A) good
   (B) fluidly
   (C) fluency
   (D) fluently

47. Those years were not _____ pleasant as many people think.

   (A) so
   (B) as
   (C) very
   (D) that

48. Mr. and Mrs. Lake moved _____ a new apartment on the first of the month.

   (A) at
   (B) over
   (C) into
   (D) through

49. The discovery was considered very _____.

   (A) interests
   (B) interested
   (C) interesting
   (D) interestingly

50. The judge was not _____ that the witness was telling the truth.

   (A) convince
   (B) convinced
   (C) conviction
   (D) convincing

51. He went to work elsewhere immediately _____ leaving our office.

   (A) upon
   (B) since
   (C) while
   (D) before

52. The capital is _____ city in the country.

   (A) a largest
   (B) the larger
   (C) the largest
   (D) the most large

53. The temple on the hill is over one hundred _____.

   (A) old years
   (B) year aged
   (C) years old
   (D) years ancient

54. Life in this century is very _____ from that of the last century.

   (A) unlike
   (B) differ
   (C) different
   (D) differing

55. Do not call this number _____ it is an emergency.

   (A) unless
   (B) besides
   (C) excepting
   (D) otherwise

56. This piece of equipment _____ not be left on and unattended.

   (A) should
   (B) would
   (C) could
   (D) will

57. The consul's Spanish is so good that he sounds almost _____ a native speaker.

   (A) as
   (B) like
   (C) the same
   (D) close to

58. It was _____ long conference that the staff missed their flight home and had to stay over.

   (A) too
   (B) a so
   (C) very
   (D) such a

59. When traveling abroad, there are many places worth _____.

   (A) to see
   (B) seeing
   (C) for seeing
   (D) having seen

60. Nothing seems to _____ to the new owner.

   (A) care
   (B) mean
   (C) matter
   (D) important

61. _____ with similar products, this one offers better quality at a lower price.

   (A) Compare
   (B) Compared
   (C) Comparing
   (D) To compare

62. Some people say that if you want a job
    _____ right, you have to do it yourself.

    (A) done
    (B) to do
    (C) doing
    (D) have done

63. According to the contract, _____ deposits
    must be sent to their account.

    (A) all
    (B) all of
    (C) mostly every
    (D) most of all

64. Miss Ha enjoys shopping, golfing, and _____.

    (A) to bowl
    (B) bowling
    (C) to play bowling
    (D) playing bowling

65. To understand _____ a corporate client
    needs, you must talk to him about his
    business.

    (A) if
    (B) that
    (C) what
    (D) which

66. It is _____ said that nobody wins an
    argument.

    (A) much
    (B) often
    (C) usual
    (D) frequent

67. They had four children, but waited until
    their _____ child married, before moving
    to a smaller apartment.

    (A) young
    (B) younger
    (C) youngest
    (D) most young

68. Now is the time to plan for future growth
    and _____.

    (A) develop
    (B) developed
    (C) developing
    (D) development

69. Careful management of resources _____
    the key to fiscal stability.

    (A) is
    (B) are
    (C) has
    (D) to be

70. Borrowing money at fixed rates is more
    _____ when interest rates are low.

    (A) desire
    (B) desired
    (C) desirable
    (D) to be desired

71. Our job is to find the financial opportunities
    that best _____ your situation.

    (A) suit
    (B) suits
    (C) suited to
    (D) is suited

72. _____ you are like the average person, you
    need eight hours' sleep every night.

    (A) If
    (B) As
    (C) Maybe
    (D) As if

73. Tax _____ has benefitted lower-income
    workers.

    (A) reform
    (B) reforms
    (C) reforming
    (D) reformation

74. The company's intention is to increase
    production by 40 percent _____ the next
    three years.

    (A) into
    (B) over
    (C) about
    (D) throughout

75. The Board voted to have the executive
    offices _____.

    (A) remodeled
    (B) as remodeled
    (C) by remodeling
    (D) as remodeling

76. _____ having hired additional inspectors, quality did not improve.

(A) Due to
(B) Although
(C) Because of
(D) In spite of

77. The Purchasing Department was asked when the new computers _____.

(A) arrive
(B) would arrive
(C) would arriving
(D) had been arriving

78. The man _____ suit had been torn was very upset.

(A) who
(B) whom
(C) which
(D) whose

79. _____ house was known to everybody in the region.

(A) Small red
(B) A red small
(C) The red small
(D) The small red

80. The team always does a _____ warm-up exercises before beginning practice.

(A) few
(B) some
(C) many
(D) little

81. With the arrival of the new CEO, hopes for the company's success have _____ greatly.

(A) rose
(B) risen
(C) raised
(D) been raising

82. Some people _____ the single most important factor in any business is service.

(A) say
(B) tell
(C) talk
(D) speak

83. _____ his calls come from abroad.

(A) Much
(B) Almost
(C) Most of
(D) Almost of

84. The rising costs of product promotion _____ profit margins.

(A) low
(B) lower
(C) lowest
(D) lowers

85. Twenty years ago, few people expected the _____ technological development that has taken place.

(A) drama
(B) dramatic
(C) dramatical
(D) dramatically

86. Although it experienced many difficulties, the company made _____ overall showing.

(A) good
(B) a good
(C) an good
(D) the good

87. The watchman's _____ will keep him out for at least another week.

(A) ill
(B) sick
(C) hurt
(D) illness

88. At the end of an overseas trip, one always has _____ foreign coins in one's pocket.

(A) a lot
(B) a few
(C) a little
(D) a few of

89. Public transportation is _____ for residents of the city.

(A) need
(B) neither
(C) needy
(D) necessary

90. It is said that the _____ has improved a lot in recent years.

    (A) finance
    (B) economy
    (C) financial
    (D) economical

91. He would not talk that way about the company if he _____ not the owner's son.

    (A) was
    (B) will
    (C) were
    (D) would

92. In this business a person must keep a _____ of humor.

    (A) sense
    (B) sensing
    (C) sensible
    (D) sensitive

93. There are not _____ people who dislike sweet things.

    (A) much
    (B) many
    (C) a few
    (D) a lot

94. The President will come, but says his wife will not come with _____.

    (A) he
    (B) her
    (C) him
    (D) them

95. They introduced the new equipment _____ his third year with the company.

    (A) at
    (B) over
    (C) while
    (D) during

96. The passengers were advised to _____ a long delay.

    (A) wait
    (B) expect
    (C) accept
    (D) except

97. Young people are taught to have respect _____ age.

    (A) to
    (B) for
    (C) over
    (D) through

98. Today more women hold jobs in management _____ before.

    (A) comparing
    (B) than from
    (C) than ever
    (D) comparably

99. The performers exhibited complete _____.

    (A) competent
    (B) confident
    (C) confidence
    (D) confidential

100. People _____ depend on newspapers for much of their information.

    (A) yet
    (B) keep
    (C) still
    (D) continue

101. The book _____ by a well-known management consultant.

    (A) wrote
    (B) was writing
    (C) has written
    (D) was written

102. When their masters leave, pets always wait for _____ to return.

    (A) him
    (B) them
    (C) they
    (D) their

103. Although he lives alone, he _____ not know how to cook.

    (A) do
    (B) did
    (C) can
    (D) does

104. The assistant manager was just _____ to manager.

    (A) raised
    (B) elected
    (C) promoted
    (D) promotion

105. The professor _____ wanted to visit London, but never had an opportunity.

    (A) never
    (B) always
    (C) seldom
    (D) usually

106. He lived in a small town _____ moving to the city.

    (A) that
    (B) until
    (C) later
    (D) before

107. It was so hot in the room _____ nobody could work.

    (A) as
    (B) so
    (C) that
    (D) then

108. It takes _____ time to receive shipments from them that customers have stopped placing orders.

    (A) so much
    (B) so long
    (C) too much
    (D) too long

109. They asked _____ they could take the visitors for dinner.

    (A) why
    (B) for
    (C) what
    (D) where

110. Most people become _____ when asked to speak before a group.

    (A) nervy
    (B) nervous
    (C) nervously
    (D) nervousness

111. The man did not like the dish he ordered and asked for a _____ one.

    (A) unlike
    (B) differed
    (C) differing
    (D) different

112. Employees are told they _____ arrive late for work.

    (A) do not
    (B) must not
    (C) will not
    (D) have not to

113. The engineers started a new company because they wanted to be _____.

    (A) along
    (B) freedom
    (C) independent
    (D) independence

114. Some young people feel they must always disagree _____ their teachers.

    (A) from
    (B) with
    (C) about
    (D) against

115. Management does not want workers _____ extended coffee breaks.

    (A) to do
    (B) to use
    (C) to make
    (D) to take

116. _____ his work, he has no other interests.

    (A) Inside
    (B) Aspect
    (C) Besides
    (D) Adding to

117. Taking the driving instruction _____ the woman feel more confident behind the wheel.

    (A) made
    (B) forced
    (C) help
    (D) has

118. The sign outside says the building _____ is for sale.

(A) next
(B) around
(C) next door
(D) neighboring

119. _____ depends mostly upon concentration.

(A) Memories
(B) Remember
(C) Memorable
(D) Memorization

120. He asked for an album of the artist's most _____ songs.

(A) new
(B) latest
(C) recent
(D) lately

121. The waiter assumed that the customer _____ to pay the check.

(A) will be back
(B) can come back
(C) would be back
(D) is being back

122. Weather prevented them from _____ the sunken ship.

(A) ruining
(B) ravaging
(C) intruding
(D) salvaging

123. The court clerk asked the attorney whether he _____ notice of the matter.

(A) do ever receive
(B) had ever received
(C) had never received
(D) have never received

124. The detective _____ the man to give himself up.

(A) made
(B) talked
(C) argued
(D) persuaded

125. Had the corporate officers done _____ they could not have defended their position.

(A) indeed
(B) however
(C) otherwise
(D) contrary to fact

126. The visitor did not _____ in the secure area.

(A) need
(B) keep
(C) belong
(D) possess

127. We _____ to be able to ship it within ten days.

(A) can
(B) must
(C) ought
(D) should

128. _____ he had made a mistake, he repeated the experiment.

(A) Realizing
(B) To realize
(C) Not to realize
(D) Having realize

129. When the product is considered safe, _____ and only then can it be put on the market.

(A) only
(B) then
(C) next
(D) after

130. Some people find _____ even in difficult situations.

(A) humor
(B) funny
(C) humorous
(D) laughing

131. _____ the forecast, people can expect the weather to be cold.

(A) As by
(B) Accordingly
(C) In line of
(D) According to

132. They held an elaborate _____ when they opened the new building.

   (A) celebrity
   (B) celebration
   (C) declaration
   (D) celebrating

133. The clerk _____ the office to pick up the message.

   (A) called out
   (B) entered to
   (C) looked for
   (D) stopped by

134. Workers were warned _____ down into the hole in the ground.

   (A) to go
   (B) not to go
   (C) not to going
   (D) against to go

135. If Flynn _____ to try to sell these products, he would learn it is not easy.

   (A) am
   (B) be
   (C) was
   (D) were

136. There was no _____ solution to the problem.

   (A) opaque
   (B) serious
   (C) obvious
   (D) obsolete

137. The company cannot _____ the increase demanded by the union.

   (A) paid
   (B) value
   (C) afford
   (D) approach

138. The supervisor wanted to help the worker _____ the misplaced part.

   (A) find
   (B) found
   (C) finding
   (D) having found

139. They did not become _____ the problem until it was too late.

   (A) aware of
   (B) concerned
   (C) understood
   (D) understanding

140. Please _____ the insured sign the paper and return it to the head office.

   (A) get
   (B) have
   (C) cause
   (D) invite

141. All visitors must make an appointment _____ the receptionist.

   (A) to
   (B) for
   (C) through
   (D) from

142. His friends _____ him yesterday, when he became very ill.

   (A) visited
   (B) have visited
   (C) were visiting
   (D) have been visiting

143. It was a _____ that both companies applied for a patent on the same device.

   (A) happening
   (B) similarity
   (C) confidence
   (D) coincidence

144. _____ pleased to have an opportunity to serve you again in the future, should you need us.

   (A) We will be
   (B) We could be
   (C) We might be
   (D) We would be

145. The public was _____ by the light show.

   (A) amazed
   (B) nervous
   (C) amazing
   (D) interested

146. They have not _____ finished their work.

(A) now
(B) yet
(C) still
(D) anyway

147. It looks _____ the company is bankrupt.

(A) like it
(B) although
(C) as though
(D) even though

148. The letter to Mr. Seng was opened by _____ secretary.

(A) her
(B) him
(C) his
(D) their

149. These developments _____ very closely by the Securities Exchange Commission.

(A) has watched
(B) are watching
(C) is being watched
(D) are being watched

150. When he looked for his briefcase, he discovered it was _____.

(A) gone
(B) went
(C) going
(D) missed

151. Investigators called it sabotage, as it was clear that _____ damaged the machinery on purpose.

(A) nobody
(B) anyone
(C) anybody
(D) somebody

152. They waited for the shipment _____ more than a week.

(A) for
(B) over
(C) during
(D) at least

153. It was impossible to _____ the bank check because there was no record of the bank.

(A) have
(B) cash
(C) write
(D) change

154. Except by going in, the fire fighters had no way to know if the house was _____.

(A) usual
(B) vacant
(C) visual
(D) fired

155. Our consultants are well qualified to make _____ to your company.

(A) recommend
(B) recommends
(C) recommendation
(D) recommendations

156. _____ the introduction of its new line, the company has prospered.

(A) As
(B) Since
(C) Because
(D) In order for

157. There _____ no distress signal to indicate the ship was in trouble.

(A) are
(B) had been
(C) has been
(D) have been

158. _____ more information on this new system, send for a free brochure.

(A) For
(B) With
(C) Have
(D) Order

159. The next time your company _____ with a shipping deadline, call Express Max.

(A) face
(B) facing
(C) is faced
(D) has face

160. The government found it difficult to
_____ the law against public officials
taking bribes.

(A) enforce
(B) support
(C) analyze
(D) exercise

161. They left at 10:00 A.M. and _____ a taxi to
the airport.

(A) take
(B) took
(C) are taking
(D) have taken

162. It is easy to see _____ they are ahead of
the competition.

(A) who
(B) what
(C) why
(D) whose

163. Driving their new model car is _____
driving a truck.

(A) as
(B) like
(C) similar
(D) same to

164. Our supply system makes it easy to obtain
the _____ materials at the lowest prices.

(A) most
(B) many
(C) best
(D) better

165. Company _____ include an easy-credit
home mortgage plan.

(A) benefit
(B) benefits
(C) beneficial
(D) beneficent

166. When shopping, you should always buy
the product that best _____ your needs.

(A) takes
(B) holds
(C) calls
(D) meets

167. Because of our large inventory, we _____
guarantee delivery before July 1.

(A) can
(B) did
(C) could
(D) would

168. To the expert investigator, even the most
trivial piece of information may _____
significant.

(A) prove
(B) proves
(C) proved
(D) have proven

169. We will continue to provide our customers
the same high quality for which _____.

(A) we know
(B) we have known
(C) we have come again
(D) we have come to be known

170. To guard _____ accidents, to operate this
machine you must use two hands and
press both red buttons at the same time.

(A) for
(B) about
(C) against
(D) in case of

171. The special compound allows for the
growth of far _____ nutritious vegetables.

(A) many
(B) more
(C) most
(D) much

172. This vehicle is not recommended _____
use by children under the age of seven.

(A) as
(B) to
(C) for
(D) with

173. The researchers wanted to ensure that the
experiment was carefully _____.

(A) control
(B) controls
(C) controlled
(D) controlling

174. Production costs must _____ low.

   (A) keep
   (B) be keep
   (C) be kept
   (D) keeping

175. At the first sign of a problem, contact _____ service center nearest you.

   (A) a
   (B) the
   (C) one
   (D) which

176. Discounts _____ for quick-response bulk orders.

   (A) offer
   (B) offers
   (C) are offered
   (D) are offering

177. They considered _____ they were doing to be important.

   (A) that
   (B) what
   (C) those
   (D) which

178. Every child has the right to be fed and _____.

   (A) educate
   (B) educates
   (C) educated
   (D) education

179. No one knows how many documents _____ been lost.

   (A) has
   (B) had
   (C) have
   (D) has had

180. Ours is one of only two companies that can offer the _____ technology.

   (A) late
   (B) later
   (C) lately
   (D) latest

181. Fame and power _____ different people differently.

   (A) affect
   (B) affects
   (C) are affected
   (D) having affected

182. Nobody likes to _____ requests for help.

   (A) deny
   (B) turn
   (C) tell
   (D) some

183. They wanted to find the employee _____ had made the suggestion.

   (A) who
   (B) whom
   (C) who's
   (D) whose

184. Many people in the village went to a fair in a _____ town.

   (A) neighbor
   (B) neighbored
   (C) neighboring
   (D) neighborhood

185. Month by month, with _____ exercise and fresh air his health improved greatly.

   (A) consist
   (B) constant
   (C) constantly
   (D) consistently

186. This equipment is built _____ close tolerances.

   (A) as
   (B) by
   (C) to
   (D) about

187. The day _____ his long flight from London he was back at work.

   (A) ago
   (B) since
   (C) later
   (D) after

188. _____ average, in this plant the ratio of absenteeism is 15.3:l000/mh.

   (A) At
   (B) In
   (C) On
   (D) For

189. Refer _____ refund requests to the head office.

   (A) all
   (B) few
   (C) all of
   (D) any of

190. When employees _____ a voice in setting goals, they work harder.

   (A) has
   (B) had
   (C) have
   (D) having

191. He thought he had seen _____ somewhere before.

   (A) we
   (B) her
   (C) she
   (D) they

192. Mr. Yan _____ been chosen to head up the research team.

   (A) only
   (B) just
   (C) has only
   (D) has just

193. The committee _____ by the breadth of the applicant's experience.

   (A) impressed
   (B) impression
   (C) impressing
   (D) was impressed

194. The manager returned from a business trip _____ the entire work schedule changed.

   (A) found
   (B) to find
   (C) finding
   (D) had found

195. This model has _____ new features.

   (A) much
   (B) many
   (C) a lot
   (D) little

196. The first and _____ important management skill is the ability to listen.

   (A) best
   (B) main
   (C) more
   (D) most

197. Many people are opposed to the use of _____ energy, because they are not convinced it is safe.

   (A) atom
   (B) nucleus
   (C) nuclear
   (D) automatic

198. The large tank _____ with glass to protect its contents.

   (A) lines
   (B) lined
   (C) was lined
   (D) which is lined

199. Test meters showed that lighting in the room was _____ and hazardous to the eyesight of staff.

   (A) improbable
   (B) undermined
   (C) inadequate
   (D) indeterminable

200. He said that he _____ well paid for his effort.

   (A) was
   (B) has
   (C) are
   (D) were

201. Good nutrition and adequate rest are essential for a _____ body.

   (A) health
   (B) healthy
   (C) health like
   (D) well healthy

202. The policeman agreed _____ the accident was not the motorist's fault.

    (A) if
    (B) how
    (C) that
    (D) what

203. By lunch time, Mr. Lee already _____ six hours.

    (A) worked
    (B) working
    (C) was working
    (D) had worked

204. The company was known for the quality of _____ products.

    (A) its
    (B) it's
    (C) their
    (D) their's

205. Your letter was received the week _____ last.

    (A) ago
    (B) from
    (C) after
    (D) before

206. The drive _____ is often seen even in very small children.

    (A) to excel
    (B) to success
    (C) for excess
    (D) for succeeding

207. Last Friday he _____ to Singapore.

    (A) returned
    (B) is returning
    (C) has returned
    (D) will returned

208. It is easy to learn _____ responsible for it.

    (A) that
    (B) who's
    (C) that's
    (D) whose

209. The flight _____ two hours due to fog.

    (A) delays
    (B) delaying
    (C) will delay
    (D) was delayed

210. The _____ of the discovery was not recognized during his lifetime.

    (A) importune
    (B) important
    (C) importance
    (D) importantly

211. It is necessary to ship orders _____ time.

    (A) at
    (B) on
    (C) due
    (D) with

212. This diet calls for foods with _____ salt.

    (A) few
    (B) not
    (C) many
    (D) little

213. Eighty percent of the job _____.

    (A) ending
    (B) were done
    (C) is completed
    (D) having been done

214. The _____ part of this program is that it can be run by inexperienced volunteers.

    (A) most
    (B) best
    (C) more
    (D) better

215. _____ you are worried about your health, perhaps the Parkside Wellness Clinic can help.

    (A) If
    (B) For
    (C) Why
    (D) Due to

216. The staff were all _____ happy with the latest sales reports.

(A) too
(B) best
(C) much
(D) very

217. The company was unable to get _____ debt.

(A) away
(B) over
(C) out of
(D) without

218. The Office Manager _____ his plan for the coming year.

(A) outline
(B) outlined
(C) outlining
(D) has been outlined

219. Once he started looking, he was able to find _____ new buyers.

(A) a lot
(B) big
(C) many
(D) much

220. To report an accident, _____ anybody has to do is call 911.

(A) all
(B) every
(C) all which
(D) every time

221. Violence in the workplace _____ to be dealt with as soon as it happens.

(A) needs
(B) needed
(C) is needed
(D) is necessary

222. The messenger _____ not to deliver the package to the front door.

(A) asks
(B) asked
(C) was asked
(D) was asking

223. Finding the company _____ products meet your requirements is not always easy.

(A) is
(B) that
(C) which
(D) whose

224. The workers were assigned to sections, _____ organized into teams.

(A) as
(B) then
(C) when
(D) after

225. Nine _____ out of ten, seemingly difficult problems have simple solutions.

(A) time
(B) times
(C) hours
(D) happens

226. In addition to working, Ian _____ time to take courses at the university.

(A) find
(B) found
(C) finding
(D) to find

227. If interest rates continue to rise, ABAT, Inc. _____ postpone its reorganization.

(A) have to
(B) will have to
(C) would have to
(D) should have had to

228. After _____ the necessary approvals, submit documents at this window.

(A) obtain
(B) obtains
(C) obtained
(D) obtaining

229. Both companies offer discounts on orders of over five _____ units.

(A) thousand
(B) thousands
(C) thousand of
(D) thousands of

230. Knowing the right thing to _____ can often make a sale.

(A) say
(B) said
(C) tell
(D) speak

231. _____ writing progress reports, be clear and concise.

(A) As
(B) When
(C) During
(D) Before

232. The mechanic ordered only the parts he _____.

(A) need
(B) needed
(C) has need
(D) is needing

233. The improvement was apparent _____ only one week.

(A) on
(B) from
(C) after
(D) since

234. Employees are expected to do _____ to help the company succeed.

(A) as possible as
(B) so much as possible
(C) the best as possible
(D) as much as possible

235. When in Paris, another tourist _____ him how to use the subway.

(A) show
(B) shows
(C) showed
(D) had shown

236. Last year the Los Angeles warehouse _____ down.

(A) burns
(B) burned
(C) is burning
(D) had burned

237. _____ attention to contract terms will avoid problems later.

(A) Pay
(B) To pay
(C) Paying
(D) Having paid

238. The office _____ handling complaints is on the second floor.

(A) charging
(B) charged to
(C) in charge of
(D) for charged with

239. The _____ trend in the market is toward conservatism.

(A) late
(B) current
(C) recently
(D) currently

240. Mr. Chan asked us to choose a restaurant _____ for the company banquet.

(A) suited
(B) suitably
(C) suitable
(D) suited to

241. If oil _____ go down, production will also be reduced.

(A) fee
(B) cost
(C) prices
(D) values

242. The _____ model includes design changes to improve reliability.

(A) late
(B) latest
(C) of late
(D) most late

243. Mr. Suarez was given the job _____ he is a good worker.

(A) due to
(B) owed to
(C) because
(D) after all

244. The play is _____ a man who thought his life was a failure.

    (A) over
    (B) about
    (C) relating
    (D) concerned

245. The purchasing department bought from Sweden _____ from Germany, where the price was higher.

    (A) not
    (B) instant
    (C) changing
    (D) rather than

246. Because he is very busy, he will make the call some _____.

    (A) other time
    (B) time again
    (C) another time
    (D) different period

247. The management committee has said that there _____ will be a pay raise beginning January 1.

    (A) definite
    (B) infinity
    (C) definitely
    (D) uncertainly

248. He was heard _____ on the telephone at about four o'clock.

    (A) to talk
    (B) talking
    (C) was talking
    (D) have been talking

249. People exhibiting any symptoms are _____ contact the Health Office.

    (A) must
    (B) having to
    (C) supposed to
    (D) supposing to

250. Employees must arrive at work _____ to reach their work stations before the bell.

    (A) before
    (B) timely
    (C) on time
    (D) promptness

251. Before he was fired, he was always _____.

    (A) getting anger
    (B) losing his anger
    (C) losing his temper
    (D) falling into a temper

252. Everybody was very _____ by the performance.

    (A) disillusion
    (B) discouraging
    (C) disappointed
    (D) disappointing

253. Last year, for the first time, students _____ register for courses ahead of time.

    (A) must
    (B) had to
    (C) should
    (D) ought to

254. Poor work habits will always get employees _____ trouble.

    (A) at
    (B) on
    (C) in
    (D) over

255. _____ qualities that people most admire in others is generosity.

    (A) Many
    (B) Another
    (C) One of the
    (D) Some of the

256. Driving a bus requires a great deal of _____.

    (A) patents
    (B) patient
    (C) patience
    (D) patients

257. It was their custom to go to the mountains _____ summer.

    (A) on
    (B) for
    (C) every
    (D) each one

258. _____ this design was modified to make it safer.

   (A) Some day
   (B) Every time
   (C) Not long ago
   (D) Once in a while

259. The car has two new tires, _____ are flat.

   (A) all of them
   (B) two of them
   (C) both of which
   (D) the couple of them

260. The parents are _____ having educated well their three children.

   (A) proud
   (B) pride to
   (C) proud of
   (D) boastful to

261. Working people have to deal with _____ matters.

   (A) practice
   (B) practical
   (C) practicing
   (D) practically

262. The official refuses to change his _____.

   (A) head
   (B) mind
   (C) think
   (D) opine

263. It is not right to _____ others.

   (A) critical
   (B) criticize
   (C) criticizes
   (D) criticizing

264. He _____ he were younger.

   (A) wants
   (B) hopes
   (C) wishes
   (D) desires

265. The teacher never _____ his students finish a sentence.

   (A) have
   (B) lets
   (C) allows
   (D) permits

266. It is _____ to park here without a permit.

   (A) in-law
   (B) outlaw
   (C) illegal
   (D) paralegal

267. Although they were twins, they seemed to have nothing _____.

   (A) common
   (B) the same
   (C) together
   (D) in common

268. He wishes the boss _____ give him a day off.

   (A) will
   (B) were
   (C) would
   (D) might

269. We will not buy from them because they _____ deliver on time.

   (A) often
   (B) evermore
   (C) frequently
   (D) hardly ever

270. _____ business has improved, they will hire more help.

   (A) So
   (B) Since
   (C) Due to
   (D) Even though

271. _____ by the film's ending, the audience did not leave the theater for several minutes.

   (A) Terribly
   (B) Terrified
   (C) Terrifyingly
   (D) Having terror

272. The restaurant review commented the food tasted _____.

   (A) well
   (B) better
   (C) delicious
   (D) deliciously

273. The young man claimed to have been unfairly _____.

   (A) quit
   (B) shot
   (C) fired
   (D) retired

274. Of the three alternatives, two are unacceptable, while _____ is only minimally acceptable.

   (A) both
   (B) other
   (C) another
   (D) the other

275. _____ they buy, we will produce.

   (A) Suppose
   (B) Besides
   (C) Ever since
   (D) As long as

276. The applications of the invention were too _____ to mention.

   (A) few
   (B) much
   (C) numbered
   (D) numerous

277. The office staff worked _____ they could, under the circumstances.

   (A) as hard as
   (B) harder than
   (C) as possibly
   (D) as hardly as possible

278. The committee was informed of a very _____ matter.

   (A) crisis
   (B) urgent
   (C) urgency
   (D) emergency

279. At full speed, the car _____ like an airplane.

   (A) hears
   (B) noises
   (C) sounds
   (D) listens

280. The office reported that a repair crew _____.

   (A) were sent
   (B) been sent
   (C) has been sent
   (D) have been sent

281. The promotional material states that the speakers for this series are the finest _____.

   (A) in supply
   (B) avoidable
   (C) available
   (D) on the shelf

282. He has many _____, including butterfly collecting.

   (A) jobs
   (B) games
   (C) sports
   (D) interests

283. The patient says he _____ himself while jogging.

   (A) tore
   (B) damage
   (C) injured
   (D) wounded

284. One unit has just _____ problems as another.

   (A) more
   (B) fewer
   (C) as many
   (D) as much

285. Some people _____ working, even when they are very tired.

   (A) keep
   (B) stop
   (C) stood
   (D) avoid

286. _____ of the favorites came in first at the races on Sunday.

(A) All
(B) Much
(C) Either
(D) Including

287. A complaint _____ with the Employee Relations Office.

(A) files
(B) can file
(C) is filing
(D) can be filed

288. Prices _____ may change without notice.

(A) list
(B) lists
(C) listed
(D) listings

289. Refunds cannot be made for returned appliances that carry no _____.

(A) status
(B) promise
(C) statement
(D) guarantee

290. Stress is a common _____ of headache.

(A) cause
(B) effort
(C) raisin
(D) insult

291. It was _____ for anything to move.

(A) so cold
(B) too cold
(C) very cold
(D) cold enough

292. The accident victim complained that the injury was extremely _____.

(A) pained
(B) hurting
(C) painful
(D) wonderful

293. The staff remained _____ they finished the work.

(A) until
(B) before
(C) to become
(D) by the time

294. Nobody knows what the world will be like fifty years _____.

(A) ago
(B) future
(C) from now
(D) afterwards

295. Holding onto unnecessary inventory is a _____.

(A) use of money
(B) waste of time
(C) waste of money
(D) spending of money

296. The operator likes the work, but it does not pay _____.

(A) lots
(B) good
(C) well
(D) best

297. If the directors _____ more time, they would have been able to find a better buyer for the company.

(A) had
(B) has
(C) had had
(D) would have

298. Computers pay for themselves by _____ time.

(A) using
(B) saving
(C) keeping
(D) storing

299. Independent studies showed that our product was the most reliable _____ the market.

(A) at
(B) in
(C) on
(D) for

300. One order _____ five is for the old edition.

    (A) to
    (B) in
    (C) per
    (D) out

301. In any totally new situation, common sense is generally _____ guide.

    (A) most
    (B) a best
    (C) the most
    (D) the best

302. An employee should not have to be told to _____ his work.

    (A) do
    (B) make
    (C) perform
    (D) get done

303. The driver _____ had an accident, but avoided it by reacting quickly.

    (A) near
    (B) nearly
    (C) already
    (D) closed to

304. He dislikes living in the dormitory, and _____ do his friends.

    (A) so
    (B) too
    (C) even
    (D) neither

305. It is easy to be _____ about the future.

    (A) hoping
    (B) optimistic
    (C) depressing
    (D) optometrist

306. The field day was canceled _____ it was raining.

    (A) because
    (B) in case
    (C) because of
    (D) in case of

307. She asked him to _____ her on the phone.

    (A) call
    (B) calling
    (C) call up
    (D) having called

308. It was the _____ disaster ever to strike the area.

    (A) worse
    (B) worst
    (C) baddest
    (D) most bad

309. Passengers were instructed _____ stand up.

    (A) no
    (B) do not
    (C) to not
    (D) to ever

310. They asked _____ the order was not sent.

    (A) who
    (B) why
    (C) for reason
    (D) the explanation

311. We did not see him, so he _____ left early.

    (A) has
    (B) had
    (C) must have
    (D) should have

312. He _____ go abroad often for his work, but he has changed jobs and now no longer travels.

    (A) uses
    (B) used to
    (C) was used
    (D) is used to

313. If the real owner does not claim it, someone _____ will.

    (A) else
    (B) except
    (C) besides
    (D) exception

314. The research has been _____ for nearly three years.

(A) doing
(B) going
(C) doing to
(D) going on

315. The company will build a _____ plant near the site of the old one.

(A) new
(B) anew
(C) knew
(D) newer

316. _____ further information on equipment maintenance, consult the operating manual.

(A) If
(B) For
(C) When
(D) In order to

317. No matter _____ your specifications, we can build to your requirements.

(A) then
(B) that
(C) what
(D) which

318. The new employee did not know _____ to operate the computer.

(A) so
(B) how
(C) too
(D) only

319. _____ snowed the day of the ceremony, which made parking a problem.

(A) As
(B) It
(C) Here
(D) There

320. The meeting _____ by the sound of a fire truck going by.

(A) interrupted
(B) was interrupted
(C) are interrupting
(D) was having interruption

321. The new machinery proved to be a _____ investment.

(A) worth
(B) younger
(C) youthful
(D) worthwhile

322. We have received your request for a sample and _____ it as soon as it becomes available.

(A) will ship
(B) would ship
(C) had shipped
(D) will have shipped

323. His work leaves him _____ time to be with his family.

(A) few
(B) many
(C) most
(D) little

324. Sixty percent of the employees have already _____ the training course.

(A) completed
(B) completely
(C) completion
(D) completing

325. Nothing _____ except that somebody makes it happen.

(A) happen
(B) happens
(C) happened
(D) is happening

326. Accounts overdue 15 days will _____ a penalty fee.

(A) charge
(B) be charged
(C) be charging
(D) have charged

327. _____ labor negotiations, management must be available at all times.

(A) As of
(B) Since
(C) Due to
(D) Because

328. An automobile is one of the _____ expensive purchases a person usually makes.

(A) better
(B) most
(C) best
(D) most of

329. Our company understands the _____ of service.

(A) means
(B) meant
(C) meaning
(D) meaningful

330. The past will indicate how to plan for _____.

(A) future
(B) futures
(C) a future
(D) the future

331. The airplane descended _____ to avoid the storm.

(A) quick
(B) quicker
(C) quickly
(D) quickness

332. It _____ difficult to improve quality, but really it is not.

(A) seem
(B) seems
(C) seemed
(D) seemingly

333. It is possible _____ a lot of money for only a very small computer.

(A) spending
(B) to spend
(C) having spent
(D) to be spending

334. The sign on the front of the building _____ surely be removed.

(A) can
(B) may
(C) ought
(D) already

335. Fear of failure often keeps people from doing _____ best.

(A) its
(B) his
(C) your
(D) their

336. Everything _____ well until the discussion turned to trade policy.

(A) goes
(B) went
(C) going
(D) will go

337. Mr. Harris travels three days out of _____ five.

(A) a
(B) the
(C) one
(D) every

338. The Chairman _____ the company forty years ago.

(A) began
(B) begun
(C) begins
(D) was beginning

339. The reservation was for _____ on the early flight.

(A) first class
(B) a first class
(C) the first class
(D) some first class

340. The tourism business has many _____.

(A) ups or downs
(B) ups and downs
(C) downs and ups
(D) ups with downs

341. _____ people ever achieve their full potential.

(A) Few
(B) Some
(C) Most
(D) Many

342. The office sent out the _____ advertisements.

(A) new design
(B) newer design
(C) newly designed
(D) renew designs

343. Yesterday's quality control seminar _____ exactly two hours.

(A) lasts
(B) lasted
(C) lasting
(D) has been lasting

344. The _____ the product, the greater its acceptance.

(A) good
(B) best
(C) better
(D) more better

345. _____ the orientation for new employees takes only half a day.

(A) Usual
(B) Mostly
(C) Usually
(D) Frequent

346. The sales force proposed _____ prices as of the second quarter.

(A) raise
(B) raising
(C) to raise
(D) the raising

347. The _____ for frequent equipment repairs had an impact on production.

(A) need
(B) needs
(C) needy
(D) needing

348. Having computer training, she found it _____ to get a job.

(A) easy
(B) easily
(C) more easy
(D) more easily

349. The Ministry official wondered whether the bridge would _____ be completed.

(A) ever
(B) quick
(C) never
(D) on time

350. If they _____ control 20 percent of the market, they would expand their facilities.

(A) can
(B) will
(C) could
(D) would

351. Flights leave the airport _____ every five minutes.

(A) most
(B) almost
(C) most of
(D) almost of

352. The earlier the notice can _____, the better.

(A) send
(B) sent
(C) be sent
(D) be sending

353. The director explained _____ the basics of the new plan.

(A) brief
(B) briefs
(C) briefly
(D) briefed

354. The item you ordered is no longer in _____.

(A) sight
(B) place
(C) order
(D) stock

355. The construction began _____ schedule.

(A) as
(B) in
(C) on
(D) to

356. This approach _____ to reinforce a negative attitude.

(A) tend
(B) tends
(C) tending
(D) is tending

357. _____ the economy has begun to pick up.

(A) Late
(B) Later
(C) Lately
(D) Lateness

358. In response to your inquiry, we are sending you _____ enclosed information.

(A) the
(B) this
(C) that
(D) those

359. The summit meeting brought new hope for an _____ in international cooperation.

(A) increase
(B) increased
(C) increasing
(D) increasingly

360. Recently he _____ to work very late and will have to be spoken to.

(A) come
(B) had come
(C) having come
(D) has been coming

361. We received a call _____ information on the new system.

(A) requested
(B) to request
(C) requesting
(D) for requesting

362. Member companies were asked to send a _____ to the meeting.

(A) represent
(B) representer
(C) representing
(D) representative

363. Lee went to work as _____ as he finished school.

(A) much
(B) soon
(C) quick
(D) possible

364. The much _____ changes were finally implemented.

(A) needs
(B) needed
(C) needful
(D) necessary

365. The team worked hard to make their office the _____ successful in the company.

(A) more
(B) most
(C) best
(D) biggest

366. New methods have made production a _____ easier than before.

(A) lot
(B) much
(C) very
(D) small

367. Weather _____ them to cancel their trip.

(A) force
(B) forces
(C) forced
(D) forcing

368. Language barriers _____ the greatest difficulties she faced in her travels.

(A) is
(B) was
(C) are
(D) were

369. _____ was a heated argument over who was right.

(A) The
(B) Where
(C) There
(D) These

370. He delivered the reports to the head office _____.

   (A) him
   (B) by him
   (C) his self
   (D) himself

371. He _____ to put the packages wherever he could find room.

   (A) asks
   (B) asked
   (C) was asked
   (D) was asking

372. Problems _____ as the chamber became hotter.

   (A) develop
   (B) develops
   (C) developed
   (D) developing

373. It was evening before the meeting reached _____ end.

   (A) its
   (B) his
   (C) it's
   (D) their

374. The _____ session was longer than the meeting itself.

   (A) plan
   (B) plans
   (C) planned
   (D) planning

375. They had to guess as to _____ had sent the telex.

   (A) who
   (B) whom
   (C) whose
   (D) which

376. More than anything, Chang wanted _____ promoted.

   (A) to be
   (B) to do
   (C) being
   (D) to have

377. Once they discovered which part was broken, they _____ able to replace it.

   (A) are
   (B) can
   (C) were
   (D) will be

378. Whoever removes tools from the bench _____ replace them when finished.

   (A) maybe
   (B) would
   (C) should
   (D) have to

379. Next year is always better _____ the last.

   (A) so
   (B) as
   (C) like
   (D) than

380. They reported that nothing more _____ to improve conditions.

   (A) had done
   (B) being done
   (C) had been done
   (D) is having done

381. Mr. Haslit read as much as he _____ about managing by objectives.

   (A) can
   (B) might
   (C) could
   (D) would

382. _____ ordering, please retain the bottom copy for your records.

   (A) As
   (B) For
   (C) When
   (D) During

383. _____ made over the past few months have increased production.

   (A) Improve
   (B) Improving
   (C) Improvement
   (D) Improvements

384. This receipt should _____ with your form J-56.

(A) file
(B) be filed
(C) be filing
(D) have filed

385. Be prepared to speak on _____ any subject during the interview.

(A) must
(B) almost
(C) most of
(D) almost of

386. All questions must be answered _____ and you must sign at the bottom where indicated.

(A) truth
(B) honest
(C) truthful
(D) truthfully

387. They imagined _____ to be researchers.

(A) them
(B) they
(C) themselves
(D) their selves

388. Those features are available only on the _____ priced model.

(A) height
(B) highest
(C) more high
(D) best high

389. The affected area is _____ to encompass nearly 500 square kilometers.

(A) rough
(B) roughly
(C) estimated
(D) more or less

390. The first rule of business is to give the customer his money's _____.

(A) cost
(B) value
(C) worth
(D) price

391. After the sun _____, the older people left the picnic.

(A) has set
(B) setting
(C) set
(D) was setting

392. Half of the order arrived today, and the rest _____ here next week.

(A) is
(B) came
(C) will be
(D) would be

393. _____ the word processor, she finished in half the time it usually takes her.

(A) Using
(B) To use
(C) Used to
(D) For using

394. _____ ensure prompt delivery, enclose payment with your order.

(A) To
(B) As to
(C) In ordering
(D) In order for

395. They stopped to _____ a cup of coffee before going home.

(A) eat
(B) take
(C) have
(D) think

396. Cash awards were given to employees who _____ suggestions to improve quality and raise production.

(A) offer
(B) had offered
(C) are offering
(D) had been offered

397. The girl thought the job was demanding too much of _____ time.

(A) its
(B) her
(C) the
(D) she's

398. They discovered _____ the lock was defective.

(A) if
(B) that
(C) what
(D) which

399. Everybody _____ the test, although it was difficult.

(A) passes
(B) passed
(C) was passed
(D) had been passed

400. Mr. Kit awoke _____ the plane began its descent.

(A) just
(B) only
(C) just as
(D) only as

401. Looking at the blueprint, it did not _____ to be an easy job.

(A) do
(B) try
(C) work
(D) appear

402. The invitation stated that the reception _____ begin at eight o'clock.

(A) can
(B) may
(C) could
(D) would

403. The instructions _____ to fasten the two ends together.

(A) read
(B) said
(C) told
(D) made

404. Mr. Francis has _____ at ten o'clock to meet with the director.

(A) appointment
(B) appointments
(C) an appointment
(D) the appointment

405. Two new automated systems were introduced in the _____ process.

(A) products
(B) produces
(C) producing
(D) production

406. The sporting event took place _____ the rain.

(A) due to
(B) owing to
(C) because of
(D) in spite of

407. The market showed a trend toward increased sales of home _____ items.

(A) improved
(B) improves
(C) improving
(D) improvement

408. We received many more responses _____ expected.

(A) as
(B) so
(C) like
(D) than

409. Mr. Lock _____ the assignment because he is mature and responsible.

(A) was given
(B) gave
(C) had given
(D) will give

410. The letter had been sent the day _____.

(A) ago
(B) next
(C) before
(D) previous

411. They had expected to arrive _____ than they did.

(A) soon
(B) sooner
(C) more soon
(D) the sooner

412. _____ fire, ring the alarm.

   (A) If
   (B) Instead of
   (C) In case of
   (D) According to

413. He will prepare the invoice _____ he finds the record of shipment.

   (A) since
   (B) after
   (C) while
   (D) before

414. Increased _____ in other countries has brought about a surplus of manufactured goods.

   (A) produce
   (B) products
   (C) producing
   (D) production

415. In most societies women _____ of children.

   (A) watch
   (B) take care
   (C) guard
   (D) see to

416. To stay warm in winter, a person should keep his head warm and _____ wear a wool hat.

   (A) anyway
   (B) always
   (C) somehow
   (D) therefore

417. No one from the International Office, _____ Mr. Pons, came to the meeting.

   (A) except
   (B) even
   (C) for
   (D) include

418. The salesman became discouraged, as he _____ five days without a sale.

   (A) been
   (B) had gone
   (C) went
   (D) was going

419. In Asian countries most people eat _____ chopsticks.

   (A) by
   (B) with
   (C) through
   (D) having

420. The new employee has not submitted his report _____.

   (A) now
   (B) still
   (C) yet
   (D) even

421. To survive, the company needed to _____ a lot of money.

   (A) borrow
   (B) lease
   (C) extend
   (D) loan

422. If you do not know a word, you should _____ in the dictionary.

   (A) look around
   (B) see it
   (C) look it up
   (D) look it over

423. Whether they acquire the company _____ upon government approval of the agreement.

   (A) depend
   (B) depending
   (C) depends
   (D) can depend

424. They want to know how long _____ staying.

   (A) he
   (B) he is
   (C) he will
   (D) he be

425. This equipment is _____ old to be of much use.

   (A) often
   (B) too
   (C) even
   (D) some

426. The conference was so _____ that everybody became impatient.

(A) long
(B) length
(C) bore
(D) trouble

427. The director is not familiar _____ the arbitration clause in the contract.

(A) to
(B) in
(C) with
(D) that

428. During our business trip to India, we took a few days to visit some _____ tombs and forts.

(A) very old enough
(B) too ancient
(C) very old
(D) ancient enough

429. The teacher told the student to open _____ book.

(A) he
(B) him
(C) his
(D) their

430. The president's decision was unacceptable _____ the Board of Directors.

(A) by
(B) to
(C) with
(D) over

431. The actress is known the world over, not only for her beauty _____ for her intelligence.

(A) as well as
(B) but
(C) and also
(D) but also

432. Mr. Smith has been working for the Department of State _____ he passed his law examinations.

(A) since
(B) until
(C) for
(D) when

433. The staff in the Personnel Department is too _____.

(A) high
(B) much
(C) small
(D) many

434. When ordering by mail, please _____ a check or money order.

(A) include
(B) increase
(C) admit
(D) invoke

435. The fax was _____ to Belgium yesterday.

(A) translated
(B) transmitted
(C) transformed
(D) transcribed

436. Because of new developments, it was necessary to _____ the management team.

(A) reserve
(B) require
(C) reassure
(D) reorganize

437. During the trip, he will _____ over briefly in London.

(A) stop
(B) pass
(C) work
(D) continue

438. The advisory committee is _____ in favor of funding the new computer center.

(A) overly
(B) overseeing
(C) overbearing
(D) overwhelmingly

439. Mr. Churchill quickly became _____ the demands of the new job.

(A) to get
(B) got used to
(C) accustomed to
(D) used to getting

440. The sales manager wants _____ all of the remaining units by April 30.

(A) selling
(B) by selling
(C) to sell
(D) to selling

441. Before joining the international marketing department, he _____ had worked for the company for five years.

(A) also
(B) already
(C) even
(D) still

442. The investigation required the cooperation of a _____ of different sections.

(A) several
(B) few
(C) number
(D) groups

443. The pharmacist was not able to fill the _____ right away.

(A) medication
(B) description
(C) subscription
(D) prescription

444. Golf was one of his favorite _____ pursuits.

(A) creativity
(B) recreational
(C) procreation
(D) enthusiasm

445. Job counselors are often able to _____ clients to potential employers.

(A) prefer
(B) refer
(C) reserve
(D) deter

446. The opinions expressed in this article do not necessarily _____ the views of the publishers.

(A) refract
(B) reflect
(C) distract
(D) detract

447. Employees must pay income tax on their entire _____.

(A) files
(B) brief
(C) salary
(D) paying

448. Photographs are not to be taken on the _____.

(A) policy
(B) premises
(C) premium
(D) poverty

449. After finishing your meal, you ask the waiter for the _____.

(A) tipping
(B) patron
(C) check
(D) register

450. No report that is stamped "confidential" may be _____ outside the company.

(A) disclosed
(B) detained
(C) deposed
(D) deferred

451. The athletes ran a _____ race.

(A) thousand-meter
(B) thousand meters
(C) thousand metric
(D) thousand metered

452. _____, people will use computers in their everyday activities.

   (A) More to few
   (B) More and more
   (C) Most of every
   (D) More or less

453. While he was talking _____ the telephone, someone rang the doorbell.

   (A) on
   (B) to
   (C) with
   (D) by

454. He has lived in Pusan his _____ life.

   (A) all
   (B) entire
   (C) present
   (D) total

455. It is necessary that children _____ when adults speak to them.

   (A) listen
   (B) may listen
   (C) can listen
   (D) may have to listen

456. When people are in good _____ condition, they are bound to feel good.

   (A) body
   (B) physic
   (C) bodily
   (D) physical

457. The manager wanted to _____ the plant's operations.

   (A) look over
   (B) seeing over
   (C) looking over
   (D) watching around

458. People _____ study handwriting are called graphologists.

   (A) who
   (B) what
   (C) which
   (D) whose

459. He was unable to _____ the assembly instructions.

   (A) figure
   (B) decide
   (C) check out
   (D) figure out

460. The purchasing office _____ used equipment.

   (A) must have buying
   (B) will buy
   (C) have bought
   (D) some bought

461. The night shift employees were upset because they were required _____ the afternoon meeting.

   (A) to present
   (B) to be present at
   (C) unexpected at
   (D) making

462. Please put a _____ box in the reception area.

   (A) suggestion's
   (B) suggestion
   (C) suggestions'
   (D) suggestions

463. If the wire transfer arrives _____ not be able to meet the payroll.

   (A) late, we could
   (B) lately, we would
   (C) more lately, we will
   (D) late, we will

464. Dr. Franz studied finance _____ while at the business school.

   (A) and marketing
   (B) also marketing
   (C) in addition to marketing
   (D) and marketing were studied by him

465. She has not _____ her mother in ten years.

   (A) saw
   (B) see
   (C) seen
   (D) to see

466. Please call _____ for the meeting.

    (A) he and I
    (B) the vice-president and I
    (C) the vice-president and me
    (D) we, me and the vice-president,

467. The secretary sometimes wishes that she _____ in a big corporation.

    (A) worked not
    (B) does not work
    (C) was not working
    (D) were not working

468. If there is one more such incident, Mr. Karl will have to be _____.

    (A) recessed
    (B) returned
    (C) replaced
    (D) retailed

469. Due to the poor coffee bean crop, prices are expected to _____ soon.

    (A) go up
    (B) rise up
    (C) be risen
    (D) elevate

470. When Mr. Carlo returned from Malta, he said he _____ a number of influential people.

    (A) met
    (B) had met
    (C) was meeting
    (D) has been meeting

471. The credit department can complete a credit check in only two _____.

    (A) time
    (B) times
    (C) hours
    (D) of them

472. The committee meeting has been _____ until Thursday.

    (A) moved
    (B) reviewed
    (C) replaced
    (D) postponed

473. Please dispose of this _____ properly when finished.

    (A) contact
    (B) contents
    (C) conductor
    (D) container

474. The buyers want to order more of the product because of its high _____ in most of their stores.

    (A) turnover
    (B) turn off
    (C) turn up
    (D) turnout

475. Captain Young, our pilot, has been _____ for twenty-two years.

    (A) flying
    (B) flight
    (C) to fly
    (D) flew

476. With proper treatment, gradual improvement is _____.

    (A) hope
    (B) wished
    (C) wanted
    (D) expected

477. Economists do not agree as to exactly _____ causes recessions.

    (A) what
    (B) which
    (C) whatever
    (D) whenever

478. New York, _____ skyscrapers and millions of people, is always an exciting place.

    (A) has
    (B) some
    (C) with its
    (D) there are

479. The top universities _____ a unique type of graduate.

    (A) produce
    (B) produces
    (C) products
    (D) producing

480. Some businesses operate in such a way as to suggest that economic growth _____ the movement of the stars.

(A) depend
(B) depends upon
(C) which depends on
(D) directly correlative

481. The first automobile _____ in England cost less than two hundred pounds.

(A) was made
(B) manufacture
(C) manufactured
(D) was manufactured

482. A young businessman with an MBA is _____ for his potential for growth.

(A) value
(B) valued
(C) valuing
(D) to be valuable

483. Why does the new man make the same mistakes time after _____?

(A) that
(B) time
(C) again
(D) another

484. The Business Affairs Department _____ such a move at this time.

(A) discouraging
(B) was discouraged
(C) are discouraged
(D) strongly discourages

485. If I had known about the funeral, I _____ too.

(A) would go
(B) had gone
(C) will have gone
(D) would have gone

486. What is the best way to get _____ City Hall?

(A) at
(B) to
(C) over
(D) on with

487. Dr. Lim, an expert engineer, does not need _____ advice from us.

(A) any
(B) our
(C) his
(D) some

488. Mr. Anthony found that his performance on the job improved _____ after he took the seminar.

(A) so much
(B) so great
(C) greatly
(D) that much

489. These three terminals, _____ purchased only last year, have proven to be a sound investment.

(A) all
(B) were
(C) that
(D) which

490. Because I trusted my friend, I let him _____ the loan whenever he could.

(A) repay
(B) to repay
(C) repayment
(D) repayal of

491. The new stadium cannot accommodate _____ people as the old one.

(A) as many
(B) so many
(C) so much
(D) as much

492. They should _____ to the seminar last week.

(A) had went
(B) had gone
(C) have went
(D) have gone

493. _____ the night, the tapes containing the information are fed into the computer.

(A) On
(B) For
(C) While
(D) During

494. After the contract _____, everybody celebrated.

   (A) signed
   (B) was signed
   (C) had signed
   (D) was signing

495. The project demands precision and accuracy, as well as _____.

   (A) create
   (B) creation
   (C) creatively
   (D) creativity

496. The workers met _____ management to discuss the new contract.

   (A) at
   (B) for
   (C) with
   (D) under

497. On weekdays, the library _____ at 10 A.M. and closes at midnight.

   (A) opens
   (B) opened
   (C) begins
   (D) starts

498. The new employee was told that he was out of _____ for having addressed the President at the meeting.

   (A) it
   (B) them
   (C) line
   (D) stock

499. _____ his tight schedule, Mr. Hart will not be able to visit the plant this week.

   (A) Since
   (B) According
   (C) Because of
   (D) Accordingly

500. He has a hard time _____ people, especially when they are not speaking directly to him.

   (A) understand
   (B) to understand
   (C) knowing
   (D) hearing

501. If somebody is looking for work, it is _____ checking the advertisements in the newspapers.

   (A) worth
   (B) valuable
   (C) expensive
   (D) necessary

502. On holidays, people often give gifts to _____.

   (A) another
   (B) the other
   (C) one another
   (D) the opposite

503. Three kilometers into the race, the runner _____ that he could not win.

   (A) knew
   (B) knows
   (C) had known
   (D) having known

504. Mr. Park is the kind of manager _____ will always try to listen to his workers.

   (A) who
   (B) whom
   (C) when
   (D) which

505. If the factory had not been damaged by the fire, it _____ by the end of the year.

   (A) would finish
   (B) will be complete
   (C) would be complete
   (D) would have been completed

506. Banks are a primary source _____ operating capital.

   (A) of
   (B) has
   (C) that
   (D) where

507. Algeria exports _____ many other countries.

(A) produce more than
(B) more produce than
(C) than more produce
(D) more than produce

508. _____ have become more powerful than many nations is an interesting topic of debate.

(A) Whereas typical multinational corporations
(B) When multinational corporations, they
(C) How and why multinational corporations
(D) Why and how multinational corporations, they

509. In some countries, most public money _____ on building the infrastructure for development.

(A) spends
(B) is spent
(C) that spent
(D) is spending

510. With a fax machine, _____ to send information less expensively than with telex.

(A) probes
(B) it is probable
(C) it is possible
(D) possibility that

511. There are several advantages to _____ a business partner.

(A) have
(B) order
(C) having
(D) sharing

512. He is considering starting _____ business.

(A) his
(B) himself
(C) his own
(D) his owner

513. The Director cannot go, and _____ can his assistant.

(A) too
(B) also
(C) either
(D) neither

514. They need to learn _____ the responsibilities of the union.

(A) of
(B) from
(C) about
(D) through

515. He told me I _____ the advice of a lawyer.

(A) can need
(B) will need
(C) might needed
(D) should need

516. The business has been doing well _____ it started.

(A) as
(B) since
(C) before
(D) because

517. Investors _____ fascinated by the stock market for a long time.

(A) can be
(B) has been
(C) are being
(D) have been

518. Everyone agrees that the National Insurance Company is a solid _____.

(A) place
(B) building
(C) institute
(D) institution

519. The man went to his lawyer for _____ legal advice.

(A) big
(B) some
(C) much
(D) a few

520. _____ your corporation plan adequately for the future?

(A) Is
(B) Do
(C) Are
(D) Does

521. We cannot _____ how soon it will be available.

(A) ask you
(B) say you
(C) tell you
(D) say to you

522. We have a spare, but we would _____ use it unless necessary.

(A) not prefer
(B) rather not
(C) not sooner
(D) later not

523. Heavy rains have _____ serious flooding in low areas.

(A) made
(B) done
(C) caused
(D) resulted

524. It is not _____ soon to start.

(A) too
(B) very
(C) so
(D) that

525. I _____ sales volume would increase.

(A) wish
(B) hope
(C) know
(D) want

526. She has been a design assistant _____ XYZ Cards for the past year.

(A) in
(B) at
(C) to
(D) under

527. Mr. Willis is one of our _____ talented salesmen.

(A) best
(B) very
(C) much
(D) most

528. The children are a lot _____ than when you last saw them.

(A) big
(B) bigger
(C) biggest
(D) more big

529. It is _____ unusual for companies from one country to invite experts from other countries to offer business advice.

(A) no more
(B) no longer
(C) not longer
(D) still longer

530. _____ park has been very popular with tourists from all over.

(A) A
(B) An
(C) The
(D) Some

531. If he had left by 3:00 P.M., he _____ have had time to visit.

(A) can
(B) will
(C) shall
(D) would

532. In the future please try to drive _____.

(A) carefuller
(B) more careful
(C) most carefully
(D) more carefully

533. This high-level position requires _____ secretarial experience.

(A) exterior
(B) precious
(C) extensive
(D) prevalent

534. We expect the price of bulk sugar to increase by 25 percent sometime _____ the next year.

    (A) to
    (B) for
    (C) while
    (D) during

535. The machine tool market is very _____ right now.

    (A) soft
    (B) softer
    (C) softly
    (D) softest

536. The monitoring systems are quite _____ one another.

    (A) differ from
    (B) different to
    (C) different than
    (D) different from

537. He _____ be getting enough sleep.

    (A) is not
    (B) must no
    (C) must not
    (D) probably not

538. She _____ as a full-time employee for a construction company for the past year.

    (A) did work
    (B) has worked
    (C) had worked
    (D) is working

539. He has made the same argument more than _____ before.

    (A) ever
    (B) once
    (C) never
    (D) always

540. The driver will _____ at your hotel at 7:00 P.M.

    (A) pick up you
    (B) pick you up
    (C) drive on you
    (D) drive you up

541. The director wants the report _____ possible.

    (A) as
    (B) as much as
    (C) as soon as
    (D) sooner than

542. Those cakes look _____.

    (A) well
    (B) tasteful
    (C) delicious
    (D) deliberate

543. The conference should be over _____ 3:00 P.M.

    (A) by
    (B) on
    (C) in
    (D) until

544. He called _____ his business trip because of the announcement.

    (A) on
    (B) in
    (C) for
    (D) off

545. The data is _____ complicated for him to explain in simple terms.

    (A) so
    (B) too
    (C) much
    (D) over

546. The use of computers _____ increased in recent years.

    (A) did
    (B) has
    (C) will
    (D) have

547. I _____ exercise more, but I can never find the time.

    (A) can
    (B) will
    (C) might
    (D) ought to

548. Her oldest son lives in the city, _____ her other children live at home.

(A) but
(B) for
(C) with
(D) even if

549. The supervisor would like _____ to arrive on time.

(A) they
(B) them
(C) their
(D) theirs

550. The engineers do not think the problem is anything _____.

(A) serious
(B) seriously
(C) seriousness
(D) somewhat serious

551. The film was too _____, according to one critic.

(A) depress
(B) depressed
(C) depressive
(D) depressing

552. Mr. Lee was the man with _____ we spoke.

(A) who
(B) whom
(C) what
(D) which

553. The contractor says he will _____ the building before the end of the year.

(A) complete
(B) completing
(C) to complete
(D) to completing

554. The new employees are now beginning to understand just _____ big the company is.

(A) why
(B) how
(C) what
(D) that

555. The assistant manager is said _____ an excellent report.

(A) to have wrote
(B) to have written
(C) have been writing
(D) to have not been written

556. _____ awaiting the arrival of the replacement bearings.

(A) They
(B) Them
(C) Their
(D) They're

557. Can you suggest a _____ to this problem?

(A) dilution
(B) solution
(C) reservation
(D) dissolution

558. His poor health required him to take _____ when going outdoors.

(A) causations
(B) cessations
(C) exhaustions
(D) precautions

559. It was _____ that class was held outside.

(A) so beautiful weather
(B) so beautiful a weather
(C) such beautiful weather
(D) such a beautiful weather

560. There _____ in that part of the world.

(A) is not much water
(B) is not many water
(C) are not much water
(D) are not many water

561. Wang said he wished he had not gone to work for that company, without _____.

(A) first having parents speaking
(B) first having spoken out parents
(C) first having spoken with his parents
(D) not first having spoken with his parents

562. Our supervisor _____ us to return to work.

   (A) told
   (B) he told
   (C) who told
   (D) that told

563. During his recent trip to China, Mr. Park visited Beijing, went sight-seeing, and _____ a number of government officials.

   (A) met
   (B) had met
   (C) was meeting
   (D) had been meeting

564. The department store buyers have gone to Paris _____ from among the new spring designs.

   (A) to select
   (B) for to select
   (C) for selecting
   (D) for having selected

565. A modern word processor enables a person to prepare correspondence much _____ than before.

   (A) fast
   (B) faster
   (C) fastest
   (D) more fast

566. He sent to have the film _____.

   (A) develop
   (B) developed
   (C) to develop
   (D) developing

567. The assistant asked _____ with the problem.

   (A) help
   (B) helping
   (C) helpless
   (D) for help

568. If it is _____, could you please reply immediately?

   (A) convenient
   (B) convenience
   (C) comfortable
   (D) inconvenient

569. He said I could pay him _____ I returned.

   (A) when
   (B) while
   (C) until
   (D) during

570. Before a decision could be made, it was necessary to _____ the circumstances in great detail.

   (A) initiate
   (B) instigate
   (C) interrogate
   (D) investigate

571. The Immigration Office requires originals of all documents before the registration _____ can begin.

   (A) process
   (B) prospect
   (C) progress
   (D) preference

572. The front window is still missing the _____ that blew out during the storm.

   (A) edge
   (B) pane
   (C) plane
   (D) slide

573. The developing situation in the Caribbean was not _____ in the local newspapers.

   (A) revised
   (B) petition
   (C) reported
   (D) assembled

574. To take advantage of the capabilities of a computer, _____ no need to know how to program it.

   (A) it is
   (B) you are
   (C) there is
   (D) there are

575. She likes to travel _____ she has a few days vacation.

(A) forever
(B) whomever
(C) whenever
(D) whichever

576. Anybody entering an auditorium after a performance has begun is bound to _____ the act.

(A) disrupt
(B) interact
(C) interfere
(D) intervene

577. I asked the department manager if he could _____ me as to how to respond.

(A) advise
(B) advice
(C) devise
(D) device

578. After the wedding ceremony, guests attended a _____ in the hall downstairs.

(A) lounge
(B) reservoir
(C) reception
(D) anniversary

579. To schedule the early flight, passengers have to book their _____ in person.

(A) advances
(B) resolutions
(C) restorations
(D) reservations

580. The new telephone service has not lived up to _____.

(A) experts
(B) expects
(C) expected
(D) expectations

581. When traveling abroad, a person must _____ eating different kinds of food.

(A) used to
(B) had to use
(C) get used to
(D) have use to

582. Return all completed forms in the enclosed envelope _____ January 12.

(A) by
(B) on
(C) for
(D) until

583. The supervisor in Quality Control was reprimanded because he _____ doing his job.

(A) has not
(B) should have
(C) had not been
(D) could not be

584. Mr. Lake asked his assistant to translate the report, even though he could have done it _____.

(A) for him
(B) himself
(C) all right
(D) as he says

585. The western regional office was opened only six months ago _____ is already showing a profit.

(A) or
(B) and
(C) though
(D) even if

586. The new employee hopes _____ his assignment before the deadline.

(A) finish
(B) to finish
(C) finished
(D) finishing

587. It was essential that the corporation _____ an account before it could receive shipment.

(A) open
(B) opened
(C) had opened
(D) were opening

588. _____ that the only chance for world peace may depend upon universal nuclear disarmament.

(A) Assuming
(B) To assume
(C) It is assumed
(D) The assumption

589. The large trading company of the '80s was not at all the small enterprise it _____ in the earlier decades.

(A) had
(B) had been
(C) has been being
(D) has been at one time

590. The receptionist escorted the visitor _____.

(A) the fifth floor
(B) of the floor five
(C) on the floor five
(D) to the fifth floor

591. If the members of the committee had known _____, someone could have asked him to speak at the awards ceremony.

(A) he was who
(B) who was he
(C) who he was
(D) whom was he

592. The introduction of the new telecommunications system has made business for the company _____.

(A) better
(B) more good
(C) more better
(D) much the better

593. If it _____ tomorrow, the roads will be closed.

(A) snows
(B) will snow
(C) had snowed
(D) were snowing

594. Delegate authority to _____ can do the best job.

(A) who
(B) whom
(C) whoever
(D) evermore

595. Ping sometimes wishes he _____ better qualified for his job.

(A) was
(B) can
(C) will
(D) were

596. His wife liked the painting so much that _____ decided to buy it.

(A) it
(B) her
(C) him
(D) she

597. If he had _____, he would visit London once a year.

(A) the money
(B) rich enough
(C) so much money
(D) too much money

598. For new employees, special assignments are in addition to their other responsibilities, not a _____ for them.

(A) change
(B) replacing
(C) difference
(D) substitute

599. Mr. Park moved to Hong Kong _____.

(A) a year
(B) in a year
(C) a year ago
(D) since a year ago

600. He did little of anything _____ in this department.

(A) as
(B) for
(C) while
(D) during

601. What was the first district _____ reported the problem?

   (A) what
   (B) where
   (C) that
   (D) when

602. The two companies have been in competition _____ one another for many years.

   (A) at
   (B) to
   (C) with
   (D) from

603. The manager showed an interest in _____ marketing problems.

   (A) this kind
   (B) these kind
   (C) these kind of
   (D) those kinds of

604. Despite his hard work, intelligence, and loyalty, he has not _____ been promoted.

   (A) once
   (B) much
   (C) still
   (D) enough

605. There is not much _____ in inventory.

   (A) case
   (B) goods
   (C) store
   (D) stock

606. The report will not get _____ on time because there is nobody to do the layout.

   (A) by
   (B) out
   (C) over
   (D) through

607. The printing contract is _____ by 35 percent.

   (A) underbid
   (B) underdone
   (C) underfoot
   (D) underplayed

608. The office needs a _____ of supplies.

   (A) lot
   (B) few
   (C) half
   (D) many

609. Headquarters would like to know _____ everyone thinks of the new schedule.

   (A) how
   (B) who
   (C) what
   (D) maybe

610. The planning team seldom _____ before 9:00 A.M.

   (A) met
   (B) are meeting
   (C) were meeting
   (D) have been met

611. The company expects _____ more people next year.

   (A) hire
   (B) hiring
   (C) to hire
   (D) to be hired

612. The Board meeting has been put _____ until August 21.

   (A) in
   (B) on
   (C) off
   (D) over

613. The inspectors all agree that _____ the goods were defective.

   (A) about
   (B) almost
   (C) most of
   (D) almost of

614. Most of the reply forms cannot be processed because of a variety of marking _____.

   (A) losses
   (B) errors
   (C) lateness
   (D) admissions

615. They will stay late tonight, because the project _____ completed by tomorrow.

(A) is
(B) was
(C) must be
(D) must have been

616. It was the best response we have had to a fire drill _____ March of last year.

(A) at
(B) since
(C) until
(D) before

617. While it was the only route open, it had many _____.

(A) definite
(B) deficient
(C) definitive
(D) deficiencies

618. Pricing of the new product had to take into account many _____.

(A) money
(B) various
(C) accounts
(D) variables

619. The new system will permit direct access to _____ branch offices.

(A) much
(B) most
(C) almost
(D) too many

620. Contact the Personnel Office regarding _____ employee complaints.

(A) of
(B) to
(C) any
(D) one

621. A company's ability to prosper is _____ the quality of its management.

(A) regarding
(B) in spite of
(C) in addition to
(D) dependent upon

622. The conclusions appear to _____ the outcomes.

(A) oversee
(B) overstep
(C) overreach
(D) oversimplify

623. Computers solve problems by _____ data.

(A) process
(B) procedure
(C) processing
(D) to process

624. If the laboratory had been informed earlier, they _____ saved a lot of money.

(A) would
(B) would be
(C) would have
(D) would having been

625. Everyone who wants to go should be _____ to get a ticket.

(A) able
(B) wish
(C) have
(D) must

626. The store manager wants _____ prices to move the merchandise.

(A) reduce
(B) to reduce
(C) to be reducing
(D) to have reduced

627. To credit your account, your original _____ must be sent to the bookkeeping department.

(A) remake
(B) resale
(C) release
(D) receipt

628. Tourist visa applicants must first _____ the necessary forms from the consulate.

(A) refuse
(B) request
(C) reverse
(D) register

629. The recipe on the cake package calls for a
    _____ of sugar.

    (A) cup
    (B) cube
    (C) gallon
    (D) particle

630. Please _____ seated until given
    permission to stand.

    (A) retain
    (B) detain
    (C) adjust
    (D) remain

631. His performance review said he made only
    _____ progress.

    (A) vitiated
    (B) satisfied
    (C) satisfactory
    (D) dissatisfied

632. People who _____ alcohol should not
    drive.

    (A) resume
    (B) assume
    (C) consume
    (D) presume

633. The doctor advised him to take two
    _____, three times daily.

    (A) pieces
    (B) illness
    (C) tablets
    (D) fillings

634. The radio transmission could not be
    heard, _____ the volume on the receiver
    was up as high as possible.

    (A) due to
    (B) even though
    (C) even because
    (D) the reason why

635. Their products are known not only for
    their low price, _____ for their high
    quality.

    (A) but
    (B) but also
    (C) and also
    (D) as well as

636. Their currency is devaluing at _____ the
    rate of last year.

    (A) times
    (B) doubly
    (C) double
    (D) doubles

637. There are only two alternatives, one is
    expensive, _____, time consuming.

    (A) two
    (B) another
    (C) the other
    (D) some other

638. We would like _____ to join our firm.

    (A) them
    (B) they
    (C) their
    (D) theirs

639. Visitors _____ never offend their hosts.

    (A) can
    (B) do not
    (C) should
    (D) should not

640. In many public places it is forbidden
    _____.

    (A) smokes
    (B) smoking
    (C) to smoke
    (D) will smoke

641. The presentation is so _____, it is difficult
    to understand.

    (A) confuse
    (B) confuser
    (C) confused
    (D) confusion

642. The supervisor in that department can always _____ his employees.

(A) count
(B) count on
(C) count for
(D) count with

643. They are _____ that the public will buy their new product.

(A) confiding
(B) confident
(C) confidence
(D) conference

644. _____ the company's employees live in a nearby town.

(A) Most
(B) Much
(C) Most of
(D) Majority

645. The seminar will discuss the important role management _____ in maintaining employee morale during last year's crisis.

(A) plays
(B) played
(C) playing
(D) had played

646. He has received a raise every year _____ he began working for this company.

(A) from
(B) when
(C) since
(D) while

647. You look very familiar _____ me.

(A) to
(B) on
(C) at
(D) for

648. There are no lights on in the laboratory, so they _____ left early.

(A) must be
(B) will be
(C) can have
(D) must have

649. The accident did much _____ to the machine.

(A) damper
(B) garage
(C) damage
(D) dental work

650. The insurance company refuses to _____ the project because of the many risks.

(A) underhand
(B) underline
(C) understand
(D) underwrite

651. It was only a _____ that all of the pieces were found quickly.

(A) random
(B) question
(C) ambiguity
(D) coincidence

652. The Department has not _____ much absenteeism in the past.

(A) has
(B) had
(C) having
(D) happen

653. He did not show any _____ of being ill.

(A) symmetry
(B) symptoms
(C) symposium
(D) sympathetic

654. Attendance at company functions is _____ for new employees, if they expect to advance.

(A) mandible
(B) mannerism
(C) mandatory
(D) managerial

655. Of their many retail outlets, only one has _____ to be unsuccessful.

(A) shown
(B) found
(C) proven
(D) reached

656. Do not accept delivery of any order until you have _____ it carefully.

  (A) exampled
  (B) examined
  (C) exchanged
  (D) exhausted

657. In the past, the accounting department _____ able to locate missing invoices within a few hours.

  (A) was
  (B) should be
  (C) could not have
  (D) should have been

658. _____ all goes well, the launch will take place on Tuesday.

  (A) Because
  (B) Since
  (C) When
  (D) If

659. Before going ahead, we need to _____ the total cost of the operation.

  (A) estimate
  (B) proximate
  (C) instigate
  (D) actualize

660. The vehicle was in _____ when he started it up.

  (A) retard
  (B) retort
  (C) retreat
  (D) reverse

661. The plant has been working full time from the day the contract _____.

  (A) signed
  (B) is signed
  (C) was signed
  (D) will be signed

662. All of the conferees were concerned _____ the new trade embargo.

  (A) to
  (B) for
  (C) too
  (D) about

663. If he had more time, he _____ learn to play the guitar.

  (A) can
  (B) will
  (C) would
  (D) could have

664. _____ his tight schedule, Mr. Roper will not be able to visit the plant this afternoon.

  (A) Since
  (B) According
  (C) Because of
  (D) Accordingly

665. There was no _____ how many people would be present at the reception.

  (A) tell
  (B) to tell
  (C) telling
  (D) have told

666. As difficult as it _____ seem, the shipment arrived on time.

  (A) was
  (B) can
  (C) might
  (D) could

667. The _____ time he was available was at 6:00 A.M.

  (A) only
  (B) every
  (C) simple
  (D) later

668. _____ the opportunities he had, the one he accepted was the best.

  (A) Of all
  (B) In every
  (C) With some of
  (D) Unfortunately

669. The package was received damaged, but _____.

  (A) close
  (B) quick
  (C) broken
  (D) on time

670. Time _____ more and more important as the deadline drew near.

(A) flies
(B) study
(C) became
(D) appears

671. The clock _____ the hour, and the heavy wooden door began to open.

(A) held
(B) knew
(C) called
(D) struck

672. Efforts to revive the man _____ with failure.

(A) met
(B) were
(C) ran
(D) accompanied

673. Seven of the people in the _____ could not be convinced that the motion was necessary to rescue the proposed amendment.

(A) bus
(B) land
(C) assembly
(D) line

674. _____ onto her child, the woman moved toward the back of the boat.

(A) Calling
(B) Feeding
(C) Holding
(D) Pulling

675. The latest _____ to the department is a man who will someday run the company.

(A) joiner
(B) employee
(C) addition
(D) entrance

676. There is _____ hope that there will be any survivors.

(A) few
(B) every
(C) little
(D) some

677. Parking in this area is _____ for bank customers.

(A) denied
(B) limits
(C) reserved
(D) determined

678. April is a month _____ we always expect the weather to change.

(A) for
(B) such
(C) during
(D) in which

679. Tennis is a sport that _____ a lot of pleasure.

(A) demands
(B) deprives
(C) requires
(D) provides

680. His best efforts were _____ to convince the Chairman.

(A) brought
(B) effortless
(C) interested
(D) insufficient

681. We knew it would be a very _____ experience.

(A) except
(B) excited
(C) interest
(D) difficult

682. _____ the first and the tenth, we expect to receive three new shipments.

(A) After
(B) Since
(C) Between
(D) Although

683. The telephone _____ three times, but when I answered, nobody was there.

(A) was
(B) bell
(C) rang
(D) sounds

684. _____ anybody travels there, they always have a good experience.

(A) As
(B) Every
(C) Anyway
(D) Whenever

685. When I crossed the street, I _____ him out of the corner of my eye.

(A) see
(B) regard
(C) decided
(D) noticed

686. By ten A.M., the man knew that on that day he should have _____ in bed.

(A) stood
(B) held
(C) stayed
(D) slept

687. The students thought very _____ of their teacher.

(A) good
(B) best
(C) highly
(D) excellently

688. The team was interviewed by the newspaper _____.

(A) report
(B) reporter
(C) reported
(D) reporting

689. The man liked the product _____ much he bought the company.

(A) so
(B) as
(C) too
(D) very

690. They _____ for Rome last night.

(A) loft
(B) left
(C) leave
(D) laughed

691. The _____ problem was the price—it was too high.

(A) too
(B) only
(C) later
(D) unique

692. Small children _____ everything they are told.

(A) ask
(B) said
(C) talk
(D) accept

693. In the crowded bus station, the man _____ and somebody took his seat.

(A) on foot
(B) standing
(C) stood up
(D) goes walking

694. _____ traveling to France should check whether there are any visa requirements.

(A) He
(B) Who
(C) Every
(D) Anyone

695. After _____ ten years, he did not recognize the town where he was born.

(A) gone
(B) a prisoner
(C) being away
(D) travel abroad

696. Anybody _____ the man in the photo is asked to call the police.

(A) knows
(B) calls
(C) recognizing
(D) a friend of

697. Guests are asked to not _____ towels from the hotel.

(A) sell
(B) keep
(C) have
(D) remove

698. This product is not _____ for small children.

(A) safe
(B) make
(C) help
(D) safely

699. Every new vehicle must _____ a rigorous inspection.

(A) be
(B) do
(C) undergo
(D) requires

700. Production has _____, but sales remain low.

(A) increased
(B) go down
(C) become big
(D) been best

701. Many people worked _____ to make the city beautiful.

(A) lot
(B) some
(C) lately
(D) together

702. The _____ person to leave the office shut and locked the door.

(A) left
(B) last
(C) past
(D) lost

703. The car was unable to _____ the bridge.

(A) over
(B) cover
(C) cross
(D) travel

704. The woman wanted to buy a new _____ of shoes.

(A) two
(B) pair
(C) couple
(D) double

705. One of the lights was _____ out.

(A) ever
(B) burned
(C) turned
(D) switched

706. By eleven o'clock the people were _____ of waiting for the store to open.

(A) still
(B) tired
(C) afraid
(D) wanting

707. A _____ for making a cake is on the package of flour.

(A) way
(B) how
(C) recipe
(D) direction

708. The driver took the _____ route to the center of the city.

(A) worse
(B) fasting
(C) improve
(D) shortest

709. None of the workers understood the _____ plan.

(A) complicated
(B) constructed
(C) replicated
(D) restricted

710. This piece cannot be manufactured with _____ than twelve operations.

(A) less
(B) fewer
(C) lower
(D) minimum

711. Opportunities such as this one do not present _____ often.

(A) some
(B) each one
(C) everything
(D) themselves

712. Employees were not _____ to seeing the company president.

(A) accepted
(B) concluded
(C) accustomed
(D) concentrated

713. The contract was _____ by all parties.

(A) signed
(B) shaped
(C) shipped
(D) signaled

714. It was not clear why the investigator _____ upon having more information.

(A) sought
(B) decided
(C) insisted
(D) requested

715. The supervisor was not _____ who was responsible for the loss of the tools.

(A) even
(B) sure
(C) present
(D) decided

716. Nobody _____ how to open the combination lock.

(A) knew
(B) came
(C) tried
(D) advised

717. The Administration _____ informed of the problem before the accident.

(A) is
(B) will be
(C) had been
(D) having been

718. It is difficult to find films that are _____ for the entire family.

(A) accepting
(B) exceptions
(C) determined
(D) appropriate

719. _____ about the new technology, the Chairman asked for a complete report on its applications.

(A) Learned
(B) He read
(C) Had studied
(D) Having heard

720. _____ people enjoy working under dangerous conditions.

(A) Few
(B) None
(C) Much
(D) Every

721. Musicians are _____ very well paid.

(A) some
(B) enjoy
(C) rarely
(D) popular

722. The child was hurt _____ his parents were careless.

(A) upon
(B) where
(C) despite
(D) because

723. _____ can run faster than he.

(A) No
(B) Any
(C) Every
(D) Nobody

724. When the supervisor _____, they were already working.

(A) saw
(B) come
(C) calling
(D) arrived

725. The clothes were _____ in the closet.

(A) keep
(B) hung
(C) hanged
(D) putting

726. All of the passengers, _____ one, were accounted for immediately.

(A) even
(B) every
(C) except
(D) without

727. The man said he was _____ in 1972.

(A) born
(B) brown
(C) bought
(D) brought

728. They arrived at the gate _____ late to board the plane and had to wait for the next flight.

(A) so
(B) too
(C) very
(D) much

729. The department did not receive the manual and had to begin their work _____ it.

(A) to
(B) on
(C) over
(D) without

730. Knowing what I know now, I _____ not have spoken that way.

(A) had
(B) was
(C) will
(D) would

731. This shirt is guaranteed _____ shrinkage.

(A) to
(B) for
(C) with
(D) against

732. Few, _____, of the employees liked the new schedule.

(A) again
(B) of all
(C) if any
(D) certainly

733. The Board _____ not to invest in the project.

(A) decided
(B) refused
(C) continued
(D) accounted

734. The company _____ its offer.

(A) withdrew
(B) announce
(C) repetition
(D) transferred

735. Financial analysts called the buy-out a very _____ opportunity.

(A) rare
(B) unique
(C) unsure
(D) responsibility

736. The rain came much _____ than expected, and caught many small boats out of port.

(A) more
(B) heavy
(C) harder
(D) earlier

737. The stock market _____ quickly to the news.

(A) sold
(B) closed
(C) reacted
(D) reported

738. They were late for their ten o'clock _____.

(A) meter
(B) depart
(C) minutes
(D) appointment

739. The coupling fits _____ over the shank.

(A) once
(B) loose
(C) fasten
(D) tightly

740. For best results, the surface must be _____ smooth.

    (A) total
    (B) wholly
    (C) eventually
    (D) absolutely

741. In appearance they were _____, but in behavior very different.

    (A) closer
    (B) similar
    (C) on time
    (D) together

742. Although he did not like the ocean, he often _____ his son to the beach.

    (A) took
    (B) went
    (C) drives
    (D) enjoyed taking

743. Fashion designers often _____ of people's vanity.

    (A) appeal to
    (B) concentrate
    (C) sell designs
    (D) take advantage

744. Parents should _____ children to think for themselves.

    (A) reward
    (B) helping
    (C) identify
    (D) encourage

745. The immigration officer _____ upon reviewing everybody's documents.

    (A) asked
    (B) watched
    (C) decided
    (D) insisted

746. _____ having recently visited the museum, the teacher was glad to return with her class.

    (A) Ever after
    (B) Because of
    (C) In spite of
    (D) Declining to

747. Pass the wire (a) through the hole (b) and _____ it to the base (c) with a screw.

    (A) put
    (B) move
    (C) have
    (D) secure

748. Clouds are good _____ of the weather.

    (A) pictures
    (B) elements
    (C) indicators
    (D) predictions

749. People traveling abroad must _____ to protect their belongings.

    (A) ask
    (B) always
    (C) promise
    (D) be careful

750. Not all accidents can be _____.

    (A) known
    (B) expect
    (C) avoided
    (D) reminded

751. The car stopped because it was _____ gasoline.

    (A) no
    (B) empty
    (C) out of
    (D) vacant

752. Newly _____ pharmaceuticals bring relief to the ill.

    (A) device
    (B) declined
    (C) developed
    (D) detrimental

753. In situations of _____, people must learn to remain calm.

    (A) effort
    (B) stress
    (C) anxious
    (D) pleasure

754. The Audit Department had no _____ on the situation.

(A) auditors
(B) comment
(C) interest
(D) decided

755. Environmental scientists are _____ about the water quality in the world's rivers and lakes.

(A) determined
(B) commented
(C) assembled
(D) concerned

756. Good mechanics are rarely entirely _____ taught.

(A) only
(B) self
(C) usual
(D) somewhat

757. Until man could fly, relatively _____ people traveled great distances.

(A) few
(B) any
(C) much
(D) every

758. Having begun, and faced with an approaching storm, the team could not _____in its attempt to climb the mountain.

(A) plan
(B) delay
(C) hurry
(D) postpone

759. Your _____ of parts is in Customs at the airport.

(A) new
(B) sales
(C) request
(D) shipment

760. The economic forecast _____ the next three years is very good.

(A) in
(B) for
(C) after
(D) during

761. Architects sometimes _____ the obvious, designing buildings without plumbing, stairways, or electrical outlets.

(A) work
(B) design
(C) overlook
(D) forgotten

762. The concrete did not dry sufficiently before it rained, _____ the surface.

(A) hitting
(B) ending
(C) ruining
(D) finishing

763. No amount of argument could _____ him otherwise.

(A) hurt
(B) change
(C) remind
(D) convince

764. The last flight from Athens _____ two hours ago.

(A) is
(B) since
(C) departs
(D) arrived

765. In the distance, huge cranes _____ to be great mechanical monsters.

(A) saw
(B) tried
(C) became
(D) appeared

766. The Olympic Games are one effort to _____ mankind in the spirit of healthy competition.

(A) play
(B) make
(C) bring
(D) unify

767. Capital and labor are of equal _____ in the modern corporation.

 (A) need
 (B) certain
 (C) importance
 (D) availability

768. Not _____ the announcement of the delay, they went to the gate to board the plane.

 (A) to hear
 (B) by hearing
 (C) having heard
 (D) to have heard

769. New employees usually work very hard to _____ their supervisors and coworkers.

 (A) learn
 (B) train
 (C) impress
 (D) convince

770. This garment needs no _____ to retain its shape and tailored appearance.

 (A) sewing
 (B) ironing
 (C) washing
 (D) wearing

771. Newspapers should not be _____ by government if the public is to learn the truth.

 (A) printed
 (B) controlled
 (C) subsidized
 (D) recycled

772. A man who is not _____ to work should never go hungry.

 (A) doing
 (B) angry
 (C) afraid
 (D) willing

773. Some airplanes have such _____ shapes, it is surprising that they are able to fly.

 (A) pendulum
 (B) peculiar
 (C) perennial
 (D) perpendicular

774. To avoid accidents and crime, in most countries citizens are not _____ to own small guns.

 (A) liked
 (B) returned
 (C) allowed
 (D) forbidden

775. Never in the history of the World _____ such a terrible disaster.

 (A) had seen
 (B) was to be
 (C) were there
 (D) has there been

776. The ladder _____ when the man was near the top.

 (A) slip
 (B) hold
 (C) falls
 (D) broke

777. Some countries have very cold winters, _____ others have no winter at all.

 (A) if
 (B) when
 (C) while
 (D) including

778. Mr. Carter _____ to get involved in the matter.

 (A) hope
 (B) tried
 (C) invited
 (D) wanting

779. The staff had _____ worked very hard.

 (A) some
 (B) always
 (C) recent
 (D) every

780. Opportunities _____ cultivated, if they are to be of value.

 (A) to be
 (B) should
 (C) must be
 (D) ought to

781. The trailer became _____ from the truck that was pulling it.

(A) lose
(B) damaged
(C) detached
(D) fastened

782. Safety in the home is _____ it is in the workplace.

(A) important to
(B) also important
(C) as important as
(D) every important

783. The police _____ the man in a crowded store.

(A) entered
(B) answered
(C) apprehended
(D) understood

784. The flight was _____ because of poor weather conditions that developed after takeoff.

(A) late
(B) cancel
(C) taking off
(D) overbooked

785. The author, a man of principle, _____ to change what he had written.

(A) refused
(B) eagerly
(C) withdraw
(D) absolutely

786. The domestic automobile costs the same as _____ imported models.

(A) required
(B) eventual
(C) controlled
(D) comparable

787. Tire pressure should be _____ at 32 pounds.

(A) under
(B) remain
(C) reduce
(D) maintained

788. The _____ decision to be made is whether to go.

(A) all
(B) only
(C) now
(D) some

789. Mr. Hanks _____ time off work to take care of some personal business.

(A) was given
(B) gave
(C) had given
(D) will give

ANSWER SHEET—PART V

1. Ⓐ Ⓑ Ⓒ Ⓓ
2. Ⓐ Ⓑ Ⓒ Ⓓ
3. Ⓐ Ⓑ Ⓒ Ⓓ
4. Ⓐ Ⓑ Ⓒ Ⓓ
5. Ⓐ Ⓑ Ⓒ Ⓓ
6. Ⓐ Ⓑ Ⓒ Ⓓ
7. Ⓐ Ⓑ Ⓒ Ⓓ
8. Ⓐ Ⓑ Ⓒ Ⓓ
9. Ⓐ Ⓑ Ⓒ Ⓓ
10. Ⓐ Ⓑ Ⓒ Ⓓ
11. Ⓐ Ⓑ Ⓒ Ⓓ
12. Ⓐ Ⓑ Ⓒ Ⓓ
13. Ⓐ Ⓑ Ⓒ Ⓓ
14. Ⓐ Ⓑ Ⓒ Ⓓ
15. Ⓐ Ⓑ Ⓒ Ⓓ
16. Ⓐ Ⓑ Ⓒ Ⓓ
17. Ⓐ Ⓑ Ⓒ Ⓓ
18. Ⓐ Ⓑ Ⓒ Ⓓ
19. Ⓐ Ⓑ Ⓒ Ⓓ
20. Ⓐ Ⓑ Ⓒ Ⓓ
21. Ⓐ Ⓑ Ⓒ Ⓓ
22. Ⓐ Ⓑ Ⓒ Ⓓ
23. Ⓐ Ⓑ Ⓒ Ⓓ
24. Ⓐ Ⓑ Ⓒ Ⓓ
25. Ⓐ Ⓑ Ⓒ Ⓓ
26. Ⓐ Ⓑ Ⓒ Ⓓ
27. Ⓐ Ⓑ Ⓒ Ⓓ
28. Ⓐ Ⓑ Ⓒ Ⓓ
29. Ⓐ Ⓑ Ⓒ Ⓓ
30. Ⓐ Ⓑ Ⓒ Ⓓ
31. Ⓐ Ⓑ Ⓒ Ⓓ
32. Ⓐ Ⓑ Ⓒ Ⓓ
33. Ⓐ Ⓑ Ⓒ Ⓓ
34. Ⓐ Ⓑ Ⓒ Ⓓ
35. Ⓐ Ⓑ Ⓒ Ⓓ
36. Ⓐ Ⓑ Ⓒ Ⓓ
37. Ⓐ Ⓑ Ⓒ Ⓓ
38. Ⓐ Ⓑ Ⓒ Ⓓ
39. Ⓐ Ⓑ Ⓒ Ⓓ
40. Ⓐ Ⓑ Ⓒ Ⓓ
41. Ⓐ Ⓑ Ⓒ Ⓓ

42. Ⓐ Ⓑ Ⓒ Ⓓ
43. Ⓐ Ⓑ Ⓒ Ⓓ
44. Ⓐ Ⓑ Ⓒ Ⓓ
45. Ⓐ Ⓑ Ⓒ Ⓓ
46. Ⓐ Ⓑ Ⓒ Ⓓ
47. Ⓐ Ⓑ Ⓒ Ⓓ
48. Ⓐ Ⓑ Ⓒ Ⓓ
49. Ⓐ Ⓑ Ⓒ Ⓓ
50. Ⓐ Ⓑ Ⓒ Ⓓ
51. Ⓐ Ⓑ Ⓒ Ⓓ
52. Ⓐ Ⓑ Ⓒ Ⓓ
53. Ⓐ Ⓑ Ⓒ Ⓓ
54. Ⓐ Ⓑ Ⓒ Ⓓ
55. Ⓐ Ⓑ Ⓒ Ⓓ
56. Ⓐ Ⓑ Ⓒ Ⓓ
57. Ⓐ Ⓑ Ⓒ Ⓓ
58. Ⓐ Ⓑ Ⓒ Ⓓ
59. Ⓐ Ⓑ Ⓒ Ⓓ
60. Ⓐ Ⓑ Ⓒ Ⓓ
61. Ⓐ Ⓑ Ⓒ Ⓓ
62. Ⓐ Ⓑ Ⓒ Ⓓ
63. Ⓐ Ⓑ Ⓒ Ⓓ
64. Ⓐ Ⓑ Ⓒ Ⓓ
65. Ⓐ Ⓑ Ⓒ Ⓓ
66. Ⓐ Ⓑ Ⓒ Ⓓ
67. Ⓐ Ⓑ Ⓒ Ⓓ
68. Ⓐ Ⓑ Ⓒ Ⓓ
69. Ⓐ Ⓑ Ⓒ Ⓓ
70. Ⓐ Ⓑ Ⓒ Ⓓ
71. Ⓐ Ⓑ Ⓒ Ⓓ
72. Ⓐ Ⓑ Ⓒ Ⓓ
73. Ⓐ Ⓑ Ⓒ Ⓓ
74. Ⓐ Ⓑ Ⓒ Ⓓ
75. Ⓐ Ⓑ Ⓒ Ⓓ
76. Ⓐ Ⓑ Ⓒ Ⓓ
77. Ⓐ Ⓑ Ⓒ Ⓓ
78. Ⓐ Ⓑ Ⓒ Ⓓ
79. Ⓐ Ⓑ Ⓒ Ⓓ
80. Ⓐ Ⓑ Ⓒ Ⓓ
81. Ⓐ Ⓑ Ⓒ Ⓓ
82. Ⓐ Ⓑ Ⓒ Ⓓ

83. Ⓐ Ⓑ Ⓒ Ⓓ
84. Ⓐ Ⓑ Ⓒ Ⓓ
85. Ⓐ Ⓑ Ⓒ Ⓓ
86. Ⓐ Ⓑ Ⓒ Ⓓ
87. Ⓐ Ⓑ Ⓒ Ⓓ
88. Ⓐ Ⓑ Ⓒ Ⓓ
89. Ⓐ Ⓑ Ⓒ Ⓓ
90. Ⓐ Ⓑ Ⓒ Ⓓ
91. Ⓐ Ⓑ Ⓒ Ⓓ
92. Ⓐ Ⓑ Ⓒ Ⓓ
93. Ⓐ Ⓑ Ⓒ Ⓓ
94. Ⓐ Ⓑ Ⓒ Ⓓ
95. Ⓐ Ⓑ Ⓒ Ⓓ
96. Ⓐ Ⓑ Ⓒ Ⓓ
97. Ⓐ Ⓑ Ⓒ Ⓓ
98. Ⓐ Ⓑ Ⓒ Ⓓ
99. Ⓐ Ⓑ Ⓒ Ⓓ
100. Ⓐ Ⓑ Ⓒ Ⓓ
101. Ⓐ Ⓑ Ⓒ Ⓓ
102. Ⓐ Ⓑ Ⓒ Ⓓ
103. Ⓐ Ⓑ Ⓒ Ⓓ
104. Ⓐ Ⓑ Ⓒ Ⓓ
105. Ⓐ Ⓑ Ⓒ Ⓓ
106. Ⓐ Ⓑ Ⓒ Ⓓ
107. Ⓐ Ⓑ Ⓒ Ⓓ
108. Ⓐ Ⓑ Ⓒ Ⓓ
109. Ⓐ Ⓑ Ⓒ Ⓓ
110. Ⓐ Ⓑ Ⓒ Ⓓ
111. Ⓐ Ⓑ Ⓒ Ⓓ
112. Ⓐ Ⓑ Ⓒ Ⓓ
113. Ⓐ Ⓑ Ⓒ Ⓓ
114. Ⓐ Ⓑ Ⓒ Ⓓ
115. Ⓐ Ⓑ Ⓒ Ⓓ
116. Ⓐ Ⓑ Ⓒ Ⓓ
117. Ⓐ Ⓑ Ⓒ Ⓓ
118. Ⓐ Ⓑ Ⓒ Ⓓ
119. Ⓐ Ⓑ Ⓒ Ⓓ
120. Ⓐ Ⓑ Ⓒ Ⓓ
121. Ⓐ Ⓑ Ⓒ Ⓓ
122. Ⓐ Ⓑ Ⓒ Ⓓ
123. Ⓐ Ⓑ Ⓒ Ⓓ

124. Ⓐ Ⓑ Ⓒ Ⓓ
125. Ⓐ Ⓑ Ⓒ Ⓓ
126. Ⓐ Ⓑ Ⓒ Ⓓ
127. Ⓐ Ⓑ Ⓒ Ⓓ
128. Ⓐ Ⓑ Ⓒ Ⓓ
129. Ⓐ Ⓑ Ⓒ Ⓓ
130. Ⓐ Ⓑ Ⓒ Ⓓ
131. Ⓐ Ⓑ Ⓒ Ⓓ
132. Ⓐ Ⓑ Ⓒ Ⓓ
133. Ⓐ Ⓑ Ⓒ Ⓓ
134. Ⓐ Ⓑ Ⓒ Ⓓ
135. Ⓐ Ⓑ Ⓒ Ⓓ
136. Ⓐ Ⓑ Ⓒ Ⓓ
137. Ⓐ Ⓑ Ⓒ Ⓓ
138. Ⓐ Ⓑ Ⓒ Ⓓ
139. Ⓐ Ⓑ Ⓒ Ⓓ
140. Ⓐ Ⓑ Ⓒ Ⓓ
141. Ⓐ Ⓑ Ⓒ Ⓓ
142. Ⓐ Ⓑ Ⓒ Ⓓ
143. Ⓐ Ⓑ Ⓒ Ⓓ
144. Ⓐ Ⓑ Ⓒ Ⓓ
145. Ⓐ Ⓑ Ⓒ Ⓓ
146. Ⓐ Ⓑ Ⓒ Ⓓ
147. Ⓐ Ⓑ Ⓒ Ⓓ
148. Ⓐ Ⓑ Ⓒ Ⓓ
149. Ⓐ Ⓑ Ⓒ Ⓓ
150. Ⓐ Ⓑ Ⓒ Ⓓ
151. Ⓐ Ⓑ Ⓒ Ⓓ
152. Ⓐ Ⓑ Ⓒ Ⓓ
153. Ⓐ Ⓑ Ⓒ Ⓓ
154. Ⓐ Ⓑ Ⓒ Ⓓ
155. Ⓐ Ⓑ Ⓒ Ⓓ
156. Ⓐ Ⓑ Ⓒ Ⓓ
157. Ⓐ Ⓑ Ⓒ Ⓓ
158. Ⓐ Ⓑ Ⓒ Ⓓ
159. Ⓐ Ⓑ Ⓒ Ⓓ
160. Ⓐ Ⓑ Ⓒ Ⓓ
161. Ⓐ Ⓑ Ⓒ Ⓓ
162. Ⓐ Ⓑ Ⓒ Ⓓ
163. Ⓐ Ⓑ Ⓒ Ⓓ
164. Ⓐ Ⓑ Ⓒ Ⓓ

165. Ⓐ Ⓑ Ⓒ Ⓓ	210. Ⓐ Ⓑ Ⓒ Ⓓ	255. Ⓐ Ⓑ Ⓒ Ⓓ	300. Ⓐ Ⓑ Ⓒ Ⓓ
166. Ⓐ Ⓑ Ⓒ Ⓓ	211. Ⓐ Ⓑ Ⓒ Ⓓ	256. Ⓐ Ⓑ Ⓒ Ⓓ	301. Ⓐ Ⓑ Ⓒ Ⓓ
167. Ⓐ Ⓑ Ⓒ Ⓓ	212. Ⓐ Ⓑ Ⓒ Ⓓ	257. Ⓐ Ⓑ Ⓒ Ⓓ	302. Ⓐ Ⓑ Ⓒ Ⓓ
168. Ⓐ Ⓑ Ⓒ Ⓓ	213. Ⓐ Ⓑ Ⓒ Ⓓ	258. Ⓐ Ⓑ Ⓒ Ⓓ	303. Ⓐ Ⓑ Ⓒ Ⓓ
169. Ⓐ Ⓑ Ⓒ Ⓓ	214. Ⓐ Ⓑ Ⓒ Ⓓ	259. Ⓐ Ⓑ Ⓒ Ⓓ	304. Ⓐ Ⓑ Ⓒ Ⓓ
170. Ⓐ Ⓑ Ⓒ Ⓓ	215. Ⓐ Ⓑ Ⓒ Ⓓ	260. Ⓐ Ⓑ Ⓒ Ⓓ	305. Ⓐ Ⓑ Ⓒ Ⓓ
171. Ⓐ Ⓑ Ⓒ Ⓓ	216. Ⓐ Ⓑ Ⓒ Ⓓ	261. Ⓐ Ⓑ Ⓒ Ⓓ	306. Ⓐ Ⓑ Ⓒ Ⓓ
172. Ⓐ Ⓑ Ⓒ Ⓓ	217. Ⓐ Ⓑ Ⓒ Ⓓ	262. Ⓐ Ⓑ Ⓒ Ⓓ	307. Ⓐ Ⓑ Ⓒ Ⓓ
173. Ⓐ Ⓑ Ⓒ Ⓓ	218. Ⓐ Ⓑ Ⓒ Ⓓ	263. Ⓐ Ⓑ Ⓒ Ⓓ	308. Ⓐ Ⓑ Ⓒ Ⓓ
174. Ⓐ Ⓑ Ⓒ Ⓓ	219. Ⓐ Ⓑ Ⓒ Ⓓ	264. Ⓐ Ⓑ Ⓒ Ⓓ	309. Ⓐ Ⓑ Ⓒ Ⓓ
175. Ⓐ Ⓑ Ⓒ Ⓓ	220. Ⓐ Ⓑ Ⓒ Ⓓ	265. Ⓐ Ⓑ Ⓒ Ⓓ	310. Ⓐ Ⓑ Ⓒ Ⓓ
176. Ⓐ Ⓑ Ⓒ Ⓓ	221. Ⓐ Ⓑ Ⓒ Ⓓ	266. Ⓐ Ⓑ Ⓒ Ⓓ	311. Ⓐ Ⓑ Ⓒ Ⓓ
177. Ⓐ Ⓑ Ⓒ Ⓓ	222. Ⓐ Ⓑ Ⓒ Ⓓ	267. Ⓐ Ⓑ Ⓒ Ⓓ	312. Ⓐ Ⓑ Ⓒ Ⓓ
178. Ⓐ Ⓑ Ⓒ Ⓓ	223. Ⓐ Ⓑ Ⓒ Ⓓ	268. Ⓐ Ⓑ Ⓒ Ⓓ	313. Ⓐ Ⓑ Ⓒ Ⓓ
179. Ⓐ Ⓑ Ⓒ Ⓓ	224. Ⓐ Ⓑ Ⓒ Ⓓ	269. Ⓐ Ⓑ Ⓒ Ⓓ	314. Ⓐ Ⓑ Ⓒ Ⓓ
180. Ⓐ Ⓑ Ⓒ Ⓓ	225. Ⓐ Ⓑ Ⓒ Ⓓ	270. Ⓐ Ⓑ Ⓒ Ⓓ	315. Ⓐ Ⓑ Ⓒ Ⓓ
181. Ⓐ Ⓑ Ⓒ Ⓓ	226. Ⓐ Ⓑ Ⓒ Ⓓ	271. Ⓐ Ⓑ Ⓒ Ⓓ	316. Ⓐ Ⓑ Ⓒ Ⓓ
182. Ⓐ Ⓑ Ⓒ Ⓓ	227. Ⓐ Ⓑ Ⓒ Ⓓ	272. Ⓐ Ⓑ Ⓒ Ⓓ	317. Ⓐ Ⓑ Ⓒ Ⓓ
183. Ⓐ Ⓑ Ⓒ Ⓓ	228. Ⓐ Ⓑ Ⓒ Ⓓ	273. Ⓐ Ⓑ Ⓒ Ⓓ	318. Ⓐ Ⓑ Ⓒ Ⓓ
184. Ⓐ Ⓑ Ⓒ Ⓓ	229. Ⓐ Ⓑ Ⓒ Ⓓ	274. Ⓐ Ⓑ Ⓒ Ⓓ	319. Ⓐ Ⓑ Ⓒ Ⓓ
185. Ⓐ Ⓑ Ⓒ Ⓓ	230. Ⓐ Ⓑ Ⓒ Ⓓ	275. Ⓐ Ⓑ Ⓒ Ⓓ	320. Ⓐ Ⓑ Ⓒ Ⓓ
186. Ⓐ Ⓑ Ⓒ Ⓓ	231. Ⓐ Ⓑ Ⓒ Ⓓ	276. Ⓐ Ⓑ Ⓒ Ⓓ	321. Ⓐ Ⓑ Ⓒ Ⓓ
187. Ⓐ Ⓑ Ⓒ Ⓓ	232. Ⓐ Ⓑ Ⓒ Ⓓ	277. Ⓐ Ⓑ Ⓒ Ⓓ	322. Ⓐ Ⓑ Ⓒ Ⓓ
188. Ⓐ Ⓑ Ⓒ Ⓓ	233. Ⓐ Ⓑ Ⓒ Ⓓ	278. Ⓐ Ⓑ Ⓒ Ⓓ	323. Ⓐ Ⓑ Ⓒ Ⓓ
189. Ⓐ Ⓑ Ⓒ Ⓓ	234. Ⓐ Ⓑ Ⓒ Ⓓ	279. Ⓐ Ⓑ Ⓒ Ⓓ	324. Ⓐ Ⓑ Ⓒ Ⓓ
190. Ⓐ Ⓑ Ⓒ Ⓓ	235. Ⓐ Ⓑ Ⓒ Ⓓ	280. Ⓐ Ⓑ Ⓒ Ⓓ	325. Ⓐ Ⓑ Ⓒ Ⓓ
191. Ⓐ Ⓑ Ⓒ Ⓓ	236. Ⓐ Ⓑ Ⓒ Ⓓ	281. Ⓐ Ⓑ Ⓒ Ⓓ	326. Ⓐ Ⓑ Ⓒ Ⓓ
192. Ⓐ Ⓑ Ⓒ Ⓓ	237. Ⓐ Ⓑ Ⓒ Ⓓ	282. Ⓐ Ⓑ Ⓒ Ⓓ	327. Ⓐ Ⓑ Ⓒ Ⓓ
193. Ⓐ Ⓑ Ⓒ Ⓓ	238. Ⓐ Ⓑ Ⓒ Ⓓ	283. Ⓐ Ⓑ Ⓒ Ⓓ	328. Ⓐ Ⓑ Ⓒ Ⓓ
194. Ⓐ Ⓑ Ⓒ Ⓓ	239. Ⓐ Ⓑ Ⓒ Ⓓ	284. Ⓐ Ⓑ Ⓒ Ⓓ	329. Ⓐ Ⓑ Ⓒ Ⓓ
195. Ⓐ Ⓑ Ⓒ Ⓓ	240. Ⓐ Ⓑ Ⓒ Ⓓ	285. Ⓐ Ⓑ Ⓒ Ⓓ	330. Ⓐ Ⓑ Ⓒ Ⓓ
196. Ⓐ Ⓑ Ⓒ Ⓓ	241. Ⓐ Ⓑ Ⓒ Ⓓ	286. Ⓐ Ⓑ Ⓒ Ⓓ	331. Ⓐ Ⓑ Ⓒ Ⓓ
197. Ⓐ Ⓑ Ⓒ Ⓓ	242. Ⓐ Ⓑ Ⓒ Ⓓ	287. Ⓐ Ⓑ Ⓒ Ⓓ	332. Ⓐ Ⓑ Ⓒ Ⓓ
198. Ⓐ Ⓑ Ⓒ Ⓓ	243. Ⓐ Ⓑ Ⓒ Ⓓ	288. Ⓐ Ⓑ Ⓒ Ⓓ	333. Ⓐ Ⓑ Ⓒ Ⓓ
199. Ⓐ Ⓑ Ⓒ Ⓓ	244. Ⓐ Ⓑ Ⓒ Ⓓ	289. Ⓐ Ⓑ Ⓒ Ⓓ	334. Ⓐ Ⓑ Ⓒ Ⓓ
200. Ⓐ Ⓑ Ⓒ Ⓓ	245. Ⓐ Ⓑ Ⓒ Ⓓ	290. Ⓐ Ⓑ Ⓒ Ⓓ	335. Ⓐ Ⓑ Ⓒ Ⓓ
201. Ⓐ Ⓑ Ⓒ Ⓓ	246. Ⓐ Ⓑ Ⓒ Ⓓ	291. Ⓐ Ⓑ Ⓒ Ⓓ	336. Ⓐ Ⓑ Ⓒ Ⓓ
202. Ⓐ Ⓑ Ⓒ Ⓓ	247. Ⓐ Ⓑ Ⓒ Ⓓ	292. Ⓐ Ⓑ Ⓒ Ⓓ	337. Ⓐ Ⓑ Ⓒ Ⓓ
203. Ⓐ Ⓑ Ⓒ Ⓓ	248. Ⓐ Ⓑ Ⓒ Ⓓ	293. Ⓐ Ⓑ Ⓒ Ⓓ	338. Ⓐ Ⓑ Ⓒ Ⓓ
204. Ⓐ Ⓑ Ⓒ Ⓓ	249. Ⓐ Ⓑ Ⓒ Ⓓ	294. Ⓐ Ⓑ Ⓒ Ⓓ	339. Ⓐ Ⓑ Ⓒ Ⓓ
205. Ⓐ Ⓑ Ⓒ Ⓓ	250. Ⓐ Ⓑ Ⓒ Ⓓ	295. Ⓐ Ⓑ Ⓒ Ⓓ	340. Ⓐ Ⓑ Ⓒ Ⓓ
206. Ⓐ Ⓑ Ⓒ Ⓓ	251. Ⓐ Ⓑ Ⓒ Ⓓ	296. Ⓐ Ⓑ Ⓒ Ⓓ	341. Ⓐ Ⓑ Ⓒ Ⓓ
207. Ⓐ Ⓑ Ⓒ Ⓓ	252. Ⓐ Ⓑ Ⓒ Ⓓ	297. Ⓐ Ⓑ Ⓒ Ⓓ	342. Ⓐ Ⓑ Ⓒ Ⓓ
208. Ⓐ Ⓑ Ⓒ Ⓓ	253. Ⓐ Ⓑ Ⓒ Ⓓ	298. Ⓐ Ⓑ Ⓒ Ⓓ	343. Ⓐ Ⓑ Ⓒ Ⓓ
209. Ⓐ Ⓑ Ⓒ Ⓓ	254. Ⓐ Ⓑ Ⓒ Ⓓ	299. Ⓐ Ⓑ Ⓒ Ⓓ	344. Ⓐ Ⓑ Ⓒ Ⓓ

345. Ⓐ Ⓑ Ⓒ Ⓓ
346. Ⓐ Ⓑ Ⓒ Ⓓ
347. Ⓐ Ⓑ Ⓒ Ⓓ
348. Ⓐ Ⓑ Ⓒ Ⓓ
349. Ⓐ Ⓑ Ⓒ Ⓓ
350. Ⓐ Ⓑ Ⓒ Ⓓ
351. Ⓐ Ⓑ Ⓒ Ⓓ
352. Ⓐ Ⓑ Ⓒ Ⓓ
353. Ⓐ Ⓑ Ⓒ Ⓓ
354. Ⓐ Ⓑ Ⓒ Ⓓ
355. Ⓐ Ⓑ Ⓒ Ⓓ
356. Ⓐ Ⓑ Ⓒ Ⓓ
357. Ⓐ Ⓑ Ⓒ Ⓓ
358. Ⓐ Ⓑ Ⓒ Ⓓ
359. Ⓐ Ⓑ Ⓒ Ⓓ
360. Ⓐ Ⓑ Ⓒ Ⓓ
361. Ⓐ Ⓑ Ⓒ Ⓓ
362. Ⓐ Ⓑ Ⓒ Ⓓ
363. Ⓐ Ⓑ Ⓒ Ⓓ
364. Ⓐ Ⓑ Ⓒ Ⓓ
365. Ⓐ Ⓑ Ⓒ Ⓓ
366. Ⓐ Ⓑ Ⓒ Ⓓ
367. Ⓐ Ⓑ Ⓒ Ⓓ
368. Ⓐ Ⓑ Ⓒ Ⓓ
369. Ⓐ Ⓑ Ⓒ Ⓓ
370. Ⓐ Ⓑ Ⓒ Ⓓ
371. Ⓐ Ⓑ Ⓒ Ⓓ
372. Ⓐ Ⓑ Ⓒ Ⓓ
373. Ⓐ Ⓑ Ⓒ Ⓓ
374. Ⓐ Ⓑ Ⓒ Ⓓ
375. Ⓐ Ⓑ Ⓒ Ⓓ
376. Ⓐ Ⓑ Ⓒ Ⓓ
377. Ⓐ Ⓑ Ⓒ Ⓓ
378. Ⓐ Ⓑ Ⓒ Ⓓ
379. Ⓐ Ⓑ Ⓒ Ⓓ
380. Ⓐ Ⓑ Ⓒ Ⓓ
381. Ⓐ Ⓑ Ⓒ Ⓓ
382. Ⓐ Ⓑ Ⓒ Ⓓ
383. Ⓐ Ⓑ Ⓒ Ⓓ
384. Ⓐ Ⓑ Ⓒ Ⓓ
385. Ⓐ Ⓑ Ⓒ Ⓓ
386. Ⓐ Ⓑ Ⓒ Ⓓ
387. Ⓐ Ⓑ Ⓒ Ⓓ
388. Ⓐ Ⓑ Ⓒ Ⓓ
389. Ⓐ Ⓑ Ⓒ Ⓓ
390. Ⓐ Ⓑ Ⓒ Ⓓ

391. Ⓐ Ⓑ Ⓒ Ⓓ
392. Ⓐ Ⓑ Ⓒ Ⓓ
393. Ⓐ Ⓑ Ⓒ Ⓓ
394. Ⓐ Ⓑ Ⓒ Ⓓ
395. Ⓐ Ⓑ Ⓒ Ⓓ
396. Ⓐ Ⓑ Ⓒ Ⓓ
397. Ⓐ Ⓑ Ⓒ Ⓓ
398. Ⓐ Ⓑ Ⓒ Ⓓ
399. Ⓐ Ⓑ Ⓒ Ⓓ
400. Ⓐ Ⓑ Ⓒ Ⓓ
401. Ⓐ Ⓑ Ⓒ Ⓓ
402. Ⓐ Ⓑ Ⓒ Ⓓ
403. Ⓐ Ⓑ Ⓒ Ⓓ
404. Ⓐ Ⓑ Ⓒ Ⓓ
405. Ⓐ Ⓑ Ⓒ Ⓓ
406. Ⓐ Ⓑ Ⓒ Ⓓ
407. Ⓐ Ⓑ Ⓒ Ⓓ
408. Ⓐ Ⓑ Ⓒ Ⓓ
409. Ⓐ Ⓑ Ⓒ Ⓓ
410. Ⓐ Ⓑ Ⓒ Ⓓ
411. Ⓐ Ⓑ Ⓒ Ⓓ
412. Ⓐ Ⓑ Ⓒ Ⓓ
413. Ⓐ Ⓑ Ⓒ Ⓓ
414. Ⓐ Ⓑ Ⓒ Ⓓ
415. Ⓐ Ⓑ Ⓒ Ⓓ
416. Ⓐ Ⓑ Ⓒ Ⓓ
417. Ⓐ Ⓑ Ⓒ Ⓓ
418. Ⓐ Ⓑ Ⓒ Ⓓ
419. Ⓐ Ⓑ Ⓒ Ⓓ
420. Ⓐ Ⓑ Ⓒ Ⓓ
421. Ⓐ Ⓑ Ⓒ Ⓓ
422. Ⓐ Ⓑ Ⓒ Ⓓ
423. Ⓐ Ⓑ Ⓒ Ⓓ
424. Ⓐ Ⓑ Ⓒ Ⓓ
425. Ⓐ Ⓑ Ⓒ Ⓓ
426. Ⓐ Ⓑ Ⓒ Ⓓ
427. Ⓐ Ⓑ Ⓒ Ⓓ
428. Ⓐ Ⓑ Ⓒ Ⓓ
429. Ⓐ Ⓑ Ⓒ Ⓓ
430. Ⓐ Ⓑ Ⓒ Ⓓ
431. Ⓐ Ⓑ Ⓒ Ⓓ
432. Ⓐ Ⓑ Ⓒ Ⓓ
433. Ⓐ Ⓑ Ⓒ Ⓓ
434. Ⓐ Ⓑ Ⓒ Ⓓ
435. Ⓐ Ⓑ Ⓒ Ⓓ
436. Ⓐ Ⓑ Ⓒ Ⓓ

437. Ⓐ Ⓑ Ⓒ Ⓓ
438. Ⓐ Ⓑ Ⓒ Ⓓ
439. Ⓐ Ⓑ Ⓒ Ⓓ
440. Ⓐ Ⓑ Ⓒ Ⓓ
441. Ⓐ Ⓑ Ⓒ Ⓓ
442. Ⓐ Ⓑ Ⓒ Ⓓ
443. Ⓐ Ⓑ Ⓒ Ⓓ
444. Ⓐ Ⓑ Ⓒ Ⓓ
445. Ⓐ Ⓑ Ⓒ Ⓓ
446. Ⓐ Ⓑ Ⓒ Ⓓ
447. Ⓐ Ⓑ Ⓒ Ⓓ
448. Ⓐ Ⓑ Ⓒ Ⓓ
449. Ⓐ Ⓑ Ⓒ Ⓓ
450. Ⓐ Ⓑ Ⓒ Ⓓ
451. Ⓐ Ⓑ Ⓒ Ⓓ
452. Ⓐ Ⓑ Ⓒ Ⓓ
453. Ⓐ Ⓑ Ⓒ Ⓓ
454. Ⓐ Ⓑ Ⓒ Ⓓ
455. Ⓐ Ⓑ Ⓒ Ⓓ
456. Ⓐ Ⓑ Ⓒ Ⓓ
457. Ⓐ Ⓑ Ⓒ Ⓓ
458. Ⓐ Ⓑ Ⓒ Ⓓ
459. Ⓐ Ⓑ Ⓒ Ⓓ
460. Ⓐ Ⓑ Ⓒ Ⓓ
461. Ⓐ Ⓑ Ⓒ Ⓓ
462. Ⓐ Ⓑ Ⓒ Ⓓ
463. Ⓐ Ⓑ Ⓒ Ⓓ
464. Ⓐ Ⓑ Ⓒ Ⓓ
465. Ⓐ Ⓑ Ⓒ Ⓓ
466. Ⓐ Ⓑ Ⓒ Ⓓ
467. Ⓐ Ⓑ Ⓒ Ⓓ
468. Ⓐ Ⓑ Ⓒ Ⓓ
469. Ⓐ Ⓑ Ⓒ Ⓓ
470. Ⓐ Ⓑ Ⓒ Ⓓ
471. Ⓐ Ⓑ Ⓒ Ⓓ
472. Ⓐ Ⓑ Ⓒ Ⓓ
473. Ⓐ Ⓑ Ⓒ Ⓓ
474. Ⓐ Ⓑ Ⓒ Ⓓ
475. Ⓐ Ⓑ Ⓒ Ⓓ
476. Ⓐ Ⓑ Ⓒ Ⓓ
477. Ⓐ Ⓑ Ⓒ Ⓓ
478. Ⓐ Ⓑ Ⓒ Ⓓ
479. Ⓐ Ⓑ Ⓒ Ⓓ
480. Ⓐ Ⓑ Ⓒ Ⓓ
481. Ⓐ Ⓑ Ⓒ Ⓓ
482. Ⓐ Ⓑ Ⓒ Ⓓ

483. Ⓐ Ⓑ Ⓒ Ⓓ
484. Ⓐ Ⓑ Ⓒ Ⓓ
485. Ⓐ Ⓑ Ⓒ Ⓓ
486. Ⓐ Ⓑ Ⓒ Ⓓ
487. Ⓐ Ⓑ Ⓒ Ⓓ
488. Ⓐ Ⓑ Ⓒ Ⓓ
489. Ⓐ Ⓑ Ⓒ Ⓓ
490. Ⓐ Ⓑ Ⓒ Ⓓ
491. Ⓐ Ⓑ Ⓒ Ⓓ
492. Ⓐ Ⓑ Ⓒ Ⓓ
493. Ⓐ Ⓑ Ⓒ Ⓓ
494. Ⓐ Ⓑ Ⓒ Ⓓ
495. Ⓐ Ⓑ Ⓒ Ⓓ
496. Ⓐ Ⓑ Ⓒ Ⓓ
497. Ⓐ Ⓑ Ⓒ Ⓓ
498. Ⓐ Ⓑ Ⓒ Ⓓ
499. Ⓐ Ⓑ Ⓒ Ⓓ
500. Ⓐ Ⓑ Ⓒ Ⓓ
501. Ⓐ Ⓑ Ⓒ Ⓓ
502. Ⓐ Ⓑ Ⓒ Ⓓ
503. Ⓐ Ⓑ Ⓒ Ⓓ
504. Ⓐ Ⓑ Ⓒ Ⓓ
505. Ⓐ Ⓑ Ⓒ Ⓓ
506. Ⓐ Ⓑ Ⓒ Ⓓ
507. Ⓐ Ⓑ Ⓒ Ⓓ
508. Ⓐ Ⓑ Ⓒ Ⓓ
509. Ⓐ Ⓑ Ⓒ Ⓓ
510. Ⓐ Ⓑ Ⓒ Ⓓ
511. Ⓐ Ⓑ Ⓒ Ⓓ
512. Ⓐ Ⓑ Ⓒ Ⓓ
513. Ⓐ Ⓑ Ⓒ Ⓓ
514. Ⓐ Ⓑ Ⓒ Ⓓ
515. Ⓐ Ⓑ Ⓒ Ⓓ
516. Ⓐ Ⓑ Ⓒ Ⓓ
517. Ⓐ Ⓑ Ⓒ Ⓓ
518. Ⓐ Ⓑ Ⓒ Ⓓ
519. Ⓐ Ⓑ Ⓒ Ⓓ
520. Ⓐ Ⓑ Ⓒ Ⓓ
521. Ⓐ Ⓑ Ⓒ Ⓓ
522. Ⓐ Ⓑ Ⓒ Ⓓ
523. Ⓐ Ⓑ Ⓒ Ⓓ
524. Ⓐ Ⓑ Ⓒ Ⓓ
525. Ⓐ Ⓑ Ⓒ Ⓓ
526. Ⓐ Ⓑ Ⓒ Ⓓ
527. Ⓐ Ⓑ Ⓒ Ⓓ
528. Ⓐ Ⓑ Ⓒ Ⓓ

529. Ⓐ Ⓑ Ⓒ Ⓓ   575. Ⓐ Ⓑ Ⓒ Ⓓ   621. Ⓐ Ⓑ Ⓒ Ⓓ   667. Ⓐ Ⓑ Ⓒ Ⓓ
530. Ⓐ Ⓑ Ⓒ Ⓓ   576. Ⓐ Ⓑ Ⓒ Ⓓ   622. Ⓐ Ⓑ Ⓒ Ⓓ   668. Ⓐ Ⓑ Ⓒ Ⓓ
531. Ⓐ Ⓑ Ⓒ Ⓓ   577. Ⓐ Ⓑ Ⓒ Ⓓ   623. Ⓐ Ⓑ Ⓒ Ⓓ   669. Ⓐ Ⓑ Ⓒ Ⓓ
532. Ⓐ Ⓑ Ⓒ Ⓓ   578. Ⓐ Ⓑ Ⓒ Ⓓ   624. Ⓐ Ⓑ Ⓒ Ⓓ   670. Ⓐ Ⓑ Ⓒ Ⓓ
533. Ⓐ Ⓑ Ⓒ Ⓓ   579. Ⓐ Ⓑ Ⓒ Ⓓ   625. Ⓐ Ⓑ Ⓒ Ⓓ   671. Ⓐ Ⓑ Ⓒ Ⓓ
534. Ⓐ Ⓑ Ⓒ Ⓓ   580. Ⓐ Ⓑ Ⓒ Ⓓ   626. Ⓐ Ⓑ Ⓒ Ⓓ   672. Ⓐ Ⓑ Ⓒ Ⓓ
535. Ⓐ Ⓑ Ⓒ Ⓓ   581. Ⓐ Ⓑ Ⓒ Ⓓ   627. Ⓐ Ⓑ Ⓒ Ⓓ   673. Ⓐ Ⓑ Ⓒ Ⓓ
536. Ⓐ Ⓑ Ⓒ Ⓓ   582. Ⓐ Ⓑ Ⓒ Ⓓ   628. Ⓐ Ⓑ Ⓒ Ⓓ   674. Ⓐ Ⓑ Ⓒ Ⓓ
537. Ⓐ Ⓑ Ⓒ Ⓓ   583. Ⓐ Ⓑ Ⓒ Ⓓ   629. Ⓐ Ⓑ Ⓒ Ⓓ   675. Ⓐ Ⓑ Ⓒ Ⓓ
538. Ⓐ Ⓑ Ⓒ Ⓓ   584. Ⓐ Ⓑ Ⓒ Ⓓ   630. Ⓐ Ⓑ Ⓒ Ⓓ   676. Ⓐ Ⓑ Ⓒ Ⓓ
539. Ⓐ Ⓑ Ⓒ Ⓓ   585. Ⓐ Ⓑ Ⓒ Ⓓ   631. Ⓐ Ⓑ Ⓒ Ⓓ   677. Ⓐ Ⓑ Ⓒ Ⓓ
540. Ⓐ Ⓑ Ⓒ Ⓓ   586. Ⓐ Ⓑ Ⓒ Ⓓ   632. Ⓐ Ⓑ Ⓒ Ⓓ   678. Ⓐ Ⓑ Ⓒ Ⓓ
541. Ⓐ Ⓑ Ⓒ Ⓓ   587. Ⓐ Ⓑ Ⓒ Ⓓ   633. Ⓐ Ⓑ Ⓒ Ⓓ   679. Ⓐ Ⓑ Ⓒ Ⓓ
542. Ⓐ Ⓑ Ⓒ Ⓓ   588. Ⓐ Ⓑ Ⓒ Ⓓ   634. Ⓐ Ⓑ Ⓒ Ⓓ   680. Ⓐ Ⓑ Ⓒ Ⓓ
543. Ⓐ Ⓑ Ⓒ Ⓓ   589. Ⓐ Ⓑ Ⓒ Ⓓ   635. Ⓐ Ⓑ Ⓒ Ⓓ   681. Ⓐ Ⓑ Ⓒ Ⓓ
544. Ⓐ Ⓑ Ⓒ Ⓓ   590. Ⓐ Ⓑ Ⓒ Ⓓ   636. Ⓐ Ⓑ Ⓒ Ⓓ   682. Ⓐ Ⓑ Ⓒ Ⓓ
545. Ⓐ Ⓑ Ⓒ Ⓓ   591. Ⓐ Ⓑ Ⓒ Ⓓ   637. Ⓐ Ⓑ Ⓒ Ⓓ   683. Ⓐ Ⓑ Ⓒ Ⓓ
546. Ⓐ Ⓑ Ⓒ Ⓓ   592. Ⓐ Ⓑ Ⓒ Ⓓ   638. Ⓐ Ⓑ Ⓒ Ⓓ   684. Ⓐ Ⓑ Ⓒ Ⓓ
547. Ⓐ Ⓑ Ⓒ Ⓓ   593. Ⓐ Ⓑ Ⓒ Ⓓ   639. Ⓐ Ⓑ Ⓒ Ⓓ   685. Ⓐ Ⓑ Ⓒ Ⓓ
548. Ⓐ Ⓑ Ⓒ Ⓓ   594. Ⓐ Ⓑ Ⓒ Ⓓ   640. Ⓐ Ⓑ Ⓒ Ⓓ   686. Ⓐ Ⓑ Ⓒ Ⓓ
549. Ⓐ Ⓑ Ⓒ Ⓓ   595. Ⓐ Ⓑ Ⓒ Ⓓ   641. Ⓐ Ⓑ Ⓒ Ⓓ   687. Ⓐ Ⓑ Ⓒ Ⓓ
550. Ⓐ Ⓑ Ⓒ Ⓓ   596. Ⓐ Ⓑ Ⓒ Ⓓ   642. Ⓐ Ⓑ Ⓒ Ⓓ   688. Ⓐ Ⓑ Ⓒ Ⓓ
551. Ⓐ Ⓑ Ⓒ Ⓓ   597. Ⓐ Ⓑ Ⓒ Ⓓ   643. Ⓐ Ⓑ Ⓒ Ⓓ   689. Ⓐ Ⓑ Ⓒ Ⓓ
552. Ⓐ Ⓑ Ⓒ Ⓓ   598. Ⓐ Ⓑ Ⓒ Ⓓ   644. Ⓐ Ⓑ Ⓒ Ⓓ   690. Ⓐ Ⓑ Ⓒ Ⓓ
553. Ⓐ Ⓑ Ⓒ Ⓓ   599. Ⓐ Ⓑ Ⓒ Ⓓ   645. Ⓐ Ⓑ Ⓒ Ⓓ   691. Ⓐ Ⓑ Ⓒ Ⓓ
554. Ⓐ Ⓑ Ⓒ Ⓓ   600. Ⓐ Ⓑ Ⓒ Ⓓ   646. Ⓐ Ⓑ Ⓒ Ⓓ   692. Ⓐ Ⓑ Ⓒ Ⓓ
555. Ⓐ Ⓑ Ⓒ Ⓓ   601. Ⓐ Ⓑ Ⓒ Ⓓ   647. Ⓐ Ⓑ Ⓒ Ⓓ   693. Ⓐ Ⓑ Ⓒ Ⓓ
556. Ⓐ Ⓑ Ⓒ Ⓓ   602. Ⓐ Ⓑ Ⓒ Ⓓ   648. Ⓐ Ⓑ Ⓒ Ⓓ   694. Ⓐ Ⓑ Ⓒ Ⓓ
557. Ⓐ Ⓑ Ⓒ Ⓓ   603. Ⓐ Ⓑ Ⓒ Ⓓ   649. Ⓐ Ⓑ Ⓒ Ⓓ   695. Ⓐ Ⓑ Ⓒ Ⓓ
558. Ⓐ Ⓑ Ⓒ Ⓓ   604. Ⓐ Ⓑ Ⓒ Ⓓ   650. Ⓐ Ⓑ Ⓒ Ⓓ   696. Ⓐ Ⓑ Ⓒ Ⓓ
559. Ⓐ Ⓑ Ⓒ Ⓓ   605. Ⓐ Ⓑ Ⓒ Ⓓ   651. Ⓐ Ⓑ Ⓒ Ⓓ   697. Ⓐ Ⓑ Ⓒ Ⓓ
560. Ⓐ Ⓑ Ⓒ Ⓓ   606. Ⓐ Ⓑ Ⓒ Ⓓ   652. Ⓐ Ⓑ Ⓒ Ⓓ   698. Ⓐ Ⓑ Ⓒ Ⓓ
561. Ⓐ Ⓑ Ⓒ Ⓓ   607. Ⓐ Ⓑ Ⓒ Ⓓ   653. Ⓐ Ⓑ Ⓒ Ⓓ   699. Ⓐ Ⓑ Ⓒ Ⓓ
562. Ⓐ Ⓑ Ⓒ Ⓓ   608. Ⓐ Ⓑ Ⓒ Ⓓ   654. Ⓐ Ⓑ Ⓒ Ⓓ   700. Ⓐ Ⓑ Ⓒ Ⓓ
563. Ⓐ Ⓑ Ⓒ Ⓓ   609. Ⓐ Ⓑ Ⓒ Ⓓ   655. Ⓐ Ⓑ Ⓒ Ⓓ   701. Ⓐ Ⓑ Ⓒ Ⓓ
564. Ⓐ Ⓑ Ⓒ Ⓓ   610. Ⓐ Ⓑ Ⓒ Ⓓ   656. Ⓐ Ⓑ Ⓒ Ⓓ   702. Ⓐ Ⓑ Ⓒ Ⓓ
565. Ⓐ Ⓑ Ⓒ Ⓓ   611. Ⓐ Ⓑ Ⓒ Ⓓ   657. Ⓐ Ⓑ Ⓒ Ⓓ   703. Ⓐ Ⓑ Ⓒ Ⓓ
566. Ⓐ Ⓑ Ⓒ Ⓓ   612. Ⓐ Ⓑ Ⓒ Ⓓ   658. Ⓐ Ⓑ Ⓒ Ⓓ   704. Ⓐ Ⓑ Ⓒ Ⓓ
567. Ⓐ Ⓑ Ⓒ Ⓓ   613. Ⓐ Ⓑ Ⓒ Ⓓ   659. Ⓐ Ⓑ Ⓒ Ⓓ   705. Ⓐ Ⓑ Ⓒ Ⓓ
568. Ⓐ Ⓑ Ⓒ Ⓓ   614. Ⓐ Ⓑ Ⓒ Ⓓ   660. Ⓐ Ⓑ Ⓒ Ⓓ   706. Ⓐ Ⓑ Ⓒ Ⓓ
569. Ⓐ Ⓑ Ⓒ Ⓓ   615. Ⓐ Ⓑ Ⓒ Ⓓ   661. Ⓐ Ⓑ Ⓒ Ⓓ   707. Ⓐ Ⓑ Ⓒ Ⓓ
570. Ⓐ Ⓑ Ⓒ Ⓓ   616. Ⓐ Ⓑ Ⓒ Ⓓ   662. Ⓐ Ⓑ Ⓒ Ⓓ   708. Ⓐ Ⓑ Ⓒ Ⓓ
571. Ⓐ Ⓑ Ⓒ Ⓓ   617. Ⓐ Ⓑ Ⓒ Ⓓ   663. Ⓐ Ⓑ Ⓒ Ⓓ   709. Ⓐ Ⓑ Ⓒ Ⓓ
572. Ⓐ Ⓑ Ⓒ Ⓓ   618. Ⓐ Ⓑ Ⓒ Ⓓ   664. Ⓐ Ⓑ Ⓒ Ⓓ   710. Ⓐ Ⓑ Ⓒ Ⓓ
573. Ⓐ Ⓑ Ⓒ Ⓓ   619. Ⓐ Ⓑ Ⓒ Ⓓ   665. Ⓐ Ⓑ Ⓒ Ⓓ   711. Ⓐ Ⓑ Ⓒ Ⓓ
574. Ⓐ Ⓑ Ⓒ Ⓓ   620. Ⓐ Ⓑ Ⓒ Ⓓ   666. Ⓐ Ⓑ Ⓒ Ⓓ   712. Ⓐ Ⓑ Ⓒ Ⓓ

713. Ⓐ Ⓑ Ⓒ Ⓓ
714. Ⓐ Ⓑ Ⓒ Ⓓ
715. Ⓐ Ⓑ Ⓒ Ⓓ
716. Ⓐ Ⓑ Ⓒ Ⓓ
717. Ⓐ Ⓑ Ⓒ Ⓓ
718. Ⓐ Ⓑ Ⓒ Ⓓ
719. Ⓐ Ⓑ Ⓒ Ⓓ
720. Ⓐ Ⓑ Ⓒ Ⓓ
721. Ⓐ Ⓑ Ⓒ Ⓓ
722. Ⓐ Ⓑ Ⓒ Ⓓ
723. Ⓐ Ⓑ Ⓒ Ⓓ
724. Ⓐ Ⓑ Ⓒ Ⓓ
725. Ⓐ Ⓑ Ⓒ Ⓓ
726. Ⓐ Ⓑ Ⓒ Ⓓ
727. Ⓐ Ⓑ Ⓒ Ⓓ
728. Ⓐ Ⓑ Ⓒ Ⓓ
729. Ⓐ Ⓑ Ⓒ Ⓓ
730. Ⓐ Ⓑ Ⓒ Ⓓ
731. Ⓐ Ⓑ Ⓒ Ⓓ
732. Ⓐ Ⓑ Ⓒ Ⓓ

733. Ⓐ Ⓑ Ⓒ Ⓓ
734. Ⓐ Ⓑ Ⓒ Ⓓ
735. Ⓐ Ⓑ Ⓒ Ⓓ
736. Ⓐ Ⓑ Ⓒ Ⓓ
737. Ⓐ Ⓑ Ⓒ Ⓓ
738. Ⓐ Ⓑ Ⓒ Ⓓ
739. Ⓐ Ⓑ Ⓒ Ⓓ
740. Ⓐ Ⓑ Ⓒ Ⓓ
741. Ⓐ Ⓑ Ⓒ Ⓓ
742. Ⓐ Ⓑ Ⓒ Ⓓ
743. Ⓐ Ⓑ Ⓒ Ⓓ
744. Ⓐ Ⓑ Ⓒ Ⓓ
745. Ⓐ Ⓑ Ⓒ Ⓓ
746. Ⓐ Ⓑ Ⓒ Ⓓ
747. Ⓐ Ⓑ Ⓒ Ⓓ
748. Ⓐ Ⓑ Ⓒ Ⓓ
749. Ⓐ Ⓑ Ⓒ Ⓓ
750. Ⓐ Ⓑ Ⓒ Ⓓ
751. Ⓐ Ⓑ Ⓒ Ⓓ
752. Ⓐ Ⓑ Ⓒ Ⓓ

753. Ⓐ Ⓑ Ⓒ Ⓓ
754. Ⓐ Ⓑ Ⓒ Ⓓ
755. Ⓐ Ⓑ Ⓒ Ⓓ
756. Ⓐ Ⓑ Ⓒ Ⓓ
757. Ⓐ Ⓑ Ⓒ Ⓓ
758. Ⓐ Ⓑ Ⓒ Ⓓ
759. Ⓐ Ⓑ Ⓒ Ⓓ
760. Ⓐ Ⓑ Ⓒ Ⓓ
761. Ⓐ Ⓑ Ⓒ Ⓓ
762. Ⓐ Ⓑ Ⓒ Ⓓ
763. Ⓐ Ⓑ Ⓒ Ⓓ
764. Ⓐ Ⓑ Ⓒ Ⓓ
765. Ⓐ Ⓑ Ⓒ Ⓓ
766. Ⓐ Ⓑ Ⓒ Ⓓ
767. Ⓐ Ⓑ Ⓒ Ⓓ
768. Ⓐ Ⓑ Ⓒ Ⓓ
769. Ⓐ Ⓑ Ⓒ Ⓓ
770. Ⓐ Ⓑ Ⓒ Ⓓ
771. Ⓐ Ⓑ Ⓒ Ⓓ
772. Ⓐ Ⓑ Ⓒ Ⓓ

773. Ⓐ Ⓑ Ⓒ Ⓓ
774. Ⓐ Ⓑ Ⓒ Ⓓ
775. Ⓐ Ⓑ Ⓒ Ⓓ
776. Ⓐ Ⓑ Ⓒ Ⓓ
777. Ⓐ Ⓑ Ⓒ Ⓓ
778. Ⓐ Ⓑ Ⓒ Ⓓ
779. Ⓐ Ⓑ Ⓒ Ⓓ
780. Ⓐ Ⓑ Ⓒ Ⓓ
781. Ⓐ Ⓑ Ⓒ Ⓓ
782. Ⓐ Ⓑ Ⓒ Ⓓ
783. Ⓐ Ⓑ Ⓒ Ⓓ
784. Ⓐ Ⓑ Ⓒ Ⓓ
785. Ⓐ Ⓑ Ⓒ Ⓓ
786. Ⓐ Ⓑ Ⓒ Ⓓ
787. Ⓐ Ⓑ Ⓒ Ⓓ
788. Ⓐ Ⓑ Ⓒ Ⓓ
789. Ⓐ Ⓑ Ⓒ Ⓓ

Answer Key—Part V

1. (A) whose
2. (B) out
3. (B) has lead
4. (C) colorful
5. (B) as
6. (B) could
7. (C) terribly
8. (D) Disappointment
9. (C) leaped
10. (B) Many
11. (A) special
12. (B) To avoid
13. (D) with
14. (B) efficiency
15. (C) hardly ever
16. (D) against
17. (B) to improve
18. (B) received
19. (B) and
20. (D) probably
21. (A) incident
22. (B) protest
23. (D) appreciate
24. (B) to get
25. (A) for
26. (B) feel
27. (C) never
28. (B) more comfortable
29. (D) between
30. (C) anybody
31. (D) effect
32. (A) by
33. (B) off
34. (C) impression
35. (A) need
36. (C) small enough
37. (B) advice
38. (B) harder
39. (D) themselves
40. (B) that
41. (A) may
42. (C) leave
43. (C) two months ago
44. (B) take a trip
45. (C) no longer
46. (D) fluently
47. (B) as
48. (C) into
49. (C) interesting
50. (B) convinced
51. (A) upon
52. (C) the largest
53. (C) years old
54. (C) different
55. (A) unless
56. (A) should
57. (B) like

58. (D) such a
59. (B) seeing
60. (C) matter
61. (B) Compared
62. (A) done
63. (A) all
64. (B) bowling
65. (C) what
66. (B) often
67. (C) youngest
68. (D) development
69. (A) is
70. (C) desirable
71. (A) suit
72. (A) If
73. (A) reform
74. (B) over
75. (A) remodeled
76. (D) In spite of
77. (B) would arrive
78. (D) whose
79. (D) The small red
80. (A) few
81. (B) risen
82. (A) say
83. (C) Most of
84. (B) lower
85. (B) dramatic
86. (B) a good
87. (D) illness
88. (B) a few
89. (D) necessary
90. (B) economy
91. (C) were
92. (A) sense
93. (B) many
94. (C) him
95. (D) during
96. (B) expect
97. (B) for
98. (C) than ever
99. (C) confidence
100. (C) still
101. (D) was written
102. (B) them
103. (D) does
104. (C) promoted
105. (B) always
106. (D) before
107. (C) that
108. (A) so much
109. (D) where
110. (B) nervous
111. (D) different
112. (B) must not
113. (C) independent
114. (B) with

115. (D) to take
116. (C) Besides
117. (A) made
118. (C) next door
119. (D) Memorization
120. (C) recent
121. (C) would be back
122. (D) salvaging
123. (B) had ever received
124. (D) persuaded
125. (C) otherwise
126. (C) belong
127. (C) ought
128. (A) Realizing
129. (B) then
130. (A) humor
131. (D) According to
132. (B) celebration
133. (D) stopped by
134. (B) not to go
135. (D) were
136. (C) obvious
137. (C) afford
138. (A) find
139. (A) aware of
140. (B) have
141. (C) through
142. (C) were visiting
143. (D) coincidence
144. (D) We would be
145. (A) amazed
146. (B) yet
147. (C) as though
148. (C) his
149. (D) are being watched
150. (A) gone
151. (D) somebody
152. (A) for
153. (B) cash
154. (B) vacant
155. (D) recommendations
156. (B) Since
157. (B) had been
158. (A) For
159. (C) is faced
160. (A) enforce
161. (B) took
162. (C) why
163. (B) like
164. (C) best
165. (B) benefits
166. (D) meets
167. (A) can
168. (A) prove
169. (D) we have come to be known
170. (C) against

171. (B) more
172. (C) for
173. (C) controlled
174. (C) be kept
175. (B) the
176. (C) are offered
177. (B) what
178. (C) educated
179. (C) have
180. (D) latest
181. (A) affect
182. (A) deny
183. (A) who
184. (C) neighboring
185. (B) constant
186. (C) to
187. (D) after
188. (C) On
189. (A) all
190. (C) have
191. (B) her
192. (D) has just
193. (D) was impressed
194. (B) to find
195. (B) many
196. (D) most
197. (C) nuclear
198. (C) was lined
199. (C) inadequate
200. (A) was
201. (B) healthy
202. (C) that
203. (D) had worked
204. (A) its
205. (D) before
206. (A) to excel
207. (A) returned
208. (B) who's
209. (D) was delayed
210. (C) importance
211. (B) on
212. (D) little
213. (C) is completed
214. (B) best
215. (A) If
216. (D) very
217. (C) out of
218. (B) outlined
219. (C) many
220. (A) all
221. (A) needs
222. (C) was asked
223. (D) whose
224. (B) then
225. (B) times
226. (B) found
227. (B) will have to
228. (D) obtaining
229. (A) thousand
230. (A) say
231. (B) When
232. (B) needed
233. (C) after
234. (D) as much as possible
235. (C) showed
236. (B) burned
237. (C) Paying
238. (C) in charge of
239. (B) current
240. (C) suitable
241. (C) prices
242. (B) latest
243. (C) because
244. (B) about
245. (D) rather than
246. (A) other time
247. (C) definitely
248. (B) talking
249. (C) supposed to
250. (C) on time
251. (C) losing his temper
252. (C) disappointed
253. (B) had to
254. (C) in
255. (C) One of the
256. (C) patience
257. (C) every
258. (C) Not long ago
259. (C) both of which
260. (C) proud of
261. (B) practical
262. (B) mind
263. (B) criticize
264. (C) wishes
265. (B) lets
266. (C) illegal
267. (D) in common
268. (C) would
269. (D) hardly ever
270. (B) Since
271. (B) Terrified
272. (C) delicious
273. (C) fired
274. (D) the other
275. (D) As long as
276. (D) numerous
277. (A) as hard as
278. (B) urgent
279. (C) sounds
280. (C) has been sent
281. (C) available
282. (D) interests
283. (C) injured
284. (C) as many
285. (A) keep
286. (A) All
287. (D) can be filed
288. (C) listed
289. (D) guarantee
290. (A) cause
291. (B) too cold
292. (C) painful
293. (A) until
294. (C) from now
295. (C) waste of money
296. (C) well
297. (C) had had
298. (B) saving
299. (C) on
300. (B) in
301. (D) the best
302. (A) do
303. (B) nearly
304. (A) so
305. (B) optimistic
306. (A) because
307. (A) call
308. (B) worst
309. (C) to not
310. (B) why
311. (C) must have
312. (B) used to
313. (A) else
314. (D) going on
315. (A) new
316. (B) For
317. (C) what
318. (B) how
319. (B) It
320. (B) was interrupted
321. (D) worthwhile
322. (A) will ship
323. (D) little
324. (A) completed
325. (B) happens
326. (B) be charged
327. (C) Due to
328. (B) most
329. (C) meaning
330. (D) the future
331. (C) quickly
332. (B) seems
333. (B) to spend
334. (A) can
335. (D) their
336. (B) went
337. (D) every
338. (A) began
339. (A) first class
340. (B) ups and downs
341. (A) Few
342. (C) newly-designed
343. (B) lasted
344. (C) better
345. (C) Usually
346. (B) raising
347. (A) need
348. (A) easy
349. (A) ever
350. (C) could
351. (B) almost
352. (C) be sent
353. (C) briefly
354. (D) stock
355. (C) on
356. (B) tends
357. (C) Lately
358. (A) the
359. (A) increase

360. (D) has been coming
361. (C) requesting
362. (D) representative
363. (B) soon
364. (B) needed
365. (B) most
366. (A) lot
367. (C) forced
368. (D) were
369. (C) There
370. (D) himself
371. (C) was asked
372. (C) developed
373. (A) its
374. (D) planning
375. (A) who
376. (A) to be
377. (C) were
378. (C) should
379. (D) than
380. (C) had been done
381. (C) could
382. (C) When
383. (D) Improvements
384. (B) be filed
385. (B) almost
386. (D) truthfully
387. (C) themselves
388. (B) highest
389. (C) estimated
390. (C) worth
391. (C) set
392. (C) will be
393. (A) Using
394. (A) To
395. (C) have
396. (B) had offered
397. (B) her
398. (B) that
399. (B) passed
400. (C) just as
401. (D) appear
402. (D) would
403. (B) said
404. (C) an appointment
405. (D) production
406. (D) in spite of
407. (D) improvement
408. (D) than
409. (A) was given
410. (C) before
411. (B) sooner
412. (C) In case of
413. (B) after
414. (D) production
415. (B) take care
416. (B) always
417. (A) except
418. (B) had gone
419. (B) with
420. (C) yet
421. (A) borrow
422. (C) look it up

423. (C) depends
424. (B) he is
425. (B) too
426. (A) long
427. (C) with
428. (C) very old
429. (C) his
430. (B) to
431. (D) but also
432. (A) since
433. (C) small
434. (A) include
435. (B) transmitted
436. (D) reorganize
437. (A) stop
438. (D) overwhelmingly
439. (C) accustomed to
440. (C) to sell
441. (B) already
442. (C) number
443. (D) prescription
444. (B) recreational
445. (B) refer
446. (B) reflect
447. (C) salary
448. (B) premises
449. (C) check
450. (A) disclosed
451. (A) thousand-meter
452. (B) More and more
453. (A) on
454. (B) entire
455. (A) listen
456. (D) physical
457. (A) look over
458. (A) who
459. (D) figure out
460. (B) will buy
461. (B) to be present at
462. (B) suggestion
463. (D) late, we will
464. (A) and marketing
465. (C) seen
466. (C) the vice president and
          me
467. (D) were not working
468. (C) replaced
469. (A) go up
470. (B) met
471. (C) hours
472. (D) postponed
473. (D) container
474. (A) turnover
475. (A) flying
476. (D) expected
477. (A) what
478. (C) with its
479. (A) produce
480. (B) depends upon
481. (C) manufactured
482. (B) valued
483. (B) time
484. (D) strongly discourages

485. (D) would have gone
486. (B) to
487. (A) any
488. (C) greatly
489. (A) all
490. (A) repay
491. (A) as many
492. (D) have gone
493. (D) During
494. (B) was signed
495. (D) creativity
496. (C) with
497. (A) opens
498. (C) line
499. (C) Because of
500. (D) hearing
501. (A) worth
502. (C) one another
503. (A) knew
504. (A) who
505. (D) would have been
          completed
506. (A) of
507. (B) more produce than
508. (C) How and why
          multinational
          corporations
509. (B) is spent
510. (C) it is possible
511. (C) having
512. (C) his own
513. (D) neither
514. (C) about
515. (B) will need
516. (B) since
517. (D) have been
518. (D) institution
519. (B) some
520. (D) Does
521. (C) tell you
522. (B) rather not
523. (C) caused
524. (A) too
525. (A) wish
526. (B) at
527. (D) most
528. (B) bigger
529. (B) no longer
530. (C) The
531. (D) would
532. (D) more carefully
533. (C) extensive
534. (D) during
535. (A) soft
536. (D) different from
537. (C) must not
538. (B) has worked
539. (B) once
540. (B) pick you up
541. (C) as soon as
542. (C) delicious
543. (A) by
544. (D) off

545. (B) too
546. (B) has
547. (D) ought to
548. (A) but
549. (B) them
550. (A) serious
551. (D) depressing
552. (B) whom
553. (A) complete
554. (B) how
555. (B) to have written
556. (D) They're
557. (B) solution
558. (D) precautions
559. (C) such beautiful weather
560. (A) is not much water
561. (C) first having spoken with his parents
562. (A) told
563. (A) met
564. (A) to select
565. (B) faster
566. (B) developed
567. (D) for help
568. (A) convenient
569. (A) when
570. (D) investigate
571. (A) process
572. (B) pane
573. (C) reported
574. (C) there is
575. (C) whenever
576. (A) disrupt
577. (A) advise
578. (C) reception
579. (D) reservations
580. (D) expectations
581. (C) get used to
582. (A) by
583. (C) had not been
584. (B) himself
585. (B) and
586. (B) to finish
587. (A) open
588. (C) It is assumed
589. (B) had been
590. (D) to the fifth floor
591. (C) who he was
592. (A) better
593. (A) snows
594. (C) whoever
595. (D) were
596. (D) she
597. (A) the money
598. (D) substitute
599. (C) a year ago
600. (C) while
601. (C) that
602. (C) with
603. (D) those kinds of
604. (A) once
605. (D) stock
606. (B) out

607. (A) underbid
608. (A) lot
609. (C) what
610. (A) met
611. (C) to hire
612. (C) off
613. (C) most of
614. (B) errors
615. (C) must be
616. (B) since
617. (D) deficiencies
618. (D) variables
619. (B) most
620. (C) any
621. (D) dependent upon
622. (D) oversimplify
623. (C) processing
624. (C) would have
625. (A) able
626. (B) to reduce
627. (D) receipt
628. (B) request
629. (A) cup
630. (D) remain
631. (C) satisfactory
632. (C) consume
633. (C) tablets
634. (B) even though
635. (B) but also
636. (C) double
637. (C) the other
638. (A) them
639. (C) should
640. (C) to smoke
641. (C) confused
642. (B) count on
643. (B) confident
644. (C) Most of
645. (B) played
646. (C) since
647. (A) to
648. (D) must have
649. (C) damage
650. (D) underwrite
651. (D) coincidence
652. (B) had
653. (B) symptoms
654. (C) mandatory
655. (C) proven
656. (B) examined
657. (A) was
658. (D) If
659. (A) estimate
660. (D) reverse
661. (C) was signed
662. (D) about
663. (C) would
664. (C) Because of
665. (C) telling
666. (C) might
667. (A) only
668. (A) Of all
669. (D) on time

670. (C) became
671. (D) struck
672. (A) met
673. (C) assembly
674. (C) Holding
675. (C) addition
676. (C) little
677. (C) reserved
678. (D) in which
679. (D) provides
680. (D) insufficient
681. (D) difficult
682. (C) Between
683. (C) rang
684. (D) Whenever
685. (D) noticed
686. (C) stayed
687. (C) highly
688. (B) reporter
689. (A) so
690. (B) left
691. (B) only
692. (D) accept
693. (C) stood up
694. (D) Anyone
695. (C) being away
696. (C) recognizing
697. (D) remove
698. (A) safe
699. (C) undergo
700. (A) increased
701. (D) together
702. (B) last
703. (C) cross
704. (B) pair
705. (B) burned
706. (B) tired
707. (C) recipe
708. (D) shortest
709. (A) complicated
710. (B) fewer
711. (D) themselves
712. (C) accustomed
713. (A) signed
714. (C) insisted
715. (B) sure
716. (A) knew
717. (C) had been
718. (D) appropriate
719. (D) Having heard
720. (A) Few
721. (C) rarely
722. (D) because
723. (D) Nobody
724. (D) arrived
725. (B) hung
726. (C) except
727. (A) born
728. (B) too
729. (D) without
730. (D) would
731. (D) against
732. (C) if any

733. (A) decided
734. (A) withdrew
735. (A) rare
736. (D) earlier
737. (C) reacted
738. (D) appointment
739. (D) tightly
740. (D) absolutely
741. (B) similar
742. (A) took
743. (D) take advantage
744. (D) encourage
745. (D) insisted
746. (C) In spite of
747. (D) secure
748. (C) indicators
749. (D) be careful
750. (C) avoided
751. (C) out of

752. (C) developed
753. (B) stress
754. (B) comment
755. (D) concerned
756. (B) self
757. (A) few
758. (B) delay
759. (D) shipment
760. (B) for
761. (C) overlook
762. (C) ruining
763. (D) convince
764. (D) arrived
765. (D) appeared
766. (D) unify
767. (C) importance
768. (C) having heard
769. (C) impress
770. (B) ironing

771. (B) controlled
772. (C) afraid
773. (B) peculiar
774. (C) allowed
775. (D) has there been
776. (D) broke
777. (C) while
778. (B) tried
779. (B) always
780. (C) must be
781. (C) detached
782. (C) as important as
783. (C) apprehended
784. (A) late
785. (A) refused
786. (D) comparable
787. (D) maintained
788. (B) only
789. (A) was given

PART VI: DISCUSSION

Questions in this part of the test are similar in concept to questions in Part V in that they do not test your global knowledge of English. Rather, they test discrete points of grammar, vocabulary, and usage.

Each question consists of a single sentence. The sentence has four underlined parts, sometimes an individual word, other times up to as many as four words. Each underlined part has a letter written under it, (A), (B), (C), or (D).

From among the underlined words or phrases, you are asked to identify the word or phrase that is incorrect and mark your answer on the answer sheet. If something is not underlined, you *must* assume that it is correct.

In each case, read the entire sentence before deciding which part is incorrect. You will find that often what you think is incorrect on first reading will prove to be correct because of something that follows in the sentence. Each sentence has only one incorrect part.

As with all parts of the TOEIC, there is no penalty for wrong answers on Part VI. Any answer you may not be sure of, you should guess.

On the TOEIC®, this part of the test consists of twenty questions.

The directions for Part VI of the TOEIC read as follows:

PART VI

Directions: In Questions 141–160 each sentence has four words or phrases underlined. The four underlined parts of the sentence are marked (A), (B), (C), (D). You are to identify the <u>one</u> underlined word or phrase that should be corrected or rewritten. Then, on your answer sheet, find the number of the question and mark your answer.

Example

    All <u>employee</u> are required <u>to wear</u> their
         A   B
    <u>identification</u> badges <u>while</u> at work.
       C   D

Sample Answer

Choice (A), the underlined word "employee," is not correct in the sentence. The sentence should read, "All employees are required to wear their identification badges while at work." Therefore, you should choose answer (A).

Now begin work on the questions.

1. He <u>refused</u> <u>to tell</u> <u>us</u> why <u>was he</u> crying.
        A   B   C   D

2. That new person from the head office <u>who</u>
                                    A
   <u>is working</u> with us reminds <u>me</u> <u>to</u> my uncle.
      B   C D

3. I was <u>surprised</u> to see <u>those</u> number of
          A   B
  <u>people</u> at <u>the show</u>.
    C   D

4. On our <u>trip</u> to Central America, we <u>spent</u> a
       A   B
 lot of time visiting <u>too old</u> Mayan ruins.
               D

5. The <u>future</u> of <u>our</u> company <u>depends finishing</u>
      A   B   C
 the project <u>quickly</u>.
         D

6. Be sure to wake <u>Paul and I</u> at 8:00 A.M.,
          A   B
 <u>before</u> you <u>leave</u> for the station.
   C   D

7. The supervisor <u>showed</u> a <u>noticeable</u> dislike
         A   B   C
 for employees <u>which</u> were late.
            D

8. If it <u>will rain</u> in the afternoon, the flight
     A   B
 <u>will have</u> <u>to be</u> canceled.
    C   D

9. The new CEO worked the night long,
                           A
   attempting to find a way to avoid laying off
      B   C   D
   any employees.

10. The company rules are establishing
                    A   B
    to increase morale and profits.
       C   D

11. The communication center will have moved
                                A
    as soon as the reception area
      B   C
    nears completion.
        D

12. Be certain to provide the manager with a
             A   B
    analysis of the problems you face
              C
    in carrying out your duties.
        D

13. Park seemed tiredly when he filled out
            A   B   C
    the shipping documents to give them
                       D
    to the customs officer.

14. They have not still paid the annual retainer
         A B C   D
    that we agreed upon.

15. When he was younger, it was said he is an
           A   B   C
    inventive and loyal employee.
             D

16. The cartel has little opportunities to keep
            A   B
    prices at a level that they feel is
             C   D
    appropriate.

17. Did they hear many news about the
             A
    nation's economy while they were abroad
             B   C   D
    for the conference?

18. The company gave him a bonus
                       A
    for to compensate the extra days
          B
    he had been spending in the office.
        C   D

19. Having heard the visiting consultant's
        A   B
    speech many times, all of us were
          C
    bored of it.
        D

20. We set the merchandise next to the
        A   B
    window to keep it from get in our way.
            C   D

21. Our supervisor has gone to London
        A   B
    for meeting with the head office.
        C   D

22. My brother has been pursuing a career in
                 A   B
    medical research until he graduated
              C   D
    last May.

23. He had his tailor made a pair of dress pants
        A   B   C
    for him to wear to the opening ceremony.
                D

24. By next year, a majority of the office staff
               A   B
    have been trained on the new computer
       C   D
    system.

25. My friend found the life style in Bali as
                        A   B   C
    satisfying that he wished he could stay
                        D
    there forever.

26. Their office is always late to remitting
                            A
    payment, regardless of how small the
                B   C
    amount.
    D

27. This year the company picnic will be
    A   B
    held on Thursday, July twenty-two.
        C   D

28. Their friends sometimes wish that
                    A   B
    they are not living in the city.
    C   D

29. It is important that employees turned off
    A   B
    the office electrical equipment every

    evening when they leave work.
            C   D

30. If the team had been in better physical
                    A   B
    condition, they might enjoyed the hike more.
            C   D

31. The manager's projection relies to a great
                            A
    extent to our market survey, which was
            B   C
    completed only yesterday.
            D

32. Mr. Suda has been the chief officer of the
                A
    firm before he was fired five years ago.
                        B   C   D

33. Professor Tong will depend on his research
                        A   B
    assistants while he will take a leave of
                            C
    absence next year.
    D

34. The consignor instructed them who
                            A
    had received their goods to apply for an
        B   C   D
    additional discount.

35. Their company vacation, which include
                                    A
    one week in Europe, is nearly always the
        B   C
    best experience of the year for managers.
    D

36. There were never any secrets among my
                                A
    brother and me when we were
            B   C
    growing up.
    D

37. Even if they have been looking for an
    A   B
    apartment for a month, they have not been
            C
    able to find one anywhere.
                        D

38. The interesting-designed stairway led
        A
    directly to a large dining room, where
    B
    everyone met for dinner Thursday
            C
    evenings.
    D

39. You cannot compare economics, with

their emphasis on money matters, with
    A   B   C
political science, which examines how
                                    D
power is used.

40. Our director understood that it was we,
                                    A   B
Roko and me, who had made
        C   D
the business successful.

41. All of the secretaries were quiet frustrated
    A   B   C
with their new responsibilities, which they
     D
did not understand.

42. It is essential to turned off the power before
         A   B   C
throwing the main switch.
D

43. The bill of lading was setting on the counter
        A   B
when Jon returned to the office.
C   D

44. It is not longer necessary for employees
        A   B
to wear an I.D.badge to work in the
C   D
high-security area.

45. The passenger had only a twenty-dollars
                   A   B
bill with him when he boarded the bus.
C   D

46. I asked them to repair my room's
    A   B
door's knob before my return.
C   D

47. Anybody willing to spend the necessary
    A
time will find these workshop to be a
     B   C
rewarding experience.
D

48. During the storm the police demanded that
    A   B
people stayed off the beach except in cases
       C   D
of emergency.

49. By the end of the year, much of the
    A   B
workers who were laid off should have
             C   D
good employment opportunities.

50. While working in Tokyo, the new salesman
    A
was able not only to follow up on inquiry
                  B
letters, but as well as to find promising
             C   D
marketing opportunities.

51. The machinery's poorly design inevitably
        A   B
led to breakdowns, which always occurred
                   C
when customers were waiting for delivery.
     D

52. They might enjoyed the training course if
         A   B
they had studied more diligently during
         C   D
their college years.

53. Because of the financial difficulties of the
                                        A
company, it is doubtful weather
                        B
they will remain solvent until the
     C   D
end of the year.

54. After graduating, Carlos hopes to become
             A   B
    an engineer, as his brother, and join a
               C
    construction firm somewhere.
                        D

55. Please be sure that everybody has a ticket
            A   B
    ready to give to the lady in the door.
      C   D

56. According to the newspaper, the securities
        A
    firm had had financial problems in the
          B
    passed and was not well regarded
      C   D
    in the industry.

57. John stayed up all night trying to solve a
         A   B   C
    physic problem.
      D

58. As soon as they will finish the new
        A   B
    administration building, our offices are
         C
    going to be renovated.
         D

59. To break even on one's investment, you
               A   B
    should always pay attention to the net
         C   D
    profit.

60. Anybody who studies economics at the
           A   B
    university will have no difficulties finding
                 C
    a position in a corporation.
           D

61. Life in modern society lacks the sense of
                     A
    permanent that is so important to social
       B   C
    stability.
      D

62. In the chapter one of the report there is a
             A   B
    full explanation of this year's staff
      C   D
    reduction.

63. The salesman told me that a good set of
             A   B
    tires was supposed to least forty-thousand
           C   D
    kilometers.

64. Since the instructor had been seriously ill
      A   B
    for several months, the staff were
      C
    concerned about she returning to work.
                  D

65. If Kim would have sent in his application
            A
    sooner, he would have been accepted for
         B   C
    this seminar.
      D

66. By the beginning of next year, much of the
        A   B
    people who live in that area may have
         C
    difficulty finding employment.
           D

67. Having ran for three kilometers, I was
        A   B
    exhausted, but I felt good.
          C   D

68. In spite of the <u>wonderfully</u> fine weather,
        A   B
    my mother now wishes <u>she were not</u> living
                                    C
    in the South by <u>himself</u>.
                     D

69. <u>Ever since</u> he arrived, he <u>has been</u>
        A   B
    <u>complaining</u> <u>about constantly</u> the weather.
        C   D

70. When he <u>visited</u> the doctor, <u>the doctor</u> <u>told</u>
            A   B   C
    Mr. Park that <u>he should gone</u> to the
                     D
    hospital immediately.

71. How <u>much</u> <u>times</u> must he <u>ask you</u> not
          A   B   C
    <u>to do</u> that?
       D

72. A better accountant <u>then</u> Mr. Blanco
        A   B
    <u>would be</u> <u>hard</u> to find.
        C   D

73. When <u>completed</u>, the new plant <u>will be</u>
          A   B
    the <u>larger</u> facility of <u>its</u> kind in the nation.
         C   D

74. Mr. Gomes was <u>the kind of</u> teacher <u>which</u>
                    A   B
    tried to <u>motivate</u> his students through
            C
    <u>his own</u> enthusiasm.
        D

75. His attorney <u>advised</u> <u>him</u> <u>that sign</u> the
               A   B   C
    contract <u>immediately</u>.
            D

76. Board members <u>will discuss</u> about the
                   A
    <u>proposed</u> budget <u>at</u> <u>next month's</u> meeting.
       B   C   D

77. The secretary and the receptionist <u>takes</u>
                                   A
    their lunch break <u>whenever</u> <u>it is</u>
                   B   C
    <u>most convenient</u>.
        D

78. The new <u>sales</u> campaign <u>has obvious</u> <u>been</u>
             A   B   C
    <u>well</u> planned.
     D

79. <u>Since</u> six months, Mr. Sun <u>has been</u>
      A   B
    <u>handling</u> <u>all</u> new accounts.
       C   D

80. Mr. Grey is <u>most</u> intelligent than <u>anyone</u>
                 A   B
    <u>else</u> <u>working</u> in his field.
     C   D

81. <u>Over</u> a <u>four-years</u> period our international
      A   B
    sales <u>have increased</u> <u>by</u> more than
            C   D
    60 percent.

82. The <u>weather</u> has <u>never</u> been as <u>worse</u> as
          A   B   C
    <u>it is</u> now.
     D

83. No matter <u>how many</u> <u>time</u> it takes to find
          A   B   C
    the error in the calculation, it
    <u>must be done</u> right.
        D

84. By the end of the week, all applicants
    A   B
    have had a preliminary interview.
        C   D

85. The presentation was made by Mr. Suk,
                           A
    which is the man I told you about last
      B   C   D
    week.

86. Most experts agree that sufficient break-
       A
    time significantly increases a productivity
                         B   C
    of an employee.
       D

87. Standard Co. is looking for a
            A
    highly qualifying office manager who is
          B
    willing to take on a broad range of
       C   D
    responsibilities.

88. The typist asked to have some time more
                    A   B
    to finish preparing the letters.
        C   D

89. Although the man pretended
       A
    to have innocence, when the police saw the
         B   C
    evidence they considered him a suspect.
                   D

90. The air conditioner is very old to keep the
        A   B   C
    office cool.
          D

91. The director of the department advised the
                                   A
    new employees to avoid to waste time
                           B
    studying methods that were so
       C   D
    out-of-date.

92. His speech was a careful-worded attempt
                     A
    to evade responsibility in the matter.
       B   C   D

93. Teo and Alan must have ate some bad food
                  A   B
    in the cafeteria because they became
                           C
    very ill shortly after they left.
             D

94. I was very disappointed that you
              A
    do not send your representative
       B
    to watch the test of the new model
       C
    last week.
       D

95. Acme Company has been withdrawing its
                                       A
    bid since the last time we spoke.
        B   C   D

96. The businessmen went always to lunch at
                     A   B
    their favorite restaurant.
      C   D

97. The students cannot go to the movies often
                 A   B
    because they do not have many money
            C   D
    to spend.

98. She said she <u>likes</u> her new boss better
    A
    because his explanations are <u>clearer</u> and
    B
    <u>it's</u> <u>much more</u> patient.
    C   D

99. The package <u>will arrive</u> <u>first</u>, either
    A   B
    <u>in this morning</u> or afternoon, and <u>then</u>
    C   D
    the invoice will be sent.

100. The bank <u>cut</u> its interest <u>rate</u> <u>by</u> a quarter
     A   B   C
     of a <u>percent point</u> last week.
     D

101. The Ministry <u>estimates</u> that the workers
     A
     <u>who</u> <u>will be covered</u> by the new law
     B   C
     <u>is now making</u> less than the minimum
     D
     wage.

102. <u>Economics</u>, with <u>their</u> widespread range of
     A   B
     practical application, <u>is</u> a field of study
     C
     of interest to business people <u>everywhere</u>.
     D

103. The partners <u>got</u> a <u>government loan</u>
     A   B
     <u>for to expand</u> <u>their</u> company.
     C   D

104. They <u>never get</u> <u>upset</u> <u>about</u> <u>work</u>
     A   B   C   D
     overtime.

105. He was <u>amazed</u> to see <u>how much</u> the city
     A   B
     <u>it had changed</u> since the last time he
     C
     visited.
     D

106. The consultant <u>described about</u> <u>how</u> the
     A   B
     new system <u>would</u> function.
     C   D

107. What we must do <u>immediate</u> <u>is</u> inform
     A   B
     our customers, even <u>before trying</u>
     C
     <u>to solve</u> the problem.
     D

108. She <u>had a vacation</u> <u>one years ago</u> and
     A   B
     <u>went</u> <u>to visit</u> Canada.
     C   D

109. Mr. Chun said he <u>would have given</u> a
     A
     lecture <u>at</u> the conference, <u>if</u> he
     B   C
     <u>had been ask</u>.
     D

110. My associate <u>was studying</u> the financial
     A
     report <u>very</u> <u>hardly</u> when I saw him <u>last</u>.
     B   C   D

111. Mr. Park <u>should</u> have met Mr. Lee at the
     A
     airport, but he <u>could</u> not, so he
     B
     <u>would have</u> <u>to go</u> to the hotel instead.
     C   D

112. The <u>Commerce</u> Department <u>encourages</u>
 A B
 businesses to export <u>to</u> whenever
 C
 they <u>can</u>.
 D

113. You will have <u>an opportunity</u> <u>to test</u>,
 A B
 <u>compare</u>, and <u>for choosing</u> the
 C D
 equipment that is best for you.

114. <u>In</u> the Board's opinion, <u>that</u> candidate is
 A B
 <u>enough resourceful</u> to be <u>a</u> branch
 C D
 manager.

115. Some members <u>of the committee</u> were
 A
 opposed <u>to use</u> the <u>members'</u> money for
 B C
 <u>charitable contributions</u>.
 D

116. <u>Although</u> they have been <u>advertising for</u> a
 A B
 broker for over a year, they have been

 <u>unable at finding</u> one who was <u>suitable</u>.
 C D

117. The computer program <u>is</u> a detailed set of
 A
 <u>instruction</u> that <u>tell</u> a computer what to
 B C
 do with the information it <u>is given</u>.
 D

118. Our new manager, Ms. Marbin, <u>said</u> that
 A
 <u>he</u> will want all her new employees
 B
 <u>to meet</u> <u>one another</u> at the reception.
 C D

119. He did not <u>remain</u> for the <u>entire</u>
 A B
 presentation because it was not

 <u>interested</u> <u>for</u> him.
 C D

120. <u>They think</u> their office furniture <u>are</u> very
 A B
 <u>old, so</u> they want to <u>remodel</u>.
 C D

121. <u>During</u> the interview, the student <u>said</u> he
 A B
 <u>planned</u> to study <u>harder than</u> learn a
 C D
 lot.

122. <u>Among</u> my boss and <u>me</u>, there are
 A B
 <u>only a few</u> aspects of our relationship
 C
 that are <u>dissatisfying</u>.
 D

123. <u>These</u> clause guarantees <u>that</u> under no
 A B
 circumstances <u>will there be</u> an
 C
 abrogation <u>of</u> our contract.
 D

124. <u>Determined</u> to <u>meet his appointment</u> as
 A B
 agreed, the manager left <u>for catching</u> a
 C
 flight <u>for</u> Geneva.
 D

125. Our agent <u>prepares</u> the documentation for
 A
 all of our <u>shipment</u> and is in the <u>customs</u>
 B C D
 office every day.

126. The quality of <u>this material</u> is <u>more better</u>
                 A   B
than the quality of <u>that</u> received
                 C
<u>previously</u>.
  D

127. The union cannot <u>last much longer</u>
                    A
without <u>any</u> pay, because <u>they</u> have
       B   C
been on strike for <u>near</u> a year.
              D

128. <u>Even though</u> he was not <u>a blame</u>, Paul
     A   B
wrote a memorandum <u>to his supervisor</u>
                  C
<u>explaining</u> the situation.
  D

129. They <u>must have</u> <u>a</u> exact count of the
        A   B
<u>number of people</u> <u>expected</u> to attend
      C   D
the opening ceremonies.

130. The <u>increased</u> in revenue <u>was greater</u> <u>than</u>
      A   B   C
<u>had been</u> forecast.
  D

131. The mail <u>usually</u> <u>arrived</u> <u>before</u> we
         A   B   C
<u>were opening</u> the office.
    D

132. <u>Them</u> <u>who</u> have the greatest incentive
   A   B
<u>always</u> find a way to get the job <u>done</u>.
  C   D

133. <u>During</u> the past <u>five years</u>, our company
    A   B
has <u>grown</u> <u>rapid</u>.
    C   D

134. I <u>lent</u> Kim's typewriter <u>a few days ago</u> but
   A   B
<u>have</u> not <u>yet</u> had time to return it to him.
  C   D

135. <u>It is</u> difficult to <u>distinct</u> the difference
  A   B
<u>between</u> the new model and the old <u>one</u>.
  C   D

136. The method <u>they chose</u> was different <u>than</u>
          A   B
the one <u>that</u> <u>was suggested</u> by the
      C   D
director.

137. Some labor <u>relations</u> workers, <u>who</u> are
         A   B
required to have law degrees, <u>are</u> often
                         C
responsible for <u>negotiate</u> contract terms.
            D

138. A computer can <u>process</u> data by <u>add</u>
             A   B
numbers, for instance, or by <u>storing</u>
                    C
information for future <u>use</u>.
                D

139. Mr. Hong <u>has been</u> in <u>his</u> position
         A   B
<u>as managing director</u> <u>since</u> two years.
      C   D

140. Every employee <u>receives</u> a <u>two-weeks</u>
            A   B
<u>paid</u> vacation in the summer, <u>as well as</u>
  C   D
all official holidays.

141. Negotiations should have been completed
                      A   B
    before the end of a year ago.
          C   D

142. When the commission representative
     A
    began his new job, he had very difficult
     B   C
    time staying within his budget.
     D

143. The irrevocable letter of credit is clearly a
         A   B
    most effective method of payment than
     C
    any other used in the past.
                    D

144. Mr. Smith was the kind of foreign service
                      A
    officer who insist on investigating every
          B   C
    complaint brought to his attention.
              D

145. Claims for damages have decline
                      A
    precipitously when compared to this time
     B   C   D
    last year.

146. It is unusual to meet a salesman who has
                                  A
    such a thorough understanding of their
     B   C   D
    product.

147. Unfortunately, I have not been able to
                    A   B
    consult with our attorney because he is
            C
    at vacations.
     D

148. Our southern branch is quick becoming
        A   B   C
    the first in the nation.
             D

149. The advertising copy was extreme poorly
         A   B   C
    written.
     D

150. The Director instructed his assistant draft a
                  A   B
    letter to the arbitration tribunal on
                  C
    the best method to settle the dispute.
         D

151. I am optimistic about your new position
                   A
    and intend to help you in any way
        B   C
    possible when a member of our staff.
             D

152. The representatives have forgotten that it
                      A   B
    is them who initially introduced the
        C   D
    product line.

153. The agent was able to negotiate only a
                 A   B
    couple of contract before he was given a
              C   D
    new assignment.

154. By the end of the day, near all of the
                          A   B
    orders had been shipped.
          C   D

155. Committees were formed to report on
                              A
the budget, long-range planning, industry
     B   C
trends, and to increase productivity.
              D

156. The last final decision will be made earlier
         A   B   C
than anticipated.
     D

157. He was walking down the street when the
        A   B   C
wind blew on his hat.
     D

158. Despite how much long it took to make
     A   B   C
the preparations, the project

was completed before the deadline.
    D

159. The speaker was pleased because
                  A   B
too many people came to the lecture.
C   D

160. The manager leafed the office before
                 A   B
receiving the message from the branch
C
office that it had been robbed.
                D

161. It is important to get what you expect for
A   B   C
his money
D

162. The advice of experts can help us
        A   B
for avoiding many mistakes.
C   D

163. Most of decisions require detailed study of
     A   B
both sides of a problem.
C   D

164. As a boy, Han dreamed of someday to fly.
     A   B   C   D

165. After coming home from work, Chan lied
          A   B   C
down and took a nap.
         D

166. Mrs. Kurz searched the marketplace since
                A   B
an hour looking for the things she needed.
        C   D

167. The children had been said not to go near
         A   B   C   D
the water.

168. Mr. Yan could not figure out what to
              A   B   C
repair the broken machine.
           D

169. While the plane landed, it was surrounded
      A   B   C
by police.
D

170. The cold wind blew the broke door
      A   B   C
back and forth.
     D

171. As time passes, Ms. Lee became more
     A   B   C
comfortable in the new office.
            D

172. A fruit was delivered fresh as had been
    A   B   C   D
    promised.

173. Mr. Park very enjoys the food prepared by
         A   B   C
    the chef very much.
        D

174. The family used the holiday to visit
                A   B
    relatives whom lived in the country.
              C   D

175. Since the plant neared completion,
     A   B
    management began making preparations
              C
    for its opening.
        D

176. Several week had passed since the
            A   B
    information was requested.
        C   D

177. Even though the goods were sent two
          A   B
    weeks before, they have not arrived.
          C   D

178. Fortunate, the taxi driver knew the
         A   B
    location of the theater.
        C   D

179. The free vacation trip, which they won in
              A   B   C
    a lottery, include a week in Hawaii.
               D

180. The financing was needed now most than
         A   B   C
    ever before.
        D

181. Art proposed keeping the production line
                  A
    in operation every twenty-four hours a day.
        B   C   D

182. There is not many industry in that region
                 A   B   C
    at present.
        D

183. He has been feeling badly since he got the
         A   B   C   D
    divorce.

184. Management decided to put a new
                 A   B
    air conditioning in the Board Room.
        C   D

185. Since his car was being repaired, Mr. Lee
     A   B
    asked to borrow me.
        C   D

186. The director remembered the office
                  A
    celebration and sent to along some
        B   C   D
    flowers.

187. The plans for the new subway system

    were drawn up last year, but they still
     A   B
    have not been approving
        C   D

188. Mr. Paul <u>will</u> <u>most like</u> come, but his wife
         A   B
<u>will</u> <u>probably</u> stay home.
 C   D

189. The doctor <u>recommended</u> <u>that</u> Miko <u>lay</u>
                      A   B   C
down <u>every</u> afternoon.
       D

190. Our professor told <u>us</u> <u>we must</u> <u>turn in</u> our
                          A   B   C
papers <u>since</u> next week.
          D

191. It <u>was</u> <u>essential that</u> <u>our</u> sign the lease
       A   B   C
<u>before</u> the end of the month.
   D

192. The opening of the new expressway <u>has</u>
                                         A
made traffic <u>conditions</u> in the city
                  B
<u>much more</u> <u>better</u>.
   C   D

193. If our plane <u>arrives</u> <u>lately</u>, <u>we will miss</u>
                     A   B   C
our <u>connection</u> to Jakarta.
       D

194. When <u>traveling</u> in a foreign country, one
            A
<u>should</u> <u>be careful</u> to carry <u>ones</u> passport at
   B   C   D
all times.

195. Only employees <u>who</u> work in <u>those</u>
                      A   B
departments that <u>meeting</u> their
                     C
production goals <u>can be</u> promoted next
                    D
year.

196. Lawrence <u>ever</u> showed respect <u>for</u> his
                A   B
parents, who <u>struggled</u> so hard
                  C
<u>to put him through</u> college.
         D

197. It is <u>advisable</u> to <u>checked</u> the oil and <u>water</u>
              A   B   C
in the engine <u>at least</u> every 1000
                  D
kilometers.

198. I <u>wish</u> I <u>had not signed</u> that contract <u>with</u>
      A   B   C
first <u>having consulted</u> my lawyer.
         D

199. He <u>would rather</u> play classical music <u>by</u>
              A   B
the piano <u>than</u> to listen to others <u>play</u>.
             C   D

200. The reason <u>they are</u> not <u>coming</u> is <u>as</u> they
                   A   B   C
are angry with <u>us</u>.
                  D

201. The student <u>asked</u> <u>his advisor</u> <u>which</u>
                   A   B   C
courses <u>will he</u> take.
           D

202. <u>Of all the sports</u> <u>in which</u> he <u>participated</u>,
        A   B   C
he liked tennis <u>less</u>.
                   D

203. Drivers should always <u>avoid</u> <u>to change</u>
                             A   B
lanes <u>without</u> first <u>signaling</u>.
         C   D

204. The supertanker was shipwrecked on
      A   B
    the rocks from the coast of France.
      C   D

205. The town was no longer the sleepy little
      A   B   C
    village it has been.
                D

206. For she practiced constantly, she became
      A   B   C
    an expert golfer.
      D

207. The custom in that country is to call the
      A   B
    first child after the paternal grandfather.
                C   D

208. My roommate studies very hardly and is
      A   B   C
    always at the library.
      D

209. Physics is a demanding field that
                  A
    has challenged many people to probe
          B   C
    their mysteries.
      D

210. Next year he is planning to run in the
      A   B   C
    ten-kilometers race.
      D

211. He is said to have be an excellent athlete
              A   B   C
    in his youth.
      D

212. The company's decision will depend
          A
    largely to its ability to find a competent
          B   C
    person to take charge of the branch office.
                    D

213. He has been their sales representative
          A   B
    before he quit a year ago.
      C   D

214. The ushers asked all of the audience to
                  A   B   C
    leave as quick as possible.
          D

215. Having slept for nine hours, Mr. Seng
              A   B
    woke up feeling many better.
      C   D

216. They have the highest per capita rate of
                    A   B
    crime of any industrialization nation.
      C   D

217. Sometime Tan would take long walks
          A   B
    alone on the sandy beach below his
      C   D
    house.

218. All of students were asked to come to
      A   B   C
    school early on the first day of the
                  D
    semester.

219. There is many more paper in the boxes
              A   B
    next to that wall.
      C   D

220. A few days <u>before</u>, the president
              A
<u>passed thought</u> on <u>his way</u> <u>to meet</u> the
   B   C   D
ministers.

221. Feng worked <u>overtime</u> three nights
             A
<u>on a row</u> <u>to complete</u> the project <u>on time</u>.
  B   C   D

222. The flowers <u>on the trees</u> <u>began to open</u>
             A   B
<u>one after one</u> as the days <u>became</u> warmer.
     C   D

223. The concert was <u>good</u> <u>attended</u> and the
             A   B
music <u>was performed</u> <u>superbly</u>.
        C   D

224. A <u>common</u> <u>held</u> belief is that <u>man</u>
     A   B   C
<u>has evolved from</u> lower forms of life.
       D

225. His parents <u>are planning</u> <u>to move</u> <u>to</u> a
            A   B   C
warmer climate as soon as <u>they will retire</u>
                        D
next year.

226. I had to tell her <u>that</u> she <u>looked</u> so
   A   B   C
<u>beautifully</u> in her new dress.
  D

227. A bouquet of <u>lovely</u> flowers
      A   B
<u>were displayed</u> <u>in</u> the lobby of the hotel.
   C   D

228. That class <u>has had</u> <u>little</u> opportunities <u>for</u>
          A   B   C
education <u>or</u> advancement.
       D

229. <u>On</u> our <u>last</u> trip we drove nearly one
   A   B
hundred kilometers <u>in the way</u>, after
               C
<u>taking</u> a wrong turn.
  D

230. His problem is <u>that</u> he knows <u>hardly ever</u>
            A   B
English and <u>cannot</u> be <u>understood</u>.
         C   D

231. He <u>was</u> looking <u>to</u> a way <u>to complete</u> the
    A   B   C
job rapidly, without going <u>over budget</u>.
                   D

232. Returning <u>home</u> from work, he <u>was bite</u>
    A   B   C
by a dog and <u>had to go</u> to the hospital.
         D

233. <u>When</u> only a small child, he <u>was taken</u> to
     A   B
the circus <u>with</u> his father.
  C   D

234. Parents should be careful <u>when</u> <u>selecting</u> a
                    A   B
<u>child's</u> toys and furniture, <u>as avoiding</u> the
  C   D
consequences of an accident.

235. When Mrs. Chung <u>went</u> to Brazil, she
    A   B
<u>had bought</u> an <u>exquisitely</u> carved bowl.
  C   D

236. They all worked hardly and saved enough
     A   B   C
money to invest in a small business.
     D

237. This product should be left out in the rain
                    A   B
as moisture will irreparably damage the
C   D
surface.

238. After arriving in Tokyo three years ago,
     A   B   C
Mr. Lupus has been to all of the major
                      D
tourist sites.

239. Modern technologies have allowed
                         A
businesses to improve its ability to
           B   C
communicate with their clients.
                 D

240. He works as a maintenance man because
             A
he never had the opportunity to learn
        B   C
another skills.
   D

241. The letter requesting samples of the new
            A   B
line was received the day ago yesterday.
        C   D

242. The man at the front row looked like a
            A   B
businessman attending a convention,

too tired to appreciate the performance.
   C   D

243. Most students than usual registered for
     A   B
the class in economics, requiring a change
                        C
in the lecture room.
D

244. The greatest amount of freedom for the
     A
majority of the people seem to be the goal
                        B   C
of democracies around the world.
                   D

245. When he had applied by August 15, the
     A   B
university would have accepted him
         C
for the next school year.
   D

246. The autumn mornings are cool and fresh
     A   B
and inviting a person to travel to the
    C   D
countryside.

247. His mother could never understand him
                A   B
wanting to become a stage actor.
         C   D

248. I often think back to when our parents
               A   B
would take my brother and I to the park
   C   D
to play.

249. When the famous pianist was young, he

was accustomed to practicing
     A   B
during many hours a day.
       C   D

250. When we finally bought stock in the
          A
company, the market had already reached
                       B
its peak and the stock was declined
                            C
in value.
  D

251. Jogging, walking, and go swimming are all
                         A   B
excellent ways to improve one's health.
          C   D

252. The boy tried to help his mother, but
              A
success only in breaking two of her
  B   C   D
favorite dishes.

253. For the weather became cooler,
  A   B
more and more birds left for warmer areas
       C
where food was more abundant.
                  D

254. There were many different kinds of fruit
                A   B   C
on the table and many more food in the
                 D
kitchen.

255. The occasion marked by parades and
        A   B
celebrations across the country.
             C   D

256. Just when she thought she was finished
        A
for the day, her supervisor brought her
  B   C
three more letters for typing.
                      D

257. The nation's economic prosperity led to a
                  A   B
generally satisfaction with the
  C
administration in power.
               D

258. Fifty people were invited to the dinner
                A
gave in honor of the man who
  B   C
had been awarded a Nobel Prize.
       D

259. He stopped to smoke a year ago and has
                 A   B   C
not started again.
    D

260. Negotiations broke off after it become
                 A   B
clear that neither side was willing to
           C   D
compromise.

261. For several years now, the
        A
student body has been attempting to gain
     B   C
many influences over university policies.
     D

262. Much to his surprise, when Jan arrived in
        A   B   C
London he had found several friends
           D
waiting for him at the airport.

263. Having read several books on those
     A   B
subject, the man considered himself
                   C
something of an expert.
  D

264. The traveler was later advised that he
              A   B
    should not have drank the tap water in
         C   D
    the hotel.

265. The doctor was too surprised that his
                    A   B
    patient had let his condition deteriorate so
            C
    much before calling him.
                   D

266. Park showed up fifteen minutes lately and
            A   B
    missed the first part of the presentation.
      C   D

267. Ms. Ford had a hard time to find her way
                A   B   C
    around the unfamiliar streets of the new
      D
    city.

268. While Lin was out of town on business,
         A   B
    several new employee were hired to work
                   C   D
    in the shipping department.

269. The family members are gathering
                         A
    together during the holiday and shared
      B   C
    their adventures and memories.
      D

270. To the restaurant, Mr. Kim ordered a cup
      A   B
    of coffee and his wife a pot of tea.
                   C   D

271. Page two of the operation manual

    contains instructions in how to correct
      A   B   C
    problems that may occur.
             D

272. Anybody had heard of the plan to sell the
      A   B   C
    company before last night's meeting, but

    today everybody knows.
               D

273. The director finally agreed to

    go forward with the project,
      A
    even though he did not agree with few of
      B   C
    its recommendations.
      D

274. Mr. Lee said Ms. Jan to mail the letters
              A   B
    as soon as she could find time to go to the
      C   D
    post office.

275. The office was arranged as that each
                 A   B
    worker had his own desk and was located
             C   D
    near a window.

276. All of the buildings on the north side of
      A
    the street were made of brick, except the
               B   C
    one across to the bank.
         D

277. Employees are required to report to his
               A   B
    supervisor at the latest by 7:50 A.M.,
               C
    prepared to work.
      D

278. Chung <u>was bore</u> on August 12, 1965, <u>in</u> a
          A   B   C
small <u>town</u> near the border.
     D

279. The <u>bus stop</u> is on <u>a</u> next street,
       A   B
<u>on the corner</u> <u>opposite</u> the parking lot.
     C   D

280. He was a <u>dynamic</u> figure
            A
<u>who inspired awe</u> and devotion, and <u>build</u>
     B   C
an empire that lasted <u>for</u> many years.
                D

281. While <u>I was</u> shopping at the market, I
       A
realized that the prices of <u>many</u> items
    B   C
<u>had been risen</u> in recent weeks.
     D

282. The public opinion polls <u>indicated</u> that
                    A
most people <u>were not as much</u>
          B
<u>in favor with</u> the new law as <u>had been</u>
     C   D
previously thought.

283. We <u>were asked</u> to try <u>to image</u> <u>what</u> life
      A   B   C
was like for <u>people who lived</u> in our area
           D
three hundred years ago.

284. <u>Two weeks ago</u> Mr. Bram rented a car and
     A
<u>drove</u> <u>up</u> to the mountain resort to spend
   B   C
<u>a</u> time skiing.
 D

285. The noisy children <u>kept asking</u> their father
                 A
<u>for little money</u>, but <u>he said he</u> did not
     B   C
have <u>any</u>.
    D

286. There <u>were</u> a large <u>crowd</u> of people in
      A   B
front of the store, <u>waiting</u> <u>to be let</u> in when
              C   D
it opened.

287. Mr. Kim <u>keeps informed</u> on political
           A
matters <u>by reading</u> <u>a</u> newspaper <u>ever</u>
        B   C   D
morning at breakfast.

288. We <u>had to arrive</u> <u>before</u> the main office
      A   B
<u>closes</u> or we <u>will</u> <u>not be able</u> to meet the
  C   D
president.

289. As the old man <u>went on</u>, the children
    A   B
<u>became very</u> interested in <u>a</u> story.
    C   D

290. The invitation <u>asked us</u> <u>for joining</u> a club
           A   B
for people with <u>similar</u> interests.
  C   D

291. We <u>regret</u> that <u>we are able</u> to order <u>any</u>
     A   B   C
more items at this time <u>as</u> we are
               D
overstocked.

292. They were <u>hardly able</u> to get <u>settled</u> in the
                A   B
 room before <u>there</u> was time for the
                C
 meeting <u>to begin</u>.
          D

293. Jane said that she <u>had never visited</u> Cairo,
                       A
 <u>or</u> that if she ever <u>did</u>, she <u>would</u> call us.
  B   C   D

294. This is the <u>most frequent</u> requested item
              A
 <u>in</u> the entire line and we are pleased
  B
 <u>to offer</u> <u>it to you</u> at a 25 percent discount.
   C   D

295. The <u>mother</u> went to <u>the finest store</u> in the
       A   B
 city <u>for to get</u> presents for her children,
      C
 <u>nieces</u>, and nephews.
   D

296. I <u>did not understand</u> their predicament
          A
 <u>until</u> Mary <u>explained me</u> all the details of
  B   C
 the mishap.
    D

297. The company <u>have</u> not <u>responded</u> <u>yet</u> to
          A   B   C
 <u>our proposal</u>.
  D

298. Ms. Kim <u>was planning</u> to send <u>me</u> a
         A   B
 package from New York <u>as soonest as</u> she
                   C
 <u>arrived</u>.
  D

299. His father <u>mentioned</u> to me that Chan
          A
 <u>had wrote</u> <u>to him</u> <u>asking</u> for money to buy
    B   C   D
 a car.

300. He did not tell <u>anything to me</u>
                A
 <u>about having</u> to stay <u>late</u> at the office
    B   C
 <u>to work</u> on the project.
   D

301. Although Ms. Sato <u>has been</u> here <u>longer</u>,
              A   B
 Ms. Park is <u>in charge for</u> this department,
          C
 and the next department <u>as well</u>.
                   D

302. After <u>working out</u>, I was <u>so</u> hungry that I
      A   B
 <u>could have</u> <u>ate</u> everything in the
   C   D
 refrigerator.

303. <u>When</u> it <u>became apparent</u> that the project
  A   B
 was not <u>practically</u>, all of the investors
         C
 <u>backed out</u>.
   D

304. Increased sales, new clients, and
 <u>inexpensive labor</u> <u>added up</u> to
     A   B
 <u>much profits</u> for the <u>young</u> company.
   C   D

305. It is <u>far better</u> to be honest <u>than</u> <u>trying</u> to
     A   B   C
 obtain favors <u>through</u> deception.
          D

306. Mr. Finn <u>told</u> the agent <u>to check to see</u> if
             A   B   C
     the order had been shipped <u>still</u>.
                                   D

307. <u>Among</u> these two products, <u>the one</u> on
       A   B
     the right <u>is better</u> for <u>a number of</u> reasons.
              C   D

308. The father was very <u>disappointing</u> in the
                          A
     <u>boy's</u> behavior at the reception and
      B
     <u>said he would</u> speak with him <u>later</u>.
           C   D

309. We <u>went</u> to eat at a restaurant and
          A
     thought the <u>meal</u> was <u>too delicious</u>.
       B   C   D

310. I <u>did not have</u> enough <u>experiences</u>
          A   B
     <u>to get</u> the job I applied for, but I was
      C
     given <u>another one</u>.
           D

311. He is <u>no going</u> on vacation this year
           A
     because he <u>spent</u> <u>too much</u> money <u>on</u> his
             B   C   D
     new furniture.

312. The teacher <u>told</u> the students to sit <u>quiet</u>
              A   B
     and not to open their <u>books</u> until
                  C
     <u>told to do so</u>.
          D

313. They <u>foolishly</u> <u>drove</u> into the <u>desert</u>
           A   B   C
     without <u>none</u> water.
            D

314. The plane <u>was leaving</u> San Francisco on
              A
     time, but <u>was unable</u> to land <u>due to</u> the
              B   C
     weather <u>conditions</u> at Narita airport.
            D

315. It was important <u>for</u> them to <u>arrive</u> <u>before</u>
                  A   B   C
     the curtain <u>goes up</u> last night.
              D

316. <u>Because</u> many guests <u>do not arrive</u>, the
       A   B
     hotel requires <u>for</u> reservations be
                 C
     confirmed <u>at least</u> one day before arrival.
             D

317. Pam's house <u>was located</u> on the <u>right</u>
                A   B
     <u>side of</u> the street, <u>across to</u> the music
       C   D
     store.

318. Football, or soccer, <u>has become</u> a sport
                     A
     that <u>is enjoyed</u> by <u>millions</u> <u>through</u> the
         B   C   D
     world.

319. The company <u>headquarters</u> have been in
               A
     that city <u>before</u> the company <u>began</u>, <u>over</u>
           B   C   D
     ten years ago.

320. The warm weather brought
                          A
    much swimmers out to enjoy the
         B   C
    sunshine and the pleasant beaches.
                    D

321. Jung had read magazines often
              A
    when he was a student, but now he ever
         B   C
    seems to find the time.
         D

322. The cars sped along the expressway like if
                A   B
    it were a racetrack and they were all
       C
    trying to take first place.
      D

323. Playing skiing has become Mr. Anders'
         A   B
    favorite sport, since he took it up last year.
                    C   D

324. Thera noticed many peoples who
                     A   B
    had been waiting hours to buy their
              C   D
    tickets.

325. It is asked that English can be a very
          A   B
    difficult language for a person to learn in
                      C
    his later years.
     D

326. Any approach to economics, whether
                              A
    liberal or conservative, relies on the will of
                             B   C
    the people for their success.
                D

327. The father, looking for his young son
                  A
    at the park, called at him in a loud voice.
        B   C   D

328. The Ministry of Energy is pushing for the
                              A
    immediately construction of a nuclear
         B   C
    power plant, but people who live in the
                      D
    area where it is to be built do not like it.

329. After the computer printouts have
         A   B
    finished, they will have to be handed out
                      C   D
    to the participants.

330. The park, locating as it was, among the
                  A   B
    trees on the south side of the mountain,

    was small, clean, and ideal as a place
       C
    for meditation.
         D

331. As soon as these misunderstandings
         A   B
    will be straightened out, we will be able
       C   D
    to proceed.

332. The brochure summed out the value
            A   B
    and quality of the new line of materials.
       C   D

333. The two groups were asked to team up so
                     A   B   C
    the report could be completed more quick.
                                        D

334. Most of common mistakes can be avoided
    —A—   —B—
    by careful planning and attention to
       —C—
    detail.
    —D—

335. Ms. Abe will be unavailable for the
              —A—
    rest of day, because she has
       —B—   —C—
    meetings scheduled until 6:30 this
    ——D——
    evening.

336. The dog who belonged to the man
            —A—— —B—
    living next door was caught chasing
    ——C——   —D—
    chickens.

337. This is one of the best easy tests that I
    ——A——   —B—   —C—
    have taken since entering college.
               —D—

338. He gave me so good advice that I was
              —A—   —B—   —C—
    able to solve all my problems.
    —D—

339. As the after dinner meeting became more
    —A—   —B—
    and more bored, several of the people
            —C—
    attending it fell asleep.
               —D—

340. It is tradition to have flowers
       —A— —B—   —C—
    at a wedding.
    —D—

341. On the way to their place in the country,
    ——A——   —B—
    they were injured in an automobile
        —C—
    incident and had to be taken to a hospital.
    —D—

342. Teachers usually spend many hours
                    —A—
    correcting paper, a task that few of them
             —B—   —C— —D—
    enjoy.

343. Doctors have to going to school for
                —A—
    many years to complete their education,
    —B—
    and even then they must study to keep up
        ——C——   —D—
    with new developments.

344. He is intelligence enough to do well in
          —A—   —B—   —C—
    school, but he does not apply himself.
                               —D—

345. He has instructed them time and again
                     —A—
    to be careful how to get the formulas
       —B—   —C— —D—
    mixed up.

346. When the results were tabulated, it was
    —A—   —B—
    obviously which candidate the people
    —C—   —D—
    preferred.

347. The secretary tries to reach him at his
                  —A— —B—
    other office, but was not able to
                       —C—
    get in touch with him.
    —D—

348. The clients paid promptly, as their
                 A   B   C
    accounts came due to.
                   D

349. As much young as he was, he was
     A   B   C   D
    surprisingly well qualified for the position.

350. The local newspaper is delivered by
                          A   B
    6 o'clock every morning, and Saturday.
               C   D

351. There was no children in the playground
     A
    yesterday afternoon, which explains why
                          B   C
    it was so quiet.
           D

352. She was unable to remember where
                A   B
    she did leave her hat and gloves, but was
        C
    confident she would find them.
                     D

353. The author, whose book we had been
                 A   B
    discussing, came for giving a lecture at the
                     C
    university and invited the public.
                    D

354. A greatest deal of pleasure and satisfaction
       A   B
    can be found in a job well done.
     C   D

355. Mr. James was able to find medicine at a
                A   B
    drugstore to relieve his stomach aching.
             C   D

356. The letter had to be typed and retyped
                  A
    several time before it could be sent.
       B   C   D

357. This building was more expensive as that
                      A   B
    one, but it is not nearly as beautiful.
                       C   D

358. Paul had the rather difficult time, and it
                A   B
    was a miracle that he survived at all.
           C   D

359. I have been told that yesterday was the
         A   B
    colder day of the year.
      C   D

360. Professor Young was the best-read man I
                            A
    have ever met, until I met his father.
      B   C   D

361. The doctor had too many patients that she
                   A   B   C   D
    could not see them all.

362. Ling took carefully notes of all the
                A   B
    presentations throughout the conference,

    to be able to refer to them later.
      C   D

363. The bookkeeping department have
             A   B
    reported several errors in the financial
             C
    reports received from regional offices last
           D
    month.

364. While all goes as planned, construction
     ___A___   ___B___
     can begin on the new warehouse before
     ___C___
     the end of the year.
     _____D_____

365. Either the foreman nor the workers
     __A__
     were able to explain how the fire was able
     ___B___   ___C___
     to go unnoticed for so long.
     _____D_____

366. The blue car had been parked in front of
                   ___A___ ___B___ ___C___
     the house since at least an hour.
              ___D___

367. Mark was hired for the position on the
          ___A___ ___B___   ___C___
     base of his computer background.
     __D__

368. My advice is, doing it carefully, if not
        __A__   ___B__ ___C___   __D__
     rapidly.

369. All the employees looked very nervously
     ___A___   ___B___   ___C___
     before the visit of the company president

     to their plant.
     ___D___

370. My uncle Theo is an avid student of
                      ___A___ ___B___
     politic, and has considered running for
     __C__   ___D___
     local office.

371. The airport had been fogged in all
                   ___A___ ___B___
     morning, but by afternoon

     it was beginning to clear through.
            ___C___   ___D___

372. They had to took four fifty-minute classes
          __A__ __B__   ___C___
     every school day.
     __D__

373. Those kind of woman is likely to have a
     __A__   __B__ __C__
     lot of success in business.
     __D__

374. Speaking on behalf of entirely the
                         ___A___
     committee, Clark reported the findings and
                                ___B___
     conclusions, adding his own
                  ___C___
     recommendation for further study.
                    __D__

375. He has had no chance to come up with a
         __A__   ___B___
     good answer to the question before his
                             ___C___
     time was up, so he lost the contest.
       ___D___

376. The teacher asked the students to bring in
                 __A__   ___B___
     some photographs of his family.
          __C__   __D__

377. These forms must be completed and sent
                 __A__   ___B___
     back to the office as much as possible.
     __C__   ___D___

378. The police captured the thief after
         __A__ __B__
     had chased him for ten kilometers.
     ___C___   __D__

379. The office was <u>lately</u> <u>expanded</u> to
                      A   B
    <u>allow for</u> the new equipment, which is
         C
    now <u>on order</u>.
             D

380. <u>Speaking</u> on behalf of <u>all</u> the staff, Mr. Plat
         A   B
    <u>thanked</u> the manager for his <u>kind</u>.
         C   D

381. We <u>were shown</u> around the new facility
             A
    by <u>two of the men</u> who worked there, and
           B
    <u>with whom</u> we have since <u>became</u> friends.
         C   D

382. Everyone should have <u>a equal</u>
             A   B
    opportunity <u>to get</u> an education and to
               C
    earn <u>a livelihood</u>.
              D

383. We <u>still</u> do not have <u>much</u> <u>informations</u>
           A   B   C
    on the disaster, but will inform you as

    soon as we receive <u>word</u>.
                   D

384. <u>Moving</u> from a warm climate to a cold
         A
    one, the family <u>had</u> <u>few</u> winter clothing
        B   C   D
    when they arrived.

385. <u>On arrival</u> at the airport, all passengers
          A
    <u>should</u> proceed to <u>gate the eighth</u> to pick
         B   C
    up <u>their</u> new boarding passes.
          D

386. I <u>would like</u> to have an apartment
         A
    <u>as the one</u> my friend <u>has</u>, but I cannot
         B   C
    afford <u>it</u>.
          D

387. Her job pays <u>a higher</u> salary than <u>my</u>, <u>but</u>
              A   B   C
    of course I have <u>better</u> hours.
                 D

388. It is hard to believe <u>that</u> they <u>are</u> exactly
         A   B   C
    the same <u>weigh</u>.
            D

389. The new maid <u>cleaned up</u> the room, <u>made</u>
                A   B
    the bed, <u>pick up</u> the trash, and <u>put away</u>
             C   D
    the books.

390. <u>Even as</u> he <u>had been told</u> not <u>to</u>, the boy
         A   B   C
    insisted <u>upon</u> playing near the trucks in
             D
    the yard.

391. <u>Many</u> different <u>kind</u> of <u>fish</u> can be seen <u>in</u>
        A   B   C   D
    the aquarium at the new zoo.

392. <u>Here</u> is a large selection of restaurants in
        A
    the downtown area of <u>both cities</u>, for the
                       B
    <u>pleasure</u> of residents and visitors <u>alike</u>.
         C   D

393. The typhoon <u>damaged</u> <u>nearly</u> every house
                A   B
    on <u>a</u> west <u>side</u> of the island.
          C   D

394. To ensure <u>long</u> life, these flowers
            A
<u>should be put</u> in a place out <u>in</u> direct
    B   C
sunlight and watered <u>every</u> three days.
                     D

395. The <u>writer upset</u> because the editor
        A
<u>left out</u> a <u>large</u> and important part of <u>her</u>
   B   C   D
story.

396. He took <u>much</u> language courses <u>when</u> he
        A   B
was <u>studying</u> at the university, but <u>still</u>
     C   D
speaks only English.

397. <u>Organization</u>, cleanliness, and <u>prompt</u> are
    A   B
important <u>traits</u> to <u>develop</u> in the field of
        C   D
business.

398. <u>When</u> he found his suitcase <u>opened</u> and
   A   B
his wallet <u>missing</u>, he was sure that
        C
someone <u>had broke</u> into his room.
        D

399. The conference <u>began</u> with
           A
<u>an introduction</u> of the main speaker, after
   B
<u>that</u> the agenda <u>was reviewed</u>.
  C   D

400. The doctor <u>wanted to check</u> the <u>child's</u>
           A   B
medical <u>records</u> before <u>having run</u> any
     C   D
tests.

401. The police <u>respected</u> a <u>thirty-year old</u>
        A   B
pharmacist <u>of</u> <u>committing</u> the crime.
       C   D

402. Sam scored the <u>less</u> points <u>in</u> the
           A   B
basketball game, but he played <u>hard,</u>
                         C
<u>nevertheless.</u>
 D

403. The map <u>failing</u> to offer any help
        A
<u>in finding</u> the airport, <u>requiring</u> visitors to
  B   C
ask <u>directions</u> of policemen and other
    D
public servants.

404. The houses <u>that</u> <u>were destroyed</u> by the
        A   B
typhoon <u>had been</u> built <u>more a</u> hundred
       C   D
years before.

405. In an antique shop <u>he found</u> an
            A
interesting sculpture, <u>as the one</u> he
                B
<u>had seen</u> <u>on</u> a trip to India.
  C   D

406. We were all <u>looked</u> forward <u>to going</u> on
           A   B
our <u>class</u> picnic on the last day of the year,
    C
<u>but</u> weather prevented it.
 D

407. <u>Fortunately,</u> it was <u>not yet too late</u> to
    A   B
correct the mistake <u>before</u> the report was
              C
<u>send</u> out.
 D

ANSWER SHEET—PART VI

1. Ⓐ Ⓑ Ⓒ Ⓓ	43. Ⓐ Ⓑ Ⓒ Ⓓ	85. Ⓐ Ⓑ Ⓒ Ⓓ	127. Ⓐ Ⓑ Ⓒ Ⓓ
2. Ⓐ Ⓑ Ⓒ Ⓓ	44. Ⓐ Ⓑ Ⓒ Ⓓ	86. Ⓐ Ⓑ Ⓒ Ⓓ	128. Ⓐ Ⓑ Ⓒ Ⓓ
3. Ⓐ Ⓑ Ⓒ Ⓓ	45. Ⓐ Ⓑ Ⓒ Ⓓ	87. Ⓐ Ⓑ Ⓒ Ⓓ	129. Ⓐ Ⓑ Ⓒ Ⓓ
4. Ⓐ Ⓑ Ⓒ Ⓓ	46. Ⓐ Ⓑ Ⓒ Ⓓ	88. Ⓐ Ⓑ Ⓒ Ⓓ	130. Ⓐ Ⓑ Ⓒ Ⓓ
5. Ⓐ Ⓑ Ⓒ Ⓓ	47. Ⓐ Ⓑ Ⓒ Ⓓ	89. Ⓐ Ⓑ Ⓒ Ⓓ	131. Ⓐ Ⓑ Ⓒ Ⓓ
6. Ⓐ Ⓑ Ⓒ Ⓓ	48. Ⓐ Ⓑ Ⓒ Ⓓ	90. Ⓐ Ⓑ Ⓒ Ⓓ	132. Ⓐ Ⓑ Ⓒ Ⓓ
7. Ⓐ Ⓑ Ⓒ Ⓓ	49. Ⓐ Ⓑ Ⓒ Ⓓ	91. Ⓐ Ⓑ Ⓒ Ⓓ	133. Ⓐ Ⓑ Ⓒ Ⓓ
8. Ⓐ Ⓑ Ⓒ Ⓓ	50. Ⓐ Ⓑ Ⓒ Ⓓ	92. Ⓐ Ⓑ Ⓒ Ⓓ	134. Ⓐ Ⓑ Ⓒ Ⓓ
9. Ⓐ Ⓑ Ⓒ Ⓓ	51. Ⓐ Ⓑ Ⓒ Ⓓ	93. Ⓐ Ⓑ Ⓒ Ⓓ	135. Ⓐ Ⓑ Ⓒ Ⓓ
10. Ⓐ Ⓑ Ⓒ Ⓓ	52. Ⓐ Ⓑ Ⓒ Ⓓ	94. Ⓐ Ⓑ Ⓒ Ⓓ	136. Ⓐ Ⓑ Ⓒ Ⓓ
11. Ⓐ Ⓑ Ⓒ Ⓓ	53. Ⓐ Ⓑ Ⓒ Ⓓ	95. Ⓐ Ⓑ Ⓒ Ⓓ	137. Ⓐ Ⓑ Ⓒ Ⓓ
12. Ⓐ Ⓑ Ⓒ Ⓓ	54. Ⓐ Ⓑ Ⓒ Ⓓ	96. Ⓐ Ⓑ Ⓒ Ⓓ	138. Ⓐ Ⓑ Ⓒ Ⓓ
13. Ⓐ Ⓑ Ⓒ Ⓓ	55. Ⓐ Ⓑ Ⓒ Ⓓ	97. Ⓐ Ⓑ Ⓒ Ⓓ	139. Ⓐ Ⓑ Ⓒ Ⓓ
14. Ⓐ Ⓑ Ⓒ Ⓓ	56. Ⓐ Ⓑ Ⓒ Ⓓ	98. Ⓐ Ⓑ Ⓒ Ⓓ	140. Ⓐ Ⓑ Ⓒ Ⓓ
15. Ⓐ Ⓑ Ⓒ Ⓓ	57. Ⓐ Ⓑ Ⓒ Ⓓ	99. Ⓐ Ⓑ Ⓒ Ⓓ	141. Ⓐ Ⓑ Ⓒ Ⓓ
16. Ⓐ Ⓑ Ⓒ Ⓓ	58. Ⓐ Ⓑ Ⓒ Ⓓ	100. Ⓐ Ⓑ Ⓒ Ⓓ	142. Ⓐ Ⓑ Ⓒ Ⓓ
17. Ⓐ Ⓑ Ⓒ Ⓓ	59. Ⓐ Ⓑ Ⓒ Ⓓ	101. Ⓐ Ⓑ Ⓒ Ⓓ	143. Ⓐ Ⓑ Ⓒ Ⓓ
18. Ⓐ Ⓑ Ⓒ Ⓓ	60. Ⓐ Ⓑ Ⓒ Ⓓ	102. Ⓐ Ⓑ Ⓒ Ⓓ	144. Ⓐ Ⓑ Ⓒ Ⓓ
19. Ⓐ Ⓑ Ⓒ Ⓓ	61. Ⓐ Ⓑ Ⓒ Ⓓ	103. Ⓐ Ⓑ Ⓒ Ⓓ	145. Ⓐ Ⓑ Ⓒ Ⓓ
20. Ⓐ Ⓑ Ⓒ Ⓓ	62. Ⓐ Ⓑ Ⓒ Ⓓ	104. Ⓐ Ⓑ Ⓒ Ⓓ	146. Ⓐ Ⓑ Ⓒ Ⓓ
21. Ⓐ Ⓑ Ⓒ Ⓓ	63. Ⓐ Ⓑ Ⓒ Ⓓ	105. Ⓐ Ⓑ Ⓒ Ⓓ	147. Ⓐ Ⓑ Ⓒ Ⓓ
22. Ⓐ Ⓑ Ⓒ Ⓓ	64. Ⓐ Ⓑ Ⓒ Ⓓ	106. Ⓐ Ⓑ Ⓒ Ⓓ	148. Ⓐ Ⓑ Ⓒ Ⓓ
23. Ⓐ Ⓑ Ⓒ Ⓓ	65. Ⓐ Ⓑ Ⓒ Ⓓ	107. Ⓐ Ⓑ Ⓒ Ⓓ	149. Ⓐ Ⓑ Ⓒ Ⓓ
24. Ⓐ Ⓑ Ⓒ Ⓓ	66. Ⓐ Ⓑ Ⓒ Ⓓ	108. Ⓐ Ⓑ Ⓒ Ⓓ	150. Ⓐ Ⓑ Ⓒ Ⓓ
25. Ⓐ Ⓑ Ⓒ Ⓓ	67. Ⓐ Ⓑ Ⓒ Ⓓ	109. Ⓐ Ⓑ Ⓒ Ⓓ	151. Ⓐ Ⓑ Ⓒ Ⓓ
26. Ⓐ Ⓑ Ⓒ Ⓓ	68. Ⓐ Ⓑ Ⓒ Ⓓ	110. Ⓐ Ⓑ Ⓒ Ⓓ	152. Ⓐ Ⓑ Ⓒ Ⓓ
27. Ⓐ Ⓑ Ⓒ Ⓓ	69. Ⓐ Ⓑ Ⓒ Ⓓ	111. Ⓐ Ⓑ Ⓒ Ⓓ	153. Ⓐ Ⓑ Ⓒ Ⓓ
28. Ⓐ Ⓑ Ⓒ Ⓓ	70. Ⓐ Ⓑ Ⓒ Ⓓ	112. Ⓐ Ⓑ Ⓒ Ⓓ	154. Ⓐ Ⓑ Ⓒ Ⓓ
29. Ⓐ Ⓑ Ⓒ Ⓓ	71. Ⓐ Ⓑ Ⓒ Ⓓ	113. Ⓐ Ⓑ Ⓒ Ⓓ	155. Ⓐ Ⓑ Ⓒ Ⓓ
30. Ⓐ Ⓑ Ⓒ Ⓓ	72. Ⓐ Ⓑ Ⓒ Ⓓ	114. Ⓐ Ⓑ Ⓒ Ⓓ	156. Ⓐ Ⓑ Ⓒ Ⓓ
31. Ⓐ Ⓑ Ⓒ Ⓓ	73. Ⓐ Ⓑ Ⓒ Ⓓ	115. Ⓐ Ⓑ Ⓒ Ⓓ	157. Ⓐ Ⓑ Ⓒ Ⓓ
32. Ⓐ Ⓑ Ⓒ Ⓓ	74. Ⓐ Ⓑ Ⓒ Ⓓ	116. Ⓐ Ⓑ Ⓒ Ⓓ	158. Ⓐ Ⓑ Ⓒ Ⓓ
33. Ⓐ Ⓑ Ⓒ Ⓓ	75. Ⓐ Ⓑ Ⓒ Ⓓ	117. Ⓐ Ⓑ Ⓒ Ⓓ	159. Ⓐ Ⓑ Ⓒ Ⓓ
34. Ⓐ Ⓑ Ⓒ Ⓓ	76. Ⓐ Ⓑ Ⓒ Ⓓ	118. Ⓐ Ⓑ Ⓒ Ⓓ	160. Ⓐ Ⓑ Ⓒ Ⓓ
35. Ⓐ Ⓑ Ⓒ Ⓓ	77. Ⓐ Ⓑ Ⓒ Ⓓ	119. Ⓐ Ⓑ Ⓒ Ⓓ	161. Ⓐ Ⓑ Ⓒ Ⓓ
36. Ⓐ Ⓑ Ⓒ Ⓓ	78. Ⓐ Ⓑ Ⓒ Ⓓ	120. Ⓐ Ⓑ Ⓒ Ⓓ	162. Ⓐ Ⓑ Ⓒ Ⓓ
37. Ⓐ Ⓑ Ⓒ Ⓓ	79. Ⓐ Ⓑ Ⓒ Ⓓ	121. Ⓐ Ⓑ Ⓒ Ⓓ	163. Ⓐ Ⓑ Ⓒ Ⓓ
38. Ⓐ Ⓑ Ⓒ Ⓓ	80. Ⓐ Ⓑ Ⓒ Ⓓ	122. Ⓐ Ⓑ Ⓒ Ⓓ	164. Ⓐ Ⓑ Ⓒ Ⓓ
39. Ⓐ Ⓑ Ⓒ Ⓓ	81. Ⓐ Ⓑ Ⓒ Ⓓ	123. Ⓐ Ⓑ Ⓒ Ⓓ	165. Ⓐ Ⓑ Ⓒ Ⓓ
40. Ⓐ Ⓑ Ⓒ Ⓓ	82. Ⓐ Ⓑ Ⓒ Ⓓ	124. Ⓐ Ⓑ Ⓒ Ⓓ	166. Ⓐ Ⓑ Ⓒ Ⓓ
41. Ⓐ Ⓑ Ⓒ Ⓓ	83. Ⓐ Ⓑ Ⓒ Ⓓ	125. Ⓐ Ⓑ Ⓒ Ⓓ	167. Ⓐ Ⓑ Ⓒ Ⓓ
42. Ⓐ Ⓑ Ⓒ Ⓓ	84. Ⓐ Ⓑ Ⓒ Ⓓ	126. Ⓐ Ⓑ Ⓒ Ⓓ	168. Ⓐ Ⓑ Ⓒ Ⓓ

169. Ⓐ Ⓑ Ⓒ Ⓓ	214. Ⓐ Ⓑ Ⓒ Ⓓ	259. Ⓐ Ⓑ Ⓒ Ⓓ	304. Ⓐ Ⓑ Ⓒ Ⓓ
170. Ⓐ Ⓑ Ⓒ Ⓓ	215. Ⓐ Ⓑ Ⓒ Ⓓ	260. Ⓐ Ⓑ Ⓒ Ⓓ	305. Ⓐ Ⓑ Ⓒ Ⓓ
171. Ⓐ Ⓑ Ⓒ Ⓓ	216. Ⓐ Ⓑ Ⓒ Ⓓ	261. Ⓐ Ⓑ Ⓒ Ⓓ	306. Ⓐ Ⓑ Ⓒ Ⓓ
172. Ⓐ Ⓑ ● Ⓓ	217. Ⓐ Ⓑ Ⓒ Ⓓ	262. Ⓐ Ⓑ Ⓒ Ⓓ	307. Ⓐ Ⓑ Ⓒ Ⓓ
173. Ⓐ Ⓑ Ⓒ Ⓓ	218. Ⓐ Ⓑ Ⓒ Ⓓ	263. Ⓐ Ⓑ Ⓒ Ⓓ	308. Ⓐ Ⓑ Ⓒ Ⓓ
174. Ⓐ Ⓑ Ⓒ Ⓓ	219. Ⓐ Ⓑ Ⓒ Ⓓ	264. Ⓐ Ⓑ Ⓒ Ⓓ	309. Ⓐ Ⓑ Ⓒ Ⓓ
175. Ⓐ Ⓑ Ⓒ Ⓓ	220. Ⓐ Ⓑ Ⓒ Ⓓ	265. Ⓐ Ⓑ Ⓒ Ⓓ	310. Ⓐ Ⓑ Ⓒ Ⓓ
176. Ⓐ Ⓑ Ⓒ Ⓓ	221. Ⓐ Ⓑ Ⓒ Ⓓ	266. Ⓐ Ⓑ Ⓒ Ⓓ	311. Ⓐ Ⓑ Ⓒ Ⓓ
177. Ⓐ Ⓑ Ⓒ Ⓓ	222. Ⓐ Ⓑ Ⓒ Ⓓ	267. Ⓐ Ⓑ Ⓒ Ⓓ	312. Ⓐ Ⓑ Ⓒ Ⓓ
178. Ⓐ Ⓑ Ⓒ Ⓓ	223. Ⓐ Ⓑ Ⓒ Ⓓ	268. Ⓐ Ⓑ Ⓒ Ⓓ	313. Ⓐ Ⓑ Ⓒ Ⓓ
179. Ⓐ Ⓑ Ⓒ Ⓓ	224. Ⓐ Ⓑ Ⓒ Ⓓ	269. Ⓐ Ⓑ Ⓒ Ⓓ	314. Ⓐ Ⓑ Ⓒ Ⓓ
180. Ⓐ Ⓑ Ⓒ Ⓓ	225. Ⓐ Ⓑ Ⓒ Ⓓ	270. Ⓐ Ⓑ Ⓒ Ⓓ	315. Ⓐ Ⓑ Ⓒ Ⓓ
181. Ⓐ Ⓑ Ⓒ Ⓓ	226. Ⓐ Ⓑ Ⓒ Ⓓ	271. Ⓐ Ⓑ Ⓒ Ⓓ	316. Ⓐ Ⓑ Ⓒ Ⓓ
182. Ⓐ Ⓑ Ⓒ Ⓓ	227. Ⓐ Ⓑ Ⓒ Ⓓ	272. Ⓐ Ⓑ Ⓒ Ⓓ	317. Ⓐ Ⓑ Ⓒ Ⓓ
183. Ⓐ Ⓑ Ⓒ Ⓓ	228. Ⓐ Ⓑ Ⓒ Ⓓ	273. Ⓐ Ⓑ Ⓒ Ⓓ	318. Ⓐ Ⓑ Ⓒ Ⓓ
184. Ⓐ Ⓑ Ⓒ Ⓓ	229. Ⓐ Ⓑ Ⓒ Ⓓ	274. Ⓐ Ⓑ Ⓒ Ⓓ	319. Ⓐ Ⓑ Ⓒ Ⓓ
185. Ⓐ Ⓑ Ⓒ Ⓓ	230. Ⓐ Ⓑ Ⓒ Ⓓ	275. Ⓐ Ⓑ Ⓒ Ⓓ	320. Ⓐ Ⓑ Ⓒ Ⓓ
186. Ⓐ Ⓑ Ⓒ Ⓓ	231. Ⓐ Ⓑ Ⓒ Ⓓ	276. Ⓐ Ⓑ Ⓒ Ⓓ	321. Ⓐ Ⓑ Ⓒ Ⓓ
187. Ⓐ Ⓑ Ⓒ Ⓓ	232. Ⓐ Ⓑ Ⓒ Ⓓ	277. Ⓐ Ⓑ Ⓒ Ⓓ	322. Ⓐ Ⓑ Ⓒ Ⓓ
188. Ⓐ Ⓑ Ⓒ Ⓓ	233. Ⓐ Ⓑ Ⓒ Ⓓ	278. Ⓐ Ⓑ Ⓒ Ⓓ	323. Ⓐ Ⓑ Ⓒ Ⓓ
189. Ⓐ Ⓑ Ⓒ Ⓓ	234. Ⓐ Ⓑ Ⓒ Ⓓ	279. Ⓐ Ⓑ Ⓒ Ⓓ	324. Ⓐ Ⓑ Ⓒ Ⓓ
190. Ⓐ Ⓑ Ⓒ Ⓓ	235. Ⓐ Ⓑ Ⓒ Ⓓ	280. Ⓐ Ⓑ Ⓒ Ⓓ	325. Ⓐ Ⓑ Ⓒ Ⓓ
191. Ⓐ Ⓑ Ⓒ Ⓓ	236. Ⓐ Ⓑ Ⓒ Ⓓ	281. Ⓐ Ⓑ Ⓒ Ⓓ	326. Ⓐ Ⓑ Ⓒ Ⓓ
192. Ⓐ Ⓑ Ⓒ Ⓓ	237. Ⓐ Ⓑ Ⓒ Ⓓ	282. Ⓐ Ⓑ Ⓒ Ⓓ	327. Ⓐ Ⓑ Ⓒ Ⓓ
193. Ⓐ Ⓑ Ⓒ Ⓓ	238. Ⓐ Ⓑ Ⓒ Ⓓ	283. Ⓐ Ⓑ Ⓒ Ⓓ	328. Ⓐ Ⓑ Ⓒ Ⓓ
194. Ⓐ Ⓑ Ⓒ Ⓓ	239. Ⓐ Ⓑ Ⓒ Ⓓ	284. Ⓐ Ⓑ Ⓒ Ⓓ	329. Ⓐ Ⓑ Ⓒ Ⓓ
195. Ⓐ Ⓑ Ⓒ Ⓓ	240. Ⓐ Ⓑ Ⓒ Ⓓ	285. Ⓐ Ⓑ Ⓒ Ⓓ	330. Ⓐ Ⓑ Ⓒ Ⓓ
196. Ⓐ Ⓑ Ⓒ Ⓓ	241. Ⓐ Ⓑ Ⓒ Ⓓ	286. Ⓐ Ⓑ Ⓒ Ⓓ	331. Ⓐ Ⓑ Ⓒ Ⓓ
197. Ⓐ Ⓑ Ⓒ Ⓓ	242. Ⓐ Ⓑ Ⓒ Ⓓ	287. Ⓐ Ⓑ Ⓒ Ⓓ	332. Ⓐ Ⓑ Ⓒ Ⓓ
198. Ⓐ Ⓑ Ⓒ Ⓓ	243. Ⓐ Ⓑ Ⓒ Ⓓ	288. Ⓐ Ⓑ Ⓒ Ⓓ	333. Ⓐ Ⓑ Ⓒ Ⓓ
199. Ⓐ Ⓑ Ⓒ Ⓓ	244. Ⓐ Ⓑ Ⓒ Ⓓ	289. Ⓐ Ⓑ Ⓒ Ⓓ	334. Ⓐ Ⓑ Ⓒ Ⓓ
200. Ⓐ Ⓑ Ⓒ Ⓓ	245. Ⓐ Ⓑ Ⓒ Ⓓ	290. Ⓐ Ⓑ Ⓒ Ⓓ	335. Ⓐ Ⓑ Ⓒ Ⓓ
201. Ⓐ Ⓑ Ⓒ Ⓓ	246. Ⓐ Ⓑ Ⓒ Ⓓ	291. Ⓐ Ⓑ Ⓒ Ⓓ	336. Ⓐ Ⓑ Ⓒ Ⓓ
202. Ⓐ Ⓑ Ⓒ Ⓓ	247. Ⓐ Ⓑ Ⓒ Ⓓ	292. Ⓐ Ⓑ Ⓒ Ⓓ	337. Ⓐ Ⓑ Ⓒ Ⓓ
203. Ⓐ Ⓑ Ⓒ Ⓓ	248. Ⓐ Ⓑ Ⓒ Ⓓ	293. Ⓐ Ⓑ Ⓒ Ⓓ	338. Ⓐ Ⓑ Ⓒ Ⓓ
204. Ⓐ Ⓑ Ⓒ Ⓓ	249. Ⓐ Ⓑ Ⓒ Ⓓ	294. Ⓐ Ⓑ Ⓒ Ⓓ	339. Ⓐ Ⓑ Ⓒ Ⓓ
205. Ⓐ Ⓑ Ⓒ Ⓓ	250. Ⓐ Ⓑ Ⓒ Ⓓ	295. Ⓐ Ⓑ Ⓒ Ⓓ	340. Ⓐ Ⓑ Ⓒ Ⓓ
206. Ⓐ Ⓑ Ⓒ Ⓓ	251. Ⓐ Ⓑ Ⓒ Ⓓ	296. Ⓐ Ⓑ Ⓒ Ⓓ	341. Ⓐ Ⓑ Ⓒ Ⓓ
207. Ⓐ Ⓑ Ⓒ Ⓓ	252. Ⓐ Ⓑ Ⓒ Ⓓ	297. Ⓐ Ⓑ Ⓒ Ⓓ	342. Ⓐ Ⓑ Ⓒ Ⓓ
208. Ⓐ Ⓑ Ⓒ Ⓓ	253. Ⓐ Ⓑ Ⓒ Ⓓ	298. Ⓐ Ⓑ Ⓒ Ⓓ	343. Ⓐ Ⓑ Ⓒ Ⓓ
209. Ⓐ Ⓑ Ⓒ Ⓓ	254. Ⓐ Ⓑ Ⓒ Ⓓ	299. Ⓐ Ⓑ Ⓒ Ⓓ	344. Ⓐ Ⓑ Ⓒ Ⓓ
210. Ⓐ Ⓑ Ⓒ Ⓓ	255. Ⓐ Ⓑ Ⓒ Ⓓ	300. Ⓐ Ⓑ Ⓒ Ⓓ	345. Ⓐ Ⓑ Ⓒ Ⓓ
211. Ⓐ Ⓑ Ⓒ Ⓓ	256. Ⓐ Ⓑ Ⓒ Ⓓ	301. Ⓐ Ⓑ Ⓒ Ⓓ	346. Ⓐ Ⓑ Ⓒ Ⓓ
212. Ⓐ Ⓑ Ⓒ Ⓓ	257. Ⓐ Ⓑ Ⓒ Ⓓ	302. Ⓐ Ⓑ Ⓒ Ⓓ	347. Ⓐ Ⓑ Ⓒ Ⓓ
213. Ⓐ Ⓑ Ⓒ Ⓓ	258. Ⓐ Ⓑ Ⓒ Ⓓ	303. Ⓐ Ⓑ Ⓒ Ⓓ	348. Ⓐ Ⓑ Ⓒ Ⓓ

349. Ⓐ Ⓑ Ⓒ Ⓓ	364. Ⓐ Ⓑ Ⓒ Ⓓ	379. Ⓐ Ⓑ Ⓒ Ⓓ	394. Ⓐ Ⓑ Ⓒ Ⓓ
350. Ⓐ Ⓑ Ⓒ Ⓓ	365. Ⓐ Ⓑ Ⓒ Ⓓ	380. Ⓐ Ⓑ Ⓒ Ⓓ	395. Ⓐ Ⓑ Ⓒ Ⓓ
351. Ⓐ Ⓑ Ⓒ Ⓓ	366. Ⓐ Ⓑ Ⓒ Ⓓ	381. Ⓐ Ⓑ Ⓒ Ⓓ	396. Ⓐ Ⓑ Ⓒ Ⓓ
352. Ⓐ Ⓑ Ⓒ Ⓓ	367. Ⓐ Ⓑ Ⓒ Ⓓ	382. Ⓐ Ⓑ Ⓒ Ⓓ	397. Ⓐ Ⓑ Ⓒ Ⓓ
353. Ⓐ Ⓑ Ⓒ Ⓓ	368. Ⓐ Ⓑ Ⓒ Ⓓ	383. Ⓐ Ⓑ Ⓒ Ⓓ	398. Ⓐ Ⓑ Ⓒ Ⓓ
354. Ⓐ Ⓑ Ⓒ Ⓓ	369. Ⓐ Ⓑ Ⓒ Ⓓ	384. Ⓐ Ⓑ Ⓒ Ⓓ	399. Ⓐ Ⓑ Ⓒ Ⓓ
355. Ⓐ Ⓑ Ⓒ Ⓓ	370. Ⓐ Ⓑ Ⓒ Ⓓ	385. Ⓐ Ⓑ Ⓒ Ⓓ	400. Ⓐ Ⓑ Ⓒ Ⓓ
356. Ⓐ Ⓑ Ⓒ Ⓓ	371. Ⓐ Ⓑ Ⓒ Ⓓ	386. Ⓐ Ⓑ Ⓒ Ⓓ	401. Ⓐ Ⓑ Ⓒ Ⓓ
357. Ⓐ Ⓑ Ⓒ Ⓓ	372. Ⓐ Ⓑ Ⓒ Ⓓ	387. Ⓐ Ⓑ Ⓒ Ⓓ	402. Ⓐ Ⓑ Ⓒ Ⓓ
358. Ⓐ Ⓑ Ⓒ Ⓓ	373. Ⓐ Ⓑ Ⓒ Ⓓ	388. Ⓐ Ⓑ Ⓒ Ⓓ	403. Ⓐ Ⓑ Ⓒ Ⓓ
359. Ⓐ Ⓑ Ⓒ Ⓓ	374. Ⓐ Ⓑ Ⓒ Ⓓ	389. Ⓐ Ⓑ Ⓒ Ⓓ	404. Ⓐ Ⓑ Ⓒ Ⓓ
360. Ⓐ Ⓑ Ⓒ Ⓓ	375. Ⓐ Ⓑ Ⓒ Ⓓ	390. Ⓐ Ⓑ Ⓒ Ⓓ	405. Ⓐ Ⓑ Ⓒ Ⓓ
361. Ⓐ Ⓑ Ⓒ Ⓓ	376. Ⓐ Ⓑ Ⓒ Ⓓ	391. Ⓐ Ⓑ Ⓒ Ⓓ	406. Ⓐ Ⓑ Ⓒ Ⓓ
362. Ⓐ Ⓑ Ⓒ Ⓓ	377. Ⓐ Ⓑ Ⓒ Ⓓ	392. Ⓐ Ⓑ Ⓒ Ⓓ	407. Ⓐ Ⓑ Ⓒ Ⓓ
363. Ⓐ Ⓑ Ⓒ Ⓓ	378. Ⓐ Ⓑ Ⓒ Ⓓ	393. Ⓐ Ⓑ Ⓒ Ⓓ	

ANSWER KEY—PART VI

1. D he was
2. D of
3. B that
4. D very old
5. C depends upon finishing
6. B Paul and me
7. D who
8. B rains
9. A all night long
10. B established
11. A will be moved
12. B an
13. A tired
14. B yet
15. C was
16. A few
17. A any
18. B as compensation for, to compensate for
19. D with
20. D getting
21. C to meet
22. C since
23. B make
24. C will have been
25. C so
26. A in
27. D twenty-second
28. C they were not
29. B turn off
30. D might have enjoyed
31. B on
32. A was
33. C takes
34. A those who
35. A includes
36. A between
37. A Even though, Although
38. A interestingly-designed
39. A its
40. C Roko and I
41. B quite, quietly
42. B turn off
43. B sitting
44. A It is no
45. B twenty-dollar
46. C door knob
47. C this
48. C stay
49. B many
50. C also
51. B poor design
52. A might have enjoyed
53. B whether
54. C like
55. D at
56. C past
57. D physics

58. B finish
59. B he
60. C no difficulty
61. B permanence
62. A the first chapter, in Chapter One
63. D last
64. D her return, her returning
65. A had sent in
66. B many
67. A having run
68. D herself
69. D about
70. D he should go
71. A many
72. B than
73. C largest
74. B who
75. C to sign
76. A will talk (about)
77. A take
78. B has obviously
79. A For
80. A more
81. B four-year
82. C bad
83. B how much
84. C will have had
85. B who
86. C the
87. B highly-qualified
88. B some more time, more time
89. B to be innocent
90. B too
91. B wasting
92. A carefully-worded
93. B have eaten
94. B did not send
95. A has withdrawn
96. A always went
97. D much
98. C is
99. C this morning
100. D percentage point
101. D are now making
102. B its
103. C to expand
104. D working
105. C had changed
106. A described
107. A immediately
108. B one year ago
109. D had been asked
110. C hard
111. C had
112. C wherever
113. D choose
114. C resourceful enough

115. B to using, to the use of
116. C unable to find
117. B instructions
118. B she
119. C interesting
120. B is
121. D hard and
122. A Between
123. A This
124. C to catch
125. C shipping
126. B much
127. D nearly
128. B to blame
129. B an
130. A increase
131. D opened
132. A Those
133. D rapidly
134. A borrowed
135. B determine
136. B from
137. D negotiating
138. B adding
139. D for
140. B two-week
141. D last year, the year
142. C he had a very
143. C more
144. C insisted
145. A have declined
146. D his
147. D on vacation
148. B quickly
149. B extremely
150. B to draft
151. D as a member
152. C they
153. C contracts
154. A nearly
155. D how to increase productivity increasing productivity an increase in productivity
156. A final
157. D blew off
158. B how
159. C so many
160. A left
161. D your
162. C to avoid
163. A Most
164. D flying someday
165. C lay
166. B for
167. B told
168. C how
169. A When

170. C broken
171. B passed
172. A The fruit
173. A always
174. C who
175. A As
176. A weeks
177. C earlier
178. A Fortunately
179. D includes
180. C more
181. C twenty-four hours
182. B much
183. B bad
184. C air conditioner
185. D mine
186. D along
187. D approved
188. B most likely
189. C lie
190. D by
191. C we
192. C much
193. B late
194. D one's
195. C meet
196. A always
197. B check
198. C without
199. B on
200. C that
201. D he should
202. D least
203. B changing
204. D off
205. D had been
206. A As
207. B to name
208. C hard
209. D its mysteries
210. D ten-kilometer
211. B to have been
212. B on
213. A had been
214. D as quickly
215. D much
216. D industrialized
217. A Sometimes
218. A All of the
219. A a lot
220. B passed through
221. B in a row
222. C one at a time
223. A well
224. A commonly
225. D they retire
226. D beautiful
227. C was displayed
228. B few
229. C out of our way
230. B hardly any
231. B for
232. C was bitten

233. D by
234. D to avoid
235. C bought
236. B hard
237. A should not be
238. A Since
239. C their ability
240. D other
241. D day before yesterday
242. A in
243. A more
244. B seems
245. A If
246. C invite
247. B his
248. D brother and me
249. C many
250. C declining
251. A swimming
252. B succeeded
253. A As
254. D much
255. A occasion was marked
256. D to type
257. C general
258. B given
259. A smoking
260. B became
261. D influence
262. D found
263. B the, that
264. D drunk
265. A very
266. B late
267. C finding
268. C employees
269. A gathered
270. A At
271. B on
272. A No one, Nobody
273. C with any, with all, with
        most, with many
274. A told
275. B such
276. D across from
277. B their
278. A was born
279. B the
280. C built
281. D had been raised, had risen
282. C in favor of
283. B to imagine
284. D some
285. B for money, for some
        money, for a little money
286. A was
287. D every
288. A have to arrive
289. D the, his
290. B to join
291. B we are unable
292. C it
293. B but

294. A most frequently
295. C to get
296. C explained to me
297. A has
298. C as soon as
299. B had written
300. A me anything
301. C in charge of
302. D eaten
303. C practical
304. C much profit
305. C to try
306. D yet
307. A Between
308. A disappointed
309. D very delicious
310. B experience
311. A not going
312. B quietly
313. D any
314. A left
315. D went
316. C that
317. D across from
318. D around
319. B since
320. B many swimmers
321. C never
322. B as if
323. A Skiing
324. B people
325. A said
326. D for, for its
327. C to
328. B immediate
329. B are
330. A located
331. C are
332. B summed up
333. D quickly
334. A Most
335. B rest of the day
336. A that
337. B easiest
338. A such
339. C boring
340. B traditional
341. D accident
342. B papers
343. A to go
344. A intelligent
345. C not
346. C obvious
347. A tried
348. D due
349. A As
350. D including
351. A There were
352. C she left
353. C to give
354. A great
355. D stomach ache
356. B several times

357. B than
358. A a
359. C coldest
360. B had
361. A so
362. A careful
363. B has
364. A If, Since, As, Because
365. A Neither
366. D for
367. D basis
368. B do
369. C nervous
370. C politics
371. D up
372. B to take
373. A That

374. A the entire
375. A had
376. D their families
377. D as soon as
378. C chasing
379. A recently
380. D kindness
381. D become
382. B an equal
383. C information
384. D little, no
385. C Gate 8, Gate Eight
386. B like the one
387. B mine
388. D weight
389. C picked up
390. A Even though

391. B kinds
392. A There
393. C the
394. C of
395. A writer became upset
396. A many
397. B promptness
398. D had broken
399. C which
400. D running
401. A suspected
402. A fewest
403. A failed
404. D more than a
405. B like one
406. A looking
407. D sent

PART VII: DISCUSSION

For the student who knows a lot of English, this part of the test should present the most interesting material. In this part you will read a number of passages. Following each passage are up to five questions, although usually only *two* or *three* questions follow a passage. To answer the questions, you are able to refer back to the passage for information. As you work on Part VII you should pace yourself, so you do not run out of time. Remember that if you have not finished when time runs out, you will *not* be able to go back and answer any questions you may have left unanswered. Knowing that, you should be sure that depending upon how many questions you have not answered, during the last couple of minutes of the test you should mark an answer for all of the test questions. You are not penalized for any wrong answers you may mark.

The test makers try to include material that is as close to what you would find in a real life setting, and which is, at the same time, short enough and clear enough to allow for questions. This part tests your ability to understand what you read. Ability to understand written material, however, is not merely a matter of understanding vocabulary and knowing grammar.It requires an understanding of the way language fits together and how the different parts of a written piece cooperate to convey an entire message. The message in written English is not always stated as simply as a mathematical formula, or as explicitly as exercises in a grammar book might lead you to believe.

Rarely will the answer to a question depend upon a single word in the passage. Usually there will be at least two places where an answer can be found, and sometimes even more than that, so do not be concerned if you do not understand all of what you read. As you practice with these test questions, try to work without a dictionary as much as possible, guessing at meanings and attempting to answer questions based on your guesses. Remember, in the test you are not permitted to use a dictionary or other study aids. It is best that you accustom yourself here to managing without a dictionary.

On the TOEIC®, this part of the test consists of forty questions.

The directions for this part of the TOEIC® read as follows:

PART VII

Directions: Questions 161–200 are based on a variety of reading material (for example, announcements, paragraphs, and advertisements. You are to choose the <u>one</u> best answer, (A), (B), (C), or (D), to each question. Then, on your answer sheet, find the number of the question and mark your answer. Answer all questions following a passage on the basis of what is <u>stated</u> or <u>implied</u> in that passage.

Read the following example.

Example

The Museum of Technology is a "hands-on" museum designed for people to experience science at work. Visitors are encouraged to use, test, and handle the objects on display. Special demonstrations are scheduled for the first and second Wednesdays of each month at 1:30 P.M. Open Tuesday–Friday, 2:30–4:30 P.M., Saturday 11:00 A.M.–4:30 P.M., and Sunday 1:00–4:30 P.M.

When during the month can visitors see special demonstrations?

(A) Every weekend.
(B) The first two Wednesdays.
(C) One afternoon a week.
(D) Every other Wednesday.

Sample Answer

 Ⓐ ⬤ Ⓒ Ⓓ

The passage says that the demonstrations are scheduled the first and second Wednesdays of the month. Therefore, you should choose answer (B).

Now begin work on the questions.

Questions 1–4 refer to the following passage.

The Festival of Festivals

From a free, outdoor concert performance of the New York Symphony to the big band sound of Chet Bunker, the City Music Summer Festival offers a season of variety, excitement, and pleasure in this, its thirteenth year. Under the direction of William Johns, III, and presented by the Mayor's Office on the Arts, this year's program will run all summer long and has been referred to as a "Festival of Festival," by the Critics' Choice columnist, Ed Alvin.

In one mid-summer Central Park performance, the Metropolitan Opera Company will perform Verdi's *La Traviata*. There will be many other classical, jazz and pop music performances, as well as the ever-popular amateur night. By registering in advance, talented amateurs may perform, either vocally or on an instrument, any music they choose. The advance registration is not to determine a person's talent, but rather to ensure the public an enjoyable variety of music.

This year's Festival will be one to remember. Watch for further notices in the newspaper or on posters around town, or listen to your radio for program bulletins.

1. Who is responsible for organizing the Summer Festival?

   (A) Ed Alvin.
   (B) Chet Bunker.
   (C) William Johns, III.
   (D) The Mayor.

2. Which of the following words best describes the Festival?

   (A) New.
   (B) Variety.
   (C) Small.
   (D) Expensive.

3. Why must amateur performers register in advance?

   (A) To pay a fee.
   (B) To perform for the judges.
   (C) To make sure not everybody plays the same instrument.
   (D) To keep out people who have already had an opportunity to play.

4. When will the Metropolitan Opera perform?

   (A) Early in the series.
   (B) In the middle of the series.
   (C) At the end of the series.
   (D) At several times during the summer.

Questions 5–8 refer to the following passage.

The Importance of Giving

In 1992 the value of all gifts to the University totaled $6,200,340. This income, which was the generous gift of over 4300 individuals and organizations, has contributed to the development of many new activities for the larger university community. There were many sources for these funds. Some came in the form of scholarships for specific programs; others as bequests from estates for some special purpose. And still others came from a variety of sources to be added to the general revenues. All are welcome, and all are appreciated. One activity in particular has benefitted from giving this past year, and that is the President's Endowment, in support of the University's need-based scholarship program in the sciences. A 28 percent increase in funding has made it possible to award many more President scholarships this year than in past years. The Mobry Endowment has also enjoyed an increase in funding, which will help students in the field of the performing arts.

5. Where did the gift money come from?

   (A) An endowment fund.
   (B) A number of sources.
   (C) The government.
   (D) The President.

6. What will the gift money be used for?

   (A) To build a new library.
   (B) To the development of new activities.
   (C) To increase professors' salaries.
   (D) It will all go into general revenues.

7. What program will benefit particularly in the current year?

   (A) The athletic program.
   (B) The Mobry Endowment.
   (C) The President's Endowment.
   (D) The university community.

8. What course of study does the need-based scholarship fund support?

   (A) Sciences.
   (B) Business.
   (C) Performing arts.
   (D) Special studies.

Questions 9–11 refer to the following passage.

Seeds, Seeds, and More Seeds

ORDER YOUR SEED CATALOG *NOW!* This is the largest and best known seed catalog published today, featuring over 280 pages with 1500 color photographs and including more than 5000 varieties. This book tells you everything you want to know about growing anything from seed and tells you where to get the seeds. Bulbs, vegetables, cacti, potted plants, trees, perennials and annuals—you name it. This catalog includes many rare varieties that you will not find anywhere else. Yours is free by writing to Seeds, P.O. Box Y, Yubank, Texas. Allow one month for delivery. If you want first class mailing, send $3. We will credit you with $3 on your first order of $5 or more.

9. Who will order this catalog?

   (A) People who like to grow plants.
   (B) People who sell vegetables.
   (C) People who live on farms.
   (D) People who sell catalogs.

10. What does the catalog contain?

   (A) 1500 pages.
   (B) 5000 kinds of seeds.
   (C) 280 pictures.
   (D) $30 worth of gift coupons.

11. What is the lowest possible price for the catalog?

   (A) Nothing.
   (B) $1.00.
   (C) $3.00.
   (D) $5.00.

Questions 12–15 refer to the following passage.

A Hard-to-play Golf Hole: The 16th at Blue Mountain

In an age when a 275-yard drive no longer causes comment on the golf tour and holes of 420 yards are only par 4, it is uncommon to find a par-4, 350-yard hole that requires great skill to master. The 16th hole at Blue Mountain is just such a hole, and one that presents as many problems for the local golfer as for the visitor. The difficulty of the hole is not apparent, but on attempting it the obstacles seem to magnify themselves. There are sand traps to the right and left, a moat surrounds 80 percent of the green, and there is a wooded area beyond. The green, though spacious, is sloped away, making par extremely difficult. The golfer who plays this one with confidence is either very good or very foolish.

12. According to the passage, which of the following does NOT cause amazement on the golf tour?

   (A) A par-4, 350-yard hole.
   (B) A 275-yard drive.
   (C) A hole that presents problems for local golfers.
   (D) A hole with difficulties that are not apparent.

13. What is said about the obstacles of the 16th hole discussed above?

   (A) They look worse than they are.
   (B) They make the hole impossible to see except from the tee.
   (C) Their difficulty becomes apparent on playing the hole.
   (D) They are hidden from view.

14. What special problem does the green present?

   (A) It is small.
   (B) It has a slope.
   (C) It is surrounded by woods.
   (D) It is across a bridge.

15. How do most golfers play the 16th hole?

   (A) Foolishly.
   (B) Many strokes above par.
   (C) With little confidence.
   (D) The way local golfers play it.

Questions 16–20 refer to the following passage.

The Super Tomato

   The Tomato Growers Association, or TGA, has set out to grow a super tomato at an experimental farm near San Diego, California. Employing biotechnology and developments in DNA research, the TGA has determined to grow the "tomato of tomorrow." By emitting a repellent in the form of an odor, the tomato plant would be able to fight off attacks by insects. It would resist disease and rot, and would maintain its shape when shipped at the bottom of a load of tons of tomatoes.

   The skin would be tough, to permit it to be harvested by machine without damage. Its heavy, thick leaves would prevent it from becoming sunburned. All tomatoes on a plant would ripen at the same time, to prevent the loss from machine harvest of under- or overripened fruit. And it would be just as juicy and tasty as the consumer wants it to be.

   While development of this plant will prove to be extremely expensive, TGA scientists believe that if they can achieve their goal, the industry will eventually benefit from the many advantages and cost savings, particularly from harvest labor expenses and shipping loss, that the new tomato will bring.

16. How do scientists believe the new tomato will fight off insects?

   (A) They will not like the taste.
   (B) The plant will give off a smell.
   (C) They will die upon eating the leaves.
   (D) A new insecticide will be sprayed on the plants.

17. How will the new tomato be shipped?

   (A) In special protective containers.
   (B) In newly-designed trucks.
   (C) In bulk shipments.
   (D) By plane to far away markets.

18. How will the tomato avoid becoming sunburned?

   (A) Farmers will cover the plant with cloth.
   (B) All tomatoes will be grown with artificial light.
   (C) The plant will provide dense leaves.
   (D) The tomato skin will not burn in the sun.

19. How do scientists propose to create this new tomato?

   (A) Through biotechnology.
   (B) By testing many varieties.
   (C) By contracting with university scientists.
   (D) The article does not say.

20. What is a disadvantage to the creation of the new tomato?

   (A) The tomato will not taste very good.
   (B) The research will be very costly.
   (C) Foreign researchers may achieve it first.
   (D) The tomato is not popular in many countries.

Questions 21–24 refer to the following passage.

The Callahan Report

As mentioned in last week's Report, this week's Callahan Report discusses the implications of the 250 deaths and thousands of injuries caused each year as the result of high-speed police chases of criminals or suspected criminals. Police officers cause more deaths with their vehicles each year than they do with their weapons. The curious fact of the matter is that most chases that police engage in are for minor traffic violations, where the person chased becomes afraid and tries to outrun the police. Police are also killed or injured in these incidents, along with innocent bystanders or motorists who happen to be in the path.

It is not surprising, then, that there is a movement to prevent most kinds of police chases from taking place. Beginning in Texas, as the result of an incident in which fourteen people were injured and three killed, thirty-two states now have organized efforts to legislate controls on police chases. Needless to say, police forces oppose this legislation.

21. How often is the Callahan report published?

(A) Every week.
(B) Every month.
(C) Every year.
(D) Not stated.

22. How many deaths result from police chases?

(A) Three per week.
(B) Thirty-two per month.
(C) Two-hundred fifty per year.
(D) Thousands every year.

23. Who are the people police chase in cars?

(A) Known criminals.
(B) Frightened motorists.
(C) Young people.
(D) People who have been drinking.

24. Why did a movement begin to end police chases?

(A) A single incident injured and killed many people.
(B) A mother became angry when her child was killed.
(C) A police department formed a group for their own protection.
(D) Lawmakers decided it was time to end the practice.

Questions 25–27 refer to the following passage.

Excellence in the Classroom

Mathematics can be a cold and unforgiving classroom subject, but as Dr. G. Elwood Kris has shown, it does not have to be. Dr. Kris is one of this year's three winners of the Governor's Award for Excellence. His accomplishment has been that he demonstrates to young learners the practical applications of mathematics, to arouse their interest in learning the subject. Dr. Kris maintains that any teacher can give students rote learning exercises. If teachers want to make mathematics interesting, they must show how math problems are part of the student's real world, thereby giving the student a challenge and an obstacle to overcome.

The Governor's Award for Excellence is awarded to those teachers in schools who do most each year to make their students eager to learn. Besides being a great teacher, Dr. Kris is also known for his mathematical theories, and has published in a number of journals.

25. Why was Dr. Kris given an award?

    (A) For training mathematics teachers.
    (B) For inventing mathematical applications.
    (C) For making students interested in learning math.
    (D) For devising mathematical theories.

26. What is the key to Dr. Kris' approach?

    (A) Making learning useful.
    (B) Increasing the rewards of success.
    (C) Identifying the best students.
    (D) Hard work and much study.

27. Who is eligible for the Governor's Award for Excellence?

    (A) The one educator who makes the greatest contribution to learning.
    (B) Teachers who make their students want to learn.
    (C) Anyone who contributes to society in any way.
    (D) Residents who make significant humanitarian efforts or outstanding contributions to their fields of endeavor.

Questions 28–29 refer to the following passage.

Visit Paradise Cove

For adults who wish to stay at Paradise Cove, weekly rates during the season range from $700 to $800 per person; for children six to twelve, $600 to $650. A special children's program is available for children three through five for $400 each. Children two years old and younger stay free. Rates include three family-style meals daily, and all regularly scheduled Cove activities. Rates are discounted 15 percent from May 21 to June 20 and 10 percent from September 1 to 24.

If you would like to preview Paradise Cove before you make a decision to visit, a video is available free of charge by contacting the Cove at the address or phone number below. The Cove requests that you return the video when you are through with it.

28. Using the rate schedule above, what is the least amount that two adults and three children, ages two, eight and ten, could expect to pay for the week of September 6 to September 13 at Paradise Cove?

    (A) $2340.
    (B) $2600.
    (C) $2610.
    (D) $2880.

29. Which of the following statements about Paradise Cove is true?

    (A) A person receives a free video when registering at the Cove.
    (B) A three-year-old child stays for free.
    (C) The Cove is open from May 21 until September 24.
    (D) The Cove accepts only adult guests.

Questions 30–33 refer to the following passage.

Take Care of Your Heart

High blood pressure indicates the heart is working too hard to pump the blood throughout the body. Eventually, in an attempt to keep the blood flowing, the heart muscle enlarges. Unless blood pressure is lowered, the heart may dilate and stop beating altogether. Ironically, hypertension also causes blood vessels to thicken, further increasing resistance and elevating blood pressure. This process, known as reactive arteriosclerosis, jeopardizes the entire cardiovascular system.

Under these circumstances, everybody is potentially at risk for heart disease, stroke, and kidney failure. When people suffer from hypertension, the effects are subtle and they are usually not aware of it. That is why regular check-ups are necessary. In the event of high blood pressure, doctor and patient must work together to ensure that the patient works to (1) reduce blood pressure quickly and safely, (2) change lifestyles to eliminate stress (3) maintain correct weight, (4) eat the right foods, and (5) ensure proper vitamin intake, by capsule if necessary.

Hypertension, the "silent killer," is the major heart problem facing adults today. Caught in time, it can be treated and its threat can be greatly reduced.

30. What does it mean if a person has high blood pressure?

(A) He needs to change his diet.
(B) He is getting old.
(C) His heart is working too hard.
(D) His heart is weak.

31. According to the passage, what causes "reactive arteriosclerosis?"

(A) Kidney failure.
(B) Hypertension.
(C) An enlarged heart muscle.
(D) High blood pressure.

32. According to the passage, when does a heart muscle enlarge?

(A) When it must strain to pump blood to the entire body.
(B) When a person exercises too much.
(C) When a person does not get proper vitamins.
(D) When it is about to stop beating.

33. Why is hypertension referred to as the "silent killer"?

(A) Because it makes no noise.
(B) Because it is often not recognized by doctors.
(C) Because people do not know they have it.
(D) Because it accompanies other diseases that are more readily recognized.

Questions 34–37 refer to the following passage.

Medication: Sometimes a Hard Pill to Swallow

Patients often devise ingenious methods as aids to remember to take medication. These range from something as simple as placing each day's supply of pills in small containers in a specific order, with the times for taking the medication noted in each container, to something as elaborate as entering color-coded pill-taking schedules in an appointment book. People who use a beeper service for business purposes sometimes ask to be signaled at times they are supposed to take a pill.

Martha Jonas, a professor of nursing at the University of Virginia, teaches her patients to coordinate pill-taking with routine tasks, so it becomes a habit. Other patients need incentives to maintain their drug-taking schedules. One approach is to draw up a contract, with a reward to the patient adhering to the contract to take pills as required. A slight revision of the contract enlists a neighbor or family member who agrees to help a patient remember. Not everybody is suited to the task, however. Studies show that people who are intrusive, critical, or overly anxious will alienate the patient to the degree that he or she will rebel and refuse to take any medication.

34. What is the subject of this passage?

   (A) Discoveries in the field of medicine.
   (B) People avoid their medicine.
   (C) Remembering to take medicines.
   (D) Science and the art of healing.

35. How do some people use their beepers, according to the passage?

   (A) To be reminded.
   (B) To call the doctor.
   (C) To call home for help.
   (D) To learn when it is dinner time.

36. How does Martha Jonas use contracts?

   (A) To ensure patients do not take too many pills.
   (B) To avoid needing to send doctors' bills to patients.
   (C) To encourage people to do as they ought.
   (D) To charge patients for special services.

37. Why are some people not suited to help patients?

   (A) They are too critical and have a negative effect.
   (B) They charge too much for their service.
   (C) They cannot be trusted to do as they should.
   (D) They do not understand the full role of the nurse.

Questions 38–41 refer to the following passage.

Tivoli: Golf with Class

One of the best courses in the Santo Mountains of Arizona is the Tivoli Country Club course, a short distance north of the resort city of Hot Springs. The Tivoli was a busy place in the 1930s, when a casino flourished at the spot where the 18th tee now stands. A small golf course was nearby, but served only as an excuse for the existence of the casino. In 1960, however, the governor of the state banned casino gambling, and the course was expanded. The Club underwent a major redesign and turned the uninspired old 6,497-yard course into a demanding 6,770-yard course.

The Tivoli has a number of condominiums along the 18th fairway for visitors, who are given access to all of the Club's facilities.

38. Where is the Tivoli Country Club located?

   (A) In the town of Tivoli.
   (B) Near the town of Hot Springs.
   (C) Near a casino.
   (D) North of the Santo Mountains.

39. Why was Tivoli such an active place in the 1930s?

   (A) It was the site of hot springs.
   (B) It had a well-known golf course.
   (C) People went there to gamble.
   (D) People liked the mountain air.

40. How was Tivoli Country Club redesigned in the 1960s?

   (A) New professional tennis courts were built.
   (B) A new clubhouse was built.
   (C) A casino was built there.
   (D) The golf course was changed substantially.

41. Who is allowed to stay in apartments along the 18th fairway?

   (A) Visitors to Tivoli.
   (B) Club members.
   (C) Government officials.
   (D) Professional golfers.

Questions 42–44 refer to the following passage.

Program Neighborhood Watch

The next time you get together with your neighbors or local citizens group, talk to them about ways to prevent crime in your neighborhood. When it comes to fighting crime, you are all in it together.

The police may be able to help you start a prevention program or alert you to programs in other neighborhoods or nearby towns. They can also give you direction on the most effective approaches to take to involve citizens in a crime watch program. All that is needed for most of these programs is your eyes, your ears, an interest in crime prevention, and a little of your time.

42. What does the above notice suggest that a person do?

   (A) Call a meeting to discuss local crime.
   (B) Mention the issue of crime at citizens' meetings.
   (C) Ask the police department to organize citizens.
   (D) Visit neighbors to discuss crime in the area.

43. How can the police contribute to a crime watch effort?

   (A) By providing useful information.
   (B) By giving department support to activities.
   (C) By providing radios and weapons to the neighborhood.
   (D) By training people in how to apprehend criminals.

44. What does the notice say a crime watch program requires of citizens?

   (A) A little money.
   (B) Interest.
   (C) An automobile.
   (D) Courage.

Questions 45–48 refer to the following passage.

Nutrition is the Key to Good Health

Nutrition is the single most important key to vigorous long lives, says Charles M. Rosenblut, director of National Center for Nutrition Research (NCNR). "A decline in muscle mass is the most dramatic change to come with age, but this condition gets little press coverage because the condition has no name, unlike osteoporosis and other diseases usually associated with aging," says Rosenblut.

The loss of muscle strength affects mobility, vigor, breathing, and independence. Thus, intensive attention to nutrition and aging is becoming one of the major issues of the day in health research and information dissemination circles. Readers are advised to watch for changes in the required daily amounts of vitamins and minerals for the elderly, to address their special needs. As muscle mass declines with age, energy (calorie requirements) declines, and the elderly eat less and miss more of their required daily amounts of vitamins and minerals. Exercise helps to combat this condition, but nutrition and vitamin absorption among the elderly is to be given greater attention.

45. What is the most important requirement for good health?

   (A) Much exercise.
   (B) The right food.
   (C) Genetic foundation.
   (D) A positive attitude.

46. What is the most significant physical change to come with aging?

   (A) Loss of brain capacity.
   (B) Loss of sex drive.
   (C) Loss of muscle tissue.
   (D) Breakdown of calcium in bones and teeth.

47. What changes will come about in the way the elderly are advised to take care of themselves?

   (A) Their nutrient and vitamin intake needs will be redefined.
   (B) They will be encouraged to spend more time in public.
   (C) They will be asked to exercise more.
   (D) They will be asked to monitor their vital signs.

48. Why do the elderly eat less than the young?

   (A) They do not exercise.
   (B) They have less muscle mass.
   (C) They can no longer taste food.
   (D) They absorb food into their system more slowly.

Questions 49–53 refer to the following passage.

Is Gasohol the Answer?

Over the years gasohol—10 percent ethanol blended with 90 percent gasoline—has become a big political issue. Once considered a cure for oil import problems, today it is also being seen as a partial solution to air pollution concerns.

While these are admirable social goals, for many people there are everyday personal concerns about using gasohol in vehicles engineered to run on only gasoline. Some locales require oxygenated fuels for at least part of the year, to help reduce air pollution. Gasohol is one of two such fuels available. The other, MTBE enriched gasoline, is considered normal gasoline and should cause no problems.

Use of gasohol presents a few problems. First is driveability. Ethanol vaporizes at a temperature lower than gasoline, and in warm weather this could have an effect on how a vehicle responds to the fuel. Next is water in fuel. Unlike gasoline, ethanol mixes with water and, if not properly stored, in cold climates can become contaminated in ways that gasoline cannot. Also, ethanol is a solvent that will prevent deposits from forming in a fuel system, but may plug fuel filter systems. Worse than that, however, is that it corrodes rubber, and could ruin fuel lines. These are only a few of the problems associated with ethanol, one of the ingredients of gasohol, which should be kept in mind when driving a gasohol-fueled vehicle.

49. Why do some places require special fuels?

   (A) To reduce dependence on foreign oil.
   (B) To reduce the number of accidents.
   (C) To reduce air pollution.
   (D) To reduce noise pollution.

50. How is gasohol different from MTBE enriched fuel?

   (A) MTBE has higher ethanol content.
   (B) Gasohol is more available than MTBE.
   (C) MTBE is just like gasoline.
   (D) Gasohol is a lot less expensive.

51. How does the article define "driveability"?

   (A) How fast a vehicle can go.
   (B) How readily available fuel is.
   (C) How a vehicle responds to its fuel.
   (D) How often a vehicle refuses to start.

52. What property does ethanol have that gasoline does not?

   (A) It can be mixed with water.
   (B) It fires at a low temperature.
   (C) It has no odor to it.
   (D) It evaporates very slowly.

53. Which of the following is NOT given as a negative aspect of ethanol?

   (A) It will damage rubber fuel lines.
   (B) It will become contaminated if precautions are not taken.
   (C) It will reduce effectiveness of fuel filters.
   (D) It will reduce the life of an engine.

Questions 54–58 refer to the following passage.

Inventory May be Eating your Profits

It is only when a company knows its cash-flow patterns that it can make the right cash decisions in all of its areas. Accounts payable, sales, receivables, and production are all areas that will yield significant benefits to cash flow. But the area where greatest strides can be made is inventory management. For many companies, inventory is the major investment. Total assets for the average manufacturer are about 30 percent inventory. For wholesalers and retailers, the figure goes up to 60 percent. And these are assets that involve risk in that they can become damaged in storage, they can become obsolete, and they cost money to hold.

Most companies review their inventories once a year. By checking inventory between those reviews, you can spot ahead of time those points where too large an inventory is cutting into cash flow, and action can be taken. Here are some other cash saving tips:

❏ Check for your most expensive inventory items. Monitor their traffic closely.

❏ Ask employees how to move the slow-moving items.

❏ Look for employees in production areas who are hoarding parts. Get them back in the parts room.

❏ Check production schedules against orders.

Most of all, make sure that all employees are aware of the cost of inventories, and that they are on the lookout to effect savings.

54. What is necessary for making the right cash decisions?

(A) Knowing cash-flow patterns within the company.
(B) Maintaining high inventories of fast-moving items.
(C) Controlling inventories.
(D) Working closely with all department heads.

55. Why is it said that inventories involve risk?

(A) They may not sell well.
(B) They can be stolen.
(C) They may become outdated.
(D) By the time they sell, they may be priced too low.

56. How does this article say managers anticipate inventory problems?

(A) By putting the best people to manage inventories.
(B) By making checks between annual reviews.
(C) By computerizing the inventory system.
(D) By removing the most expensive items.

57. What is an employee problem that the author says affects cash flow?

(A) Production employees hold onto spare parts to have replacements.
(B) Employee theft is difficult to control.
(C) Employees may arrive late or leave early, reducing production.
(D) Employees do not maintain equipment properly.

58. What is the most important factor in controlling inventories?

(A) Good records.
(B) Employee awareness.
(C) Alert managers.
(D) Company policy.

Questions 59–62 refer to the following passage.

The Convenient Garden

The traditional place for vegetable gardening is in a large rectangular plot near the back of a property. This form evolved for practical reasons. A rectangle is easily fenced, cultivated, and irrigated. Also, weeds can grow, late tomato vines can hang on the stakes, and corn stalks can turn brown, all out of view of the public. But there are disadvantages, too. Far from the house also means it is difficult to get to and the distant garden does not call for attention the way a garden close to the house often does.

The logical place for a vegetable garden is right outside the kitchen door. This makes it easier to reach and encourages use of garden products. It also means, however, that the kitchen view is not always very pleasant, especially when the gardener is not a very tidy person. But that need not be the case, and the advantages of having the garden close by are worth putting extra effort into it to make it as beautiful a place as it is practical. With planning, flowers can be planted, as well as fruit trees, hedges, and other formal and informal plants, to achieve a visually agreeable effect.

59. According to the passage, what has long been considered the proper place for a vegetable garden?

   (A) On the sunny side of a property.
   (B) Near the rear of a property.
   (C) Close to the building where tools are kept.
   (D) Behind a beautifying hedge.

60. What was the main advantage of the traditional location?

   (A) The garden could not be seen.
   (B) Water was readily available.
   (C) It was easier to work on it.
   (D) It gave excellent results.

61. What is the best place for a vegetable garden?

   (A) Near the front gate.
   (B) Away from shade trees.
   (C) Close to the kitchen door.
   (D) The same place as in previous years.

62. What is required to make a garden pleasant to view?

   (A) Colorful vegetables.
   (B) New kinds of seeds.
   (C) A few special tools.
   (D) Planning in advance.

Questions 63–66 refer to the following passage.

How Diet Affects Your Golf Game

While most people are careful to consider what they eat, few golfers think that when they eat can have much of an impact on their score. The time of day when a golfer is to play should determine when he will eat. For instance, if he is to tee off at 1:00 P.M., he should eat at around 11:30 A.M., and no later than noon. A meal of 550 calories is ideal, according to nutritionists, and will see a golfer through a three and one half or four hour round. "Golf is a low-energy sport, yet it demands concentration," says Edith Guerney, a sports nutritionist working at the University of Arizona sports center. "You need a steady flow of energy to the brain." A golfer should not have more than 550 calories or fewer than 400. Getting hungry half way through a round will affect concentration and energy levels. A candy bar and a sandwich both have about 300 calories, but they have different nutrient qualities—"Take the sandwich and your game will be better," advises Guerney. Caffeine intake also should be controlled. In hot weather it can cause dehydration and lead to overheating, and even to heat stroke. If golfers are serious about their game, they should watch not only what they eat, but when they eat it.

63. When should a golfer eat?

   (A) Shortly before beginning play.
   (B) At least an hour before beginning play.
   (C) During first half of play, but not during second half.
   (D) Within four hours of beginning play.

64. Why do nutritionists say a golfer should take 550 calories for play?

   (A) Because golf is a low-energy, high concentration sport.
   (B) Because golfers rarely have enough calories when they begin play.
   (C) Because that is how many calories are in a sandwich and a candy bar.
   (D) Because that is an average lunch calorie count.

65. What is as important as calories to a golfer?

   (A) Vitamins.
   (B) Balanced diet.
   (C) Milk products.
   (D) Nutrients.

66. What is a disadvantage of caffeine for the golfer?

   (A) It causes the heart to pump faster.
   (B) It reduces reaction time.
   (C) It causes dehydration.
   (D) It negatively affects vision.

Questions 67–70 refer to the following passage.

General Strike in Cromatia

The nation of Cromatia had its first general strike in thirty years last Tuesday, to protest the President's recently announced austerity policies. Readers will recall that it was these policies that prompted the bloodiest riots in the country's democratic history. The main trade union group, the half-million member Trade Worker Union (TWU), called a dawn-to-dusk strike to protest the presidential decree that raised prices for gasoline, transportation, food, and electricity. The TWU seeks to lift price controls and liberalize the heavily centralized economy, a position that is at odds not only with the administration but with the World Bank as well.

"We are holding this strike because during his first one-hundred days in office President Vroka has done nothing for the labor movement, the workers, or the middle class," said the union spokesman, Mario Pinalta. Analysts also maintain that the strike is to emphasize that the government can no longer count on union support, which was so important for Vroka's successful bid for the presidency last fall.

67. Why did the people of Cromatia riot?

   (A) To protest union activity.
   (B) To protest price controls.
   (C) To protest a presidential decree.
   (D) To protest recent elections.

68. What does the TWU seek to achieve?

   (A) Lift price controls.
   (B) President Vroka's resignation.
   (C) A return to democracy.
   (D) An end to bloody riots.

69. What is the World Bank position on the direction of Cromatia?

   (A) Greater centralization is needed.
   (B) The economy requires price controls.
   (C) The government must listen to the TWU.
   (D) The government must stop the riots.

70. What does the general strike demonstrate?

   (A) That the TWU controls the country.
   (B) That the political left controls the TWU.
   (C) That the government's policies have failed.
   (D) That the government is not supported by the TWU.

Questions 71–73 refer to the following passage.

The Best Bargain in Town

Most people are spoiled when it comes to household water supplies. For many years people have paid such a low price for the liquid that flows from the tap that they never worried about how much they were wasting. Now, however, the days of inexpensive water are over, and people are having to take notice.

One recent survey of municipalities showed that water rates have increased an average of 10 percent in the past two years, and as much as 37 percent in some large cities. Before long, some homeowners may be paying more for the water they use each year than they do for their property taxes. It is in the interest of everybody to learn the reasons for this phenomenal increase and to take steps to diminish use.

71. What is the view most people have with regard to water use?

(A) They do not think about it.
(B) They are angry with rising prices.
(C) They are conserving water as much as possible.
(D) They think there is nothing that can be done about it.

72. What is happening to the price of water?

(A) While in many places it is going up, generally the price is dropping.
(B) It is going up gradually everywhere.
(C) It appears to be going up, but considering inflation, it is remaining stable.
(D) It is going up all over, in some places quite rapidly.

73. With what does the article compare some water prices?

(A) The price of air.
(B) The price of property taxes.
(C) The price of houses.
(D) The price of water supplies.

Questions 74–76 refer to the following passage.

Research into Plant Closings

When a company goes out of business, reaction among employees will range from anger with managers to sadness and apprehension about the future. Employers fear the response and what they expect to become a drop in productivity, and therefore delay informing employees about plant closings until the latest possible moment. Recent legislation that requires sixty-day notice of a plant closing was attacked as being unreasonable, opponents thinking that workers would become lazy and sabotage the operation.

A just-concluded study has shown, however, that the period between the announcement of a plant closing and the closing itself can be a time of improved productivity. A survey including a diverse sample of eight companies showed that the tense period during which workers both ran a company and prepared to close it down was one when worker efforts did not diminish, but in fact improved, among employees at all levels, senior and junior.

74. Why do employers NOT want to inform employees of a plant closing?

(A) They think workers will go out on strike.
(B) They think workers will harm them physically.
(C) They do not like to give people bad news.
(D) They think workers will work less.

75. What law has been passed to deal with the problem of plant closings?

(A) Employees must be informed two months in advance.
(B) Nobody is allowed to enter a plant once it closes.
(C) Government must approve plant closings before they can take place.
(D) If a plant closes, jobs must be found for employees.

76. What was learned in a recent study?

(A) Employees leaving a closed plant will take any work, just to have a job.
(B) Employees of a plant about to close will work harder than before.
(C) In 90 percent of the cases, the main reason plants close is employees demand too much of management.
(D) Employees treat a plant closing like the death of a close friend and become very depressed.

Questions 77–80 refer to the following passage.

Alzheimer's Origins

New research points to a finding that children who are born to older parents are more likely than children born to younger parents to develop Alzheimer's disease, a degeneration of brain tissue causing memory loss, senility, and disorientation in old age. A team of researchers studied 103 Alzheimer's patients, all of whom were over 82 years of age. At the time of the patients' birth, the average age of their fathers was 32.5 years. This is nearly six years older than the average age of fathers of a comparison group of healthy elderly people with similar social backgrounds. Mothers of the Alzheimer's patients averaged 26.8 years when the children were born, several years older than mothers of the healthy group.

In a companion study, both parents of Alzheimer's patients were also substantially older, by an average of two to four years, than both parents of another comparison group of sixty-seven patients who were suffering from a different type of memory loss.

Given the demographics of modern society, this is particularly important research. People today are waiting longer to have children, and it is expected that these findings will lead to new initiatives to better understand Alzheimer's disease and how to avoid it.

77. What causes Alzheimer symptoms in patients?

(A) Thickness of skull.
(B) Loss of vitality of brain tissue.
(C) Dehydration of brain cavity.
(D) Malformation of inner ear.

78. What is the major new understanding to result from this study?

(A) All elderly people exhibit some of the signs of Alzheimer's disease.
(B) People over 82 are more likely to get Alzheimer's than people under 82.
(C) Older parents are more likely than younger parents to have children who will get Alzheimer's disease.
(D) Possibility of Alzheimer's is lower in children whose parents are about the same age.

79. What besides age of parents was considered important and controlled for in this study?

(A) Town or region of residence.
(B) Living environment.
(C) Health of brothers and sisters.
(D) Social background.

80. Why is this research said to be important?

(A) Because younger people are starting to come down with Alzheimer's.
(B) Because the age at which people have children is rising.
(C) Because new types of Alzheimer's are being discovered, and we do not even understand the old types.
(D) Because Alzheimer's patients are healthy otherwise, live long, and are expensive to take care of.

Questions 81–83 refer to the following passage.

Are Acquisitions for You?

With profitable growth becoming more and more problematic for all businesses, small businesses selling into mature markets are finding it particularly difficult to go forward. For some time, larger companies have acquired other businesses in an effort to expand rapidly. With good planning, small businesses can do the same. Acquisitions can bring small businesses increased sales, new products and technologies, access to new markets, and a great many other benefits in less time, cheaper, and with less effort than it would take to create them.

This approach is not without its risks, however, and while a mistake for a large company could mean reduced income for the year, for a small company it could mean a loss of the company itself. The key to the success of takeovers, for all companies, is in the quality of the target company, the fit it makes in the new parent company, and the terms of the financing.

81. What does this passage discuss?

(A) How to avoid being taken over by a larger company.
(B) How to obtain profitable corporate growth.
(C) How to pay for a takeover using other people's money.
(D) How to sell a small business for a high price.

82. What does the passage say is a risk of a takeover for a large company?

(A) Employee morale and production go down.
(B) Temporary decline in income.
(C) Credit becomes more difficult.
(D) The company may be lost to a smaller company.

83. Which of the following is NOT listed as determining the success of a takeover?

(A) Source and availability of money.
(B) The size of the takeover company.
(C) How good the target company is.
(D) How the target and takeover companies work together.

Questions 84–86 refer to the following table.

U.S. Trade
With Eastern Europe
(in millions of U.S.$)
Total U.S. Exports

	1991	1990
Albania	7.2	3.3
Bulgaria	127.2	88.6
Czechoslovakia	55.1	47.2
East Germany	109.2	53.9
Hungary	77.5	95.3
Poland	303.7	238.8
Romania	202.4	192.6

Total U.S. Imports

	1991	1990
Albania	2.5	2.4
Bulgaria	31.5	47.0
Czechoslovakia	95.9	86.1
East Germany	126.7	96.2
Hungary	321.3	305.5
Poland	417.1	329.7
Romania	741.2	781.6

84. Which country's imports from the U.S. were smaller in 1991 than in 1990?

(A) Albania.
(B) Romania.
(C) Hungary.
(D) Bulgaria.

85. Which of the following countries imported more from the U.S. in 1991 than they exported to the U.S.?

(A) Romania.
(B) Poland.
(C) Czechoslovakia.
(D) Bulgaria.

86. Which of the following countries exported to the U.S. more than any of the others in 1990?

(A) Romania.
(B) Poland.
(C) East Germany.
(D) Hungary.

Questions 87–90 refer to the following passage.

Good News for Bicycle Racers

In an effort to bring together amateur and professional racing activities, the National Cycling Federation (NCF) and the Federated Professional Cycling Association (FPCA) have agreed to stop the competition that has kept their memberships apart in recent years. A new National Cycle Racing Commission (NCRC) will handle matters that concern both amateur and professional racing, oversee national professional racing, and represent the nation's cyclists at the UCI Congress, the annual international meeting of national cycling federations.

The Commission is made up of NCF President Dick Di Pietro and two NCF board members, as well as two representatives elected from the FPCA. The executive directors of both NCF and FPCA are both *ex-officio* members of the Commission. The advantage of having strong representation from FPCA on the Commission is that sponsorship of all cycling activities can be handled through one office.

And finally, the greatest advantage of the NCRC is that the two major cycling organizations in the country will no longer argue over dates, regulations, and locations for racing events. In the past, events have been cancelled or postponed because of lack of agreement, and many that have been run have not been well run, for the same reason. Now the difference between amateur and professional will be clear, activities will be sanctioned by both associations, and the cyclists, their sponsors, and the public will benefit.

87. What has happened that is important for cyclists?

(A) NCF and FPCA have merged to become the NCRC.
(B) NCF has decided to disband to avoid further disputes with the FPCA.
(C) FPCA has decided to disband to avoid further disputes with the NCF.
(D) NCF and FPCA have created the NCRC to deal with matters of interest to both.

88. What is a major advantage of involvement of the FPCA on the NCRC?

(A) Corporate sponsors no longer need to deal directly with the FPCA and the NCF.
(B) The FPCA has always controlled racing, and will continue to do so through the NCRC.
(C) It will make it easier for NCF members to join the FPCA.
(D) The UCI Congress refused to recognize the NCRC without the FPCA involvement.

89. Who makes up the board of the NCRC?

(A) Former NCF officers.
(B) Former FPCA board members.
(C) UCI Congress members.
(D) A variety of NCF and FPCA officials.

90. What problem will be overcome by the NCRC?

(A) Cyclists will know when events will take place.
(B) Racing events will be separate from promotional and hobby events.
(C) There will be no more arguments concerning race dates and places.
(D) Sponsors will not have to decide who to support.

Questions 91–95 refer to the following communication.

Olympia Shoes, Inc.
200 La Brea Avenue
Los Angeles, CA 91455

15 October, 19 – –

Long Manufacturing Co.
P.O. Box 2212A
Chonabat, Thailand

Dear Sirs:

Per our telephone conversation, today's date, and effective immediately, please cancel our recent order for monthly deliveries of rubber shoes. We have received two shipments for which we will pay, and by our agreed-upon schedule you will receive this letter before you make the third shipment. We are sending today a telex message to this same effect.

We regret having to take this step, particularly after you have been so cooperative with regard to both price and terms of payment. It is made necessary, however, by our current financial situation, which is forcing us to discontinue some of our product lines before our debt becomes too great. We believe that by this measure, with you as well as with some of our other suppliers, we will be able to avoid difficulties that have appeared on our horizon.

Thank you for your understanding. Should our situation improve, we will place another order with you. We trust that we are remaining on your list of customers qualifying for liberal credit terms.

Sincerely,

John P. Moreno
John P. Moreno

91. How is Long Manufacturing being notified of this development?

(A) By letter only.
(B) By letter and telex only.
(C) By letter, telex and telephone only.
(D) By letter, telex, telephone, and fax transmission.

92. What is the business of Olympia?

(A) A footwear wholesaler.
(B) A shoe retailer.
(C) A rubber company.
(D) A tire company.

93. What is the purpose of this letter?

(A) To ask permission to return goods to the seller.
(B) To complain about the quality of goods received.
(C) To cancel an order placed earlier.
(D) To postpone delivery of an order.

94. Why is this letter necessary?

(A) Because of bad quality.
(B) Because of money problems.
(C) Because of late shipments.
(D) Because of poor sales.

95. What does the writer ask of Olympia?

(A) Other credit terms.
(B) A letter of credit.
(C) Immediate payment.
(D) Continued good credit.

Questions 96–98 refer to the following passage.

Aquaculture in the Philippines

In the Philippines, an archipelago of over 7000 islands, many investors have been taking a close look at aquaculture, or the breeding or cultivation of animals or plants in confined bodies of water. Because of the high protein content of fish and a vastly undersupplied market, profits are plentiful in this booming industry.

By the mid 1980s, aquaculture harvesting in Asia reached over five million tons of fish annually, which is nearly 75 percent of the world aquaculture output and over 15 percent of all the fish produced in the region. World demand for fish and seafood in the year 2000 will be five times what it was in 1950. Couple the growing demand with the decline in harvests from the sea, and aquaculture becomes a very attractive investment.

96. Why is aquaculture a good investment?

(A) Fish is cheaper than meat.
(B) Fish farms do not cost a lot to establish.
(C) There is a big market for fish.
(D) More kilos of fish than animals can be raised on a hectare of land.

97. Which of the following statements is made about fish?

(A) Fish are high in protein.
(B) Fish do not get sick like cattle.
(C) Fish are easy to move to market.
(D) Fish reproduce very rapidly.

98. Which of the following points to aquaculture as a good investment?

(A) Many people are investing in it.
(B) The sea produces fewer fish every year.
(C) The Philippine government supports aquaculture.
(D) Aquaculture supplies 75 percent of the world's fish.

Questions 99–101 refer to the following article.

Arson Suspected at Lincoln High

Police think two students started a fire at the Lincoln High School on Friday night. They drove away in a Ford station wagon, but police have two of the numbers from the license plate—18. The school janitor said the two young men were both around sixteen years of age. One had curly light brown hair and the other had straight blond hair. Anyone with further information should call Detective Robert Holmes at 555-2948.

99. Why are two boys being sought?

(A) To be given a reward.
(B) Because they robbed someone.
(C) To be asked some questions.
(D) They set fire to a school.

100. How old are the boys who are being sought?

(A) Ten or twelve.
(B) Thirteen or fourteen.
(C) Fifteen or sixteen.
(D) Seventeen or eighteen.

101. What color hair do the boys have?

(A) One dark, the other light.
(B) Both dark.
(C) Both light.
(D) It is not known.

Questions 102–104 refer to the following passage.

Carlos Adams Performs Tonight

The Office for the Arts of the City Council is proud to present saxophonist Carlos Adams, performing with the Midnight Jazz band, and special guest artists Charles Brown, Everett Miller, Gimmie Guarano, and Dave Simpson tonight at 8:00 P.M. in Shelly Theater. The concert is a culmination of "A Salute to Carlos Adams," a series of events honoring this extraordinarily versatile jazz artist. Tickets are $4 for students and $6 for nonstudents and are available at the College Center Ticket Office and through ConcertCharge at 555-1111.

Revered as a peerless alto saxophonist whose elegance of tone shaped the sound and style of the instrument for generations of musicians, Carlos Adams is also known as an innovative composer/arranger, bandleader, and trumpeter. Last December he received a Lifetime Achievement Grammy Award from the National Academy of Recording Arts and Sciences for his "contribution of outstanding artistic significance."

102. Why is Carlos Adams called "an extraordinarily versatile jazz artist?"

   (A) Because he has excelled in playing many different jazz styles over a long period of time.
   (B) Because of his influence on later jazz musicians.
   (C) Because he is accomplished in many different areas of jazz music.
   (D) Because he plays a number of jazz instruments.

103. Who will perform at the evening's concert?

   (A) ConcertCharge and Carlos Adams.
   (B) Midnight Jazz Band, Carlos Adams, and others.
   (C) Only the Midnight Jazz Band and Carlos Adams.
   (D) Carlos Adams, alone.

104. Referring to the above article, which of the following statements can be made about Carlos Adams?

   (A) His style is the definition of alto saxophone jazz playing.
   (B) His uniqueness is in that his compositions have been adapted to be performed by all jazz instruments.
   (C) His last performance will not be his best, but it will be long remembered.
   (D) By his example, he has opened the eyes of many students of music to the qualities of jazz.

Questions 105–106 refer to the following communication.

```
3376 RF
86770 MILIM
10/1414:25
CBZNTP.100

S. ROBINSON

RE UR TLX 10/12 NO RECORD OF SAID ITEM IN OUR
CATALOG WHERE DID U HEAR OF SUCH? DON'T HAVE.
CAN'T SHIP. CD SEND SUBSTITUTE IF REQUESTED.

CATALOG FOLLOWS
PLS REPLY IF OTHER ITEM DESIRED

E EFFELMAN
```

105. The above telex is in reply to what communication?

(A) A letter requesting a catalog.
(B) A fax transmission requesting certain documents.
(C) A telex ordering some item.
(D) A telephone request for information.

106. What is being sent?

(A) A catalog.
(B) A substitute item.
(C) A revised document.
(D) A written reply.

Questions 107–108 refer to the following passage.

Compact Disc Club

Sign up today to join the Compact Disc Club, and we will send you any three CDs chosen by you from our up-to-date subscriber list of 1500 CDs, which you may listen to during a ten-day trial period. At the end of the ten days, you may return them with no further obligation—or keep them and send just three pounds fifty pence to enroll your membership in the Club. We will mail you monthly catalogues from which you need to purchase only three more CDs at the regular price, during the next two years, as a CD Club member.

107. What is the purchase requirement for CD Club members?

(A) Six CDs at full price.
(B) Three CDs at full price.
(C) Three CDs at half price.
(D) There is no requirement.

108. What does the three pounds fifty pence membership fee cover?

(A) The cost of three CDs and monthly catalogues.
(B) The cost of shipping and handling six CDs of the person's choice.
(C) The cost of three CDs sent for a ten-day period.
(D) The cost of annual membership.

Questions 109–112 refer to the following letter.

358 High Street, Apt.6
El Camino, CA

September 12, 19 – –

Benco Camera Corporation
92 Diamond Street
Ellsworth, NJ

Dear Sir or Madam:

A year ago I bought a Benco camera secondhand. It's an SJ 605 model and I think it's about ten years old. I don't know what the problem is, but the automatic light meter doesn't seem to operate, and my pictures are coming out too dark. I checked the batteries and they are still good. I took the camera to several repair shops, but they said they couldn't repair it because the model is too old, and they don't have any parts for it.

Do you have parts in stock for this model? If so, could I send you the camera for repairs? How much would the repairs cost? I'm going to buy your new SJ 1005 model soon, but I would still like to fix this old one.

Thank you very much.

Sincerely,
Eva Kovacs
Eva Kovacs

109. What is wrong with the camera?

(A) The flash is broken.
(B) The light meter does not work.
(C) Acid from the batteries has ruined it.
(D) Some parts are missing.

110. How old does Eva say the camera is?

(A) It is new.
(B) Five years.
(C) Ten years.
(D) She has no idea.

111. Where is the Benco Camera Corporation?

(A) In New Jersey.
(B) In California.
(C) In New York.
(D) In New Mexico.

112. What does Eva want?

(A) A new camera in exchange.
(B) A refund.
(C) Free repairs.
(D) To ask about repairs.

EXEL ENGINEERING COMPANY
333 Valley Boulevard
Bering City, WA

January 14, 19 – –

Ms. Margaret F. Thompson
4561 Merkel Street
Tacoma, WA

Dear Ms. Thompson:

After careful consideration, I am pleased to offer you the position of director of our Data Processing Division, under the terms we discussed at our meeting. I would appreciate it if you could notify us at your earliest convenience whether you accept this offer. If you do accept, please plan to report to Jack Douglas, our personnel manager, at 9:00 A.M., on Monday, January 30.

I look forward to working with you and trust our association will be a long and mutually beneficial one.

Sincerely,
Charles Jamison
Charles Jamison
General Manager

113. What is the purpose of this letter?

   (A) To make an appointment with a client.
   (B) To provide information that was requested.
   (C) To offer a job to an applicant.
   (D) To release an employee from employment against her will.

114. What must Ms. Thompson decide?

   (A) To visit Exel Engineering.
   (B) Terms that she would find acceptable.
   (C) What to tell Mr. Jamison.
   (D) Which materials to send.

115. What must Ms. Thompson do on January 30?

   (A) Make a delivery.
   (B) Phone Mr. Jamison.
   (C) Return a form to Exel.
   (D) Visit Mr. Douglas.

Questions 116-117 refer to the following passage.

The Carter-Milder Law Scholarships

The Carter-Milder Scholarships are awarded to entering students on the basis of merit by the Oceola University School of Law, located in the City of Oceola. The scholarship covers two-thirds of tuition. Each Carter-Milder scholar pursues a program of involvement outside the classroom to develop an awareness of the public service potential of a career in law. The deadline for applications is December 2. Further information is available from the Carter-Milder Scholarship Committee, Oceola University School of Law.

116. Who awards the Carter-Milder Scholarships?

(A) The City of Oceola.
(B) The Oceola University School of Law student body.
(C) The Oceola University School of Law.
(D) Mr. Carter-Milder and his Scholarship Committee.

117. What is the designated purpose of the scholarship program?

(A) To encourage more students to apply to study law at Oceola University.
(B) To reduce the price of tuition for poor students.
(C) To encourage law students to think about careers that serve the public.
(D) To encourage future lawyers to accept cases of poor clients for little or no fee.

Questions 118–119 refer to the following notice.

Notice to traveler:

You have purchased a non-refundable, non-transferable plane ticket good for one round-trip up to one year from the date of purchase. If any scheduling changes should be made on the coupon after reservations have been made and prior to flight, the holder will be subject to a 25 percent penalty surcharge on the original purchase price. Should any changes be made once flight has actually begun, there will be a 50 percent penalty surcharge on the remaining portion.

118. Which of the following statements is true?

(A) Penalties for scheduling changes prior to flight are more severe than those for changes made after one-way flight.
(B) Penalties for scheduling changes after one-way flight are more severe than for those made prior to flight.
(C) The purchased ticket is valid any time.
(D) There are no penalties assigned for scheduling changes, but reservations cannot be guaranteed.

119. What does "non-refundable, non-transferable" mean?

(A) The ticket can be used by anyone, but if unused it will not be bought back by the airline.
(B) The ticket cannot be used by another person, but if unused may be sold back to the airline at half price.
(C) If unused, the ticket will be bought back by the airline at half price, but may be used by anyone.
(D) Even if unused, the airline will not buy back the ticket and it may be used only by the person to whom it was sold.

Questions 120–121 refer to the following notice.

> **Notice to Authors:**
>
> For articles to be considered for our monthly publication they must be submitted no later than the first day of the month prior to the month of the event. For example, items to be included in the May issue of World must reach our editors by April 1.
>
> Thank you
> Managing Editor

120. How often is the publication issued?

    (A) Once every two weeks.
    (B) Once each month.
    (C) Once every two months.
    (D) Four times each year.

121. If an item is submitted for publication on November 5, when is the earliest it could be published?

    (A) November.
    (B) December.
    (C) January.
    (D) February.

Questions 122–124 refer to the following memorandum.

> ## A MEMORANDUM
>
> **TO:**   Staff
>   Receiving Department
> **FROM:** Bill Barth
>
> Please note that the 10/23 shipment (Invoice #5676) from Acme Paper was not in order. Some of the invoiced goods were not received, some of the supplied goods were not requested, and other goods were not even invoiced. Furthermore, certain of the items we requested in our purchase order were not shipped. Please see to it that the goods not ordered are returned, an amended invoice is received, and that the missing requested goods are shipped immediately.
>
> This is not the first time we have had a problem with Acme. In the future, place no further orders with Acme. We will go to their competitors and be assured that these mix-ups do not occur again.

122. What does the manager want Acme Paper to do?

    (A) Take back the shipment and begin again.
    (B) Provide assurances that mix-ups will not occur.
    (C) Send the remainder of the shipment as requested on a purchase order.
    (D) Send a representative to clear up the problem.

123. What should the Supply Department do with goods that were received but not ordered?

    (A) Hold them for Acme to pickup.
    (B) Put them in stock.
    (C) Return them for credit.
    (D) Send them back to Acme.

124. What can be said about the quality of service from Acme generally?

    (A) It is usually quite good.
    (B) Acme is not a reliable shipper.
    (C) There has never been a problem with Acme before.
    (D) Acme is a new company, and has no record.

Questions 125–126 refer to the following invitation.

Visit the Special Collections at the Crowell Museum

Among the Crowell Museum's collections is the world-famous glass flower exhibit, featuring over one hundred delicate hand-blown replicas of actual floral species. The glass flower display was donated by a benefactor who was the force behind the museum in its early years, the nephew of the enigmatic Elberth Crowell, founder of the Museum. The collection is part of the Museum's permanent display of collections. It is a curious fact that although Elberth Crowell founded the museum when only forty-three, he never visited it or inquired as to the collections it housed. The collection is housed in the West Gallery and may be visited weekdays from 9:00 A.M. to 5:00 P.M.

125. Which of the Museum's special collections is discussed?

(A) Early flower paintings.
(B) Natural flower species.
(C) Delicate glass flowers.
(D) Antique flower vases.

126. Which of the following statements may be made about Elberth Crowell?

(A) He was always pleased with the way the museum exhibited his collections.
(B) He complained at meetings that the museum was costing him too much money.
(C) He and his nephew escorted important people through the museum.
(D) He never entered the museum and apparently took no interest in it.

Questions 127–129 refer to the following letter.

June 10, 19 – –

Dear Member:

   Dr. Daniel Bronstein, a world authority on the works of John Steinbeck, will give a lecture with a slide show. Dr. Bronstein is currently the director of the Harrison Institute, Chicago. The lecture, entitled "The Life and Times of John Steinbeck," will take place Thursday, June 20, at 7:00 P.M. in the Blue Room of the Downtown Culture Center.

   A reception will follow. This lecture is being given under the auspices of the Friends of American Literature Association, and will be in lieu of our monthly meeting.

Yours,
Clara Balton
Clara Balton
Secretary to the Association

127. What is the purpose of this letter?

    (A) To invite the public to a lecture.
    (B) To advise Dr. Bronstein's friends that he is speaking.
    (C) To inform people of Dr. Bronstein's area of expertise.
    (D) To invite Association members to a lecture.

128. Who is sponsoring Dr. Bronstein's visit?

    (A) The Downtown Culture Center.
    (B) Ms. Clara Balton.
    (C) The Friends of American Literature Association.
    (D) The Harrison Institute.

129. What does the lecture take the place of?

    (A) Another lecture, which was canceled.
    (B) A meeting of the Association.
    (C) A monthly string quartet recital.
    (D) A presentation on John Steinbeck.

Questions 130–132 refer to the following passage.

Dragon Bones and the Margese

The cave of Gariwanda, where the remains of Chino Man have been found, is in a limestone formation called Dragon Bone Hill. Before it became known as a site of early man, it had long been a favorite haunt of Margese dragon-bone collectors. Dragons had an important place in traditional Margese culture and their bones, actually the fossils of a variety of animals, were thought to have great medicinal properties. Indeed, it was the dragon-bone collectors who found the first evidence of Chino Man, although the significance of the find was not recognized for some 150 years, when in 1948 a team of French anthropologists investigated the dragon-bone myth.

130. Who were the first to encounter the remains of Chino Man?

    (A) People from Gariwanda.
    (B) Dragon-bone collectors.
    (C) Margese medicine men.
    (D) French anthropologists.

131. Why is the excavated limestone region referred to as Dragon-Bone Hill?

    (A) The dragon-bone collectors did not realize the importance of their find.
    (B) Dragon-bone collectors had frequented the area for a long time prior to the discovery of human remains.
    (C) Dragon-bones found there were thought to possess great medicinal value and were highly prized.
    (D) The dragon-bone collectors claimed it as their own and refused to let others near it for many years.

132. According to the article, how is the existence of "dragon bones" explained?

    (A) A prehistoric animal from the region was locally thought to have been a dragon.
    (B) Early collectors mistook the bones of Chino Man for those of dragons.
    (C) The bones were not really those of dragons but preserved bones of other animals.
    (D) Dragons have traditionally held an important position in the Margese culture.

Questions 133–135 refer to the following résumé.

Résumé

KWON, Anne Martha

Education:	Girls' High School	1959–1962
	Woman's University, B.A. in Law	1962–1966
	Woman's University, M.A. in Psychology	1985–1988

Study and Training:

Observation tour of legal and social services in U.S.	9/79-10/79
Observation tour of legal and social services in Sri Lanka	2/83-3/83
Participation in Christian Counseling Educational Program, Alor Star, Malaysia	7/84-8/84

Work Experience:

| Woman's University, Faculty Lecturer in Law | 12/65-9/70 |
| Legal Aid Center, Counselor | 10/80-6/87 |

133. According to the résumé, what was Ms. Kwon's longest work experience?

(A) Observation of legal and social services in the U.S. and Sri Lanka.
(B) Participation in an educational program sponsored by the Christian Counseling Center in Alor Star.
(C) Faculty member in the Law Department at Woman's University.
(D) Counselor at the Legal Aid Center.

134. How many total years of formal university education did Ms. Kwon receive?

(A) Five years.
(B) Seven years.
(C) Nine years.
(D) Ten years.

135. Which of the following describes Ms. Kwon's field of expertise?

(A) Christian counseling.
(B) Women's psychology.
(C) Law and psychology.
(D) Social service agency funding.

Questions 136–138 refer to the following passage.

Differing Views on Cosmetic Surgery

Dr. Alfred Delmonico of the Cosmetic Surgery Center in Milan says the human body is a living canvas, to be fashioned like a work of art. He has performed thousands of cosmetic surgical procedures. Each one presents a challenge for Dr. Delmonico, because he knows that the work he does will contribute to a person's self-concept, and help them lead more useful, productive, and happy lives.

Across town from Dr. Delmonico's practice is Dr. Roberto Fingi, a psychiatrist, who says that Dr. Delmonico is a fraud. Dr. Fingi maintains that a person's self-concept is not in superficial appearance, but in the mind. Lately these two doctors, both among the best of their profession, have been waging a war of words in the newspapers of Milan.

Curiously enough, nobody seems to be winning the war. Some 70 percent of the people polled by this journalist, who knew of the controversy, thought that both doctors had a good argument and that it was a personal choice how others chose to define self-concept. When pressed on the point, however, 43 percent of those people said that they thought appearance was very important and would consider surgery if they felt they had a problem.

136. How does Dr. Delmonico define self-concept?

(A) Physical beauty.
(B) Health and strength.
(C) Intelligence.
(D) Mental health.

137. How has Dr. Fingi been arguing with Dr. Delmonico?

(A) In public.
(B) By correspondence.
(C) On television.
(D) In newspapers.

138. What do people generally think of the argument between Dr. Fingi and Dr. Delmonico?

(A) They are unprofessional.
(B) They are both right.
(C) Nobody knows about the argument.
(D) Nobody understands what the argument is about.

Questions 139–141 refer to the following review.

Local Cuisine/A Review: Kilmer's Kitchen

Kilmer's Kitchen isn't very large, but the food is good. Kilmer Ragley does the cooking, and his menu includes a lot of New Orleans French favorites. When I was there I had gumbo. This tasty mixture of ham and fish is cooked in a heavy pot. I thought it was delicious. For dessert I had apple surprise, a mixture of cooked apples and dough, with a glazed cinnamon topping. It was too sweet for me, but you might like it if you have a taste for sweets. Kilmer offers customers several different kinds of coffee, and my espresso was a perfect end to a good dinner.

Kilmer's Kitchen, at 798 Bourbon Street, opens only for dinner, from 5:30 P.M.to 11:00 P.M., Tuesday through Sunday. The restaurant gets very busy, so be sure to make a reservation before you go.

139. Which of the following can be said about the restaurant reviewed?

(A) It is a large restaurant in New Orleans.
(B) It serves only dinners.
(C) It is open every day of the week.
(D) It does not get many customers.

140. With what did the reviewer finish his meal?

(A) A cup of coffee.
(B) Dessert.
(C) A pot of gumbo.
(D) Some fruit.

141. Which dish did the reviewer not care for?

(A) Gumbo.
(B) Ham.
(C) Fish.
(D) Apples.

Questions 142–144 refer to the following article.

Thieves Ruin Marriage Plans

South Merrick—When unidentified thieves took $4000 worth of musical equipment from the Two Tones musical duo on Tuesday, the two performers were forced to cancel their fall bookings—and plans for a December wedding.

Joyce Benedict, 25, and Donald Jarvis, 27, both of Albany, were planning to help pay for their December 20 wedding with money earned from performances here over the next four days. The couple arrived at the Stagecoach Hotel in South Merrick about 3:00 P.M. Wednesday for their first appearance. When Jarvis went to their car at about 4:30 P.M., he found a broken window and their speakers, microphones, and other sound equipment missing. The equipment was not insured and there is little hope of recovering it. Wednesday's performance was canceled.

142. What was stolen?

(A) A car.
(B) A wedding ring.
(C) Electronic equipment.
(D) Wedding gifts.

143. When were the couple planning to get married?

(A) In the fall.
(B) On Tuesday.
(C) In December.
(D) In four days.

144. Why will the couple not be paid for their loss?

(A) Because the police could not find the thieves.
(B) Because they did not have insurance.
(C) Because they did not have a record of what was stolen.
(D) Because they could have prevented the theft.

Questions 145–147 refer to the following passage.

Economics, Development, and the Independence of Nations

The nineteenth century witnessed marked contrasts among the rates of economic development of different regions of the world. While some countries made rapid strides in development, large areas of the world remained in conditions of relative economic stagnation. During the twentieth century the gap widened progressively until in the recent decade two-thirds of the world's population receives less than one-sixth of world income.

Such disparities awakened most of the nations of the underdeveloped world to seek both economic and political independence. The movement intensified during the post–World War II period, which witnessed a rise of nationalism and a rapid movement toward industrialization and secularization.

Today it is the rare country that is held as a colony against its will, while colonies are referred to as commonwealths or as some other harmless political appendage to the mother country. Also, colonialist governments today take a much more enlightened view toward the captive citizens than did their predecessors, and development is seen as being in everybody's interest.

145. How does the author of this passage characterize economic development in the nineteenth century?

(A) Uneven.
(B) Gradual.
(C) Flourishing.
(D) Exploiting.

146. What is the author's main concern?

(A) Spread of democracy.
(B) Freedom of religion.
(C) Distribution of wealth.
(D) Independence from colonialist governments.

147. According to the author, what was a major effect of World War II?

(A) People traveled overseas more.
(B) Nations developed political awareness.
(C) Industrialized nations began to exploit their colonies.
(D) All nations lost a great deal as a result of the war.

Questions 148–151 refer to the following passage.

Selecting the Best Rope or Line for Use on Boats

Selecting the correct rope or line for an application can be confusing because of the enormous selection available. Rope has many qualities to be taken into consideration: strength, weight, stretch, cost, abrasion resistance, sunlight sensitivity, and so forth. Each application onboard demands certain qualities in the line that may be entirely different from another application.

How should you use these properties to choose the correct line for an application? The most general rule is that rope that is used for anchoring, towing, and mooring should be made from nylon, because it has lots of stretch to absorb the shock of changing loads, while rope that is used for running rigging on sailboats should be Dacron, because it has minimal stretch to ensure that sail adjustments do not change.

Nylon and Dacron have almost the same strength, while newer materials like Kevlar and Spectra are substantially stronger. Nylon will stretch about three times as much as Dacron for a given size and construction. Also, three-strand line stretches three times more than double braid construction. Kevlar and Spectra lines can be used in any application where stretch is not acceptable.

148. Why is it difficult to select the correct rope for an application?

(A) There is no standardization in the rope industry.
(B) Rope manufacturers do not adequately label rope.
(C) The alternatives for material and qualities are great.
(D) To have some qualities in a rope, you cannot have certain other qualities.

149. Which of the following materials is described as being acceptable for anchoring?

(A) Nylon.
(B) Kevlar.
(C) Dacron.
(D) Spectra.

150. Which of the following lines will stretch more than the others?

(A) A three-strand Nylon line.
(B) A double braided Dacron line.
(C) A three-strand Kevlar line.
(D) A double braided Spectra line.

151. According to the passage, how can a sailor avoid changes in the sail adjustment, once the sails are set?

(A) By using Dacron lines.
(B) By using heavier weight lines.
(C) By using newly-developed wire lines.
(D) By experimenting with a variety of lines and selecting the best.

Question 152 refers to the following passage.

How to Use CYN-X Film

CYN-X film is a high-speed panchromatic film especially useful for photographing existing-light subjects, fast action, and subjects requiring good depth of field and high shutter speeds. This film has a fine grain and excellent quality for such a high speed.

152. Which of the following would NOT be an appropriate subject to photograph with CYN-X film?

(A) Horses racing.
(B) Cave paintings.
(C) An outdoor sculpture.
(D) A mountain.

Questions 153–155 refer to the following passage.

Come to the Harper Museum Folk Fest May 15–18

Town and country crafts of the eighteenth and nineteenth centuries will be demonstrated by over ninety skilled artisans using clay, fibers, paint, paper, wood, and metal. Special demonstrations include pioneer home crafts at the log dwelling, flax breaking to linen, and operation of a pit saw.

Folk music and dancing, a quilting bee, a militia encampment, jugglers, a medicine show, a plant show, and a picnic basket lunch auction are attractions that will be held in the open air on the village green.

Hands-on crafts and entertainment for children will be featured. As in years past, it is clear that this year's Folk Fest will provide entertainment and education for visitors of all ages. Families are encouraged to attend.

153. What will be demonstrated at the Folk Fest?

(A) Striking artisans.
(B) Early crafts skills.
(C) New designs in shop equipment.
(D) Efficient techniques to achieve old designs.

154. Where will the medicine show, the plant show, and the picnic basket lunch auction take place?

(A) At the military encampment.
(B) Inside a building.
(C) Outside.
(D) In a pioneer home.

155. What is the purpose of the Folk Fest?

(A) To entertain and educate.
(B) To raise money for charity.
(C) To determine the prize winners.
(D) To bring professional artisans together.

Questions 156–158 refer to the following advertisement.

The Dangers of Hazardous Waste:

Whether or not we like to admit it, each of our homes contains numerous household hazardous waste items. In fact, it is estimated that the average household contains between ten and fifteen liters of hazardous waste materials.

The potential dangers of carelessly storing and discarding household hazardous wastes are no secret. In an effort to prevent these wastes from finding their way into local sanitary landfills and water sources, many groups of concerned citizens and city leaders are aggressively seeking ways to organize household hazardous waste collection and disposal programs.

HWG—Hazardous Waste General—is is an organization committed to the effective management of household hazardous wastes. We can advise your community on imaginative and safe approaches to waste disposal. Our managers are trained experts. If your community is considering organizing a hazardous waste disposal program, call us before you act.

156. What is the source of hazardous waste with which HWG primarily concerns itself?

(A) Industry.
(B) Private homes.
(C) Public power plants.
(D) Military installations.

157. Who is the article trying to reach?

(A) Community groups.
(B) Hazardous waste disposal companies.
(C) Government officials.
(D) Industrial managers.

158. What is HWG's business?

(A) Hazardous waste removal.
(B) Analysis of wastes to determine content.
(C) Consulting services in waste disposal.
(D) Identifying the source of illegally disposed-of waste products.

Questions 159–161 refer to the following passage.

Sopo V: The Worker

The Sopo V office copier will not win any prizes for being the fastest, or the most versatile, or the most compact, or the most beautiful in the industry. Those qualities all cost money. When we analyzed the copier market, we learned that most people do not need copiers that produce at the rate of 3 copies per second—one copy per second is enough. People do not need to copy in four colors—black and white will do just fine, thank you. People rarely need to reduce their work by 30% or by 50%—plain 1:1 copy is sufficient. And people have room in their office for copiers that are slightly larger than their typewriter. No need for a compact.

So why pay for all the extras, when what you want is a simple copier that is reliable and inexpensive? That's the Sopo V. It's the least expensive copier on the market and has an average down time of less than two days per year. We know because we have 22,000 corporate clients with maintenance contracts on over 100,000 copiers. Call your Sopo V dealer today. Buy a Sopo V copier tomorrow.

159. What is advertised in this article?

(A) A typewriter.
(B) A computer.
(C) A copy machine.
(D) A camera.

160. What is the advantage of the Sopo V over the competition?

(A) Size.
(B) Weight.
(C) Price.
(D) Speed.

161. How did the Sopo V company determine the Sopo V's design?

(A) By studying the market.
(B) By improving on a competitor's model.
(C) By genius of the company's chief designer.
(D) By asking their 100,000 corporate clients.

Questions 162–164 refer to the following passage.

Eater Beware!

A bold nutrition claim on the front of a package—such as "high in fiber" or "reduced calories"—demands close reading. For example, some soups labeled "1/3 less sodium" still contain more than 600 milligrams of sodium per serving. That is about 25 percent of the amount recommended for an entire day.

For clarity, consider the following example. If you buy a lunchmeat marked "80 percent fat free," will you be getting only 20 percent of your calories from fat—well below the recommended 30 percent level? The answer is no. This label statement means that 20 percent of the weight of the lunchmeat is fat. So how does one slice of it really measure up? Four grams of fat per slice times 9 calories per gram = 36 calories from fat: 36 calories divided by 50 total calories per slice = 72 percent of calories from fat. Calculate your fat intake and remember that the percentage of fat in an individual food is less important than the percentage of fat in a meal or in a full day's meals.

162. What is the purpose of this article?

   (A) To discourage people from eating certain foods.
   (B) To encourage people to read labels carefully.
   (C) To convince people that they need to know arithmetic.
   (D) To get people to eat less fat.

163. According to this article, what percentage of calories is recommended to be from fat?

   (A) 20 percent
   (B) 30 percent
   (C) 50 percent
   (D) 72 percent

164. Why can it be assumed that the author discusses the lunchmeat example?

   (A) Because lunchmeat contains a higher percentage of fat than other foods.
   (B) Because people eat too much lunchmeat.
   (C) Because lunchmeat labels do not tell the truth.
   (D) Because it presents an easily calculated problem.

Questions 165–166 refer to the following passage.

Foreign Source Capital Gains

The sale of investment securities may involve special tax considerations in connection with an overseas assignment. If securities are expected to be sold at a gain, consideration should be given to arranging the sale so as to create foreign source income. Capital gain income may not be taxable or may be taxed at low rates under the laws of the country in which you reside. If the gains are foreign source capital gains, they may enable you to increase your foreign tax credit limitations so that a greater amount of the foreign taxes imposed on your employment income could be applied against your federal tax liability. Any capital losses from foreign sources and any net excess of national source capital losses over national source capital gains will reduce foreign source capital gain income for this purpose.

165. What is the primary focus of this passage?

   (A) The need to invest in foreign corporations.
   (B) The sale of investment securities.
   (C) Taxable income from sales of real estate
   (D) Taxable interest on domestic investments.

166. What would the author of this passage advise?

   (A) Investigating the foreign capital gains tax rates for foreign source capital gains.
   (B) Liquidation of all assets before overseas assignment.
   (C) Hiding income as domestic source income rather than foreign source income, wherever possible.
   (D) Selling securities with minimum gain to avoid exorbitant taxes.

Questions 167–169 refer to the following advertisement.

Try "The Explorer" Receiver

The Explorer Receiver gives you crisp reception over the full ten bands of the radio spectrum, including, of course, the entire AM/FM range. At your leisure, you can also roam the entire spectrum of international shortwave and ham radio bands for information from all over the world. And you can pick up the TV-audio from channels 2 through 13, a great way to keep up with your favorite programs. But there is more. Listen to 24-hour reports from your home country, regardless of where you live or where you may be. And get news of all support services—police, fire, ships and civil defense. You may also access all forty channels of the CB band. The explorer works off your 110-volt house current, off batteries, or off any external 12-V DC source. This radio is a must for anybody in remote locations or anyone who spends a lot of time on the road.

167. Which of the following is NOT listed as being able to be listened to on the Explorer?

   (A) Aircraft communications.
   (B) Civil defense alerts.
   (C) Marine communications.
   (D) Local stations.

168. Which of the following is listed as an advantage of the Explorer?

   (A) It can reverse tapes automatically.
   (B) It can tape from radio programs.
   (C) It can play off a variety of power sources.
   (D) It screens static with sophisticated electronics.

169. Who will buy this radio?

   (A) City dwellers who have a lot of interference.
   (B) Government offices.
   (C) People who live among hills.
   (D) People who live far out in the country.

Questions 170–172 refer to the following passage.

A One-Day Seminar

You'll learn many new and exciting ways to improve your newsletter and save time, effort, and money producing it. You'll get advice from the pros on layout, design, writing, typography, photography, editing and production—everything you need to know to upgrade and update your publication. In one intensive day you'll learn things you couldn't pick up in years on the job. As a special bonus you will take away a spectacular collection of six books and manuals you'll treasure for years to come.

This seminar is a great opportunity to discover new approaches and confirm current ones. Whether you're a seasoned pro or creating your first newsletter, you'll come away with good ideas you can put to use immediately. Look over our agenda and see for yourself. We're sure you'll agree this is a seminar you will want to attend.

170. What does this statement promote?

   (A) Advertising for newsletters.
   (B) Printing facilities.
   (C) Information on publishing a newsletter.
   (D) A seminar on how to conduct a meeting.

171. Who should benefit most from responding to this advertisement?

   (A) Managers.
   (B) Editors.
   (C) Photographers.
   (D) Secretaries.

172. What is the opinion of the writer of the advertisement?

   (A) Everybody can learn.
   (B) If you know how to do something, you can teach it.
   (C) People learn by doing.
   (D) Working fast can be wasteful.

Questions 173–175 refer to the following news article.

Recent Developments in the Republic of Salming

At the time of the coup last August, the Republic of Salming was entering a boom era that had been developing under a democratic government for the past decade. The government had diversified the country's agricultural base to introduce food processing and had established shipping centers from which to ship the processed goods. The promises for a developed tourism industry, so attractive to neighboring nations, as well as silver mining, were beginning to bear fruit. Then in December a second coup sealed the nation's fate, as all development stopped. Tourism dropped precipitously, and foreign credits became impossible to come by. Currency was devalued by 22.8 percent in a five-month period and has not yet recovered. The economy of Salming is no longer going forward, and rumors of still a third coup are common.Unfortunately for the inhabitants of Salming, the leaders are unable to form a coalition government that could improve the situation, leaving the nation with an uncertain future.

173. What had the democratic government done to provide for the Republic of Salming's future?

(A) It had established a citrus fruit industry.
(B) It had formed alliances with neighboring nations.
(C) It had diversified the nation's rural economy.
(D) It had secured low-interest foreign credit.

174. What created the current situation in the Republic of Salming?

(A) The opposition party won the general election.
(B) The military took over the government.
(C) Storms destroyed the nation's agricultural base.
(D) Devaluation of the currency by 22.8 percent.

175. What does the author see as an avenue to rescue the Republic of Salming?

(A) Establishment of a coalition government.
(B) Foreign loans to rebuild the economy.
(C) Currency devaluation to raise the value of exports.
(D) A concentrated effort to improve tourism.

Questions 176–178 refer to the following passage.

Athletics as a Political Barometer

In the modern age, a nation's history can be read in the development of professional sports. As cities and nations gain in importance and become wealthier, they support more and more professional athletic teams—football, baseball, hockey, rugby. The development of international and intercity transportation enhances the possibility of competition among teams in a larger league, and the faster the transportation, the more reasonable it becomes that teams should travel great distances to compete.

Political alliances are formed through athletic contact. A willingness to engage in athletic contests is a show of trust that the other party will play fairly. By the same token, withholding competition can indicate a strong negative political position. The nation against which nobody will compete on the athletic field is the nation that stands alone in the world.

176. What does the writer say about athletic competition?

    (A) It is one of the few remaining areas in which people behave fairly toward one another.
    (B) It is above politics.
    (C) It results from political and technological developments.
    (D) It makes nations equal.

177. What does it mean when one nation refuses to compete with another nation?

    (A) Economic differences.
    (B) Lack of good health.
    (C) Poor transportation facilities.
    (D) Unwillingness to trust.

178. What does the writer think about athletic competition?

    (A) It is good for everybody.
    (B) It makes some people feel inferior.
    (C) Rightly or wrongly, it encourages nationalism.
    (D) It encourages athletes to act unfairly.

Questions 179–181 refer to the following passage.

Legal Clinic for Women

Women who need low-cost legal advice can attend day or evening legal clinics offered by Clavet College's Advisory Services for Women. The clinics, which will be held throughout the spring, are staffed by licensed attorneys and are held at the Clavet Women's Center, 345 Maple Street. There is no fee for the first consultation.

Evening clinics are scheduled from 6:00 P.M. to 8:00 P.M. on the first and third Wednesdays of each month, through June. Daytime clinics are from 9:30 A.M. to noon on the second Wednesday of each month, also through June.

Appointments are required and can be made by calling the Clavet Women's Center at (312) 555-1666.

179. Who would attend one of these clinics?

    (A) Anybody who is sick.
    (B) Women who need to understand the law.
    (C) Both men and women who have problems at work.
    (D) Female students at the college.

180. What is the price of the clinic?

    (A) There is no charge for the first consultation.
    (B) Whatever a person can afford.
    (C) Price is not discussed in the notice.
    (D) A person must work an unspecified amount of time for the Women's Center.

181. At which of the following times is the clinic open?

    (A) Wednesday, June 7, at 6:30 P.M.
    (B) Monday, June 12, at 7:45 P.M.
    (C) Friday, June 17, at 9:30 A.M.
    (D) Wednesday, June 30, at 7:00 P.M.

Questions 182–184 refer to the following horoscope.

Sagittarius (Nov. 23–Dec. 21)

The New Moon accents both health and job interests; a change in either area is in the works. Diet and fitness are reviewed, appearance may need to be spruced up, and avoid signing any binding agreements for a few weeks. Later, daily dealings may be testy. Authority or control may be key issues now.

Capricorn (Dec. 22 –Jan. 20)

Romantic, creative, or children's interests are spotlighted under the New Moon's influence, job or health interests may need careful handling now, and differences within key relationships aren't easily dismissed. Later this week, second-chance opportunities are favored, and you can now cut certain ties once and for all.

182. Which of the following is recommended for Sagittarius?

(A) Visit friends.
(B) Dress better.
(C) Avoid crowds.
(D) Work harder.

183. Which of the following could present a problem for Sagittarius?

(A) Signing contracts.
(B) Telling somebody what to do.
(C) Bicycle riding.
(D) Making a large purchase.

184. Which of the following might be of interest to Capricorn?

(A) Reading.
(B) Foreign travel.
(C) Saving money.
(D) Dancing.

Questions 185–187 refer to the following passage.

The Importance of Oral Hygiene

Thumbsucking and swallowing are related as they both affect the tongue, teeth, and overall oral hygiene. Why is this important to adults and children alike? One of the prominent causes of dental problems is due to a facial muscle imbalance and/or a deviate swallowing pattern. If dental and facial muscle problems are left untreated, they can lead to many unnecessary problems, including difficulty swallowing pills, difficulty wearing dentures, or protruding and maligned teeth. Problems with swallowing air, a feeling of "a lump in your throat," or facial pain and headaches can occur as well.

185. How are thumbsucking and swallowing similar?

(A) They are childish behavior.
(B) They bother people around you.
(C) They make eating difficult.
(D) They affect the health of the mouth.

186. What does the author of this article want the reader to avoid?

(A) Becoming unpopular.
(B) Mouth diseases.
(C) Problems with teeth.
(D) Mental illness.

187. Which of the following is NOT listed as a problem that can result from thumbsucking and swallowing?

(A) Deformed teeth.
(B) A painful face.
(C) Poorly fitting false teeth.
(D) Inability to chew.

Questions 188–189 refer to the following notice.

PROFESSIONAL TYPING SERVICE—Complete secretarial service; word/data processing on IBM-PC; repetitive letters; résumé preparation; photocopying/printing; mailing list maintenance; spiral binding. Established in 1976. Rapid service at reasonable rates.
Phone 555-9009.

188. Who might respond to this advertisement?

(A) A school teacher.
(B) An office with too much secretarial work.
(C) A typewriter salesperson.
(D) A secretary looking for work.

189. Which of the following is offered as a service?

(A) Copying in colors.
(B) Pickup and delivery.
(C) Preparation of curriculum vitae.
(D) Telephone answering.

Questions 190–191 refer to the following passage.

Sunny Greece!

The Greece you've always imagined—sunny, white-washed villages, long quiet beaches, hills covered with olive trees—is the Greece you'll see with World Travel. The Greece where the ancient past exists side by side with today. In our Grecian Holiday you'll see such classical highlights as the Parthenon, the Acropolis, and Apollo's Temple, while our Athens Holiday shows you the sights, restaurants, and shops of modern Athens. No other country offers so much in one vacation—natural beauty, astounding history, and a warm welcome wherever you go.

190. What does this advertisement want people to do?

(A) Visit a restaurant.
(B) See a film.
(C) Tour a foreign land.
(D) Take a special class.

191. When would the activity take place?

(A) On a week-end.
(B) On a vacation.
(C) One evening.
(D) Several evenings.

Questions 192–194 refer to the following news article.

Sultan of Brunei Invests in Beverly Hills

The Sultan of Brunei is reported to have bought two new houses next to his Beverly Hills Hotel in California. The Sultan purchased the famous hotel in 1987 for $186 million. Together the new houses, both pink like the hotel, cost around $10 million and have added to the Sultan's list of possessions eight new bedrooms and two acres of prized Beverly Hills land. According to sources, the Sultan has bought the houses for his personal use, so that he can partake of the hotel's amenities without taking any rooms away from the landmark's many splendid guests.

192. How much did the houses cost?

(A) Ten million dollars each.
(B) A total of ten million dollars.
(C) One hundred eighty-six million dollars.
(D) The article does not say.

193. Why were the two houses bought?

(A) As an investment.
(B) As a gift for friends.
(C) For the Sultan's use.
(D) To expand the hotel.

194. Which of the following statements is NOT made about the hotel?

(A) It is famous.
(B) It is painted pink.
(C) It is owned by the Sultan.
(D) It is visited by kings and queens.

Question 195 refers to the following passage.

Step into the designer showroom at AJAX Plumbing Supply and depart from the ordinary. Our designers can create a room that personifies your character. Choose from the Keller collection of quality fixtures. From classic traditional to a high-tech environment master bath, your personal room will be one of comfort, function, and convenience. Visit us soon, and convert your house into a living environment.

195. What do AJAX designers say they do?

(A) Design rooms to match personalities.
(B) Repair problems in house designs.
(C) Design efficient computer facilities.
(D) Work with architects to improve energy efficiency.

Questions 196–197 refer to the following diagram.

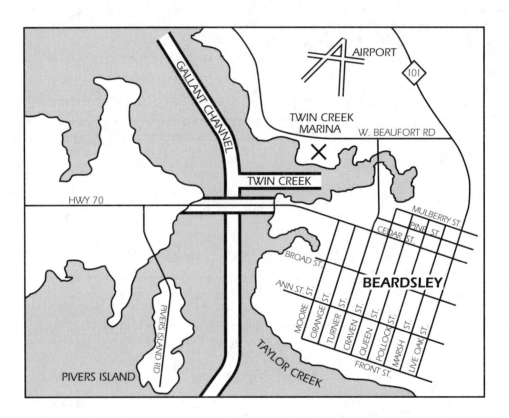

196. What streets could a person take to go from the corner of Marsh and Ann to Twin Creek Marina?

(A) Ann - Craven - Mulberry.
(B) Broad - Live Oak - 101.
(C) Ann - Turner - Beaufort.
(D) Marsh - Broad - Live Oak - Beaufort.

197. What street crosses Gallant Channel?

(A) Turner Street.
(B) Cedar Street.
(C) Pivers Island Road.
(D) Moore Street.

Questions 198–200 refer to the following passage.

Agricultural Research Falls Behind

The share of agricultural research in scientific journals is relatively small. To encourage efficient and prompt publication of agricultural research papers and reports, more financial support should be directed to current journals. Also, the establishment of new journals is necessary. *The New World Journal of Agricultural Sciences*, discontinued for lack of funds in 1983 after only four numbers were published, should be revived and its outlook expanded to include all areas of agriculture, including horticulture, viniculture, and reforestation.

198. What is the primary concern of the author of this passage?

(A) The quality of agricultural research is low.
(B) Agricultural research is too restricted in its outlook.
(C) More publication of agricultural research is needed.
(D) Agricultural journals are not widely distributed.

199. Why did the *New World Journal of Agricultural Sciences* stop publication?

(A) It did not receive any articles to publish.
(B) It did not have enough money.
(C) There was not enough interest in it.
(D) It published in only a limited field.

200. What appears to be one of the problems with current publication of agricultural research?

(A) Articles are slow in being published.
(B) Articles are not clearly written.
(C) Articles do not report original research.
(D) Only certain researchers are allowed to publish.

Questions 201–203 refer to the following announcement.

Entremont College
Alumni Association Spring Reception
Wednesday, May 24
5:30–7:30 P.M.

Share an enjoyable moment with other Entremont College graduates on Wednesday, May 24, at your Alumni Association's annual Spring Reception. The event takes place in Cardiff's new and popular Harbour League Club, from 5:30 to 7:30 P.M, and offers you an opportunity to gather with friends in a relaxed, elegant social setting.

This special annual event will be highlighted by the presentation of the Arthur Aldridge Distinguished Alumni Award to Joseph P. Napto, Jr., '56, for his years of service to the community and his many contributions to the College.

The Spring Reception is only $15 per person and includes an abundance of delicious hors d'oeuvres and a beverage of your choice. Make your reservations no later than May 21 by returning the enclosed card with your remittance to the Alumni Association. If you have any questions, phone the secretary of the Alumni Association at 555-3000.

---

201. What is the purpose of the reception?

(A) To ask for contributions to the College.
(B) To honor a graduate of the College.
(C) To introduce the College president to alumni.
(D) It is an annual activity to bring alumni together.

202. Who is Arthur Aldridge?

(A) A distinguished alumnus.
(B) President of the College.
(C) Secretary of the Alumni Association.
(D) The information is not provided in the passage.

203. How do alumni reserve admission to the event?

(A) By telephoning the Alumni Association.
(B) By sending payment and a request notice.
(C) By notifying the Harbour League Club.
(D) It is not necessary to reserve admission.

Algerian Population Classes and Incomes, 1956

Income per person	Muslim	European	Total	Class
$45	5,840,000	—	5,840,000	Traditional agriculture
$121	1,600,000	—	1,600,000	Urban Muslims
$240	510,000	440,000	950,000	Small- and medium-wage earners, craftsmen, & businessmen
$502	50,000	545,000	595,000	Middle class
$3181	—	15,000	15,000	Wealthy class
	8,000,000	1,000,000	9,000,000	**Total**

204. According to the chart, in 1956 what was the mean annual income for Algerian urban Muslims?

   (A) $45.
   (B) $121.
   (C) $240.
   (D) $502.

205. According to the chart, in 1956 how many small- and medium-wage earners, craftsmen, and businessmen were there in Algeria?

   (A) 440,000.
   (B) 510,000.
   (C) 545,000.
   (D) 950,000.

206. According to the chart, in 1956 how many Algerians were engaged in traditional agriculture?

   (A) Fewer than 1,000,000.
   (B) 1,600,000.
   (C) 5,840,000.
   (D) 9,000,000.

207. According to the chart, in 1956 how many Algerian Muslims were classified as being of the middle class?

   (A) 5,000.
   (B) 15,000.
   (C) 50,000.
   (D) 595,000.

Questions 208–211 refer to the following passage.

Why Big Disk Floppies are the *Best*

The more important your data is to you, the more you will value Big Disk. When it comes to high performance and data protection, Big Disk has the combination of qualities that no other floppy can imitate.

Consider this: Big Disk floppies are engineered to perform an average of 50 million revolutions. That's fifteen times the industry standard. Then consider that Big Disk disks were the first floppies to be factory formatted. Big Disk floppies also give you plenty to consider when it comes to data protection. We know that nearly 50 percent of all computer users have lost time and money from accidental data loss due to static charges. That's why Big Disk offers advantages such as anti-static liners, to disperse static charges before they have a chance to build up. And the patented Telap coating enables you to wipe spills and finger prints off the recording surface.

All Big Disk disks are guaranteed for life and tested to be 100 percent error free when they leave the plant. We're ahead of everybody, so what are you waiting for? Buy Big Disk next time!

208. What does Big Disk promise customers?

(A) Low prices.
(B) Quick delivery.
(C) High performance.
(D) More space on the disk than other disks.

209. What is the industry standard for number of revolutions for a disk?

(A) 3 or 4 million.
(B) 15 million.
(C) 50 million.
(D) 65 million.

210. According to the article, what is a common cause for loss of data on a disk?

(A) Telap flaws.
(B) Static charges.
(C) Interrupted current.
(D) Spills and fingerprints on recording surface.

211. Which of the following claims is NOT made by Big Disk?

(A) They are 100% error free.
(B) They carry a lifetime warranty.
(C) They surpass industry engineering standards.
(D) They can withstand extremes of heat and cold.

Questions 212–214 refer to the following passage.

Neuromuscular Electrical Stimulation

Recent research in sports medicine has discovered a way to increase muscle strength through jolts of high-intensity electricity. The technique, called neuromuscular electrical stimulation (NMES), was originally devised by Soviet medical researchers and used with teams from the Soviet Union and Eastern Bloc nations. Western researchers were at a loss to understand the procedure, because electric shocks that were strong enough to be effective resulted in excruciating pain.

A researcher at Washington University has learned that pain can be blocked by use of very high-frequency current, interrupted some fifty times per second, which permits the subject to endure previously impossibly high-level charges of current. Through the use of a special generator, current can be applied to the human body at levels twenty times stronger than earlier thought possible.

212. From where were the researchers who first discovered NMES?

   (A) The West.
   (B) The Soviet Union.
   (C) Eastern Bloc nations.
   (D) Washington University.

213. According to the passage, why did science want to apply high-level jolts of electricity to the human body?

   (A) To reduce pain from sports injuries.
   (B) To increase the strength of muscles.
   (C) To make muscles more elastic to avoid injury.
   (D) To train athletes to endure greater pain.

214. What is the purpose of the special generator?

   (A) To produce high-level electric charges.
   (B) To administer shocks with interruptions.
   (C) To add higher pain levels to electric shocks.
   (D) To temporarily short circuit pain centers.

Questions 215–216 refer to the following passage.

   Many vegetable growers, in an attempt to get larger growth and yield, delay harvesting vegetables until the stage of best quality has passed. No vegetable should be allowed to become tough, coarse, overgrown, and unpalatable before being harvested. Quantity is important, but so is quality. Large size in a product is of little value in itself. Indeed, excessive size is generally associated with mediocre, if not low, quality.

   The sooner after harvest that vegetables can be used, the better. If they cannot be marketed for a while, they should be kept in a cool, moist place. Any overproduction or surplus of fresh vegetables, where there is no foreseeable market for them, should be preserved or stored for later use.

215. What is the main subject of this passage?

   (A) How to obtain quality in vegetables.
   (B) Proper harvest methods can increase profits in vegetable farming.
   (C) Larger vegetables mean greater income.
   (D) How to preserve vegetables.

216. What should a farmer do if he has a crop that is too large to market?

   (A) Use it for fertilizer for future crops.
   (B) Donate the excess to the poor.
   (C) Sell it at low prices to get rid of it.
   (D) Store or preserve it for later sale.

Questions 217–218 refer to the following article.

Marbletown Craftsmen, Ltd., Designs

Inspired by the popularity of ferns during the Victorian period, cast iron fern-leaf garden furniture was first introduced in Great Britain in the 1870s. Now, more than a century later, it thrives again, thanks to Marbletown Craftsmen, Ltd., which in cooperation with the Appleton Institution has issued heavy cast aluminum versions of licensed adaptations of the historic leafy-design garden furniture. Although Garden White is the most popular color, the replica furniture is also available in Appleton Green, Baltimore Blue, and Federal City Yellow.

217. What inspired the design on the furniture?

(A) Ladies' fashions
(B) A kind of plant
(C) Art from Ancient Greece
(D) Egyptian tomb paintings

218. What does the article say is available for the public?

(A) A book discussing the furniture.
(B) An exposition of original furniture.
(C) Authentic pieces over one-hundred years old.
(D) Reproductions of early pieces.

Questions 219–222 refer to the following passage.

Cruise Industry in Disarray

The number of people taking cruises continues to rise, and so does the number of complaints about cruise lines. A prime concern that has arisen with the proliferation of cruise-line mergers—as it did with airline consolidation—is the apparent decline in staff courtesy, service, and cuisine. One reader reported "less than coffee-shop quality." Another writes that food "was never hot." Travel arrangements like fly/cruise programs, late port arrival, and confusing disembarkation procedures were also criticized. When asked about these irregularities, industry spokespeople say they are trying to improve their service and ask that the public report dissatisfaction to the appropriate management. Out of fairness to the industry, we must say that we have also received letters that commend specific companies for excellent service. That will be the subject of a future article, in which we will evaluate all cruise companies operating today.

219. What does the article say is the cause of the problems with cruise lines?

(A) There are too many small lines.
(B) Owners do not manage the lines.
(C) Small lines have joined together to become large companies.
(D) Lines are owned by foreign companies that do not know the public.

220. What is happening in the cruise line industry?

(A) Fewer and fewer people are taking cruises.
(B) Lawsuits from accidents have raised prices.
(C) The government is reviewing the situation.
(D) The number of people taking cruises is increasing.

221. How are cruise lines responding to public dissatisfaction?

(A) They want to hear about problems that people experience.
(B) They claim they can do nothing about the problems.
(C) They claim that there are no problems.
(D) The people responsible are never available for comment.

222. What will be reported upon in the future?

(A) A case study of an inefficient cruise line.
(B) A review of cruise line offerings, quality of service, and prices.
(C) A report of major accidents and their causes on board cruise ships.
(D) One person's bad experience with a cruise line.

Questions 223–225 refer to the following notice.

Johnson Directory of Corporate Communications

Once again, the Johnson Directory of Corporate Communications is being made available to the public. This award-winning annual publication is a comprehensive directory of the nation's top corporate communications professionals. A necessary handbook for all information services directors, the presentation lists contacts in public relations, investor relations, and media relations for over 3,000 companies and trade associations. The book is published by Johnson Publications, Inc., which also publishes the Johnson CC Update, a weekly newsletter covering the public relations industry. *Available only from the company.*

223. How often is the Johnson Directory published?

(A) Every week.
(B) Every month.
(C) Every year.
(D) It is a one-time publication.

224. Who will purchase the Directory?

(A) Board chairmen.
(B) Association members.
(C) Newspaper publishers.
(D) Directors of information services.

225. Where can the publication be bought?

(A) In bookstores.
(B) On newsstands.
(C) Through book wholesalers.
(D) Only from Johnson Publications, Inc.

Questions 226–228 refer to the following advice.

Construction Contracts—What to Watch Out For

Small companies that want to grow have to watch carefully their balance sheet, but also often need to build facilities to allow for expansion. When contracting for construction, there are a number of steps that should be followed to ensure value for money and to not have problems later because of somebody's failure to perform or because of misunderstandings. Here are some of those steps:

❏ Have a good idea of what you want done and how much you can afford to pay.
❏ Solicit bids from several companies.
❏ Ask for references, and follow through with a phone call to each.
❏ Find out how long the company has been in business, and ask to see guarantees of solvency.
❏ Inquire about the company's complaint policy, and know who is responsible for the project.
❏ Make sure your contract clearly defines what is to be done, the time frame for completion, and the payment schedule.
❏ Do not rush into a contract you are not comfortable with. If you sign and then change your mind, it will cost you money to avoid your obligations.

226. For whom is this advice intended?

(A) For lawyers.
(B) For homeowners.
(C) For small businesses.
(D) For construction companies.

227. Why would somebody want to follow this advice?

(A) To avoid difficulties.
(B) To make more money.
(C) To avoid going to jail.
(D) To avoid bankruptcy.

228. What does this passage discuss?

(A) How to expand a company.
(B) Construction contract terms.
(C) Ways to finance expansion.
(D) Advertising techniques that work.

Questions 229–232 refer to the following passage.

The Table Saw

A table saw consists of a motor and arbor assembly, housed in a base cabinet or stand. The saw blade is mounted to the arbor, which is connected to the motor by a pulley and belt. Blade height and angle adjustments are controlled by two handwheels. One handwheel controls the blade's height above the saw table, the other adjusts the bevel angle of the blade, to a maximum of forty-five degrees. The rip fence, which slides on front and rear guide bars, can be locked anywhere along the bars at the desired distance from the blade.

Table saws are classified by the diameter of blade used. Models are available in a variety of sizes, from eight inches to fourteen inches, with the ten-inch size being the most popular.

229. According to the passage, how can a saw blade be raised and lowered?

(A) By moving a lever.
(B) By turning a crank.
(C) By turning a wheel.
(D) By moving the motor.

230. Which of the following angles absolutely can NOT be cut by the saw described?

(A) Left 10 degrees.
(B) Right 20 degrees.
(C) Right 45 degrees.
(D) Left 50 degrees.

231. According to the passage, where can the rip fence be locked?

(A) To the table, in an upright position.
(B) At any point on the guides.
(C) Beginning at eight inches from the blade.
(D) At the highest level for the blade.

232. Which size of saw sells more than any other?

(A) The table saw.
(B) The sixty-degree model.
(C) The ten-inch saw.
(D) The smallest one.

Questions 233–234 refer to the following notice.

Protect Your Credit Card

Never give your credit card number to anyone who has called you on the telephone. Remember that the person on the other end of the line, if a stranger to you, may or may not be who they say the are, may not represent the organization they claim to represent, and may not be honest. When you phone a theater or a mail order company and give your credit card number to pay for an order of tickets or merchandise, you know who you are talking to. That is not the case when you are being telephoned. Over the telephone or in person, always know with whom you are dealing.

233. What is the purpose of this statement?

(A) To help people avoid losing money to dishonest people.
(B) To discourage the use of credit cards.
(C) To identify dishonest people and to arrest them.
(D) To promote credit card insurance to card users.

234. When does the statement say NOT to give a credit card number over the telephone?

(A) When buying something over the telephone.
(B) When somebody telephones the card holder.
(C) When talking to somebody not known to the card holder.
(D) Under no circumstances should a person ever give a credit card number over the telephone.

Questions 235–238 refer to the following passage.

Draco Keyboard Training:

It has not been so long since the electric typewriter and photocopying machine were the most complicated pieces of equipment in an office, and managers rarely touched them. If a person knew how to type, they were a secretary and, by office standards generally, poorly paid. Today many older managers are having to go back to school to learn typing skills that they thought they would never need, to be able to use computers that are now on every manager's desk.

This need has created a new business—computer keyboard training courses—and Mary Draco, a former secretary from Phoenix, is becoming wealthy by filling that need. Her Draco Keyboard Training (DKT) business is now franchised to three hundred forty locations across the country, and growing daily. Franchises can hardly keep up with the demand for their program, as word of the effectiveness of the DKT course spreads. In only fifteen self-paced hours of training, most managers are able to perform all of the strokes necessary to their work, and can type accurately an average of forty words per minute. From then they are on their own.

Draco has one requirement for her franchisees. In order to effectively demonstrate the system, they need to be able to type a minimum of eighty words per minute. Needless to say, many former secretaries are no longer poorly paid office workers.

235. According to the passage, who has had to learn new skills?

(A) Secretaries.
(B) New managers.
(C) Older managers.
(D) Draco franchisees.

236. How has Mary Draco become rich?

(A) By teaching people how to type.
(B) By demonstrating the DKT course.
(C) By selling DKT franchises.
(D) By selling computers.

237. How many hours of training does it take for most people to learn sufficient strokes to perform adequately?

(A) Fifteen.
(B) Forty.
(C) Eighty.
(D) One hundred forty.

238. To whom does Draco usually award franchises?

(A) To young managers.
(B) To former secretaries.
(C) To people who can type forty words per minute.
(D) To office workers.

Questions 239–241 refer to the following passage.

Vox Populi

If you are like other people, you have always wanted to have an opportunity to talk to famous people. While Vox Populi (Latin for "the voice of the people") may not be exactly that, it will let you listen to famous people speak on a variety of topics. A philosopher will speak on religion, a statesman will speak on political issues, and a rock star will speak about music. These are just three of the personalities that Vox Populi, a London-based company in which the national telephone company holds the major interest, will offer to people who call in to listen to recorded messages, each three minutes long and changed every week.

The taped speakers will talk to callers personally, as if speaking with a friend. The recordings will be available 24-hours a day and can be dialed from anywhere in the world. If the program is a success, Vox Populi says they will add other programs—tennis personalities, television and cinema stars, and perhaps even famous criminals. That would be one way to help pay for the nation's prison system.

239. What will Vox Populi offer?

(A) Recorded telephone messages.
(B) Opportunity to talk by phone with famous people.
(C) A radio show where listeners can phone in.
(D) A television show where the audience asks questions of famous people.

240. Who expects to benefit from Vox Populi?

(A) A recording studio.
(B) A telephone company.
(C) Some famous voices.
(D) The City of London.

241. What would be the advantage of having famous criminals on Vox Populi?

(A) It would make better citizens of the criminals.
(B) It would teach young people that crime is wrong.
(C) It would help pay the expenses of keeping them in prison.
(D) It would help the public understand that criminals are human beings, just like everybody else.

Questions 242–244 refer to the following passage.

Public fears about the lack of competition in American industry have reached their lowest levels in fifteen years, for everything from telephone service to oil. The only exception to this downward trend is in the airline industry, for which 15 percent of the people surveyed now say there is too little competition. This figure compares with 10 percent eight years ago.

Public attitudes toward corporate America remain quite favorable, with 75 percent saying they have a positive inclination toward most large corporations, and 89 percent saying they approve of most small companies.

Meanwhile, the public images of most industries remain quite close to what they were a year ago, except for the drug and oil industries, which have lost some favor over the past year, and airlines, which have improved their image. Add Exxon's tanker spill in Valdez, Alaska, and analysts speculate that the oil industry's image is bound to become even worse.

242. What is the subject of this passage?

(A) The public image of corporations.
(B) How corporations manipulate the public.
(C) Opinion surveys can be wrong.
(D) Lack of competition in American business.

243. What appears to have happened in the airline industry?

(A) Airplane accidents have created a loss of confidence in the airlines.
(B) There are too few airlines operating.
(C) Fewer people are traveling by air now than in the past.
(D) Airplane tickets have become too expensive.

244. Based on the information provided in the passage, which of the following statements is true?

(A) Telephone service has improved over the past fifteen years.
(B) Public perception of corporations changes a lot within a very short time.
(C) People approve more of small corporations than they do of large ones.
(D) Oil companies are among the most successful at maintaining a good image.

Questions 245–247 refer to the following statement.

Handbook of Chemical Machine Operators
By George Fabry

The book surveys the machine equipment used in the field of petrochemical industry, providing useful guidance to designers, inventors, and operators of such machines. This volume is not recommended for the casual reader.

1520 pp
Paper
In French
ISBN 963-10-6583-1

245. What is the above statement?

(A) A book order.
(B) Notice of a delivery.
(C) A library entry.
(D) Information on a publication.

246. Who would read this book?

(A) Professors.
(B) People involved with the machinery.
(C) People interested in history of technology.
(D) Anyone who reads and has interest in machines.

247. What does the book do?

(A) It provides a history of petrochemical industry machinery.
(B) It reviews all machinery currently in use in the petrochemical industry.
(C) It provides designs for improving machinery used in the petrochemical industry.
(D) It promotes new equipment for the petrochemical industry.

Questions 248–249 refer to the following notice.

Notice: The control of insects attacking vegetables assumes more importance than with most other crops because even minor damage may lower the crop's value or render it unfit for sale. Commercial vegetable growers should recognize the different insects in their various growth stages to be able to begin control measures before damage occurs. The earlier these pests can be effectively controlled, the more valuable the crop will be.

248. For whom is this notice intended?

(A) People who buy vegetables.
(B) Farmers who grow vegetables.
(C) Stores that sell vegetables.
(D) People who have home gardens.

249. What does the notice concern?

(A) Destroying insects in early stages.
(B) Identifying insects to monitor progress.
(C) Avoiding pesticides as harmful to consumers.
(D) How to buy vegetables that may appear to be damaged by insects.

Questions 250–252 refer to the following passage.

Macromarkets and Macromarketing

A profound change is taking place in the way goods and services are advertised, promoted, and sold to businesses. The untargeted approach of traditional mass marketing is giving way to a new, more accountable and personal approach.

Before they approach their market, marketers of the '90s will know by name and address the person they want to sell to. After they make the sale, they will know who bought. They will create their own private marketplace where they can close the doors to competition and build long-term customer loyalty. Now, in the international best-seller, *Macromarkets and Macromarketing*, Thomas Jarrell, one of the best known names in the field of market development, has systematized this new trend in a marketing model that anybody can apply.

Thomas Jarrell will discuss his model at a seminar to be offered in a number of cities across the country. Watch for notices in your local newspaper. In the meantime, buy *Macromarkets and Macromarketing*, and get ahead of the competition.

250. What has Jarrell done in the field of marketing?

(A) He has spoken in a number of cities.
(B) He has established a private marketplace.
(C) He has learned the names of his customers.
(D) He has devised a model for a new approach.

251. According to the passage, what is the key to macromarketing?

(A) Knowing the product.
(B) Identifying the market.
(C) Knowing the competition.
(D) Advertising in newspapers.

252. Which of the following is mentioned as an advantage to be gained from macromarketing?

(A) Long-term customer loyalty.
(B) Greater return on investment.
(C) Enhanced product name recognition.
(D) Better organization of marketing plans.

Questions 253–255 refer to the following passage.

Fishing Is Not Easy

Neither is finding buyers for fishing gear. Water levels in many places are down, the price of fishing tackle is up, and the fish are just as smart as ever. Still, experienced fishermen are catching some big ones. But those fishermen are not as many as they used to be, and they are not as young. And as John Landis, owner of Fishing World Center in Anderson, South Carolina, says, "If you're selling fishing tackle, bait, and services for fresh-water fishing, you're in trouble."

Young people today are not anxious to go to the lake with grandfather as they once were, as more exciting activities compete for their leisure time. The tranquility of mountain streams and lakes is not as attractive as a day at the beach or an afternoon at the mall. Vacations are for travel abroad or for amusement parks, not for sitting in a canoe. Deep sea fishing, fly casting, and foreign fishing still hold a certain attraction, but even those areas are showing market weakening. If sport fishing is going to survive as a growth industry, something besides a good rain will have to come along.

253. Why is the sport fishing industry having difficulty?

(A) Water level in lakes is too low.
(B) There are few people who want to fish.
(C) Fish have been contaminated by pollutants.
(D) Fishing tackle has become too expensive.

254. What segment of the population does not go fishing?

(A) Women.
(B) Urban dwellers.
(C) Young people.
(D) The middle class.

255. What kind of sport fishing is experiencing greatest difficulty?

(A) Deep sea.
(B) Fresh water.
(C) Fly casting.
(D) Foreign fishing.

Publishing in the Peoples Republic of Duslaba

In the socialist Duslaba Peoples Republic, book publishing and distribution are state-controlled activities. That control, however, is limited to the principles of publishing and financial support. The publishing houses, themselves, enjoy full editorial independence, making their own editorial decisions and accepting responsibility for adhering to state guidelines.

Publishing in Duslaba is not a commercial activity. Rather, it is an arm of national cultural policy, and therefore subsidized by the government. Its major purpose is to make books available to everyone. It has a variety of minor purposes, as well, such as promotion of the arts, maintaining the national literary patrimony, ensuring availability of a variety of reading material, and other purposes.

Its goal of making books available determines pricing, meaning that most publications remain inexpensive. Prices are established on the basis of a set of uniform principles, taking into account the character, or genre, and the length of a publication, rather than on real production costs. Different pricing applies to fiction and poetry, children's and juvenile books, non-fiction, scientific and technical literature, and bibliophile books, or those published in limited editions for collectors.

While this system is little understood in non-socialist countries, it has clear advantages over other systems, considering its primary function.

256. Who determines editorial policy in Duslaba?

(A) Authors.
(B) A government office.
(C) A committee of publishers.
(D) Individual publishing houses.

257. What is the primary purpose of publishing in Duslaba?

(A) Promotion of government policies.
(B) Universal availability of inexpensive reading.
(C) Accommodation of public interest in many areas.
(D) Maintaining national cultural principles.

258. How are book prices established?

(A) By determining cost and projecting income.
(B) By a set of principles unrelated to costs.
(C) By demand for the works among the reading public.
(D) By a formula based on quality of materials and book length.

259. What class of books are said to be published in small numbers?

(A) Poetry books.
(B) Children's books.
(C) Technical books.
(D) Bibliophile editions.

Questions 260–262 refer to the following report.

Ventriloquism is Alive and Well

This year, as every year, the Annual Ventriloquist Convention will be held the last weekend in June at Fort Mitchell, Kentucky. For four days and nights, men, women, and dummies will converse, debate, argue, and generally enjoy themselves. Ventriloquism is the art of speaking in such a way that the voice seems to come from some source other than the speaker. That means speaking without moving the lips, and having close by an apparent source for the voice, such as a dummy for whom the speech and attitude would be appropriate.

When watching ventriloquists perform, it is clear that they have a very close relationship with their dummies. Some people speculate that this is because often ventriloquists were lonely as children and invented an alter ego, a separate personality, that followed them around and kept them company. If that is true, when ventriloquism was added to the companion personality, the alter ego became useful in other ways. Today ventriloquism is big business, as can be seen in the variety and versatility of the 650 professional ventriloquists who attend this convention every year.

260. What is ventriloquism?

   (A) The art of making people laugh.
   (B) A form of psychological counseling.
   (C) An annual meeting.
   (D) Speaking without appearing to speak.

261. According to the passage, what is a "dummy"?

   (A) A neighbor.
   (B) An alter ego.
   (C) A pet animal.
   (D) A child actor.

262. Why is it suggested that people participate in ventriloquism?

   (A) To earn money.
   (B) To attend the convention.
   (C) To have somebody to talk to.
   (D) To avoid contact with others.

Questions 263–266 refer to the following passage.

The Credit Card Market in the United States

Fifty percent of the households in the United States own a Visa card. The nearest competitor is MasterCard, with 40 percent of the households. American Express has 20 percent, the Discover Card has a close 18 percent, and the high-end Optima has 1 percent. When including all forms of credit cards, including those issued by department stores, better than 75 percent of the public buy with plastic on a regular basis.

While this may seem like a lot of credit cards, particularly considering the new tax laws that discourage credit buying, experts in the field claim the market is not yet saturated and there are still a lot of people who could use plastic, or use it more often, and who do not— and the race is on to get them.

263. According to the passage, what credit card is used by more people in the U.S. than any other?

(A) American Express.
(B) MasterCard.
(C) Visa.
(D) Discover.

264. What percent of the U.S. public use credit cards?

(A) 40 percent.
(B) 50 percent.
(C) 75 percent.
(D) Information not provided.

265. How is credit buying treated by tax laws?

(A) It is encouraged.
(B) Large credit buying is discouraged, but small credit buying is encouraged.
(C) It is not considered.
(D) It is discouraged.

266. How do experts view the future for credit cards?

(A) People will gradually stop using them.
(B) There are many people who do not use them who could.
(C) Many people who are credit risks hold credit cards.
(D) It is impossible to say, because of changing tax laws.

Questions 267–269 refer to the following passage.

Several ways of recording and displaying our past are traditional and have become established over the centuries, ranging from oral heritage and historiography, or the writing of history, to the systematic collection and exhibition of works of art and other objects. With the rise of Romanticism in the West, there emerged still another previously unrecognized source, that of folk tradition, or the collection and display of objects of folk art as representations of the daily life and history of a people, and ultimately the self awareness of a nation. It was this realization of ethnic identity that forged many nationalist movements around the world, but it was in Europe where it manifested itself with vigor and where it eventually met with greatest success.

267. According to the passage, which of the following is NOT a traditional way to display a nation's history?

(A) Oral heritage.
(B) Representation of daily life.
(C) Collection of works of art.
(D) Historiography.

268. Which of the following gave rise to nationalism?

(A) The Romantic movement.
(B) Art collections.
(C) Europe.
(D) The West.

269. What is the "self awareness of a nation"?

(A) Inspirational art.
(B) Ethnic identity.
(C) Oral heritage.
(D) The writing of history.

Questions 270–273 refer to the following passage.

Filippo Does it Again!

Status seekers will surely be tempted to loosen those fashionable Filippo purse strings when they see the new Filippo Casa designed collection of fine furniture. Best known for their trendy and expensive handbags, furs, scarves, and accessories, the three Filippo brothers worked with Genoa architect Mario Larini and fashion designer Carlo Mazarro to develop a line of contemporary wood, leather, and signature-fabric furnishings for the home and office.

Manufactured by Futuro Bello, the forty-two-piece furniture collection includes the Diamante chair, at $3,350. Other exquisitely designed pieces make up the complete household line, from living room to dining room to bedroom to den, and there is even a bench for the sauna! The Filippo organization has an entire office plan on the drawing board, but at the prices quoted, they will not have many clients. Strangely, that does not seem to bother them in the least.

270. According to the passage, who will buy the Filippo Casa line of furniture?

(A) Wealthy people.
(B) Status seekers.
(C) Architects and designers.
(D) Office managers.

271. Who makes the Filippo Casa line of furniture?

(A) Diamante.
(B) Filippo Casa.
(C) Futuro Bello.
(D) Carlo Mazarro.

272. What are the Filippo brothers best known for having designed in the past?

(A) Office furniture.
(B) Household furniture.
(C) Handbags, furs and scarves.
(D) Signature-fabric items.

273. What is the reader led to believe that the Filippo brothers think of their image?

(A) They want to change it sometime in the future.
(B) They do not concern themselves with image.
(C) They are pleased with it.
(D) They are careful to ensure that they have no image, so they can change directions in design every year.

The following message to the test taker is printed in the test book following test question number 200, the last question on the test:

Stop! This is the end of the test. If you finish before time is called, you can go back to Parts V, VI, and VII and check your work.

1. Ⓐ Ⓑ Ⓒ Ⓓ
2. Ⓐ Ⓑ Ⓒ Ⓓ
3. Ⓐ Ⓑ Ⓒ Ⓓ
4. Ⓐ Ⓑ Ⓒ Ⓓ
5. Ⓐ Ⓑ Ⓒ Ⓓ
6. Ⓐ Ⓑ Ⓒ Ⓓ
7. Ⓐ Ⓑ Ⓒ Ⓓ
8. Ⓐ Ⓑ Ⓒ Ⓓ
9. Ⓐ Ⓑ Ⓒ Ⓓ
10. Ⓐ Ⓑ Ⓒ Ⓓ
11. Ⓐ Ⓑ Ⓒ Ⓓ
12. Ⓐ Ⓑ Ⓒ Ⓓ
13. Ⓐ Ⓑ Ⓒ Ⓓ
14. Ⓐ Ⓑ Ⓒ Ⓓ
15. Ⓐ Ⓑ Ⓒ Ⓓ
16. Ⓐ Ⓑ Ⓒ Ⓓ
17. Ⓐ Ⓑ Ⓒ Ⓓ
18. Ⓐ Ⓑ Ⓒ Ⓓ
19. Ⓐ Ⓑ Ⓒ Ⓓ
20. Ⓐ Ⓑ Ⓒ Ⓓ
21. Ⓐ Ⓑ Ⓒ Ⓓ
22. Ⓐ Ⓑ Ⓒ Ⓓ
23. Ⓐ Ⓑ Ⓒ Ⓓ
24. Ⓐ Ⓑ Ⓒ Ⓓ
25. Ⓐ Ⓑ Ⓒ Ⓓ
26. Ⓐ Ⓑ Ⓒ Ⓓ
27. Ⓐ Ⓑ Ⓒ Ⓓ
28. Ⓐ Ⓑ Ⓒ Ⓓ
29. Ⓐ Ⓑ Ⓒ Ⓓ
30. Ⓐ Ⓑ Ⓒ Ⓓ
31. Ⓐ Ⓑ Ⓒ Ⓓ
32. Ⓐ Ⓑ Ⓒ Ⓓ
33. Ⓐ Ⓑ Ⓒ Ⓓ
34. Ⓐ Ⓑ Ⓒ Ⓓ
35. Ⓐ Ⓑ Ⓒ Ⓓ
36. Ⓐ Ⓑ Ⓒ Ⓓ
37. Ⓐ Ⓑ Ⓒ Ⓓ
38. Ⓐ Ⓑ Ⓒ Ⓓ
39. Ⓐ Ⓑ Ⓒ Ⓓ
40. Ⓐ Ⓑ Ⓒ Ⓓ
41. Ⓐ Ⓑ Ⓒ Ⓓ
42. Ⓐ Ⓑ Ⓒ Ⓓ

43. Ⓐ Ⓑ Ⓒ Ⓓ
44. Ⓐ Ⓑ Ⓒ Ⓓ
45. Ⓐ Ⓑ Ⓒ Ⓓ
46. Ⓐ Ⓑ Ⓒ Ⓓ
47. Ⓐ Ⓑ Ⓒ Ⓓ
48. Ⓐ Ⓑ Ⓒ Ⓓ
49. Ⓐ Ⓑ Ⓒ Ⓓ
50. Ⓐ Ⓑ Ⓒ Ⓓ
51. Ⓐ Ⓑ Ⓒ Ⓓ
52. Ⓐ Ⓑ Ⓒ Ⓓ
53. Ⓐ Ⓑ Ⓒ Ⓓ
54. Ⓐ Ⓑ Ⓒ Ⓓ
55. Ⓐ Ⓑ Ⓒ Ⓓ
56. Ⓐ Ⓑ Ⓒ Ⓓ
57. Ⓐ Ⓑ Ⓒ Ⓓ
58. Ⓐ Ⓑ Ⓒ Ⓓ
59. Ⓐ Ⓑ Ⓒ Ⓓ
60. Ⓐ Ⓑ Ⓒ Ⓓ
61. Ⓐ Ⓑ Ⓒ Ⓓ
62. Ⓐ Ⓑ Ⓒ Ⓓ
63. Ⓐ Ⓑ Ⓒ Ⓓ
64. Ⓐ Ⓑ Ⓒ Ⓓ
65. Ⓐ Ⓑ Ⓒ Ⓓ
66. Ⓐ Ⓑ Ⓒ Ⓓ
67. Ⓐ Ⓑ Ⓒ Ⓓ
68. Ⓐ Ⓑ Ⓒ Ⓓ
69. Ⓐ Ⓑ Ⓒ Ⓓ
70. Ⓐ Ⓑ Ⓒ Ⓓ
71. Ⓐ Ⓑ Ⓒ Ⓓ
72. Ⓐ Ⓑ Ⓒ Ⓓ
73. Ⓐ Ⓑ Ⓒ Ⓓ
74. Ⓐ Ⓑ Ⓒ Ⓓ
75. Ⓐ Ⓑ Ⓒ Ⓓ
76. Ⓐ Ⓑ Ⓒ Ⓓ
77. Ⓐ Ⓑ Ⓒ Ⓓ
78. Ⓐ Ⓑ Ⓒ Ⓓ
79. Ⓐ Ⓑ Ⓒ Ⓓ
80. Ⓐ Ⓑ Ⓒ Ⓓ
81. Ⓐ Ⓑ Ⓒ Ⓓ
82. Ⓐ Ⓑ Ⓒ Ⓓ
83. Ⓐ Ⓑ Ⓒ Ⓓ
84. Ⓐ Ⓑ Ⓒ Ⓓ

85. Ⓐ Ⓑ Ⓒ Ⓓ
86. Ⓐ Ⓑ Ⓒ Ⓓ
87. Ⓐ Ⓑ Ⓒ Ⓓ
88. Ⓐ Ⓑ Ⓒ Ⓓ
89. Ⓐ Ⓑ Ⓒ Ⓓ
90. Ⓐ Ⓑ Ⓒ Ⓓ
91. Ⓐ Ⓑ Ⓒ Ⓓ
92. Ⓐ Ⓑ Ⓒ Ⓓ
93. Ⓐ Ⓑ Ⓒ Ⓓ
94. Ⓐ Ⓑ Ⓒ Ⓓ
95. Ⓐ Ⓑ Ⓒ Ⓓ
96. Ⓐ Ⓑ Ⓒ Ⓓ
97. Ⓐ Ⓑ Ⓒ Ⓓ
98. Ⓐ Ⓑ Ⓒ Ⓓ
99. Ⓐ Ⓑ Ⓒ Ⓓ
100. Ⓐ Ⓑ Ⓒ Ⓓ
101. Ⓐ Ⓑ Ⓒ Ⓓ
102. Ⓐ Ⓑ Ⓒ Ⓓ
103. Ⓐ Ⓑ Ⓒ Ⓓ
104. Ⓐ Ⓑ Ⓒ Ⓓ
105. Ⓐ Ⓑ Ⓒ Ⓓ
106. Ⓐ Ⓑ Ⓒ Ⓓ
107. Ⓐ Ⓑ Ⓒ Ⓓ
108. Ⓐ Ⓑ Ⓒ Ⓓ
109. Ⓐ Ⓑ Ⓒ Ⓓ
110. Ⓐ Ⓑ Ⓒ Ⓓ
111. Ⓐ Ⓑ Ⓒ Ⓓ
112. Ⓐ Ⓑ Ⓒ Ⓓ
113. Ⓐ Ⓑ Ⓒ Ⓓ
114. Ⓐ Ⓑ Ⓒ Ⓓ
115. Ⓐ Ⓑ Ⓒ Ⓓ
116. Ⓐ Ⓑ Ⓒ Ⓓ
117. Ⓐ Ⓑ Ⓒ Ⓓ
118. Ⓐ Ⓑ Ⓒ Ⓓ
119. Ⓐ Ⓑ Ⓒ Ⓓ
120. Ⓐ Ⓑ Ⓒ Ⓓ
121. Ⓐ Ⓑ Ⓒ Ⓓ
122. Ⓐ Ⓑ Ⓒ Ⓓ
123. Ⓐ Ⓑ Ⓒ Ⓓ
124. Ⓐ Ⓑ Ⓒ Ⓓ
125. Ⓐ Ⓑ Ⓒ Ⓓ
126. Ⓐ Ⓑ Ⓒ Ⓓ

127. Ⓐ Ⓑ Ⓒ Ⓓ
128. Ⓐ Ⓑ Ⓒ Ⓓ
129. Ⓐ Ⓑ Ⓒ Ⓓ
130. Ⓐ Ⓑ Ⓒ Ⓓ
131. Ⓐ Ⓑ Ⓒ Ⓓ
132. Ⓐ Ⓑ Ⓒ Ⓓ
133. Ⓐ Ⓑ Ⓒ Ⓓ
134. Ⓐ Ⓑ Ⓒ Ⓓ
135. Ⓐ Ⓑ Ⓒ Ⓓ
136. Ⓐ Ⓑ Ⓒ Ⓓ
137. Ⓐ Ⓑ Ⓒ Ⓓ
138. Ⓐ Ⓑ Ⓒ Ⓓ
139. Ⓐ Ⓑ Ⓒ Ⓓ
140. Ⓐ Ⓑ Ⓒ Ⓓ
141. Ⓐ Ⓑ Ⓒ Ⓓ
142. Ⓐ Ⓑ Ⓒ Ⓓ
143. Ⓐ Ⓑ Ⓒ Ⓓ
144. Ⓐ Ⓑ Ⓒ Ⓓ
145. Ⓐ Ⓑ Ⓒ Ⓓ
146. Ⓐ Ⓑ Ⓒ Ⓓ
147. Ⓐ Ⓑ Ⓒ Ⓓ
148. Ⓐ Ⓑ Ⓒ Ⓓ
149. Ⓐ Ⓑ Ⓒ Ⓓ
150. Ⓐ Ⓑ Ⓒ Ⓓ
151. Ⓐ Ⓑ Ⓒ Ⓓ
152. Ⓐ Ⓑ Ⓒ Ⓓ
153. Ⓐ Ⓑ Ⓒ Ⓓ
154. Ⓐ Ⓑ Ⓒ Ⓓ
155. Ⓐ Ⓑ Ⓒ Ⓓ
156. Ⓐ Ⓑ Ⓒ Ⓓ
157. Ⓐ Ⓑ Ⓒ Ⓓ
158. Ⓐ Ⓑ Ⓒ Ⓓ
159. Ⓐ Ⓑ Ⓒ Ⓓ
160. Ⓐ Ⓑ Ⓒ Ⓓ
161. Ⓐ Ⓑ Ⓒ Ⓓ
162. Ⓐ Ⓑ Ⓒ Ⓓ
163. Ⓐ Ⓑ Ⓒ Ⓓ
164. Ⓐ Ⓑ Ⓒ Ⓓ
165. Ⓐ Ⓑ Ⓒ Ⓓ
166. Ⓐ Ⓑ Ⓒ Ⓓ
167. Ⓐ Ⓑ Ⓒ Ⓓ
168. Ⓐ Ⓑ Ⓒ Ⓓ

169. Ⓐ Ⓑ Ⓒ Ⓓ   196. Ⓐ Ⓑ Ⓒ Ⓓ   223. Ⓐ Ⓑ Ⓒ Ⓓ   250. Ⓐ Ⓑ Ⓒ Ⓓ
170. Ⓐ Ⓑ Ⓒ Ⓓ   197. Ⓐ Ⓑ Ⓒ Ⓓ   224. Ⓐ Ⓑ Ⓒ Ⓓ   251. Ⓐ Ⓑ Ⓒ Ⓓ
171. Ⓐ Ⓑ Ⓒ Ⓓ   198. Ⓐ Ⓑ Ⓒ Ⓓ   225. Ⓐ Ⓑ Ⓒ Ⓓ   252. Ⓐ Ⓑ Ⓒ Ⓓ
172. Ⓐ Ⓑ Ⓒ Ⓓ   199. Ⓐ Ⓑ Ⓒ Ⓓ   226. Ⓐ Ⓑ Ⓒ Ⓓ   253. Ⓐ Ⓑ Ⓒ Ⓓ
173. Ⓐ Ⓑ Ⓒ Ⓓ   200. Ⓐ Ⓑ Ⓒ Ⓓ   227. Ⓐ Ⓑ Ⓒ Ⓓ   254. Ⓐ Ⓑ Ⓒ Ⓓ
174. Ⓐ Ⓑ Ⓒ Ⓓ   201. Ⓐ Ⓑ Ⓒ Ⓓ   228. Ⓐ Ⓑ Ⓒ Ⓓ   255. Ⓐ Ⓑ Ⓒ Ⓓ
175. Ⓐ Ⓑ Ⓒ Ⓓ   202. Ⓐ Ⓑ Ⓒ Ⓓ   229. Ⓐ Ⓑ Ⓒ Ⓓ   256. Ⓐ Ⓑ Ⓒ Ⓓ
176. Ⓐ Ⓑ Ⓒ Ⓓ   203. Ⓐ Ⓑ Ⓒ Ⓓ   230. Ⓐ Ⓑ Ⓒ Ⓓ   257. Ⓐ Ⓑ Ⓒ Ⓓ
177. Ⓐ Ⓑ Ⓒ Ⓓ   204. Ⓐ Ⓑ Ⓒ Ⓓ   231. Ⓐ Ⓑ Ⓒ Ⓓ   258. Ⓐ Ⓑ Ⓒ Ⓓ
178. Ⓐ Ⓑ Ⓒ Ⓓ   205. Ⓐ Ⓑ Ⓒ Ⓓ   232. Ⓐ Ⓑ Ⓒ Ⓓ   259. Ⓐ Ⓑ Ⓒ Ⓓ
179. Ⓐ Ⓑ Ⓒ Ⓓ   206. Ⓐ Ⓑ Ⓒ Ⓓ   233. Ⓐ Ⓑ Ⓒ Ⓓ   260. Ⓐ Ⓑ Ⓒ Ⓓ
180. Ⓐ Ⓑ Ⓒ Ⓓ   207. Ⓐ Ⓑ Ⓒ Ⓓ   234. Ⓐ Ⓑ Ⓒ Ⓓ   261. Ⓐ Ⓑ Ⓒ Ⓓ
181. Ⓐ Ⓑ Ⓒ Ⓓ   208. Ⓐ Ⓑ Ⓒ Ⓓ   235. Ⓐ Ⓑ Ⓒ Ⓓ   262. Ⓐ Ⓑ Ⓒ Ⓓ
182. Ⓐ Ⓑ Ⓒ Ⓓ   209. Ⓐ Ⓑ Ⓒ Ⓓ   236. Ⓐ Ⓑ Ⓒ Ⓓ   263. Ⓐ Ⓑ Ⓒ Ⓓ
183. Ⓐ Ⓑ Ⓒ Ⓓ   210. Ⓐ Ⓑ Ⓒ Ⓓ   237. Ⓐ Ⓑ Ⓒ Ⓓ   264. Ⓐ Ⓑ Ⓒ Ⓓ
184. Ⓐ Ⓑ Ⓒ Ⓓ   211. Ⓐ Ⓑ Ⓒ Ⓓ   238. Ⓐ Ⓑ Ⓒ Ⓓ   265. Ⓐ Ⓑ Ⓒ Ⓓ
185. Ⓐ Ⓑ Ⓒ Ⓓ   212. Ⓐ Ⓑ Ⓒ Ⓓ   239. Ⓐ Ⓑ Ⓒ Ⓓ   266. Ⓐ Ⓑ Ⓒ Ⓓ
186. Ⓐ Ⓑ Ⓒ Ⓓ   213. Ⓐ Ⓑ Ⓒ Ⓓ   240. Ⓐ Ⓑ Ⓒ Ⓓ   267. Ⓐ Ⓑ Ⓒ Ⓓ
187. Ⓐ Ⓑ Ⓒ Ⓓ   214. Ⓐ Ⓑ Ⓒ Ⓓ   241. Ⓐ Ⓑ Ⓒ Ⓓ   268. Ⓐ Ⓑ Ⓒ Ⓓ
188. Ⓐ Ⓑ Ⓒ Ⓓ   215. Ⓐ Ⓑ Ⓒ Ⓓ   242. Ⓐ Ⓑ Ⓒ Ⓓ   269. Ⓐ Ⓑ Ⓒ Ⓓ
189. Ⓐ Ⓑ Ⓒ Ⓓ   216. Ⓐ Ⓑ Ⓒ Ⓓ   243. Ⓐ Ⓑ Ⓒ Ⓓ   270. Ⓐ Ⓑ Ⓒ Ⓓ
190. Ⓐ Ⓑ Ⓒ Ⓓ   217. Ⓐ Ⓑ Ⓒ Ⓓ   244. Ⓐ Ⓑ Ⓒ Ⓓ   271. Ⓐ Ⓑ Ⓒ Ⓓ
191. Ⓐ Ⓑ Ⓒ Ⓓ   218. Ⓐ Ⓑ Ⓒ Ⓓ   245. Ⓐ Ⓑ Ⓒ Ⓓ   272. Ⓐ Ⓑ Ⓒ Ⓓ
192. Ⓐ Ⓑ Ⓒ Ⓓ   219. Ⓐ Ⓑ Ⓒ Ⓓ   246. Ⓐ Ⓑ Ⓒ Ⓓ   273. Ⓐ Ⓑ Ⓒ Ⓓ
193. Ⓐ Ⓑ Ⓒ Ⓓ   220. Ⓐ Ⓑ Ⓒ Ⓓ   247. Ⓐ Ⓑ Ⓒ Ⓓ
194. Ⓐ Ⓑ Ⓒ Ⓓ   221. Ⓐ Ⓑ Ⓒ Ⓓ   248. Ⓐ Ⓑ Ⓒ Ⓓ
195. Ⓐ Ⓑ Ⓒ Ⓓ   222. Ⓐ Ⓑ Ⓒ Ⓓ   249. Ⓐ Ⓑ Ⓒ Ⓓ

1. (C) William Johns III
2. (B) Variety
3. (C) To make sure not everybody plays the same instrument
4. (B) In the middle of the series
5. (B) From a number of sources
6. (B) To the development of new activities
7. (C) The President's Endowment
8. (A) Sciences
9. (A) People who like to grow plants
10. (B) 5000 kinds of seeds
11. (A) Nothing
12. (B) A 275-yard drive
13. (C) Their difficulty becomes apparent on playing
14. (B) It has a slope.
15. (C) With little confidence
16. (B) The plant will give off a smell.
17. (C) In bulk shipments
18. (C) The plant will provide dense leaves.
19. (A) Through biotechnology
20. (B) The research will be very costly.
21. (A) Every week
22. (C) Two-hundred fifty per year
23. (B) Frightened motorists
24. (A) A single incident injured and killed many
25. (C) For making students interested in learning math
26. (A) Making learning useful
27. (B) Teachers who make their students want to learn
28. (A) $2340
29. (C) The Cove is open from May 21 until September 24.
30. (C) His heart is working too hard.
31. (B) Hypertension
32. (A) When it must strain to pump blood to the entire body
33. (C) Because people do not know they have it.
34. (C) Remembering to take medicines
35. (A) To be reminded
36. (C) To encourage people to do as they ought
37. (A) They are too critical and have a negative effect.
38. (B) Near the town of Hot Springs
39. (C) People went there to gamble.
40. (D) The golf course was changed substantially.
41. (A) Visitors to Tivoli
42. (B) Mention the issue of crime at citizens' meetings.
43. (A) By providing useful information
44. (B) Interest
45. (B) The right food
46. (C) Loss of muscle tissue
47. (A) Their nutrient and vitamin intake needs will be redefined.
48. (B) They have less muscle mass.
49. (C) To reduce air pollution

50. (C) MTBE is just like gasoline.
51. (C) How a vehicle responds to its fuel
52. (A) It can be mixed with water.
53. (D) It will reduce the life of an engine.
54. (A) Knowing cash-flow patterns within the company
55. (C) They may become outdated.
56. (B) By making checks between annual reviews
57. (A) Production employees hold onto spare parts to have replacements.
58. (B) Employee awareness
59. (B) Near the rear of a property
60. (A) The garden could not be seen.
61. (C) Close to the kitchen door
62. (D) Planning in advance
63. (B) At least an hour before beginning play
64. (A) **Because golf is a low energy, high concentration sport.**
65. (D) **Nutrients**
66. (C) **It causes dehydration.**
67. (C) **To protest a presidential decree**
68. (A) **Lift price controls**
69. (B) **The economy requires price controls.**
70. (D) **That the government is not supported by the TWU**
71. (A) They do not think about it.
72. (D) It is going up all over, in some places quite rapidly.
73. (B) The price of property taxes
74. (D) They think workers will work less.
75. (A) Employees must be informed two months in advance.
76. (B) Employees of a plant about to close will work harder than before.
77. (B) Loss of vitality of brain tissue
78. (C) Older parents are more likely than younger parents to have children who will get Alzheimer's disease.
79. (D) Social background
80. (B) **Because the age at which people have children is rising.**
81. (B) **How to obtain profitable corporate growth**
82. (B) **Temporary decline in income**
83. (B) **The size of the takeover company**
84. (C) **Hungary**
85. (D) **Bulgaria**
86. (A) **Romania**
87. (D) NCF and FPCA have created the NCRC to deal with matters of interest to both.
88. (A) Corporate sponsors no longer need to deal directly with the FPCA and the NCF.
89. (D) A variety of NCF and FPCA officials
90. (C) There will be no more arguments concerning race dates and places.
91. (C) By letter, telex and telephone only
92. (A) A footwear wholesaler
93. (C) To cancel an order placed earlier
94. (B) Because of money problems

95. (D) Continued good credit
96. (C) There is a big market for fish.
97. (A) Fish are high in protein.
98. (B) The sea produces fewer fish every year.
99. (D) They set fire to a school.
100. (C) Fifteen or sixteen
101. (C) Both light
102. (C) Because he is accomplished in many different areas of jazz music
103. (B) Midnight Jazz Band, Carlos Adams, and others
104. (A) His style is the definition of alto saxophone jazz playing.
105. (C) A telex ordering some item
106. (A) A catalog
107. (B) Three CDs at full price
108. (A) The cost of three CDs and monthly catalogues
109. (B) The light meter does not work.
110. (C) Ten years
111. (A) In New Jersey
112. (D) To ask about repairs
113. (C) To offer a job to an applicant
114. (C) What to tell Mr. Jamison
115. (D) Visit Mr. Douglas
116. (C) The Oceola University School of Law
117. (C) To encourage law students to think about careers that serve the public
118. (B) Penalties for scheduling changes after one-way flight are more severe than for those made prior to flight.
119. (D) Even if unused, the airline will not buy back the ticket and it may be used only by the person to
120. (B) Once each month
121. (C) January
122. (C) Send the remainder of the shipment as requested on purchase order
123. (D) Send them back to Acme
124. (B) Acme is not a reliable shipper.
125. (C) Delicate glass flowers
126. (D) He never entered the museum and apparently took no interest in it.
127. (D) To invite Association members to a lecture
128. (C) The Friends of American Literature Association
129. (B) A meeting of the Association
130. (B) Dragon-bone collectors
131. (C) Dragon-bones found there were thought to possess great medicinal value and were highly prized.
132. (C) The bones were not really those dragons but preserved bones of other animals.
133. (B) Counselor at the Legal Aid Center
134. (B) Seven years
135. (C) Law and psychology
136. (A) Physical beauty
137. (D) In newspapers
138. (B) They are both right.
139. (B) It serves only dinners.
140. (A) A cup of coffee
141. (D) Apples
142. (C) Electronic equipment
143. (C) In December
144. (B) Because they did not have insurance.
145. (A) Uneven

146. (C) Distribution of wealth
147. (B) Nations developed political awareness.
148. (C) The alternatives for material and qualities are great.
149. (A) Nylon
150. (A) A three strand Nylon line
151. (A) By using Dacron lines
152. (B) Cave paintings
153. (B) Early craft skills
154. (C) Outside
155. (A) To entertain and educate
156. (B) Private homes
157. (A) Community groups
158. (C) Consulting services in waste disposal
159. (C) A copy machine
160. (C) Price
161. (A) By studying the market
162. (B) To encourage people to read labels carefully
163. (B) 30%
164. (D) Because it presents an easily calculated problem
165. (B) The sale of investment securities
166. (A) Investigating the foreign capital gains tax rates for foreign source capital gains
167. (A) Aircraft communications
168. (C) It can play off a variety of power sources
169. (D) People who live far out in the country
170. (C) Information on publishing a newsletter
171. (B) Editors
172. (A) Everybody can learn
173. (C) It had diversified the nation's rural economy.
174. (B) The military took over the government.
175. (A) Establishment of a coalition government
176. (C) It results from political and technological developments.
177. (D) Unwillingness to trust
178. (A) It is good for everybody.
179. (B) Women who need to understand the law
180. (A) There is no charge for the first consultation.
181. (A) Wednesday, June 7, at 6:30 P.M.
182. (B) Dress better
183. (A) Signing contracts
184. (D) Dancing
185. (D) They affect the health of the mouth.
186. (C) Problems with teeth
187. (D) Inability to chew
188. (B) An office with too much secretarial work
189. (C) Preparation of curriculum vitae
190. (C) Tour a foreign land
191. (B) On a vacation
192. (B) A total of ten million dollars
193. (C) For the Sultan's use
194. (D) It is visited by kings and queens.
195. (A) Design rooms to match personalities
196. (C) Ann - Turner - Beaufort
197. (B) Cedar St.
198. (C) More publication of agricultural research is needed.
199. (B) It did not have enough money.
200. (A) Articles are slow in being published.
201. (D) It is an annual activity to bring alumni together.
202. (D) The information is not provided in the passage
203. (B) By sending payment and a request notice
204. (B) $121
205. (D) 950,000

206. (C) 5,840,000
207. (C) 50,000
208. (C) High performance
209. (A) 3 or 4 million
210. (B) Static charges
211. (D) They can withstand extremes of heat and cold.
212. (B) The Soviet Union
213. (B) To increase the strength of muscles
214. (B) To administer shocks with interruptions
215. (A) How to obtain quality in vegetables.
216. (D) Store or preserve it for later sale.
217. (B) A kind of plant
218. (D) Reproductions of early pieces
219. (C) Small lines have joined together to become large companies.
220. (D) The number of people taking cruises is increasing.
221. (A) They want to hear about problems that people experience.
222. (B) A review of cruise line offerings, quality of service, and prices.
223. (C) Every year
224. (D) Directors of information services
225. (D) Only from Johnson Publications, Inc.
226. (C) For small businesses
227. (A) To avoid difficulties
228. (B) Construction contract terms
229. (C) By turning a wheel
230. (D) Left 50 degrees
231. (B) At any point on the guides
232. (C) The ten-inch saw
233. (A) To help people avoid losing money to dishonest people
234. (B) When somebody telephones the card holder
235. (C) Older managers
236. (C) By selling DKT franchises
237. (A) Fifteen
238. (B) To former secretaries
239. (A) Recorded telephone messages

240. (B) A telephone company
241. (C) It would help pay the expenses of keeping them in prison.
242. (A) The public image of corporations
243. (B) There are too few airlines operating.
244. (C) People approve more of small corporations than they do of large ones.
245. (D) Information on a publication
246. (B) People involved with the machinery
247. (B) It reviews all machinery currently in use in the petrochemical industry.
248. (B) Farmers who grow vegetables
249. (A) Destroying insects in early stages
250. (D) He has devised a model for a new approach.
251. (B) Identifying the market
252. (A) Long-term customer loyalty
253. (B) There are few people who want to fish.
254. (C) Young people
255. (B) Fresh water
256. (D) Individual publishing houses
257. (B) Universal availability of inexpensive reading
258. (B) By a set of principles unrelated to costs
259. (D) Bibliophile editions
260. (D) Speaking without appearing to speak
261. (B) An alter ego
262. (A) To earn money
263. (C) Visa
264. (C) Seventy-five percent
265. (D) It is discouraged.
266. (B) There are many people who do not use them who could.
267. (B) Representation of daily life
268. (A) The Romantic movement
269. (B) Ethnic identity
270. (B) Status seekers
271. (C) Futuro Bello
272. (C) Handbags, furs and scarves
273. (C) They are pleased with it.

THE LANGUAGE PROFICIENCY INTERVIEW

Introduction

The Language Proficiency Interview, or LPI, is a face-to-face interview conducted by a trained interviewer. The interview requires from twenty to thirty minutes to administer and for quality control purposes is usually recorded. The objective of the interview is to obtain a speech sample that can be rated on criteria set down for each of the several levels of the rating scale. The speech sample may be rated at the time of the interview—in fact, it nearly always is—or it may be rated at a later time. In most cases, when an interview is recorded it is rated twice.

The LPI tests language globally. The rating scale employs as its standard language as it is spoken by the *educated native speaker* of the language. There is no standard by profession, setting, or content. That is because native speakers are not adept in one content or professional area of language and ignorant of grammar, vocabulary, and usage as they apply to other areas. This definition of language runs counter to the often-expressed position, "My company wants me to learn English to be able to sell snowmobiles (or household appliances, or electronics), and they don't care if I can talk about an experience I had while at the university ten years ago." If that is, indeed, the case, and the speaker is charged with learning a second language only as it applies to his or her individual work activity, for levels above 1+ the LPI is not an appropriate testing procedure.

> *Fairness requires that anyone attempting to apply LPI ratings, whether in the workplace or elsewhere, have a clear understanding of the scale and what it can and cannot do.*

There are many kinds of speakers and, for measurement purposes, all must be able to be accommodated on a common scale. Some people learn English by conversing with native speakers. Generally speaking, these people usually have excellent comprehension, a broad vocabulary, good pronunciation and fluency, and a comparatively weak control of grammar. Other people study at institutes, in schools or universities, or in environments that foster an academic approach. These speakers generally have a good command of grammar, and an adequate, if limited, vocabulary, but they are comparatively weak in comprehension, fluency, and pronunciation.

The LPI scale has clear standards for all levels, based on communication skills. The strengths and limitations of all approaches to learning are taken into account, are weighed against the effect they have on overall communication, and are factored into the rating. The purpose of this section is to clarify the requirements of the levels, for language learners and users of the LPI scale alike, and to explain the interview procedure.

The language elicited during the course of an interview does not have a narrow or circumscribed focus. Interviewers do not, or should not, have a list of questions that they ask every interviewee, or even a list from which they select questions. Rather, depending upon the experience and interests of the interviewee and the content and language requirements for the interviewee's level, the interviewer approaches the interview from a wide angle, embracing as broad a sweep of language as allowed by time and the interviewee's capability.

Because during an interview the interviewee is called upon to *produce* speech, it is difficult to confound a qualified interviewer. The interviewer is trained not to assume language capability on the part of the interviewee. If a particular level of speech is not generated and sustained, the interviewee is not to be credited with it.

There are, of course, attempts on the part of interviewees to make interviewers think they know more English than they do. For instance, interviewees may prepare a discourse on a particular topic that they think will be addressed or that they will interject into the interview. While this approach is not entirely discouraged, control of the interview must always reside in the interviewer. The effect of such a discourse, regardless of how well prepared, is not what the interviewee presumes. By it, the interviewer is alerted to the possibility that the interviewee may have limitations he or she is trying to hide. Nevertheless, within the limits of time, the interviewer will usually give the interviewee time to make his or her presentation before moving on to other matters. After all, the role of the interviewer is not to intimidate or thwart the interviewees from demonstrating their ability, but to give them an opportunity to attain their highest level of sustained speech.

Format of Interview/The Interview Setting:

There are three interviewer–interviewee configurations that are possible for administration of the LPI. They are: (1) a single interviewer/rater, (2) an interviewer and a note-taker, and (3) two interviewers.

1. The first of these configurations, with a single interviewer/rater, is the most common approach and is also the most convenient logistically, if not necessarily the one best suited for providing a reliable rating. It involves a single interviewer/rater, who interviews and rates at the same time. This approach is also the most difficult of the three, from the point of view of the interviewer, as he or she must not only interview, but on completion of the interview must also provide a rating in which he or she has confidence. A recording may be made of the interview, enabling the interviewer/rater, or a second rater, to go back later to review the speech sample. Because of the expense associated with having multiple interviewers, the single interviewer approach is by far the least expensive.

    In the interview, the interviewer meets with the interviewee in an environment that is as nonthreatening as possible, perhaps sitting diagonally across the corner of a table. It is not advisable for the interviewer and the interviewee to be seated in large overstuffed chairs, or in too casual an environment, as that constitutes an intrusion on the formality and seriousness of the interview.

2. The second interview format involves two interviewers; however, in this case one is a primary interviewer and the other a secondary interviewer. With this configuration, the primary interviewer conducts the interview. Upon completion of the interview, the primary interviewer invites the secondary interviewer to address the interviewee. In this configuration, the secondary interviewer has three purposes. The first purpose is to prepare a written record of the interviewee's speech that can later be used to arrive at a consensus rating. The second purpose is to ensure that a rateable speech sample has been obtained, asking follow up questions in situations where a rateable speech sample has not been elicited by the first interviewer. The third purpose is to participate in the interview, either as an "interpreter" to help elicit higher level speech, or as a third person in a situation. Because the secondary interviewer is an observer of the interview process, his or her position is that of an uninvolved third party, and therefore is considered to allow for greater objectivity.

3. The third interview format involves two interviewers, who alternate in talking with the interviewee, while carrying out the interview. This approach is rarely taken, and if not carefully orchestrated can result in an interrogation, rather than an interview. The approach is calculated to put a certain amount of stress into the interview situation, thus requiring the interviewee to perform under conditions that could have an effect on his or her speech. This introduction of anxiety is desirable when the interviewee is going to be subjected to similar stress when called upon to work in the target language.

The Interview Process

The interview requires between twenty and thirty minutes to administer. It may be shorter than twenty minutes, particularly at the lower levels, but it should not require more than thirty minutes, in any case. Nobody except personnel involved in the interview process should be present in the interview room. The ambiance and the furnishings of the interview room should be comfortable, but not plush. The room should be away from direct noise, and indirect noise should kept be at a minimum. The interviewer and interviewee should be on equal levels. This means that the interviewer should not be in a position regarded as one of authority, behind a desk or on a higher plane than the interviewee. The optimum arrangement is that both interviewer and interviewee should be sitting at a table, on which can be placed any articles necessary for the administration of the interviews, e.g,. note paper, pens, interviewee lists, recording equipment, and so forth.

The Rating Scale

The scale on which the interview is rated is a specially devised eleven-point scale, beginning with a minimum rating of zero (0) progressing by whole numbers to 1, 2, 3, 4, and eventually reaching the maximum rating of 5. Each level from 0 to 4 also carries a plus (+) value. Hence, the possible ratings are 0, 0+, 1, 1+, 2, 2+ . . . 4+, 5. There are no minus (-) values for any of the levels, and there is no plus (+) value for level 5, which itself is the maximum.*

For levels 0–4, the accompanying plus values indicate that the speaker is almost at the next level, but for some reason does not qualify at that level. Perhaps he is able to speak at the next level for short periods of time, on certain topics, but is unable to sustain speech at that level. Or perhaps he is nearly at the next level in all aspects of speech, but lacks the language experience that would allow him to bring all of his learning to bear, preventing him from sustaining speech at the next level.

The meaning of the plus values will become clearer as the reader becomes informed about each plus level. For levels 0, 1, and 2, plus ratings can be "compensatory," meaning that exceptional strengths in certain areas, such as control of structures, breadth of vocabulary, or comprehension, can earn for the interviewee a plus rating, although he may not exhibit plus-level strengths in all areas of speech. An interviewee can in no case be compensated *over* a threshold. For technical reasons, compensatory ratings do not apply for levels 3 and above.

The distance between the levels is not scaled as an arithmetic progression, but rather as a geometric progression, becoming progressively more difficult to pass from one level to another as a person goes up the scale. It is far easier to progress from Level 1 to Level 2 than from Level 2 to Level 3, and from Level 2 to Level 3 than from Level 3 to Level 4.

Level Descriptions

Description: Level 0

Level 0 is described negatively, in that it focuses on what the interviewee is not able to do. The 0-level speaker is one who is not able to communicate in the target language at any level. He or she may know a few isolated words or phrases, may be able to tell time, recognize numbers, and make purchases, but cannot answer simple questions or even begin to survive in the language.

Interpretation: Level 0

The Level 0 is not necessarily totally ignorant of the target language. He or she is, however, the person who has *not* achieved Level 0+ proficiency. The person may know a number of words in a language, usually in isolation of their applications. He may know some numbers, politeness formulae, and certain tourist or traveler-type language. His speech does not qualify as "communication" at any level beyond the most rudimentary, and always in very predictable circumstances.

---

*At times, plus ratings are transcribed as .5, or mid-point ratings (e.g. 1.5, 2.5), for convenience in data processing. This accommodation to technology may have given rise to a false assumption on the part of the general public, that if there is a .5 rating, then surely there must also be other ratings, such as .4, .3, or .2. This is not the case. There are no intermediate decimal ratings.

Description: Level 0+

The 0+ speaker is able to satisfy immediate needs using learned utterances. He or she exhibits no real autonomy of expression, although there may be some emerging signs of spontaneity and flexibility. His speech is characterized by frequent long pauses and repetition of interlocutor's words still occur. He can ask questions or make statements with reasonable accuracy only where it involves short memorized utterances or formulae. Most of the 0+ speaker's utterances are short, and word endings are often omitted, confused, or distorted. Vocabulary is limited to areas of immediate survival needs. He can differentiate most sounds when produced in isolation, but when they are combined in words or groups of words, he commits frequent errors. Communication is severely inhibited, even with people used to dealing with speakers of limited ability. The speaker displays little development in stress and intonation.

The 0+ speaker is able to ask and answer simple questions, ask directions, initiate and respond to simple statements, and maintain very simple face-to-face conversations. He or she can understand simple questions and statements, allowing for slowed speech, repetition, and paraphrase.

Interpretation: Level 0+

The person at the 0+ level is unable to survive in the target language. That is to say, the person could not ask for directions and understand the reply. He could not board a bus, and tell the driver to let him know when the bus gets to his stop. He could not order a meal, knowing what food he is going to be served, and answer questions concerning it that he may be asked by the waiter. Of course, he may be able to go into a restaurant, order a meal that he always orders and has studied in great detail, and avoid starvation. That, however, is not an acceptable performance to merit a survival level rating.

Description: Level 1

The Level 1 speaker is able to formulate some questions, employing limited constructions and displaying much inaccuracy. Almost every utterance contains fractured syntax and grammatical errors. The speaker's vocabulary is inadequate to express anything but the most elementary needs. He experiences noticeable interference from his native language, particularly with regard to articulation, stress, and intonation. His limited vocabulary, his poor control of grammar, and his impaired phonology frequently cause misunderstandings on the part of the others. The interviewee exhibits little precision in information conveyed because of the tentative state of his grammatical development and the limited or nonexistent use of modifiers in his speech.

Interpretation: Level 1

The Level 1 speaker is the one who is able to survive by applying the language he or she has learned. He knows numbers, can ask and answer simple questions, can give and understand simple directions, and knows enough of the grammar to create structurally accurate simple sentences, whether questions, answers, or explanations. The Level 1 speaker translates in his mind nearly every utterance, thus he exhibits very poor fluency. To achieve Level 1 proficiency, the speaker's pronunciation must be adequate for others to understand. If it is not, and if his pronunciation renders his speech unintelligible, the quality of his speech or the breadth of his vocabulary are of no importance. Speakers may as well not know anything, if they cannot put it into an utterance that the listener can understand.

The degree to which a person understands English is very important at the 1 level. Not uncommonly, people who study English are able to say quite a lot, but are unable to carry on a two-way conversation because they do not understand the other person. At Level 1, the speaker can understand replies to the questions he asks, if those replies are not too elaborate. For example, at Level 1 a person should be able to ask where a post office is. He should also be able to understand a reply on the order of: "You continue on this street to the third signal. There, you turn right, and it is about 100 yards from the corner, on the right. There is parking behind the building."

The Level 1 speaker should master question words, for both production and reception. For survival purposes, it is necessary to be able to ask, to answer, and to reply to: who, what, when, where, why, how, how long/far/late/much and so forth.

Description: Level 1+

The Level 1+ speaker is able to satisfy most survival needs and limited social demands. He exhibits a developing flexibility in a range of circumstances beyond immediate survival needs. He shows spontaneity in language production, but his fluency may be quite uneven. He can initiate and sustain a general conversation, but has little understanding of the social conventions of conversation. His limited vocabulary range forces hesitation and circumlocution. In the Level 1+ speaker's speech, there is evidence of the more common structural forms, e.g.,the present, past, and future forms of verbs, but errors are common. He can employ most question forms. While for simple constructions he exhibits accurate word order, errors still occur in complex patterns. The Level 1+ speaker cannot sustain coherent structures in longer utterances or in unfamiliar situations. His ability to describe and give precise information is limited. He is aware of basic cohesive features of the language (e.g., pronouns, verb inflections), but many of his applications are unreliable, especially if less immediate in reference. The Level 1+ speaker's accuracy in elementary constructions is evident, although even there it is not consistent. To the degree that it exists, his extended discourse is, for the most part, a series of short, discrete utterances. This is usually attributable to the fact that the speaker is translating as he speaks and must pause to process his translation. His articulation is comprehensible to native speakers who are used to dealing with foreigners. He is able to combine most phonemes with reasonable comprehensibility, but he continues to have difficulty producing sounds in certain positions or combinations. The Level 1+ speaker's speech will usually be labored, and he may still have to repeat utterances frequently to be understood by the general public. He is usually able to produce fairly consistent narration in either past or future.

Interpretation: Level 1+

There are different ways for a person to reach 1+ on the LPI scale. The first learner-type is the competent student of language who studies diligently and who learns vocabulary, grammar, and other elements of speech and develops aural comprehension, at something of an even pace. He does not excel in any area, but is more or less equivalent in all. This person exhibits notions of past tenses, future, progressive forms, and perhaps passive voice, but has not internalized them. He is able to begin an utterance in an structurally appropriate way that would lead him to the "problem" part of the utterance. He then backs off, either applying a verb form randomly or reverting to the simple present tense. Occasionally, he will get it right, indicating that he is going in the right direction. This kind of a learner is referred to as a school or academic learner, whose approach is of the type fostered by a classroom learning environment.

A second learner type is very different from the first. This is the person who has been exposed to English in a work or living environment, outside of any classroom, and by force of time and opportunity develops excellent comprehension, fluency, pronunciation, and vocabulary. Rarely, however, under these circumstances, does the learner grow with regard to understanding or application of grammatical principles. In fact, as a rule this person disregards the role of grammar when it comes to communication. With regard to the rating, this speaker is given credit for his strong showing in areas other than grammar, hence the plus (+), while his or her control of grammar may be only at the minimum required to surpass the Level 1 threshold. This kind of speaker is very impressive and is often complimented on his speech. The problem is, however, that he will not be able to advance to the 2.0 level without mastering the structures that will allow him to show sequence of events in time, or the temporal relationship of events. He is often a "terminal" learner, in that his speech patterns, as wrong as they are, become fossilized, and he is unable to correct them. His comprehension will develop, as will his vocabulary and his fluency, but his control of structures will not, and he may never achieve the requirements for 2.0 level speech.

Description: Level 2

The Level 2 speaker is able to satisfy routine social demands and limited work requirements. He can handle with confidence, but not with facility, most social situations, including introductions and casual conversations about current events, as well as work, family, and autobiographical information. He can handle limited work requirements, although he requires help in handling any complications or difficulties. He is able to get the gist of most conversations on nontechnical subjects, that is, on topics requiring no specialized knowledge. He is able to give directions on how to go from one place to another. He displays a speaking vocabulary sufficient to respond simply to most questions, although often employing circumlocution. His accent, though often quite faulty, does not render his speech unintelligible. He can usually handle elementary constructions quite accurately, but he does not have a thorough or confident control of the grammar.

Interpretation: Level 2

The Level 2 threshold is very difficult for the 1+ speaker to cross. For school learners, working in an environment where they have little opportunity to practice English on a regular basis, it requires them to *internalize* speech and be able to call it forth without having to think about it. For the street, or the non-school learner, it requires him or her to accept the role of grammar in language development, at a time when for communication purposes it appears that other factors (e.g., comprehension, vocabulary, and fluency) are of greater importance. In both instances, the learner is called upon to perform in a way that is at odds with his or her experience.

It is at this level that the learner must recognize that the effective study of a language is as much a function of a person's attitude as it is of aptitude and application. To require a one-hundred eighty degree shift in attitude is to demand a lot of the learner, which is why so many learners never go beyond the 1+ level.

Description: Level 2+

The Level 2+ speaker is able to satisfy nearly all work requirements, and is able to communicate at a high level on concrete topics relating to particular interests and special fields of competence. He often displays remarkable fluency and ease of speech, but under tension or pressure his or her language may break down. He is generally very strong in either grammar or vocabulary, but not necessarily in both. His areas of weakness range from simple constructions, such as plurals, articles, prepositions, and negatives, to more complex structures, such as tense usage, passive constructions, word order, and relative clauses. Normally, he enjoys excellent control of general vocabulary, but may occasionally show some hesitation even with regard to some high-frequency vocabulary referring to common items.

Interpretation: Level 2+

The Level 2+ speaker is able to say nearly everything he or she wants to say in the target language. Culturally he or she usually appears to be very comfortable in the second language environment, and responds appropriately in nearly all social situations. Internally, however, he recognizes his limitations and realizes that he is something of an imposter. He understands some humor and only occasionally has to struggle to speak. His vocabulary is broad enough to deal with most, but not all, situations. It is only when discussing matters of an abstract or conceptual nature that he feels he is at a loss, or when attempting to unravel an unfamiliar, difficult, and complicated description or process. In these circumstances, he may be driven to silence because of the limitations of his control of structures, particularly sequence of tenses, and use of prepositions and adverbs, and his vocabulary. Luckily for the 2+ speaker, most everyday conversations do not concern material above his level. For the 2+ speaker, there are still "surprises" in the language. The range of his or her language experience is still incomplete, preventing him from drawing on what he *does* know to confront the unfamiliar.

It is worth noting that many *native* speakers fail to advance beyond this level, particularly in cases where they are never called upon to discuss abstractions or conceptualizations, where their opinion is neither offered nor solicited, and where language applications are limited to low-level employment, survival, social, and family interaction situations.

It is the rare student of English who ever achieves proficiency beyond Level 2+, and this includes many people who spend years in a native-speaker environment, at times even in academic environments.

As will be noted in the description of Level 3 speech, the 3 level speaker is able to say everything he or she wants to say in English, without exception. The speaker may have to resort to circumlocutions, meaning a "description" of what is meant, rather than the specific language, but that is of little importance, as the message is always conveyed. Furthermore, at Level 3 comprehension is nearly 100 percent for normal everyday speech. The learner who achieves a level above 2+ is in a very select group of language learners.

Description: Level 3

The Level 3 speaker is able to speak the target language with sufficient structural accuracy and vocabulary to participate effectively in most formal and informal conversations on practical, social, and professional topics. He is able to discuss particular interests and special fields of competence with ease. His comprehension is quite complete for a normal speech. His vocabulary is broad enough so that only rarely does he have to grope for a word. His accent may be obviously foreign. His control of grammar is good, and errors virtually never interfere with understanding and rarely disturb the native speaker.

Interpretation: Level 3

The Level 3 speaker is never uncomfortable with regard to his language capability. He is able to participate in high level discussions of a professional nature, understanding nearly everything that others say—unless, of course, they employ low-frequency slang terms, unfamiliar jargon, regional speech, esoteric cultural references, or slurred speech. While he may understand even some aspects of certain non-standard speech, it is not a requirement to qualify minimally for a Level 3 rating.

In most cases, this speaker has had sufficient experience with native speakers of the language that when he may not understand something that is said, he can draw on past experience to glean accurately the meaning.

The most difficult problem with regard to achieving Level 3 speech has to do with internalization of speech and structures, rather than with learning new structures. Except with regard to vocabulary, the Level 3 speaker usually does not *know* more than the 2+ speaker. The difference is that he has internalized what he knows, and does not have to think about speech to produce it. A vast array of speech is available to him without his having to concern himself with what verb tense to use, whether the verb is regular or irregular, with agreement of subject and verb, with whether a noun is countable or noncountable, singular or plural, or requires a definite, an indefinite, or any article at all. These calculations are natural to him, relieving his mind of the language task. The Level 3 speaker can devote his thinking to *what* he wants to say, rather than to *how* he wants to say it. The Level 3 speaker is able to think and speak at the same time. It is this freeing up of the mental processes, which comes at the Level 3 threshold, that enables the speaker to discuss concepts and abstractions, and to give supported opinion. At this level he also controls a vocabulary of sufficient breadth that difficult descriptions do not elude him. For instance, should he be asked to describe a boot, he could generate most of the relevant vocabulary, including: size, toe, heel, sole, laces, round, pointed, heavy, thick, stitching, leather, and rubber.

Description: Level 3+

The Level 3+ speaker is able to speak the language with sufficient structural accuracy and vocabulary to be able to use it on levels normally pertinent to professional needs. He demonstrates particular strength in vocabulary, grammar, and fluency. He may occasionally exhibit hesitancy, indicating uncertainty or effort in speech. He will most certainly display patterns of grammatical error, although his speech will impress because of its obvious strengths in pronunciation, fluency, vocabulary, and socio-linguistic cultural factors.

Description: Level 4

The Level 4 speaker is able to use the language fluently and accurately on all levels normally pertinent to professional needs. He can follow and participate in any conversation within the range of his own personal and professional experience with a high degree of fluency and precision of vocabulary. He would rarely be taken for a native speaker, but can respond appropriately even in unfamiliar situations. His errors of pronunciation and grammar are quite rare, and display no pattern of error. He can handle informal interpreting from and into the target language.

Description: Level 4+

The Level 4+ speaker displays proficiency sometimes equivalent to that of a well-educated native speaker, but cannot sustain the performance. Weaknesses may lie in breadth of vocabulary and idiom, colloquialisms, pronunciation, cultural references, or in not responding in conversation in a totally native manner.

Description: Level 5

The Level 5 speaker displays proficiency equivalent to that of a well-educated native speaker. He or she enjoys unimpeded fluency in the target language. The person's speech on all levels is fully accepted by educated native speakers in all of its features, including breadth of vocabulary and idiom, colloquialisms, and pertinent cultural references.

Conduct of the Interview

The phases of the interview:

Originally, the Language Proficiency Interview was conducted in four phases. Later, however, another phase, referred to as "the situation," was added to the sequence. The situation places the interviewee in circumstances where he or she is expected to perform a specific linguistic task, the difficulty of which is dependent upon the interviewee's level of speech.

The five phases of the interview, as it is administered today, are the following:
- ❏ Warm-up
- ❏ Level checks
- ❏ Probes
- ❏ Situation
- ❏ Wind-down

Warm-up

The interview begins with the warm-up phase, which serves several purposes. One very important purpose is to make the interviewee feel comfortable with the interview situation. It also serves to accustom the interviewee to the voice of the interviewer, his or her accent (everyone has *some* accent) and manner. A third purpose is to give the interviewer a preliminary notion as to the interviewee's level.

Any mistakes that the interviewee might make during the warm-up phase are largely ignored, as potentially the result of nervousness and not necessarily a true reflection of his speaking level. This assumes, of course, that the interviewee later demonstrates higher level proficiency. If during the course of the interview the interviewee fails to generate and sustain speech at a higher level, the warm-up phase neither adds to nor detracts from the interviewee's rating.

The warm-up phase can last from less than a minute to two or three minutes, depending upon the amount of anxiety the interviewee experiences, his level, and the ability of the interviewer to inspire trust and good feelings in the interviewee. Typical questions that a person may be asked during the warm-up phase have to do with the interviewee's name, the weather, any difficulty in finding the location, an article of clothing, and so forth. Examples of questions asked during the warm-up phase:
- ❏ What's your name?
- ❏ How do you spell your name?
- ❏ Did you have difficulty finding your way here today?
- ❏ How did you come here?
- ❏ Did you have good directions to come here?
- ❏ Your necktie (scarf, jacket, hat) is unusual. Was it a gift?
- ❏ Is it cold out?
- ❏ Is it still raining (snowing) outside?

Of course, nobody would be asked all of these questions, and the response to any of them could serve as the basis for other questions that would either constitute additional warm-up questions, provide information for later discussion, or lead the interviewee on to the next phase.

During the course of the warm-up phase of the interview, the interviewer gets a sense of the interviewee's level. If the interviewee is hesitant in his speech, if he initiates no exchanges, and if he replies to questions in single-word responses, the impression will be that his level is low. If, on the other hand, he replies in extended discourse, if he initiates exchanges or offers information beyond what was asked, and if his speech reflects a high level of comfort with the target language, the interviewer's impression will be that the interviewee speaks at a fairly high level. Rarely, by the way, does an interviewee create one impression on entering an interview and later demonstrate that his level is more than a full point above or below that level. Initial impressions are generally quite accurate.

Level Checks and Probes

Level checks take up where the warm-up leaves off. If the interviewer considers the interviewee to be a 1 or a 2.0 level speaker, following the warm-up, he will proceed to address the interviewee in speech that is at that level. His intent will be to establish that the interviewee is, indeed, at that level, by a series of confirmatory exchanges. The exchanges will focus on both content and language at a level considered appropriate for a level check. For the Level 2 speaker, for instance, the interview will cover autobiographical topics, language used in the person's work, current events, or special interests, while eliciting extended discourse in the past, present, and future. If through these exchanges it is established that the interviewee speaks at that level, the interview may then go on the next phase, the probe. If, however, it is established early in the level check that the initial assessment was too high, the interviewer abandons that level and drops to a lower level. The initial level checks should serve also to give the interviewee confidence in his speech, by not taxing him at a level beyond that of which he is capable.

Following the establishment of an interviewee's level of speech through level checks, the interviewer initiates a probe, which is conversation at the *next highest level*. A probe has as its major purpose the identification of the interviewee's highest level of sustained speech. Two lessons may be learned from the probe, depending upon the earlier sequence of the interview process. The first lesson that may be learned is that the initial assessment of the interviewee's level was too low, and that it needs to be revised upward. The second lesson that may be learned is that the interviewee has demonstrated his maximum level of sustained speech, and is unable to cope with language at the next level. In the case of the former, the initial probe is followed by a series of questions or by conversation at the same level, all of which will establish to a certainty that the interviewee can sustain speech at that level. In this case, what was initially a probe becomes another level check, accompanied by a revision in the assessment of the interviewee's level. That level check is then followed by probes at the next highest level, in a stair-step fashion. In the latter case, where the interviewee fails to uphold his end of the conversation at the level of the probe, the interviewer resorts to speech at the level of the level check, seeking thus to restore the interviewee's confidence in his speaking ability.

Following the level check is another probe, followed in turn by another level check. Before the end of the interview, the number of probes that an interviewee may be given could extend to a maximum of four, if he fails on every one. The play between the level checks and the probes continues until the interviewer is satisfied that he has both obtained a rateable speech sample and established convincingly in his own mind the speaker's proficiency level. It is here that the next phase of the interview, the situation, is introduced.

The Situation

After the interviewer arrives at his or her assessment of the interviewee's maximum level of sustained speech, a "situation" is introduced to either *confirm* the finding or betray it as being too high. The situation phase requires the interviewee to assume a role and carry on a conversation about a specific topic or concerning a particular matter. The functions, vocabulary, and structures required of the task are thought to be within range of the interviewee, judging from his performance during the level check/probe phase of the interview.

If the interviewee fails the situation, the interviewer must reassess the rating and backtrack to establish a true rating. Failure with the situation does not, as a stand-alone artifact of the interview, establish that the interviewee is to be rated at the next lowest point on the scale. In every case, there must be adequate evidence, independent of the situation, to establish the interviewee's level. It should be remembered that during the course of the interview, an interviewee must establish not only that his proficiency *is* at one level, but also that it is *not* at a higher level. Furthermore, both the interviewer and the interviewee must feel that the interviewee's language ability has been taxed to its maximum and that he has failed to meet the challenge at the higher level. This taxing of ability is referred to as "taking the interviewee to linguistic breakdown."

An interviewee should never finish an interview feeling that he has not been asked to reach with his language skills to carry his side of the interview. Given the opportunity, many interviewees reject the invitation to go beyond their level of confidence, in which case they demonstrate their limitations by their unwillingness to attempt to speak at a higher level, rather than by overt demonstration of the weaknesses in their speech. This phenomenon is common among speakers who monitor their speech carefully, in an attempt to avoid making errors. Such people tend to speak with remarkable grammatical and lexical precision and accuracy, but their speech exhibits a woodenness, or a rigidity, that renders it extremely bland and uninspired. Needless to say, interviewees who match this description exhibit a reduced level of expression.

Wind-down

Following the interview, interviewees often have an uneasy feeling about having been required to demonstrate the limitations of their language. To counter this negative feeling, the interview ends with the interviewer chatting with the interviewee about his day and about matters that seemingly have nothing to do with the interview. In this way, the interviewee feels relieved, speaking in simple language about simple topics, entirely unrelated to anything previously discussed. The wind-down is to let the interviewee breathe more easily, and to reinstate the interviewee's sense of dignity and control. This is important for everyone, and leaves the interviewee with a much better feeling about his performance than he would have were he dismissed after failing the last in a series of several probes.

Reasonable Expectations

People who have studied language for a while, sometimes three or four years, sometimes longer, are often offended by their rating, thinking it is too low. Language learners must be reasonable with regard to their expectations of themselves. As with any test of general proficiency, the LPI provides the learner with information about his level. When administered by a qualified interviewer/rater, the LPI is the equivalent of the thermometer that a person uses to determine whether he is well. It is only when a person knows the truth about his proficiency that he can address his problems. One should not be offended to learn that he has a long way to go to achieve his goal. Reasonable expectations with regard to progress, and an understanding of one's strengths and weaknesses, indicate the direction that the learner should take to advance to the next highest level.

Cheating

There is no way to "cheat" on the LPI, any more than there is a way to cheat when playing the piano before a critical audience. Interviewees attempt a variety of ruses to make an interviewer think they know more English than they do. Sometimes this is by means of a prepared presentation. Other times it is by peppering their speech with what they assume, rightly or wrongly, to be native speaker fillers. Still other times it is by using colloquial or informal speech, to simulate familiarity. And still other times it is by refusing to discuss a variety of topics, for whatever reason, requiring the interviewer, or attempting to lead the interviewer, to find a topic on which theu feel qualified to speak.

Interviewers are trained to discover a speaker's true level, through the ruses and through all of the efforts to disguise limitations. An experienced interviewer has been subjected to all of the common and to many uncommon efforts, and is not going to be fooled by the interviewee. The interviewee should understand that he will not receive credit for language he does not produce, regardless of how he approaches the interview.

Interviewees are advised to approach the interview honestly, and to demonstrate their true ability, regardless of what that ability might be. It will make the interview process more enjoyable and less anxiety-ridden, and for that may give a better result than could be had from any attempt to thwart the purpose of the interview.

TOEIC Representatives

France
Phone: 33/1-40 74 05 21
Fax: 33/1-42 56 65 27

Germany
Phone: 49/69-75 30 08 0
Fax: 49/69-75 30 08 50

Hong Kong
Phone: 852/603-5771
Fax: 852/603-5765

Indonesia
Phone: 62/21-520 0364/0365
Fax: 62/21-520 0365

Japan
Phone: 81/33-581 5663
Fax: 81/33-581 5608

Korea
Phone: 82/2-274 0509
Fax: 82/2-277 2610

Malaysia
Phone: 60/3-238 0133
Fax: 60/3-232 4585

Mexico
Phone: 52/5-545 8550
Fax: 1/503-697 3045

Spain
Phone: 34/1-345 7026 or 359 8311
Fax: 34/1-345 8608

Switzerland
Phone: 41/37-24 24 23
Fax: 41/37-24 25 75

Taiwan
Phone: 886/2-362 6385
Fax: 886/2-362 2809

Thailand
Phone: 66/2-259 8840 or 258 1132
Fax: 66/2-260 7061

United Kingdom
Phone: 44/81-748 34 18
Fax: 44/81-741 24 85

U.S.A.
Phone: 1/609-951 1600
Fax: 1/609-520 1093

Venezuela
Phone: 58/2-951 0394 or /0386 or/ 0214
Fax: 58/2-951 0592